Inwardness and Existence

SUBJECTIVITY IN/AND
HEGEL, HEIDEGGER, MARX, AND FREUD

Walter A. Davis

The University of Wisconsin Press

The University of Wisconsin Press
114 North Murray Street
Madison, Wisconsin 53715

The University of Wisconsin Press, Ltd.
1 Gower Street
London WC1E 6HA, England   .

5   4   3   2   1

Printed in the United States of America

Library of Congress Cataloging-in-Publication Data
Davis, Walter A. (Walter Albert), 1942–
   Inwardness and existence.
   Includes bibliographical references and index.
   1. Subjectivity—History.   2. Dialectic—History.
3. Hegel, Georg Wilhelm Friedrich, 1770–1831.
4. Heidegger, Martin, 1889–1976.   5. Marx, Karl,
1818–1883.   6. Freud, Sigmund, 1856–1939.   I. Title.
BD222.D38   1989   126   88-40428
ISBN 0-299-12010-4
ISBN 0-299-12014-7 (pbk.)

To Lois Tyson

Self-consciousness achieves its satisfaction
only in another self-consciousness.

—G. W. F. HEGEL

If the book we are reading does not wake us, as with a fist hammering on our skull, why then do we read it? Good God, we would also be happy if we had no books, and such books as make us happy we could, if need be, write ourselves. But what we must have are those books which come upon us like ill-fortune, and distress us deeply, like the death of one we love better than ourselves, like suicide. A book must be an ice-axe to break the sea frozen inside us.

—KAFKA

It would have to be beautiful and hard as steel and make people ashamed of their existence.

—SARTRE, *Nausea*

He who has thought most deeply
Loves what is most alive.

—HÖLDERLIN, "Socrates and Alcibiades"

Contents

Acknowledgments

IN THE sixteen years I've worked on this book I've had the help and advice of many fine colleagues. Most noteworthy: Charles Altieri, Jane Ashby, Morris Beja, Wayne Booth, John Champlin, Gretchen Cline, Allen Fitchen, Lyle Hammerberg, Stephen Lacey, Michael McCanles, Leonard Michaels, Marlene Morris, Donald Pease, Claudette Roberts, Marjorie Rowe, Kenneth Schmitz, Calvin O. Schrag, Jerrold Seigel, Lori Smart, and Molly Travis. A special word of thanks to my two best readers, Gary Heim, who edited one version of the manuscript, and Lois Tyson, who edited another. Special thanks also to Paul Almonte and David Kidd, who prepared the index. I also want to thank Hillary Foote for all the typing she did for me. Most important of all, thanks to my sons, Chris and Steve, for being so helpful and patient.

INWARDNESS AND EXISTENCE

Introduction: Toward a Hermeneutics of Engagement

THE BASIC conflict in criticism today is between humanism and deconstruction, between the poststructuralist dissolution of subject and the attempt to reaffirm traditional humanistic values. Rather than take sides in this debate, my goal is to transcend it by developing a theory of subjectivity that cuts through the conceptual limitations of both frameworks.

In so doing I attempt to construct an audience by enacting a process. My basic argument is that to attain an adequate theory of subject we need to achieve a principled dialectical integration of four contexts of thought that are usually opposed: Hegelian phenomenology, existentialism, marxism, and psychoanalysis. Such a "synthesis" faces a number of interpretive problems, and the reader may well wonder how such a relationship is possible since these movements seem unalterably opposed on so many issues. Were my purpose to write a commentary on each movement this objection would certainly prove correct. But my goal is to articulate an understanding that is contained in none of them and which entails, in fact, a quarrel with each.

Perhaps the distinction between commentary and what I will call interrogating a text will help make the point. Commentary focuses on doctrines and conclusions and reconstructs the steps that get us there; in the process it usually smooths over everything that would deter that movement. Its goal is to recapture the author's official intention, and it takes scholarly paraphrase as the proper and "objective" relationship to the text. Interrogating a text involves one in the quite different attempt to identify its contradictions, recover its vital core, and assess its contemporary relevance. The focus is on the problems in a text and the recovery of possibilities it fails to realize. The sovereignty of authorial intention is referred to a larger understanding of the complex motives that are at work in a text.

3

Because I am trying to construct a position that is found in none of my sources, each chapter presents a set of ideas that differs significantly from the official version these movements have of themselves. My goal is to free each movement from its conceptual limitations in order to extract a core theory that necessarily becomes part of a larger structure of thought. In this sense, each reading is open to the charge of misreading. Commentaries are descriptively true and that is their inherent limitation; a commentary on the four frameworks would arrest itself in the same conceptual abstractions that prevent their dialectical assimilation.

I term such a method of interpretation a hermeneutics of engagement. Its ruling assumption is that our involvement in our own subjectivity is not a barrier to interpretation but the circumstance that enables us to enter most deeply into a text. (For now I'll let the charge of subjectivism take care of itself. The nature of this hermeneutic and its justification will be worked out in the course of the book with each chapter providing a distinct illustration of how it operates.)

In practicing this method each chapter constitutes what may be regarded as a reconstruction or rescue operation. Chapter 1 frees Hegel's understanding of subjectivity from the abstract rationalism (i.e., the hypostatization of *Geist* and the imposition of conceptual abstractions on experience) he superimposed upon it. Hegel's greatest insight—that all consciousness, including Philosophy, is unhappy consciousness—is used to recapture his suppressed or repressed text. The rich existential and psychoanalytic understanding of subject that is contained in the *Phenomenology of Mind* is thereby liberated. The hermeneutic strategy employed is a close reading of Hegel's most famous text, the second chapter of the *Phenomenology*.

Chapter 2 rescues existentialism from its popular forms (relativism, subjectivism, the absurd) as well as from the neo-Kantianism of its "founder." Heidegger's Kantian insistence on formalizing the existential analytic is his central contradiction and plays a role in his thought similar to that of *Geist* in Hegel. Like Hegel, Heidegger is his own best official interpreter. He is quite right in claiming that existential readings of *Being and Time* seriously distort an intention that leads, without a real break, to the *Seinsmystik* of his later thought. There is little point in questioning this. The question, rather, is how we read Heidegger once the contradiction between analytic formalism and existential engagement becomes apparent. What, in short, constitutes an existential response to Heidegger whose greatest hermeneutic idea is that anxious attunement to our existence is the ultimate basis of any act of interpretation? That idea shatters analytic formalism and enables us to renew the experiential implications of Heidegger's investigations. The hermeneutic strategy employed to constitute this mediation might be termed an existential reading of existentialism.

Chapter 3 rescues marxism from the belief that its primary duty is to eliminate subject. By applying the theory of subject developed in the previous chapters to the internal debates that have made up the history of marxism I try to show that marxism implicitly contains one of the richest theories of situated subjectivity. The construction of this theory requires, however, combining concepts from a number of marxist thinkers who remain opposed to one another and trapped in the repetition of sterile debates (the humanism of the 1844 Manuscripts vs. scientific marxism, etc.) because marxist theorizing remains trapped in repeating the paradigm shifts of its founder. Through a hermeneutic of immanent dialectic, I explore the inherent limitations of an intellectual history—that of marxism —in order to evolve, from diverse texts, a position that transcends the contradictions in which even the most contemporary versions of marxism remain mired.

Chapter 4 rescues psychoanalysis from Freud's scientism by reconstituting its core as a theory of subject as a dramatic agent and of experience as a dramatic process. Freud's clinical insights consistently exceed the scientific framework in which he theorizes their meaning. His texts are, as we have learned, internally contradictory struggles which exemplify the very processes (defense, displacement, unconscious conflict) they attempt to comprehend. They also found a discipline and thus open themselves to a complex evolution in which new clinical insights lead to a fundamental recasting of psychoanalytic theory and of the psychoanalyst's self-understanding. No single figure or sacred text contains the key to that history. In attempting to construct its core concepts, I employ a hermeneutic strategy that draws on texts throughout that history to restate Freud's thought in the language which has gradually emerged as the one most appropriate to it. The method of historical hermeneutics developed here complements the one worked out in the previous chapter. It also redefines the nature of hermeneutic engagement by arguing, indirectly, that textual interpretation alone, however sophisticated, will never give an understanding of psychoanalysis; personal analysis is the only way into Freud's texts.

As the above summary indicates, the interrelationship of the chapters is the key to the larger argument of the book. The four investigations illuminate and complicate one another in the drive toward a single over-arching position. (Since that is so one can begin anywhere, letting interest dictate the order in which one reads the chapters.) Thus Hegel, for example, is read psychoanalytically in Chapter 2 only to return the favor when psychoanalysis is reinterpreted in dialectical terms in Chapter 4. If Freud had conceptualized his discoveries dialectically rather than scientistically he would have avoided many of the pitfalls that have continued to frustrate his discipline; if Hegel had developed the psychological implications of the *Phenomenology of Mind* rather than retreat into philosophic hyper-rationality, he would have made the major contributions to psychology that lie buried in his text still awaiting constitution. In the interdependence of the chapters no framework holds a privileged position; each contributes, rather, to an evolving theory which is greater than the sum of its parts and which requires that the four chapters be superimposed upon one another in a single comprehension.

Another word for that relationship is dialectic. Chapter 5 takes up the methodological and ontological issues that underlie the concrete investigations of the previous chapters in an effort to rethink that widely misunderstood term. Those readers concerned with theoretical foundations or with the demonstration that the more speculative flights of recent theory are warranted only by the tendency of critics to simplify the dialectical traditions they claim to represent may wish to read it first. I there show how a good deal of recent theorizing (deconstruction, semiotics, poststructuralism, French feminism) distorts and abridges what could be the experiential directions of its investigations. The credentials of dialectic as a philosophy of concrete experience are thereby rehabilitated in a way that completes our initial argument by showing that one can reject humanistic essentialism without embracing the dissolution of subject. Situated subjectivity is both the reality and the concept that cuts between these arid alternatives. The chapter thus completes the hermeneutic circle of the book—and defines the distinct nature of a hermeneutic of engagement—by referring its methodological and ontological concepts to the previous chapters for their concretization.

Premature commitment to a single position is such a distressing feature of contemporary thought precisely because it blocks the possibility of such dialectical discoveries. The fortification of one's burrow becomes the main concern, and thus opposing positions meet in sheer oppugnancy with no possibility of communication or growth beyond the narrow parameters in which we endlessly reiterate all the old tired oppositions. Thus Hegel versus Kierkegaard, marxism versus psychoanalysis, et cetera, in fruitless debates while experience awaits the conceptual integration that would alone prove adequate to it. But we are unlikely to attain such integration because the main thing we've lost in the process of scholarly interpretation is the ability to undertake the kind of reflection needed: that in which we constantly question received opinions and interpretations as the texts we read beckon us with the shock of recognition that destabilizes everything we took for granted, including everything we took for granted about their interpretation. Engaged thinking necessarily does violence to objective commentary because its goal is to reawaken that richer relationship to ourselves that is the basis for a richer relationship to texts. In an effort to transcend the abstract oppositions in which thought is currently mired, this book attempts to reconstitute the dialectical method in a specifically modern context and form. In doing so it demonstrates that, with respect to the subject, we haven't said the last word because we have not yet learned to say the first. All the really interesting questions lie on the other side of the humanist-deconstruction debate; for the true life of subjectivity comes into view only when one gets outside the terms of that debate. This book is addressed to those who would embrace our dark despairing time in love, knowing there is no other realm to which we can turn for guarantees and no way to mitigate the responsibilities we bear.

If all roads in contemporary thought lead to the question of the subject, it does not follow that the question has actually been posed in those discourses where subject is invoked only to have its death proclaimed or its existence reaffirmed only in the most abstract and ahistorical ways. Perhaps our true need is to experience this question as a question—and to keep it open as such. In any case, the death of the subject is not an event that should be celebrated as merely the latest intellectual fad, nor is it an idea we have any right to place in the category of the unthinkable. It is, rather, the primary challenge of contemporary life, and as such we should welcome it as a legitimate issue for open inquiry.

1 Hegel: The Contemporary of the Future

He [Hegel] did not know to what extent he was right.   —BATAILLE

Hegel called history the path leading to the self-liberation of the spirit, and it has become the path leading to the self-destruction of all values.
                              —HERMANN BROCH, *The Sleepwalkers*

There is no God and Mary is his mother.   —SANTAYANA

A FAREWELL TO EPISTEMOLOGY: REFLECTION ON HEGEL'S CONCEPT OF CONSCIOUSNESS

THE CRITIQUE OF RATIONALISM AND EMPIRICISM

Unless one begins with the concrete, one will never attain it.

For Hegel, the task of a concrete philosophy is to demonstrate that substance is subject: to reconcile inwardness and existence, thought and life, by showing that the self-motion of the human subject—the progression of consciousness toward freedom—necessarily entails dialectic, or a knowledge of the whole of things.

Following the tradition of post-Cartesian philosophy, Hegel begins with an examination of the knowing subject. But from the start he revolutionizes that beginning by rejecting the then-prevalent conceptions of the knower as either the instrument (*Werkzeug*) that shapes the object or the medium (*Mittel*) that receives it. In opposition to the substantializing of mind implicit in both views, he proposes a phenomenological method: he will begin in absolute skepticism with the natural consciousness (that is, consciousness in its everyday operations, independent of the categories we impose on it), and he will treat knowledge as a phenomenon that is wholly determined by the experiential process through which that consciousness evolves. Experience is "the dialectic which consciousness

8

performs on itself,"[1] and Hegel insists on generating all his concepts from that process. Adopting this method necessitates bracketing all traditional assumptions about subject, object, knowledge, truth, and the absolute. None of these concepts can be established outside the phenomenological process.

The entire project depends on establishing the possibility of self-overcoming within the immediate unity of the natural consciousness. For that to happen, the natural consciousness must in its immediacy be reflexively related to itself and thus in principle already beyond the limitations of immediate experience. This new view of consciousness grows out of Hegel's awareness of the ubiquity of reflection and his insistence on bringing reflection into direct, dynamic connection with the development of experience. As he conceives of it, consciousness is the unity of a triple relationship: consciousness of an object, consciousness of the shaping activity of consciousness, and a reflective comparison of these first two moments. As the unity of this relationship, consciousness completes itself in reflection. It thus stands in a dialectical relationship to itself: the first two moments are caught up in an act which is grounded in the possibility of continuous critique. Reflection, for Hegel, is not a pale afterthought or a private preserve. It is a disruptive force that drives right into the heart of experience.

If Hegel can center the immediacy of consciousness in such a dynamic of reflection he will have attained in principle the reconciliation of inwardness and existence. For he will have established a dialectical principle that is rooted in immediate experience in such a way that self-awareness and the overcoming of otherness become parts of a single process. It will thus be possible to write a book (*The Phenomenology of Mind*) which will trace the progressive transformation of the object through the self-overcoming activity of the subject. But to establish such a theory, Hegel's first task was to overcome the rationalist and empiricist theories of consciousness that prevailed in his time—and that have persisted in spite of his critique. The strategy he uses is one of the best examples of how a dialectical thinker operates.

While agreeing with both the rationalist and the empiricist tradition that philosophy must begin by examining the activity of the knower, Hegel realizes that in order to regain concrete experience he must reinterpret and deepen this starting point. Because they are based on severely restricted conceptions of the subject, both traditions generate correspondingly abstract conceptions of experience. Domination by the natural sciences led both to conceive subject as the objectifying knower of a world conceived of as an ensemble of physical things. To displace that model, Hegel refers the scientific attitude to a more primary mode of self-questioning which arises in immediate experience and which reveals subject not as a knower with a fixed, essential nature but as a being whose very being is at issue.

Before embarking on such an inquiry, however, Hegel must root out the substantialization of subject which shapes the thought of his predecessors. Rationalism substantializes subject by fixing the nature of mind a priori, while empiricism reifies subject by making consciousness the passive product of external relations. In the rationalist tradition, knowledge results from the application of a fixed instrument (*Werkzeug*) to phenomena, while in the empiricist tradition consciousness is a tabula rasa, the medium (*Mittel*) in which what is appears.[2] Both traditions assume that "what is" exists in sheer positivity, yet each works out a fundamentally different theory of our relation to reality. After abandoning inferential realism, the first tradition proceeds to Kant's restriction of knowledge to the construction of appearances through fixed a priori principles of mediation which mind brings to experience. The empirical tradition, on the other hand, moves inexorably toward positivism, behaviorism, and the reduction of consciousness to passivity. In opposition to both traditions, Hegel will attempt to show that consciousness can be neither predetermined nor reduced without destroying the dynamics of reflection and experience. The rationalist tradition errs by substantializing mind prior to experience, the empirical tradition by reducing consciousness to a thing among things. The first option dissolves the immediacy of experience in abstract thought, while the second, in eradicating the power of thought, reduces experience to external relations.

Rejecting both positions may, however, lead to intellectual paralysis. For if no pure subject shapes things to its preexistent demands, and if things don't simply stand beyond consciousness with fixed essential natures, then experience must be reconceived as the process of relation through which both subject and object come to be and in which both are initially and fundamentally undetermined.

THE CRITIQUE OF RATIONALISM

With its a priori determination of both consciousness and its proper object, rationalism stands directly in the way of such a phenomenological conception of knowledge. Hegel's critique focuses accordingly on the consequences of determining the nature of the knower (*Werkzeug*) a priori. If knowledge depends on a fixed instrument, we inevitably face the problem of how the mind, through its categorical activity, alters and loses the immediacy of a phenomenal world which, in Dewey's terms, is "had, enjoyed, and suffered before it is cognized."[3] Subsequent removal of what the mind contributes to experience merely returns us to the initial problem. Unable to discount the mind's categorical activity, Kant's critical philosophy accordingly restricts knowledge to the construction of appearances through predetermined principles of rational mediation. To sustain that logic Kant refuses to allow critical reflection on mind to proceed beyond the traditional concepts of science, logic, and truth whereby he fixes its nature. As a result, rationalism insulates itself from immediate experience and reduces the complexity of the lived phenomenal world to denuded appearances constructed as objects along lines set by the physical sciences.

Rationalism's most deleterious effect, however, is upon reflection. Rationalism necessarily short-circuits that principle. The logical and scientific preconceptions used to establish the nature of the mind are not open to question. As a result, it is impossible to distinguish our knowledge from what makes it possible. One can infer the consequences of rational hypotheses about mind and the world, but one has no way to question "the rationalist paradigm." Reflection is cut off precisely at the point where consciousness could enter into a fundamental debate with itself.

The rationalist assumes that through a preliminary examination of mind one can establish, prior to experience, the clear and distinct ideas or basic categories that make "scientifically valid" experience possible. Hegel argues that such criteria arise from the examination of mind only because they have already been put there. Any "critique" of mind derives from a prior conception of its nature which should be subsequently questioned. Through "critique" mind sets its own limits, but such an act contains a fertile contradiction which suggests a more dynamic concept of reflection.

Kant is Hegel's favorite example of the contradiction. *The Critique of Pure Reason* not only guarantees the applicability of a priori scientific categories to experience but also implicitly extends mind beyond those very bounds. In many ways Hegel's thought arises from an effort to radicalize the latter aspect of Kant's legacy. Why should reflection on the nature of mind stop with the categories of scientific understanding? The circularity of Kant's procedure implies the realization that any critique must criticize itself since there is no way to get back behind its questioning to a presuppositionless starting point from which apodictic knowledge, independent of the process, will flow. The act of reflecting upon its own reflective activity necessarily extends mind beyond its previous limits and introduces the possibility—which will define Hegelian thought—that through reflection consciousness effects a total transformation of itself. Reflection puts us in touch not with an a priori identity but with a radical instability. In contrast to Kant's assumptions, there is no way to limit or halt the reflective process. Any inquiry into the nature of thought which preserves the power of reflection successively (1) sets limits, (2) surmounts them, and (3) turns back upon itself to question the very basis of what it has done.

Given such complications, knowledge must be treated as an evolving phenomenon; its nature can be "known" only through a patient and total immersion in all aspects of experience. Moreover, to appropriate the dynamic of reflection, the examination of mind must be radical in both its inception and its development. Philosophy must begin at a point prior to the traditional Aristotelian distinctions that establish separate disciplines, particular problems (such as knowing the physical world), stable categories, and univocal definitions. All activities must be admitted as of equal significance to the inquiry. There is no way to set up a standard of truth outside the reflective process, nor is there any arbitrary way to limit or conclude the inquiry. Only by tracing the total development of mind's evolving determinations can we gain an adequate insight into its self-determined criteria. Reflection continually proceeds in two directions —back upon itself and beyond itself.

We thus witness the death of mind conceived of as a Cartesian cogito. Any attempt to fix the proper philosophic stance of consciousness prior to or outside the phenomenological process is an unwarranted abstraction from the natural consciousness and from all the recalcitrant aspects of experience that must be preserved in a concrete philosophy. The prereflexive cogito of desire (which is where Hegel will shortly begin) is not a ghost in a machine fitted out with innate clear and distinct ideas derived from a logical core. Nor will the world any longer find its intelligibility in this image. Rather than restrict the understanding of mind to an understanding of its rational, objectifying operations, we must reconceptualize it by immersing ourselves in all the activities that make up human experience, for any of them may reveal the ontological significance of situations that have been persistently neglected. The nature of mind now becomes the major problem for reflective thought; and the cogito that knows the world of physics emerges as one of the poorest, most abstract determinations of both self and world.

Determinations of mind and world are always reciprocal. Rationalism, for example, covertly models consciousness on a prior conception of the world that it wants to know. However, it is always difficult to "know the dancer from the dance," even in Kant. Does he construct Understanding the way he does in order to assure mind's application to a Newtonian universe, or does mind assume this form as a result of untested assumptions about the "objective" conditions of that world? Either way, for Hegel "mirror on mirror mirrored is all the show." That is, any a priori determination of the nature of mind or its objects necessarily distances us from the apprehension of immediate experience. Kant provides the perfect example. Fitting the mind a priori with concepts requisite for the construction of physical phenomena, Kant necessarily conceives of the object along Newtonian lines and models his concept of truth in the image of science. He never attains immediacy because he determines the mind, its objects, and the criteria of sound reasoning independently of the phenomenal process. It all holds together perfectly if we restrict ourselves to Kant's concept of experience. Yet, by these standards, phenomena and activities other than "scientific" become unintelligible except by analogy. As Dewey notes, Kant divides into distinct "realms" concerns that are, in immediate experience, inextricably intertwined. The primacy of "science" in his thought engenders the dualisms that mark its development. The critical philosophy thus sacrifices on the altar of physical science both the concrete world of human engagement and the dialectical drive of consciousness to unify experience by discovering essential connections among its activities.

Hegel's phenomenological method, in contrast, welcomes all forms of experience as equals in the inquiry. One mode of knowledge, such as mathematics, and one special concern, such as the problem of knowing the physical world, lose their privileged status, and previously neglected activities and modes of awareness achieve a new importance as a result of their openness to the complexities of human experience. This is why the *Phenomenology of Mind*, despite Hegel's frequent lapses into his own brand of rationalism, constitutes a fundamental turn in thought. By modeling self-knowledge on the thinking of mathematical ideas and by making physics the architectonic science, the Cartesian cogito alienated philosophy from life and conduct by implying both the ontological insignificance of existential concerns and their resolution in pure thought. One recalls Bertrand Russell's deliverance from anxiety by mathematics. Hegel's phenomenological method negates that negation. For a consciousness plunged into the world, he asks, what is a cogito which is because it thinks? Through what denudation of self and world are clear and distinct ideas arrived at? Of greater import, what is their value for the existing self? Could their greatest value lie, perhaps, in service to a self, an "unhappy consciousness," that no longer wants to exist?

Despite the insistence of these questions, there is a prior problem which may prohibit any quick abandoning of rationalism. If no criteria of knowledge or of discursive procedure can be established outside the phenomenological process, no standards of logic or truth can be established prior to the total development of consciousness. Truth itself, without a Cartesian cogito to support it, is delivered over to phenomenological determination. (This is the primary meaning of what Hegel terms his "absolute skepticism.") Truth can be discerned only as it arises out of the experience of the natural consciousness. Since that process commences at a point at which all coherence appears gone and unfolds as a history fraught with error, truth itself, depending on consciousness for its initial appearance and its final form, must retain the contradictions inhering in the activity whereby it comes to be.[4]

THE CRITIQUE OF EMPIRICISM

Renouncing the fixities of rationalist mediation, Hegel plunges consciousness into the world. The risk he runs, of course, is an empiricist emptying of consciousness that will leave it incapable of bringing anything vital to experience. To assure that in gaining the world he has not lost the dynamic of thought, he must complement the critique of rationalism with a corresponding critique of the empiricist's drive to reduce consciousness to an essentially passive thing among things.

If the reality it intends did not enter vitally into its determination, consciousness would have no reason to develop. This point is empiricism's fundamental contribution to thought. But in order to bring consciousness firmly into line with the physical world, empiricism makes mind essentially passive. Yet if mind is merely a medium (*Mittel*), there is little reason—and no way—to apply it. Lacking any genuine power of mediation, consciousness becomes, in empiricism, the product of external relations, an eternal redundancy having little to do with the development of experience and permanently unable to validate its scant activity.

Knowledge is regarded as the reproduction in consciousness of an external state of affairs, the implicit goal of empiricism being the omission of consciousness. Since consciousness, as medium, brings only minimal principles to experience, it necessarily becomes the by-product of the world of things. Empiricism is wed to the genetic fallacy and committed to the dispossession of consciousness: positivism and behaviorism are its necessary extensions. To preserve discourse the empiricist is willing to grant the unaccountable presence in experience of some minimal principles of mental activity not strictly derived from sensations or conditioned by patterns of behavior. But he really has no way to get them *into* experience—and can give them no vital force once they are there. A wholly unmediated vision is just as contradictory as a complete a priori determination of mind, but in the opposite direction. While the second never gets to experience, the first never survives it. Without sacrificing immediate experience, Hegel must reverse the basic assumption of empiricism—that the only thing capable of determining consciousness is something other than thought.

Such, in a nutshell, is the problem of "the natural consciousness." The natural consciousness on which the *Phenomenology of Mind* rests must differ fundamentally in its immediacy from the incipiently positivistic view of consciousness found in empiricism, or instead of being the field for consciousness' development, experience will become the scene of its progressive reification. Yet, contra rationalism, the mediating power of consciousness cannot be established a priori but must arise from experience. Hegel seems to face an impossible task: to discover in the spontaneity of the natural consciousness a principle of autonomy which commits mind to immediate experience for its determination and which also constitutes a dialectical principle of instability within immediacy that prevents the reduction of consciousness to a thing among things.

THE STRUCTURE OF CONSCIOUSNESS

To establish such a dialectic, Hegel must reconcile immediacy and mediation in principle within the internal structure of the natural consciousness. Doing so will effect a cancellation, preservation, and uplifting (*Aufhebung*) of both the rationalist and the empiricist traditions. Hegel will retain the rationalist emphasis on the constitutive role of consciousness in shaping experience while rejecting the abstract categories it imposes upon experience; he will maintain the empiricist emphasis on immediacy but without reducing consciousness to the play of external forces. In rejecting the Cartesian cogito, Hegel must, at a prior point, confer on consciousness an even greater power. His fundamental problem takes the following form. The natural consciousness must oppose itself to the world in the very act of intending it. That double relationship must constitute its immediate unity and provide the ground for the entire dialectical development of experience. To assure the movement from substance to subject, the natural consciousness must be *reflexively* related to itself and *negatively* related to the world; experiential self-reflexivity must define its internal constitution.

If the natural consciousness is not internally mediated it will remain a tabula rasa wholly shaped by the external world; as sheer immediacy, William James's" buzzing, blooming confusion," confines thought to a silence more total than that of Cratylus. If the world is already complete independent of consciousness, thought and discourse merely distort experience. In such a situation knowledge is condemned, as Santayana put it, to "the solipsism of the moment." Conversely, if thought does not center itself in existence, mediation, remaining wholly a priori, will ensure the nullification of experience, its dissolution in categories already unalterably fixed.

In either outcome consciousness is reified: unable to modify itself through experience or incapable of maintaining itself as a force in experience. With this problem in mind, Hegel places a series of interrelated demands upon the natural consciousness which are both methodological and ontological. Together these demands define its internal constitution as being the initial stage of a dialectic that will necessarily move from substance to subject.

To guarantee a phenomenological procedure, the natural consciousness must already be knowledge in principle and provide, in its immediate unity, all the criteria necessary to determine the course of experience. But to do so the natural consciousness must both *intend* the world and *transcend* the limitations of its own immediacy. Unlike the cogito, it is not yet adequate; to become so it must surmount or negate its initial form. Moreover, to be autonomous in principle, both the possibility and the necessity of its surmounting or negating must be contained in its immediate unity. Unaided by any principles which it does not bring to experience, the natural consciousness must constitute knowledge through an incessant (1) testing and (2) overcoming of itself by (3) its own self-determined criteria. In its immediacy the natural consciousness must, in effect, be *self-mediating* to prove capable of effecting a continuous transformation of both itself and its object. The word for that process of self-reference

—that rigorously determinate process which enacts, as the "truth" of each experience, the complete transformation of consciousness by itself— is negativity. Hegel conceives of experience as a process of continuous and comprehensive self-interrogation in which nothing remains stable, above all the interrogator.

The initial description Hegel gives of the natural consciousness is deceptively simple. Consciousness is simultaneously consciousness of an object, consciousness of itself, and a comparative consciousness of these first two moments. But the ontological import of this description is far from simple. For if only this triple relationship can appropriate the *immediacy* of consciousness, then in its immediate unity consciousness is in *mediate* relationship with itself, with reflection defining that self-reference. The three moments are interdependent: they generate and reciprocally determine one another so that in their reciprocity each is being progressively reformed. Consciousness is a process of becoming rather than a substance, a dynamic of continuous self-transformation. We must therefore apprehend each of its moments in terms of the primacy that reflection holds in consciousness' internal constitution. A fundamentally new understanding of immediacy and intentionality is the first consequence of that primacy. Is mind a tabula rasa, or does it bring fixed a priori principles to experience? Both alternatives are inadequate. If consciousness did not involve a prereflexive awareness, it could have no world. But if consciousness were only pure unmediated intentionality, it would be wholly shaped by its objects. Reflection on any prereflexive awareness always reveals, however, that intentionality is never as spontaneous or unmediated as it initially appears. Definite, albeit minimal, principles (such as the this, here, and now of sense certainty) shape even the most fleeting awareness of the world. Internalizing that realization is a crucial moment in the development of consciousness; for reflecting on its intentionality forces consciousness to modify its initial conception of intentionality. The discovery that principles shape intentions entails the basic insight of philosophic idealism: the "true" object is object-for-us and depends for its form on the activity of consciousness.

In its second moment, then, consciousness experiences "the nothingness" both of its original object and of its initial conception of itself. And for Hegel reflection can't stop at this point—with, say, the Kantian categories of rationalist mediation. Consciousness had the object it had only by determining itself in the way that it did. A genuine appropriation of reflection demands that both determinations be put into question. A reflective awareness of the principles shaping an intention is always distinct from those principles. In relating its first two moments consciousness thus incarnates a fertile contradiction within itself between its constitutive or cognitive activity and its subsequent reflection upon it. Rather than smooth over this difference Hegel's purpose is to liberate its disruptive force.

Kant, in contrast, elides it in order to arrest reflection. This is the precise point over which Hegel makes his most significant departure from Kant. Rather than conceive reflection by analogy to the scientific understanding which it simply confirms, Hegel apprehends reflection as a distinct power with a radically different office. Prior mental activities, such as categorical understanding, provide no model for its distinct principles of operation. In reflection consciousness "compares itself with itself."[5] In that act the two previous moments of consciousness, taken together as a single object, are referred to a power which sets a standard they necessarily fail to satisfy. The first two moments constitute a particular form or experience of consciousness, reflection a boundless power of self-questioning. The former is a limitation, the latter an awareness of that fact. And for Hegel, "to be aware of limitations is to be already beyond them" because reflection cannot rest until consciousness achieves a form and an experience adequate to its demands. It thus negates each experience by giving birth to a totally new form of consciousness. Reflection is not simply animated by consciousness' effort to surmount itself; it actually effects that transformation. And as consciousness alters so does its world.

In moving consciousness beyond its previous forms, reflection negates the previous objects of consciousness. Rather than removing contradictions or confirming the prior experience of consciousness, reflection proves Faustian. In creating a new consciousness and in directing that consciousness back upon immediate experience, reflection reincarnates the dialectic of subject by generating new contradictions both within consciousness and in its relationship to the world. Because this process is one of determinate negation, experience becomes a "labor of the negative" in which consciousness and its world undergo simultaneous transformation through the ongoing act of reflection.

So understood, the third moment of consciousness, the act of reflective comparison, is not a "mere reflection of consciousness into itself," a pale copy of the first two moments in which consciousness acquiesces in its previous forms, as both rationalism and empiricism would have it, but an act which produces "the total transformation of consciousness itself."[6]

THE LIFE OF REFLECTION

Rarely has reflection been given such significance. Philosophy may be defined as the practice of reflection, but for the most part philosophers and people of common sense alike regard reflection as but one aspect of experience, separable from other activities, and with strict limits placed on its power to disrupt everyday life. We all reflect once in a while and generally return from reflection to find nothing changed. We had best not overindulge in reflection, in any case, since it cuts one off from life. When reflecting one should do so in the manner of Kant or of those authorities who today would make philosophy's primary task the explanation and justification of science. Reflection since Kant has largely been a matter of solidifying those prior operations to which we give the honorific name a priori; reflection's task is to articulate the conditions of possibility underlying those operations, operations which shape distinct disciplines. Rather than casting all in doubt, reflection is seen as a conservative force which legitimizes traditional beliefs and established practices.

Rejecting such comforts, Hegel sees reflection as a principle of permanent and creative unrest. Reflection at once unifies consciousness and exists in thorough concordance with experience. Any attempt to short-circuit its disruptive effects results in the reification of both self and experience. Reflection is neither an intermittent act nor an operation with a fixed essence, but an ongoing process demanding its own continuous self-overcoming. And because reflection attains completion only by re-immersing itself in experience, it provides the ground for a philosophy of comprehensive ontological transformation, a philosophy that will move from substance to subject.

Hegel calls reflection the true or concrete infinite. In contrast to the additive mathematical infinite which simply repeats the same thing ad infinitum, each repetition of reflection enacts the total transformation of consciousness. Once one grants the possibility of such radical self-mediation, the immediate relationship between consciousness and the world becomes one of thoroughgoing discordance. The plenitude of being is before us merely as an undifferentiated totality. Corresponding to it requires the dissolution of mediation. But "thought" is "essentially the negation of that which immediately appears." With its introduction, objective being loses all positivistic moorings and is carried up into the reflective debate of consciousness with itself. Immediacy is thereby redefined. Consciousness is in the immediate situation of preserving itself by developing its negative relationship to the world. Unless both the inward and the outward dimension of this situation are maintained, the connection between inwardness and existence is sundered. Unless reflection returns a transformed consciousness to an immediate relationship with the world, self-consciousness becomes no more than a tautological inner voyage, and experience lacks the possibility of dialectical development.

But in all its moments consciousness is simultaneously intentional and reflective. Comprehending that connection is the key to understanding its unity. None of the moments that make up consciousness can be understood apart from their dialectical relationship to one another. Each must be conceived accordingly as a process of progressive and reciprocal re-formation. Consciousness does not preserve a static, identical intentionality into which it returns to commence another "bare and simple apprehension" after each pale reflection on an experience—as both empiricism and rationalism would have it. Each new consciousness which reflection produces entails a fundamentally new way of intending the world. Consciousness is a dialectical unity, an ongoing process of self-mediation in which each moment is continually and totally transformed. To use the language of quantum physics, consciousness is a force field. Substantialist thought proves incapable of conceptualizing such a reality; for consciousness is an identity not merely in difference but in self-differentiation, in becoming by self-overcoming.

A phenomenology of experience grounded in reflection leaves nothing as it initially appears, above all consciousness itself. At each stage in its progress consciousness gains a critical insight into its earlier forms, transcends them, and anticipates an awareness which will transform its relationship to experience only to then submit itself to subsequent criticism. "Consciousness is its own notion immediately";[7] it cancels, preserves, and uplifts itself in the ongoing unity of its moments, and the power so to surmount each of its determinations is the "circumstance which carries forward the whole succession of the modes or attitudes of consciousness in their necessity."[8] Reflection thus provides the principle that demands and assures the entire movement of the *Phenomenology of Mind*.

We are now in a position to see why the structuring principles of Hegel's dialectic, the concepts of contradiction and determinate negation, can be understood only when referred to their source—the internal structure of consciousness. Rather than being fixed laws of the "universe" somehow writ in triads into the "nature of things," contradiction and determinate negation are the principles of self-mediation through which consciousness simultaneously actualizes itself and structures its world. "Consciousness is what it is not and is not what it is." From its inception, consciousness' defining act is to introduce contradiction and negation, absence and nothingness into reality. The shift to this focus—which initiates the intellectual movement we term modernism—derives from Hegel's effort to liberate thought from the principle of substance. As long as thought remains bound for its formative concepts to the essences of classical metaphysics or to objectification and the scientistic picturing of "all that is the case," the substantializing of consciousness is inevitable. To establish its autonomy consciousness must have its very being emptied in principle of all determination. If consciousness is to be more than a thing among things, determined, like them, by universal principles of physical or behavioral causation, it must be self-moved by a fundamentally different logos. Consciousness successfully resists naturalization only if its internal constitution is fundamentally different from that of a substance.

Section A of the *Phenomenology of Mind* provides a clear example of how contradiction and determinate negation operate as powers implicit in consciousness. It also completes Hegel's critique of epistemology by bringing consciousness to the realization that it must leave that orientation and undertake a deeper inquiry into its subjectivity. Prior to consciousness, all simply is. With its appearance, the world becomes permeated with negations. To have any "object," consciousness must negate the undifferentiated. But, though it would like to get by with a minimum of mediation, there is no way consciousness can sustain the abstract negativity of its initial position. The "this, here, and now" of sense certainty is not an immediacy but a complex and abstract position. The lesson it teaches reflection is that it must proceed to the richer mediations which produce the world of objects reciprocally connected in space and time. Rather than removing contradictions those mediations uncover, in turn, a series of more disturbing discordances between consciousness and its objects: antinomies of the thing and its properties, the empirical and transcendental egos, the phenomenal and noumenal orders. In the movement from sense to perception to understanding traced in section A of the *Phenomenology*, consciousness extends itself beyond its previous bounds only to uncover further contradictions both within the self and in its relationship to the world.

In completing this initial movement, consciousness achieves, however, its true starting point. It becomes reflectively aware of the difference between itself and its objects, cognizant of the necessity for its shaping activity, and committed to establishing an eventual correspondence between itself and what is. These recognitions mark the transition from consciousness to self-consciousness because they imply that desire and not epistemology is the true beginning for a study of subjectivity.

Rather than steadily overcoming contradiction, the development of consciousness continually engenders more involved contradictions. The true gain of section A, for example, is a recognition of the necessity of moving from the world of epistemology to the *Lebenswelt* and the wider contexts of interpersonal and sociocultural activity. Such a progressive expansion of context and problems is the process through which dialectic proceeds toward the concrete. Consciousness overcomes the otherness of its objects and moves toward self-mastery only by accepting the determinacy of its negations and projecting upon them. There can be no retreat to a position prior to contradiction, no resting in a limited position. Consciousness must shape the contradictions it generates into a single expanding awareness that is engaged in an orderly transformation of both itself and its world.

Consciousness can do so only if it exists as a principle of ceaseless yet determinate negation. That possibility is what Hegel's intricate theory of the natural consciousness is designed to assure in principle. Contradiction and determinate negation are not predetermined realities consciousness must face but recurrent moments its development necessarily engenders. Structurally we can distinguish the intentional negation whereby consciousness establishes each relationship with what is other than it (whether the other is an object, another subject, or one of its previous attitudes) from the subsequent reflective negation whereby it transforms that experience of relationship into a new self-consciousness. These recurrent moments mark the nodal points in the development of any experience—the return of reflective consciousness to experience and the subsequent dialectic of that experience.

The way such a consciousness moves toward knowledge defies the correspondences knowledge supposedly requires. Through its activity, consciousness continually puts itself at odds with both itself and the world. Its development generates a series of progressively involved contradictions which disrupt all the correspondences in which thought could rest. The world is not what it is but what consciousness makes it. Yet consciousness is not simply shaping activity but critical reflection upon that activity. And reflection is not a contemplative end to thought but the goad to further questioning. Hegel thus stands the traditional notion of knowledge as correspondence on its head. Rather than force consciousness, by a prior cleansing of itself, into correspondence with a rational or scientific world, the problem Hegel bequeaths is to bring reality into correspondence with the inner dynamic of consciousness. The only correspondence which can satisfy consciousness is correspondence with itself, a correspondence in which the world is carried up into the subject's ongoing reflection on itself.

The irony is that in recovering radical reflection, Hegel unleashes a principle that will destroy the very system he hopes to construct. The first thing that every post-Hegelian exercise of genuine reflection (whether in Marx, Kierkegaard, Nietzsche, Heidegger, Sartre, Lacan, or Derrida) consumes is the Hegelian absolute. Having established the principle of radical reflection, Hegel spent most of his life closing the very doors he opened. In fact, already in the introduction to the *Phenomenology* Hegel superimposes on the concept of consciousness we have derived from him what is perhaps the greatest control mechanism in the history of thought —the Absolute. I have no wish to minimize the extent of this intrusion. Hegel is the founding father of existential thinking in spite of himself, not by reason of his explicit intentions.[9] His ruling intention, in fact, is to find a way to sublate everything disruptive in experience in the arch-rationalism into which his thought progressively descends. But, as Bataille said, "he did not know to what extent he was right." Except as a philosophic curiosity, the Absolute and the System have been dead for a long time. Yet Hegel lives on, a source of insight and fascination to modern thinkers as diverse as Dewey, Lukács, Sartre, Lacan, and Derrida, all of whom initiate their thought by developing a quarrel with Hegel which always takes the same form: a renewal of Hegel's radical concept of reflection to recapture the concrete investigations into subjectivity that Hegel developed in the *Phenomenology*, which can be extended in the proper direction only once they are liberated from the abstract conclusions Hegel superimposed upon them. The next chapter will carry out such an investigation by applying to Hegel's consideration of subjectivity the concept of reflection we have derived from him. As a transition we can summarize that concept in the terms that are most appropriate to it.

We are those creatures who reflect, but we enter genuine reflection only when no Cartesian cogito, no a priori Understanding, no eternal human nature comes to deliver us from the anxiety attending that act. The question reflection opens is the question of the nature of the being who undertakes this act. And when reflection is genuine there is no way to separate the question from the questioner. The depth of one's engagement in the question is the primary proof that it has been posed in an authentic manner. This is the central idea from which equally compelling ones derive—the recognition that one is going to die; the anxiety before the *why* which alone makes authentic conduct possible; passion as a function of one's appropriation of the problem of existence—as further testimonies that to be or not to be is not an academic issue but reaches into the very interiority of the subject. Reflection is that which makes us human.

But reflection is also a mere possibility—and one more honored in the breach than in the observance. That is why it is comparatively easy to dissolve the subject—and no exercise is more fashionable today—by showing all the ways in which we are determined prior to reflection and remain so in spite of the freedom reflection claims to effect. Structuralism, semiotics, and poststructuralism constitute themselves, by and large, by showing all the ways in which we are "thought" or produced by the languages, systems, and frameworks in which we find ourselves and which we remain powerless to either comprehend or alter since the very effort to do so employs rules and principles that are determined by those systems. The death of subject, the rejection of Hegel's notion that the instrument can criticize itself (a statement Nietzsche first made, presciently, with regard to language) has become the right of passage through which we proclaim our postmodernism. These are powerful discourses, and I think that to neglect them is only to lapse into the most abstract forms of contemplative and ahistorical humanism. But they are also, I hope to show, partial and often terribly one-sided, as guilty of contemplative abstraction and premature concreteness as the essentialisms and humanisms they would replace because they refuse to constitute what is their richest implication—a comprehensive understanding of our situatedness as the very condition that gives us our subjectivity and that enables us to know it as the burden we are one with. Perhaps the human race is in the process of giving itself a new definition, a definition informed by the notion that self-questioning is impossible and that the humanity we hoped to find through that discipline is an illusion and a myth. But, if so, it is we who will have to live that recognition.

SELF-CONSCIOUSNESS: THE SPIRIT THAT CUTS
BACK INTO LIFE

Hegel's chapter "Self-Consciousness" is one of the greatest acts of reflection in the history of thought. Its purpose is to account for the emergence of self-consciousness and to articulate the principles that will constitute its internal dynamics. We will interrogate it by commenting on the series of basic propositions that can be derived from it.[10]

DESIRE—AND THE OBJECT

SATISFACTION

Self-consciousness is the return out of otherness. Its first form is desire, which grounds the world in the subject. The world is before me not as object of knowledge but as field for desire.

This initial definition of desire serves as a transition; its purpose is to distinguish self-consciousness from the epistemological problematic of the previous chapter. That chapter, "Consciousness," moved from the self-contradictory positions of sense certainty and perception to the Kantian insight that consciousness is not a passive receptor given determination by the external world but the active principle whereby we construct experience by bringing mental frameworks to bear upon phenomena. The object is grounded in the subject. But this conclusion remained abstract because it remained tied to a problematic which sees knowing the world as our primary relationship to experience. Hegel now revolutionizes the Kantian turn by transcending that limitation.

Objects may be grounded in consciousness, but what is the relationship of consciousness to itself? Epistemology offers an abstract and substantialistic answer to this question by picturing experience as a knowledge affair in which a cognitive consciousness takes the knowing of objects as the act which establishes its nature. In showing that consciousness is appetitive before it is cognitive Hegel displaces that attitude. Rediscovering itself as desire, consciousness recovers that primal prereflective unity which is prior to all cogitos. Objectification, which makes knowing man's primary concern and the natural world our primary object, is thus referred to a more basic problematic of the subject.

Hegel began with epistemology as a necessary concession to the philosophic preoccupations of his time, but in tracing its dialectic he shows that this orientation is a false beginning because it abstracts from the primary relationship consciousness has both to the world and to itself. Epistemological focus depends, in fact, on suppressing the questions that arise when desire reveals knowing not as privileged or self-evident beginning but as a choice with underlying motives. Rather than fix the proper stance of consciousness to itself, classical epistemology attempts to arrest a more fundamental dialectic.

What, then, is consciousness' relationship to itself? A description of the internal structure of desire will provide a first answer, and the motives in desire will remain basic to understanding the dynamics at work in all human activities, including the epistemological attitudes previously surveyed. Everything human beings do is in some way a response to the conflicts opened up by desire. This is the deepest meaning behind Hegel's claim that the chapter on self-consciousness constitutes a return out of otherness. Once we recognize ourselves as desire we no longer seek to find the meaning of our being outside ourselves. Desire introduces a depth in subjectivity that is before and beyond the object. Desire's quarrel with the world is grounded in an effort to fathom itself. The knowledge of one's desire thus holds the key to all one will ever know about one's subjectivity. For desire is the dialectical force generating the contradictions which negate the efforts we make both to arrest and to fulfill its imperatives.

As the first form of self-consciousness, desire reveals, in a way that knowing could not, the immediacy of consciousness' relationship both to itself and to the world. The world emerges in a totally new way. The object of desire is, in Dewey's terms, "had, enjoyed, and suffered" before it is cognized. Desire isn't a false, illusory projection upon a world of objects that can be known only when one has attained the disinterested objectifying standpoint of science, as those out to reduce its significance would have it. Desire uncovers a *Lebenswelt* of appetitive investments which reveal subject as a being engrossed in the world. In desire, solipsism and science are supplanted at a stroke.

But the deeper register of desire is that it stands in a mediate or dialectical relationship to itself. This is the primary proposition Hegel will develop. It is the first form taken by the noncoincidence between subject and the emerging "logos" of experience, reflection. As such it is the watershed moment for establishing a dialectic grounded in experience as opposed to one generated a priori. It is also the first place where Hegel's text betrays a confusion that reveals the rationalistic limitations of his self-understanding.

To understand desire's internal constitution all we need do is attend to the question desire incessantly asks itself: what, ultimately, does desire desire? This question is neither abstract nor a priori. Its immediacy constitutes the nascent reflexivity of consciousness; as such it is the final step which completes every act of desire. Asking this question constitutes the distinctiveness of human desire, its difference from animal need. Living a relationship to the question forms the dialectic of the desiring consciousness.

Animals never make the detour of epistemology. Nor do they suffer the disruptiveness of human desire. As far as we know, they live the pure immediacy of desire. As Hegel says, "They fall upon the world and eat it up." Their action introduces two basic facts which are contained yet differentiated in human desire: its origin in lack and its negative attitude toward otherness.

While the animal lives the immediacy of desire it also remains trapped in immediacy. It annihilates the object's independence without transcending it. That is why the animal reproduces both the original need and the identical object in an endless cycle. Satisfaction for the animal occurs at the moment of consumption. Unlike the human being, the animal does coincide with its object. But its experience is one of repetition without self-differentiation. That is why, for all their charm, animals lack inwardness. Happiness is theirs—as is blind need—because their relationship to objects remains one of dependency.

Satisfaction doesn't work the same way for us because we live a different relationship to objects. Attainment breeds discontent because an "I want" arises in the midst of all fulfillments. We repeatedly experience the desire for something else, something more. Mere repetition introduces a vertigo into consciousness, the specter of an endless round of dependencies lacking self-differentiation in which we become indistinguishable from the objects we pursue—the self-reification of pure Giovannism. Such basic facts about the quotidian life of desire introduce a major ontological consideration.

The difference between us and the animal is that we live a question the animal never raises: does the object we desire fulfill our desire? We are condemned to this question by the fact of consciousness, for it is one with the immediacy of consciousness and is lived long before it becomes explicit. The lived experience of this question is the initial appearance of reflection as an ontological force that is present at the origin of experience —and may, in fact, be termed its origin.

Pausing over this consideration exposes the inadequacy of most traditional views of reflection. Reflection doesn't stand in wait with a fixed content which enables it to render judgment on the many false pleasures experience dangles before us; nor does it come on the scene only fairly late in the development of experience. Reflection has no a priori content. Its presence is immediate and initially lies in no more than the vague feeling that something is lacking in the object of satisfaction, something residual in consciousness that has not been fulfilled. Asserting the reflexivity of consciousness as the unmotivated first principle of his thought does not involve Hegel in an imposition of rationalist or religious values on experience because the dynamic of reflection required to initiate the dialectic arises wholly in experience and inheres in the immediacy of desire. Its a priori character is existential rather than rationalistic, originating in the feelings of boredom, lack, and emptiness that so often follow surfeit.

A phenomenological description of desire will enable us to conceptualize this internal dialectic.

Desire is the unmotivated upsurge of the existential demand we place on experience. It introduces a fundamental instability into our relationship with the world. The unrest defining subjectivity is not the result of an error, a failure at adaptation, or a lapse from one's substantial identity. Disquietude is not a derivate but the primary fact. Desire reveals that there is a radical lack of being at the heart of the subject. The first and in some ways the profoundest experience we have of our subjectivity is that of a vast and ontologically radical hunger, a gnawing emptiness bereft of substantial identity and of any secure place in the order of being. The knowledge desire harbors is that our first self-awareness is anxiety before an inner emptiness that we flee.[11] That flight is one with the upsurge of the world.

Hegel's definition of desire thus requires reformulation: subject originates not in desire but in the fundamental lack that creates desire. As desire we are wholly given over to experience for the determination of our being; experience is thereby charged with the task of addressing a fundamental emptiness. Anxiety over our lack of being initiates the quest for some object that will both fulfill and eliminate desire. This contradiction is the dynamic of desire. "Consciousness is what it is not and is not what it is." Desire both animates and nihilates all situations. We are what we are not: fleeing our emptiness we discover the world. But our discoveries prove inadequate. Every presence becomes haunted with absences: we are not what we are. No object satisfies subjectivity; it remains over and above all relationships not simply as their consciousness but as the consciousness of their inadequacy. Quotidian desire is by and large an attempt to flee this recognition, which lies in wait for us as the ineradicable burden implicit in consciousness. Desire marks the initial appearance of what will emerge as Hegel's central thought on subject: the unhappiness of all reflection, the impossibility for subject to coincide with itself in the achieved security of a substance.

DISSATISFACTION

"Dissatisfaction" is the key moment because it shows that as desire consciousness stands in a dialectical relationship with itself. Desire is defined by four moments: lack, satisfaction, dissatisfaction, and surpassing. The relationship of the second and third moments reveals the working of reflection in the immediacy of desire. In the life of desire one always needs something else, something more. Displacing oneself along the metonymic chains of this process (after a good meal a good drink then a good show and a good sleep, etc.), one misses its ontological import. Satisfaction engenders dissatisfaction not because one needs something else but because there is always a discrepancy between the object of satisfaction and the surplus of desire. Projecting a new desire flees this fact in order to avoid the moment of reflection. In the ordinary life of desire we live like Bellow's Henderson incessantly saying "I want, I want," with "What?" a suspended question whose force is reasserted each time we achieve our goal.

To grasp its significance, dissatisfaction must be internalized and its sublation made the basis for a transformation of desire itself. In that act the fundamental lack constituting desire becomes the basis not of repetition but "of a total transformation of consciousness itself" and its relationship to the world. This is the first true self-mediation of subject, the first enactment of the possibility upon which a dialectic of experience depends. Dissatisfaction internalized makes negativity determinate and reflection an act of self-overcoming. A correct understanding of dissatisfaction is thus the key to establishing the experiential credentials of these concepts, as well as of the somewhat a priori-sounding ones Hegel attaches to them. For Hegel, subject requires self-certainty, independence, and autonomy; it can achieve them only by overcoming dependency on otherness; and it is animated by a craving for absolute freedom and unconditional recognition. We are now in a position to explain the experiential genesis and meaning of these concepts.

Hegel defines desire as the negative attitude toward otherness. To attain self-certainty, desire must supersede the independence of the object. In our relationship to nature and objects of need this both works and doesn't work. Like the animal, in using the object we reproduce it and repeat our original desire. The relationship is thus one of a dependency that can be overcome only if satisfaction can survive the moment of consumption. In all object relations this does not happen. Satisfaction breeds dissatisfaction or renewed repetitive desire. To move beyond this bind our desire must become different in kind with a different object.

All relations with objects are volatilized by the presence within those objects of the imperative that defines the "who" of subject. To say that desire seeks fulfillment in the world is not the same as saying we are wholly given over to the world. One of the deepest secrets desire harbors —even from itself—is that the object will always prove inadequate because we are "always already" beyond it.[12] Dissatisfaction establishes the possibility that desire implies an experiential hierarchy. But for this hierarchy to operate, desire can't rest in quantitative difference, but must seek out a difference in kind. Desire is inherently interpersonal. The truth of the object is that it leads us to the Other. Earning these assertions requires a further interrogation of dissatisfaction.

Dissatisfaction is the key experience because through it the dialectical unrest implicit in human desire becomes explicit. Dependency isn't intolerable a priori, as it is in Sartre, but derives from a reflection that is felt long before it is cognized. As long as one is expended in passing from link to link along the chain of desire one has no identity. While defined by objects lacking all subjective character one remains like them —an object. If desire leads us not to the object but to the other, it is because the object leaves us not only empty but in a frustrated state of dependency.

Desire is thus already beyond the hedonist's attempt to arrest its dialectics. The hedonist's negative attitude toward otherness is trapped in a fundamental contradiction. Allowing no differentiation in the object allows for no self-differentiation. Relations necessarily take on the character of relations between things. Quantity arrests quality with "pleasure" assuming progressively frenetic forms. The cause of Don Giovanni's frenzy, in Mozart, is not his age but his recognition that his quest lacks genuine inwardness. All men of repetitive desire live the self-reifying consciousness of Flaubert's Rodolphe, who is unable to distinguish words, feelings, and those who utter them.[13]

Dissatisfaction establishes an experiential test which measures all our desires. Satisfaction must survive the moment of consumption. This "standing negation," rather than some a priori humanism, is what makes necessary the transition from relations with objects to interpersonal relations. Making such a transition is no easy matter, however, since the attraction of a project like Rodolphe's is the safety it promises from experiences of rejection and loss. Subjective growth is a triumph against odds because it requires surmounting such fears. Naturally most people escape the demand by successfully reifying themselves in their contradictions. But though human relationships may prove too taxing, the dialectic always exacts the price of refusal. Unable to recognize the other as other, we know when we have turned both of us into things. The hedonists' anguish is that they can never look in the face of those they make love to, can never touch with tenderness the subjectivity wanting to open before them.

Through dissatisfaction, lack and dependency generate the desire for autonomy. Contra rationalism, the desire for autonomy isn't posited as an a priori ideal to prevent subject's dispersal in experience. It grows directly out of the instability of desire's internal structure. The desperate effort to give ourselves being is informed by a "prior" experience of our emptiness.[14] This is the neglected side of the appetitive energy characterizing desire. Dissatisfaction brings forth desire by forcing a reinterpretation of the lack that informs desire. We feel the need to become certain of ourselves only when we discover that the object leaves us in the very situation we tried to overcome. This is the existential meaning of dependency. Attempting to escape our lack, we've traversed a circle which returns us in frustration to where we began. But return brings a new insight into what was already there. The lack defining us is not a biological fact but the immediate form of the inwardness that is consciousness. Loss is the driving force that destabilizes all relationships because consciousness of that outcome is the sublation of desire. Lack does not dissolve subject in the trace of irretrievable differences—that Derridean nonorigin perpetually deferred—but forces subject to project itself anew in experience.[15]

Through the self-mediation made possible by dissatisfaction, lack becomes a lack of a new kind—the experience not of emptiness but of a dependency that kills every satisfaction by making it pass under the sign of self-waste. This is the first example of how self-mediation produces a total transformation of subject's relationship to itself. Consciousness of the lack defining subject is now double. Negating the independence of the object taps our negativity, but does so incompletely as long as we stay tied to objects. To go further, we have no choice but to sublate ourselves. Our lack is now more basic than the absence of new objects. We lack something that would address the deep need for self-certainty which is not a passing mood but an essential dimension of subject. We feel the absence of the other long before the appearance of the other.

Experience teaches consciousness that it requires something that has the characteristics not of a thing but of another consciousness. The first experiential self-mediation thus produces a total transformation of both lack and desire. Lack has become loss. The need for self-certainty is doubled back upon itself in a mood of anguish which generates for experience what will become the defining human desire—the desire for recognition. There is nothing a priori, religious, or humanistic about that desire. It is not an essence that comes from on high but an existential demand that arises directly out of frustration. This distinction is crucial because it offers the concept a much more conflicted experiential development than "idealistic" interpretations of Hegel permit.

Hegel's rationalistic language, however, is the primary source of confusion. Hegel often speaks as if the need for self-certainty and absolute status must be posited before the dialectic can commence. We will find many subsequent instances of the intrusion on the inquiry of this rationalist bias; collectively they constitute both the problem of the *für uns* and the Hegelian attempt to collect under the evolving concept of Absolute Knowledge experiential complexities that resist such centering.[16] Our interpretation attempts to expose the rationalist a priori and halt its movement in order to secure and deepen the experiential credibility of Hegel's thought. Hegel often speaks as if all we need do is think things over before finding the magical concept, such as recognition, that will propel the dialectic to its next stage. But this move violates Hegel's sworn procedure to generate all of his concepts out of the experience of the natural consciousness. At this point in the *Phenomenology*, consciousness has not yet developed the capacity to engage in the abstract operations Hegel posits. The dialectic of desire is a good deal more complicated and decidedly less syllogistic. Development never proceeds simply through the detection of logical contradictions. The real contradictions, in fact, emerge only when desire, reproducing itself, suffers the vertiginous specter of living a ceaseless repetition not only of the same object but of itself in its initial form. That experience has little to do with logic.

Desire stands in mediate or dialectical relationship with itself not because the need for independence and recognition is present in consciousness a priori, but because repetition without self-differentiation is experienced as a fundamental absurdity. The object defeats us because it leaves us with the very situation we tried to overcome. This is the existential meaning of dependency: the self-waste we feel whenever satisfaction engenders only a reproduction of the need that binds us to the object. Desire is reflected back into itself only to feel, with greater urgency, the disorder that inhabits it. Independence demands both the shift to another kind of object and the overcoming of one's initial form. Self-consciousness does not await us as a cogito fitted with prearranged rational principles. Experience alone generates the desire for autonomy and establishes a radically different context for its development.

As in Kafka, consciousness is arrested and thrown back upon itself; only then does it deepen its relationship to the lack which it is. Inwardness is a nausea, not a cogito. To claim that "the act of comparing itself with itself" humanizes consciousness is a valid statement, and not a rationalist platitude, only if we recognize suffering as the logos of subjective development. Given the philosophic preoccupations of his time it is not surprising that Hegel presents his concepts in a quasi-rationalist language that serves as an imperfect vehicle for conveying their experiential meaning. The task of a reading is not to repeat his error but to liberate his repressed. In its emergence, reflection is not a logical self-presence but a suffering of being forced back upon oneself after a nauseating experience both of one's groundlessness and of how objects of experience fail to satisfy an inextinguishable ontological craving.

Consciousness has now internalized the question it is: "What does desire desire?" The recognition to which it will be led is that desire desires another desire: "Self-consciousness achieves its satisfaction only in another self-consciousness."[17] This is the second major dialectical movement of the discussion. We will now undertake its interrogation.

DESIRE—AND THE OTHER

INTERSUBJECTIVE DESIRE

The recognition that "self-consciousness achieves its satisfaction only in another self-consciousness" is not derived from an essential "human nature" or posited a priori to bail out desire, but issues directly from the contradictions that inhabit desire. Unless we reify our being, the desire for recognition imposes itself upon us. When, out of frustration with objects, desire is arrested and consciousness doubled back upon itself, the subjectivity proper to the subject is born. Internalization of this experience generates the first coherent "self" or self-feeling—the experience of oneself as a burden. One is no longer simply desire, but the awareness of oneself as desire. This recognition transcends all objects of desire because it transcends the very movement of desire toward an object. One now lives the question "why" in a more basic form: What does it mean to be desire and what, consequently, does one desire?

The transition to intersubjective desire addresses this question by complicating it. Desire desires another desire. Only another desire can give us back what we need—a recognition of the infinite and existential value of our subjectivity. We desire the consciousness of our consciousness by another consciousness. I state the principle in formalistic terms here to avoid positing a "humanistic" content. The assertion "Desire desires another desire" is initially no more than a desperate demand, born of defeat. It is not a triumphant resolution to the tortured dialectic of desire onto which we can confidently attach a storehouse of humanistic commonplaces about love. To preserve experience, the desire for recognition can be no more and no less than an effort to sublate the contradictions that define the failure of desire. Dialectic advances not by preserving solutions but by exacerbating conflicts. The transition to interpersonal experience merely ups the ante.

What would it mean for the other to give me back what I desire? My subjectivity would become the reality and the condition of another's inwardness. I would, in Proustian fashion, become the totality of the other's consciousness, with no jot of otherness. We desire an absolute affirmation of the value of our very being, requiring a subject with which we can coincide because that subject would give the unconditioned recognition we crave. We don't simply desire another consciousness. We want to write our name upon the very inwardness of that consciousness. Human relations are conflicted because in desiring one another we also desire the impossible. Given the disruptiveness of desire, the quest for love may condemn human relations to a perpetual Sartrean defeat. Interpersonal relations are necessarily characterized by struggle and mutual cruelty because they derive from a basic ontological insecurity. We want the other to fulfill our deepest need by rendering unto us the gift of their very subjectivity. Reflecting back to us our infinite value, the other must both complete and extinguish him or herself in that act.

The tensions and contradictions already present in desire become peremptory when we confront the other. It would be wonderful if we could simply see the other as our good and embark together upon the project of loving, or establish this ideal in order to chart unhappy relationships as deviations from a norm that has a firm basis in human nature. But love is a triumph against inescapable odds that have their basis, not in external obstacles or social conditions, but in the internal constitution of the subject.

Hegel's discussion is one of the first systematic attempts to explain, in principle, the tragic disorder at the center of human relationships. As he saw, experience moves in a complex circle in which nothing is lost. The stance toward the object was merely the first staging of motives and conflicts that come into their own when we find ourselves before the other. Recognition is necessary for our satisfaction, not because the other fulfills a basic need but because the other poses a fundamental threat. Dissimulating that threat is responsible for the subtleness and mendacity of human relations. Ontological insecurity and the desire for autonomy are opposite sides of the same coin. We tremble before the other because the other can seduce us into the surrender of our being. The other has the power to reject us in a way that can destroy the very sense of our value as a person. "Hell is other people," and the other is my "original sin," because the other disrupts the dream of pure inwardness even more thoroughly than the dream of unfettered desire. Our inwardness is bound up with the other. That fact entails conflicts where both parties may inevitably lose.

We are now in a position to extend the discussion in a specifically psychoanalytic direction.[18] The key to this reading is the recognition that the quest for autonomy is the other side of the fundamental insecurity that constitutes desire. As psychoanalysis shows, our first experience is abject need for a nourishing object that disappears and that we know most deeply through the fear of its loss. The breast is the first object, and relationship with the mother the genesis of a desire which is specifically human. Through prolonged dependency in a symbiotic union, our subjectivity takes form as the response to another's subjectivity. Mothering is not only a deeply subjective experience but a profoundly regressive one. Revived in fantasy and expressed through sensual togetherness, our mother's conscious and unconscious conflicts imprint themselves upon us as the relationship we come to have to our body. In specular capture, we achieve psychic cohesion by mirroring: our desire is a response not to the mother's desire but to the conflicts of her desire.[19] As Lacan puts it, desire is the desire *for* and *of* the other.[20] This is the fruit of mothering; and the experience completes itself only when the initial object, like paradise, is lost. The lack defining subjectivity isn't a biological lack, but an existential experience of irretrievable loss following total dependency. Drawing on Hegel, Heidegger, and Sartre, Lacan defines desire in the following formula: desire is the difference between need and demand. It is the difference between the fulfillment of natural biological "instincts" and the unconditional demand to be loved as the be-all and end-all of another's existence. To be a subject is to live that contradiction. The tension present in all human relations is their touch on the register of demand. Blind insistence and hysteric posturing; Proustian obsessionalism; the inability to tolerate a jot of otherness; infantile fixation and the refusal to internalize loss; the constant quest for mirroring and reassurance to prop up an ever-faltering narcissistic identity—such are some of the basic ways in which demand exerts a constant pressure on the life of human desire. The result, however, is not the inevitability of determinism, but the necessity of dialectics. The impossibility of demand does not cancel its force; nor does it confine us to repetition or "supplementarity."[21] It condemns us to desire, to the attempt to mediate the contradiction that defines us.

THE UNITY OF CONSCIOUSNESS: THE INEVITABILITY OF STRUGGLE

The contradiction between independence and dependency, between ontological insecurity and the quest for autonomy is not an oscillation between distinct and separable moments within consciousness, but the unity of consciousness itself, the tension informing the one way we feel about ourselves. This conflict is thus present in every relationship because it informs the desire of both partners. Before the other, the emptiness inhabiting desire becomes the fear of losing one's self. Strife and aggression become us because the ontological lack inhabiting desire remains permanently at work. We are always susceptible to offense because the other retains the power to make us feel in danger of being turned into a thing. This fear is the reality that keeps surfacing in the midst of Hegel's self-assured talk about the march toward independence, self-certainty, and autonomy. Quite different motives emerge in his consideration of "the struggle for recognition." And in spite of his rationalist intentions, Hegel's examination lays bare our abiding problems.

The Two Primary Forms of Interpersonal Relationship

The contradictions of interpersonal desire issue in two primary projects which inform the apparent diversity of roles and games that would be taken up in a full phenomenological description of "concrete relations with others."[22] The first project is the effort to achieve recognition and independence by becoming the subject of the other's desire. The second is the attempt to be released from the burden of subjectivity by giving one's being over to the other. Logically this sounds like a perfect match, but existentially it issues in mutual defeat. Mutual cruelty becomes the law of human relations conducted on this model, moral masochism being one of its most conspicuous triumphs. For each project generates internal contradictions which exacerbate the contradictions of the other project. In the process we witness the birth of cunning and the range of indirect behaviors in which human beings wage war under the sign of love. Cutting through the masks which sustain such behaviors depends on formulating the basic contradictions that suit the two projects so perfectly to one another.

1. *Domination.* To become the subject of the other's desire we try to seduce the other to freely render his or her subjectivity over to our infinitely more fascinating being. By keeping the other perpetually enthralled before the throne of a theatricalized narcissism he or she can only mirror, we strive to become a self-certain independent subject by turning the other into a dependent thing. We remain perpetually insecure, however, because we necessarily suspect that devotion conceals a secretly harbored otherness. We can never be sure we've conquered the other's inwardness. Perhaps all we receive is the mask. This doubt constitutes our self-consciousness. We live the suspicion that the other may, and probably must, desire the same status we claim. This explanation of the failure of domination strikes deeper than the humanistic view that in enslaving another all we get back is the defeated visage of a thing. That's what we never quite get . . . and never quite want.

2. *Submission.* To extinguish the burden of subjectivity we try to become the object who serves and idolizes the other. The restlessness of this project derives from the inability to abolish the consciousness of one's self-sacrificial activity. All attempts to achieve release through subjection harbor as their secret the awareness that in giving our being over to the other it is we who do so. They dominate, but we are dominated. They compel subservience, but we have the exalted consciousness that suffering knows the "human" truth of the relationship—its truth being the recognition we are denied. The martyr has the superior consciousness. The intense inwardness of moral masochism proves that subjectivity has not been renounced. Dissembled discontent underlies all servitude.

The two grand and self-contradictory projects outlined here make inwardness the essential term at issue in human relations. The subtle ways in which either position can triumph make it impossible to identify these projects with gender or to target one project as the cause of our ills. But there is one thing we can count on: we're in it together. The two projects feed into one another because they are opposite sides of a single dialectic that is present within each individual consciousness. They are externalizations of the two basic intrapsychic positions subject can and does take toward itself. In this sense, interpersonal experience can be seen as a projection in which we try to resolve our fundamental burden by splitting it in half. This is the suppressed truth of mutuality. The dialectic of the subject is doubled in intersubjective desire. But the subject's fate is also thereby revealed as inherently interpersonal. Whether that dialectic is a double bind condemning us to perpetual Sartrean defeat remains a topic for later investigation.[23] Nothing we say there, however, will alter the fundamental fact. In relating to the other there is no way to escape the conflicts Hegel has established because those conflicts constitute the inherent intersubjectivity of the subject.

Reflecting on the dialectic of desire, we can now grasp what could not have been known until now. The other is not a new dialectic, distinct from desire, but is already present in the earliest forms of desire as that anxiety which is displaced and momentarily arrested through fixation on the object. Hegel's apparent beginning, the desire for the object, is actually a detour, an attempt to arrest or retreat from what we already are. The truth of the object is that it leads us to the other because our relationship to it is a displaced staging of our initial attitude toward the other. When Hegel's text is read as a series of discrete chapters, rather than as an ever-deepening spiral of interrelated meaning, we are blinded to the way in which, in a dialectical discourse, subsequent developments always give a new and deeper understanding of previous ones.

Desire is inherently interpersonal because desire has its genesis in intersubjective experience. As long as our interrogation remained at the plane of object relations this fact could not emerge. We can now see that the transition from the object to the other, like so many in Hegel, is not "a leap of sentiment," but an uncovering of what is already at work, in displaced form, in the earlier experience. There is nothing necessary, however, about dialectical advance. Self-mediation through the internalization of suffering, rather than some purely rational process, is its sine qua non; and it is always possible to arrest its progress or regress to a prior moment. Desire can always be reified. That truth remains permanently outside dialectics, resisting sublation. We are thus left at this point in the analysis with a picture of human relations as a clash of contradictory projects wedded in mutual frustration. It is a chilling vision. Whether anything but sorrow can emerge from it depends on whether or not this situation also constitutes the very condition for subjective growth.

SUBJECTIVE GROWTH: MASTER-SLAVE AND THE STRUGGLE FOR RECOGNITION

The sources for such an understanding lie in the section Hegel titles "Master-Slave and the Struggle for Recognition." There the two grand projects outlined above achieve their existential context through the development of the following concepts: self-mastery (*Herr*), death, anxiety or "absolute fear," "desire restrained and checked," and labor as "universal formative activity." Through these concepts, Hegel adumbrates a theory of how interpersonal experience can produce fundamental change in the very being of the subject.

THE VANISHING ONE: THE CONCEPT OF SELF-MASTERY

Human relations suffer defeat whenever desire remains bound to its initial forms. To get beyond these binds, a new act of self-mediation is required. Through it, a new kind of experience becomes possible. But both possibilities require a reality to serve as their genesis. That reality is death. Self-mastery arises when one is willing to risk death by staking the meaning and value of one's life on the importance of one's relationship to the other.[24]

The two projects traced previously were doomed to frustration because both parties always kept something in reserve. The self was never fully engaged. And by playing it safe each subject got what it deserved —isolation rather than recognition. Human relations become significant only when one enters them without reserve, running the risk that one may be destroyed. From this perspective, death is not a physical threat but a psychological and existential reality. One of the things that makes us subjects is that we can stake our lives and lose ourselves irretrievably. This is the self-mediation which the master consciousness attempts. The *will* to do so is the act that makes one master—master over oneself. One is no longer displaced into a multitude of particular desires or condemned to manipulative, self-protecting relationships. One has centered one's desire in the desire for recognition. Putting that desire at stake in one's relationship to the other makes experience a matter of universal questions and values.

The self-consciousness of the master is poorly served when it is explained in terms of physical force and power in a struggle for the survival of the fittest. Staking one's life is a choice, an act of will. Self-mastery depends on overcoming all that prevents most of us from ever risking ourselves. The first thing to underscore is the rareness of the act. Self-mastery requires a reflection in which one stands back from the loud business of one's immediate worldly concerns to ask oneself universal questions. To succeed, that meditation must issue in an act in which one projects oneself, without reserve, into the quest for a genuine relationship with the other. Realizing that one's subjectivity is bound up with the other, not accidentally but fundamentally, one centers both one's self-consciousness and one's relationships in this awareness. Human relations thereby attain the possibility of being conducted on a new order. That is why self-mastery projects an ideal which the early Hegel termed love—or reciprocal recognition in a relationship between selves that is potentially infinite.

To understand self-mastery, the concepts of life and death must be given a specifically existential reading. The recognition of death as a possibility intrinsic to subject raises interpersonal relations to a new level. Self-mastery is the effort to embrace this fact with courage. When we transcend all particular objects of desire, realizing that the other represents our deepest concern, life is ours for the first time because we realize that to be alive is to have one's very being at issue.[25] The imperative to stake one's life or live the failure of never having done so is implicit in that awareness. Death is not a physical fact but a universalizing context constituted by the duties we bear toward one another as existing beings. Death is lived as the awareness that we can be destroyed by the other but must run the risk because the intersubjectivity of our being involves us in necessary and irreversible choices in the matter of human relationships.

In liberating this subtext I don't wish to minimize the quasi-Darwinian character of Hegel's language or to deny the historical and sociological value of the discussion as a contribution to the study of primitive sociopolitical relations. My purpose is to bring out the psychological complexities that are already at work in such struggles. Existential meanings don't come later, superimposed upon primary quasi-naturalistic experiences. The existential is already fully present in the first human encounter. That is why even the most primitive social relations can serve to illustrate fundamental principles that are operative in consciousness regardless of its historical circumstance. Historical readings of the *Phenomenology* confine the ontological-existential rather than liberate it.

But the most significant thing about the master, who was never, perhaps, more than an ideal,[26] is his disappearance. The ordinary fate of his project, whenever undertaken, is disappointment. The other proves incapable of a similar act. As Hegel shows, self-mastery no sooner announces itself than it disappears into its opposite. The master-slave struggle commences when disappointment and resentment over the cowardice of the other turn into aggression and dominance. The master's tragedy is the tragedy of a new consciousness trapped in an old position. He who understood existence, risked death, and tried to get the other to concentrate his or her being in a similar order of awareness suffers total defeat and collapses into resentment.

The notion that power and dominance rule in the master-slave dialectic because Hegel is talking about a primitive stage of human relations misses the point. Inwardness is a matter of interaction. The slave forces the sadistic role on the master by giving up; and he enacts his defeat in a way that is perfectly designed to drive the master mad. Inventing passive aggressive behavior, the slave cloaks his withdrawal from the challenge of human relationships in saintliness and humility. The master's aggression is a response to the passive aggressivity of another. In effect, the master says, "You want to remain a servile consciousness! OK, I'll give you what you want." But in doing so the master becomes the thing he feared—a reified consciousness, frozen in the defeated posture of dominance.

The dialectical dimension passes to the slave. Inwardness develops through ironic reversals; the dialectic of the servile consciousness is one of its subtlest hours. A servile consciousness is a consciousness forced back upon itself. This is the circumstance which produces each significant development of subjectivity in Hegel, for it entails a mediation in which, by withdrawing into itself, subject produces a total transformation of both itself and its relationship to experience. The irony producing this development is that the slave gets the exact opposite of what he or she desired. Servility craves complacency, rest, peace at any cost. But in experiencing absolute fear before the master, the slave is forced to face death. Wanting and being denied minimal recognition, that of the victim, the slave's desire undergoes a radical transformation into what Hegel terms *desire restrained and checked*. Through that experience, a new kind of suffering is born: self-contempt. It increases the very thing avoided

—inwardness. Although the slave tries to hide from it, an awareness of the truth is ineluctable. That consciousness demands a new kind of self-mediation. Labor becomes the *universal formative activity* through which this self-mediation will develop.

In developing these concepts, Hegel uncovers a striking reversal of the entire master-slave dialectic. The slave works but is deprived of the product of his labor which he renders to the master. But in receiving only the thing, the master regresses to a reified, nonessential relationship to objects—that of mere consumption. Thrown back to the earliest form of desire, he is frozen there. Deprived of the product of labor, the slave takes up a new development of the negative attitude toward otherness. Labor becomes for him the occasion for realizing his subjectivity—or what Marx terms our "species-being." Restrained and checked from realizing the desire for recognition, the slave projects that desire into his labor. Since he knows he will not consume his product, labor becomes for him an act of self-expression. "Universal formative activity" is the origin of art as self-mediation. The master owns the urn, but the slave realizes himself in it.

Though most discussions of the master-slave dialectic, including Marx's, end with an assertion of romantic and humanistic commonplaces about the power of enslavement to produce the desire for freedom, our interrogation shows that a much more complex process is at work. Humanistic interpretations have an a priori and idealistic ring. Establishing the experiential meaning and intersubjective genesis of the desire for freedom requires attention to a more conflicted and cunning dialectic.

THE SLAVE'S INWARDNESS

The slave's first and deepest awareness is of personal cowardice, of the failure to live up to the exacting terms of human relationships posited by the master. The task becomes to change the meaning of that failure while remaining in the subservient position. Resentment is the feeling dissembled beneath all the slave's complaints that the master refused recognition. And the true object of the slave's resentment is his or herself. Before the master, the servile consciousness recognizes one who achieved, through risk, what it itself feared to attempt—the centering of one's being in the overriding importance of recognition. Though having little understanding of the master's inner state, the slave now wants recognition. The desire for recognition is born not when recognition is denied but when one discovers one was afraid to pursue it. This reading demystifies the humanistic notion that we discover our humanity when it is denied. The servile consciousness harbors a much richer text. The slave has reached the point the master attained when, in the face of death, his or her inwardness was first tapped. But having been brought to this point unwillingly, the slave suffers it as self-awareness of his weakness. Self-loathing rather than a transparent consciousness of one's essential humanity is the self-consciousness that inhabits and transforms the slave.

The hard lesson of the dialectic is that the struggle for recognition is an offer one cannot refuse. *Absolute fear,* the feeling which constitutes the slave inwardness, is defined not by the threat of physical death but by the recognition that in giving up, in opting for a diminished subjectivity, one has already chosen death. This fear strips the servile consciousness of all particularity and delivers it over to itself in a mood of self-loathing and dread. In *absolute fear,* a consciousness forced back upon itself "trembles in the very depths of its being" because it now knows that its very being is at issue.

Once it has overcome all particularity, its relationship to the objective world becomes a "universal formative activity" in which subject meditates and attempts to mediate the inner suffering that has become its state. Labor is not a romantic act of unfettered self-expression, but the incarnation of a doubleness. It is both a nascent effort at self-liberation and a further expression of resentment toward both the master's superiority and one's own weakness. This subtext is the unhappiness that is dissembled in art, religion, and philosophy.[27]

Demystifying the slave, we recapture an insight into what is struggling to be born in his inwardness. The slave is the birth of unhappy consciousness, the grand theme of the *Phenomenology* and Hegel's essential contribution to a theory of subjectivity. The significance of the master's disappearance and the slave's resentment is that all interpersonal relations take on the character of mutual unhappiness. Though cloaked in various forms—ranging from sado-masochism to the most carefully orchestrated avowals of love—the basic problem when human beings first face one another is this: one unhappy consciousness confronts another equally unhappy consciousness in mutual dissembling. The dilemmas of intersubjective desire previously surveyed reassert themselves with a vengeance in unhappy consciousness, which is now aware of them. Such a self-consciousness doesn't tap some humanistic core that confers a beneficent order on experience, but suffers the awareness that will constitute the next stage of the dialectic. All consciousness is unhappy consciousness, the

condition of a "divided and merely contradictory being" whose activity
is always double and doubled back upon itself. As in Nietzsche, resentment and the dissembling of that resentment generate an unprecedented
development of inwardness.

Before embarking on a discussion of this inwardness we must pause
to reflect on the nature of the reading we are developing. The key is the
notion that Hegel's quasi-historical or genealogical investigations contain
a philosophic anthropology which identifies the basic experiences we all
go through in the process of achieving psychic structure. Naturally, we
do so in a variety of empirically distinct ways. But those differences are
irrelevant to the task of philosophic anthropology, as is the fact that most
people successfully arrest themselves at the earliest stage of development.
The task of a philosophic anthropology is to discover those experiences
that are essential to the development of subject and to articulate the
contribution they make to its internal constitution. In keeping with his
phenomenological method, Hegel's effort is to catch these existentials in
their first emergence and to connect them diachronically. His discourse
will thereby establish the continuity of those irreversible acts of self-
mediation that constitute the subjectivity of the fully actualized subject.
While Heidegger's analytic of existence has a formalistic and synchronic
character, Hegel's discourse takes an epigenetic and quasi-historical form
because his goal is to trace the immanent dialectic of those events in
psychic development that wed subject to experience.[28]

Our reading attempts to liberate this dimension of Hegel's thought
on subject from an exclusively historical reading. Throughout the *Phenomenology* Hegel uses history as the most convenient way to illustrate
experiences in the development of self-consciousness that are universally
true, transcending their historical occurrence. None of us goes through
the master-slave dialectic the way Ventidius and Spartacus did, but we
all go through analogous experiences countless times because master-slave
relating is one of the essential conflicts everyone faces. Contra the Hegel
of abstract reason, master-slave isn't an archaic episode we have passed
beyond in the triumphant march of a *Geist* liberated from its shackles,
but a problem we all must master. The past with its grand simplification
of issues serves as a convenient example of problems we confront in a
much broader sociohistorical context. There is a necessary historical line
to the *Phenomenology* because one of Hegel's central ideas is that "human
nature" is inherently historical: historicity isn't an accident attached to an
essence but an irreversible determination of our being as subjects. His-

tory changes us in fundamental ways. But this idea needs to be liberated from that antiquarianism which conveniently lops off the past. The past is trapped in the limits of its historical moment; in renewing it in a more developed context we strive to write the story it struggled toward. With their relationship properly established, no conflict exists between historical and anthropological readings because the former provides a specific instance of ontological principles that are articulated in the latter.

For purposes of philosophic anthropology, history is significant when it reveals experiences subject necessarily has to work through given the dynamics of its internal constitution. This is the rationale that lets Hegel play fast and loose with history throughout the *Phenomenology*, deleting facts, shuffling chronology, yoking experiences, attitudes, and philosophic positions far apart from one another in time. Were his concern primarily historical, these procedures would lack justification. But in terms of philosophic anthropology, history, suitably reconstructed, serves as a primary source of examples which, properly interrogated, yield insights into subjectivity which transcend their historical moment. The point of each investigation is to comprehend the contribution which the experience under consideration makes to the experiential self-mediation of subject. Our reading extends this procedure by situating all of Hegel's concepts in a contemporary context that necessarily takes us far beyond Hegel.

To Freedom Condemned: Stoicism and Skepticism

With the servile consciousness, achievement of an identity becomes the need that haunts consciousness. Identity becomes the peremptory desire because it is the way in which we give ourselves recognition. The use of historical examples notwithstanding, the experience Hegel discusses here is distinctively modern. Servile consciousness is the key transition in the development of subjectivity. All the themes externalized previously are now brought home as internal conflicts which subject must mediate in order to master itself. The dialectics of desire, master-slave, and recognition are repeated within consciousness as a series of relationships it assumes toward itself. The stages in the development of this self-mediation parallel the self-consciousnesses of the three attitudes—stoicism, skepticism, unhappy consciousness—that are interrogated in the chapter. These three attitudes are far more deeply conflicted and ambivalent than is generally thought because the contradictory pressures they resist generate the self-consciousness each attitude produces.

We have reached the promised land—self-consciousness—only to discover nothing resembling the comforts of the Cartesian cogito. Self-consciousness in Hegel is not a transparently rational identity that can be used to center and control the dispersiveness of desire, but an internally divided and deeply conflicted self-relationship that initially would like nothing better than to escape the awareness it keeps inflicting on itself. As Hyppolite sees, Hegel's great theme is the unhappiness of all reflection, the inability of a reflective subject to coincide with itself. Subject is defined by the impossibility of achieving the very thing it desires, the status of a substance.[29]

The irony of its situation is this: as a principle of critical unrest self-consciousness is always disruptive. The more subject strives to escape its unhappiness, the more this unhappiness is brought before it. Dialectic works not by steady logical progression, but by a movement in which each attempt to arrest the process of self-mediation produces a new inwardness which takes subject beyond its previous form. The movement from stoicism to skepticism to unhappy consciousness enables Hegel to establish this process as the general law of self-consciousness. Hegel's concern is with far more than a historical survey of early forms of self-awareness. His purpose is to articulate the necessary and irreversible movement any consciousness must go through in order to comprehend what it means to be a self-conscious being. Recapturing the contemporary relevance of the discussion turns on this point because the three attitudes Hegel surveys have identifiable contemporary adherents who would like to order the sequence quite differently. As a critique and reversal of the line of "progress" proclaimed in recent intellectual history, the following discussion restores the credentials of existential thought by showing its emergence from the contradictions of structuralist and deconstructive ways of thinking rather than the other way around.[30]

At first glance Hegel here appears to leave interpersonal experience for the study of philosophic and religious worldviews. But Hegel's concern is not with ideas as such, but with their meaning for the subject. The motives behind stoicism, skepticism, and unhappy consciousness, and not their logical truth or falsity, are what concerns him. The three interest him not as philosophic positions but as attitudes or life-styles developed to deal with a complex nest of conflicts and motives. In a sense, this discussion accounts for the birth of philosophy, yet Hegel's effort is to show that philosophy is thoroughly situated and continues, in a conceptual medium, the conflicts of desire previously studied. Hegel thus offers us a new way of understanding philosophy and of discovering the motives at work in a philosophic text. In discussing each position, his effort is to uncover what it tries to disguise and suppress. He does so by focusing on contradictions, knowing, long before Derrida beautifully formulated it, "that persistence in contradiction must express the force of a desire."[31]

Its motives constitute the heart of any philosophic position. Developing this heresy will make this discussion continuous with the previous one and give it a necessary progression which might be termed the progression of philosophy's bad conscience. Philosophy is not a matter of pure thinking but a complex, impassioned, and often utterly disguised response to life. Like a psychoanalyst, Hegel seeks out the motives beneath conceptual constructs because they give him the deepest insight into the desire animating the position. Contradictions are never solely a matter of logic. In fact, logical contradictions befall a position only because it persists in an effort to fulfill contradictory desires. In discovering contradictions one recovers the life of that desire.

This method of interpretation constitutes one of Hegel's basic and still insufficiently appreciated contributions to thought. I will illustrate its methodology in this section by offering (1) a phenomenological description which dramatizes the conflicts and motives in stoicism, skepticism, and the unhappy consciousness, followed by (2) a critique which reveals those contradictions as each position's contradictory desires. The second step will establish the contribution each attitude makes to the self-mediation of subject.

Stoicism, skepticism, and unhappy consciousness constitute the most mature examples Hegel could find of attempts to solve the central problem of servile consciousness: the fashioning of an identity that will assure one of freedom, universality, and a self-recognition that vanquishes dependency on the other. The movement to unhappy consciousness thus enacts an internalization of the entire previous dialectic. Master-slave becomes the way subject now relates to itself. Taking up, alternately, both stances toward itself, subject engages in a battle to master itself by exacerbating its unhappiness.

STOICISM—OR RETREAT . . . AND PURE VICTORY

The question that underlies the stoic dialectic is this: how does one preserve and enhance one's inwardness when the product in which one realizes it is appropriated and recognition denied? Stoicism corresponds to situations in which we can't realize ourselves in relationships and retreat to a privacy (though not a solipsism) of the self. If fashioning an identity is consciousness' task, stoicism is the first attempt to confront the universality of the problem. All of the desires that have been restrained and checked go into a single desire—the desire to attain freedom within self-consciousness. But since the stoic sees no way to realize freedom in the world, he projects it beyond the world. In stoicism one is free—"whether on the throne or in fetters"—by identifying oneself with a purely rational order of thought that transcends existence. In this sense, stoicism is the birth of philosophy, if we define philosophy as an attempt to achieve universal understanding of a purely rational order. The ascent to rationality is so conspicuous in Hegel's presentation here, in fact, that several commentators have offered decidedly nondialectical readings which view stoicism solely as an advance.[32]

But stoicism is not as innocent as it appears, nor as abstract. A complex desire is at work in it. Stoicism is not a bloodless abstraction, but the kind of choice a certain kind of person makes in the face of harsh existential imperatives for complex and contradictory psychological reasons. Rather than an archaic episode, stoicism is an option that is always with us. The attainment of reason is a fine thing, but the main thing a close scrutiny of the stoic motives offers is a situated redefinition of reason. Stoicism is the response one makes to suffering when suffering is seen as meaningless, irrational, and irremediable. Rationality then makes it unessential, depriving it of being. Powerless to deal with one's lot, one accepts it by, in effect, denying its reality.

The stoic ascent to universality thus effects a curious transformation of the slave's position. In the slave, desire becomes comprehensive, expressing itself as the effort to triumph over the whole of objective being by making labor a "universal formative activity" capable, eventually, of remaking all of nature in our image. With particularity transcended, our projects acquire—and require—a universal scope. Positing that project is the slave's achievement. But, in doing so, servile consciousness indulges in its own brand of hubris and self-delusion. It is one thing to project universality, quite another to achieve it, especially when one harbors a feeling not only of one's inadequacy but of the absurdity of such an undertaking in a world characterized by meaningless and unremitting pain. Unable to face that world, subject takes flight into pure thought. Failure to realize oneself in the world is thus the true genesis of stoicism and the repressed text that reveals its inner contradictions. It is also the complex self-consciousness that is avoided when the movement to stoicism is celebrated as an unequivocal advance. One can argue, and Hegel commentators as different as Hyppolite and Taylor do, that stoicism raises the slave's position—the ability to impress mind upon objects—to the universal by making the I that thinks absolute. But this reading is far too abstract and "idealistic" because it neglects the existential situation that generates abstract thought. If one forgets this situation, one misses both the motives and the real nature of any intellectual position. (We may set down this maxim as symptomatic of all rationalistic readings of Hegel.)

Thought is a product of the slave's situation; it's an attempt to overcome contradictions that can be dealt with in no other manner. The slave does not deny the significance of labor or simply transcend it in favor of those nobler objects, universals, which are the preserve of rational thought.[33] On the contrary, being deprived of concrete realization, the slave sustains the significance of his or her work in the only way left open to him: by turning to thought. Inwardness seeking recognition was objectified in a product; with that product wrested away, the only way to preserve inwardness is by making it a wholly private thing that exists in an order unto itself—an order of reason released from the contingencies of the world. Stoicism is the attempt of those who aren't free to persuade themselves that they are.

But the one thing the stoic cannot sublate in the innerness of consciousness is the fact of suffering. Unable to deal with suffering concretely, stoics take revenge upon their situation and themselves by denying the world any possible value. Those accounts which try to celebrate stoicism as an unequivocal gain omit this consideration. Both regression and a unique effort at self-mastery are at work in stoicism. Stoicism is bad faith, but a complex act of bad faith. On careful scrutiny stoicism presents a compelling picture not of the attainment of pure thought, but of the contradictions that underlie such a conception of thought.

In stoicism, freedom is identified with thought alone because the driving force in stoicism is to make suffering unessential. The stoic seeks peace at all costs because suffering is seen as unalterable and lacking any possible meaning. Accordingly, stoic rationality is permeated by exclusions and defined by the refusal to deal with everything that constitutes the particularity of human experience. Emotion is irrational, desire a brute force which must be extinguished. Stoic universality harbors as its subtext an abhorrence of contingency and particularity. Interpersonally, stoicism necessarily involves a retreat from concrete relations which are viewed as the primary source of suffering. All that one hoped to gain from a relationship with the other goes into fashioning a private self. To secure this self and give it the recognition it needs, identity must be located in a transcendent order of pure thought that remains untouched by the contingencies of experience. There is much to be said for Hegel commentaries that see stoicism as the beginning of philosophy, but the suppressed side of the story is philosophy's flight from life.

Stoicism identifies the I with thought, with the exercise of a rational function concerned solely with universals, because such an identification offers an independence and freedom of a very general and carefully protected order. Consciousness of oneself as reason liberates one from the horror of existence. The conception of reason stoicism advances bears all the scars of this denial. The moment we aren't blinded by the jargon of rationality and look closely at the stoic universal, the contradictions of the entire project emerge as its most significant truth. The bankruptcy of the stoic self is the absence of content. Stoicism necessarily conceives of thought abstractly because thought can have no connection to the world. The self thereby evolved remains utterly empty, an abstract tautology. Stoic universality thus expresses no more than the desire to find truths of so general an order that they will place one securely above existence. The entire movement of stoic thought is a progressive withdrawal from experience.

Hegel, like Freud, saw that you always get what you want. Stoic desire is eminently satisfied since the result of all intellectual operations is a dichotomy between the self of pure thought and the self found in experience. The true stoic has nothing to think about and nothing to do, for the goal of all efforts is, through thinking, to deny the reality of the world. Hoping to achieve everything by endorsing the pure movement of transcendence, stoicism comes up with nothing. Its tragedy is its denial of tragedy, the desire to escape suffering rather than to project upon it.

The contradictions Hegel finds in stoicism are far from purely logical. Indeed, the attitude has a perfect conceptual coherence. Contradictions emerge only when one uncovers the subjectivity beneath philosophic constructs. Dialectic happens when subject is drawn into the open and brought to a reversal through an unmasking of the hidden motives that keep it tied to a self-contradictory position. Through this process, the desire hidden beneath the cloak of reason is revealed. Persisting in its blind assertion, despite refutation, the attitude discloses its truth as the force of a desire. Dialectical interrogation of an attitude always addresses far more than reasons, because its purpose is to make us aware of the motives behind our deep investment in rationality and our use of it to marginalize other realities. Dialectical progress is thus a matter far more of pantragism (as Sartre said) than of panlogicism. In interrogating attitudes, Hegel forces the motives that went into them to undergo an immanent critique. The collapse in each case is internal to the attitude, a product of the effort to avoid contradictions generated by the failure to embrace reality in a more open and courageous way. This method of interpretation liberates the deepest subtext at work in stoicism. Stoicism is abstract thought taking revenge on experience. As an act of resentment, it confers a purely intellectual superiority on those who parade themselves as masters because they no longer care about the worldly affairs that occupy lesser beings. This insight into its inwardness brings out the true value of stoicism, which is quite different from the value it ascribes to itself.

Stoicism is an internalization of the master-slave dialectic. In stoicism, that dialectic becomes a dialectic within self-consciousness. Stoicism represents the first coherent attempt to become one's own master. This, its deepest meaning, is what a consciousness aware of stoicism's contradictions preserves as a far more important possibility than the impotent transcendence into which stoicism degenerates. The dialectic at work in stoicism is this: the stoic exalts the abstract "I" of pure contemplative identity in order to whip and punish the "empirical" self for its failures. Stoicism is a form of unhappy consciousness, and that is why all its efforts to escape itself produce only a deeper experience of its unrest.

Stoicism thus harbors the beginnings of a theory of self-knowledge as a tragic process requiring subject to undertake, at each stage of its development, an act of existential, and not purely conceptual, self-overcoming. All stoic efforts to escape suffering issue only in a more intense brooding about self and experience. In stoicism, suffering shifts its ground, becoming an internal affair. But the dissembled source of stoic unrest is that stoic self-overcoming tries to cancel personal subjectivity yet mocks itself for attempting such an easy escape. This self-consciousness, slumbering in stoicism, will erupt as the daemonic unrest of skepticism.

Stoicism is the proper beginning for a theory of subject because it shows that the first thing we do with subjectivity, once aware of its burdens, is take flight. Wanting the security of a substance, subject's first act is the effort to escape itself by fashioning an a priori identity in a realm of pure thought. The inwardness it harbors as its bad conscience is the knowledge that otherworldliness is grounded in weakness. The contradictions of stoicism produce the recognition that its entire effort has been to escape a more disruptive experience of the self. The dialectical

circle completes itself with the discovery, beneath the stoicism, of the new
and deeper consciousness and skepticism.

SKEPTICISM—OR PURE DECONSTRUCTIVE MANIA

Hegel's apparently abrupt transition to skepticism offers a prime
example of dialectical continuity. Skepticism continues the conflicts of
stoicism by inverting them. Directing the negativity of thought upon the
world, the skeptic attacks the weak, dissembled fears of the stoic self in
the name of a yet undiscovered self that will come into being through the
practice of unfettered negativity. While the stoic fled the world, the skeptic will annihilate it. Reflection was contemplative peace amid abstract
universals for the stoic; it will become an unremitting exercise of negativity for the skeptic. Whereas stoicism rested on a dichotomy between
the transcendent and the empirical selves, the dichotomies generated in
skepticism will all exist wholly inside consciousness. We thereby experience dialectical reversal not as something that happens but as something
subject brings upon itself. The paradoxes and aporias to which reflection will thereby be driven—as it repeatedly splits then negates both the
reflecting self and the self reflected upon—produce an inwardness skepticism continually intimates without being able to comprehend. It can't,
as we'll see, because doing so would reveal the deeper unhappiness the
project is designed to exorcise. At the beginning, of course, skeptic consciousness knows little of this. All it knows is that the bankruptcy of
stoicism necessitates a plunge into the unrest stoicism fled.

Hegel terms skepticism "absolute dialectical unrest" and sees it as
the first realization of a genuinely negative attitude toward experience,
the first true appropriation of negativity as the power constituting the
essence of self-consciousness. While stoicism was a retreat from the unrest
of subjectivity, skepticism is an attempt to ride it out, to give full and free
play to the internal restlessness that defines subject. "In the destructive
element immerse" is its motto. The skeptic's *desire* is to experience the
absolute freedom of thought by making thought a principle capable of
annihilating the entire phenomenal world. True to its principle, it can
complete the operation only by destroying itself.

Skepticism moves toward the feeling of *independence* denied stoicism
because here consciousness actively produces the dialectic rather than
passively suffer it. The skeptic defines himself as "the spirit that always
denies." Negation becomes the principle through which one will forge an
identity. *Self-certainty* lies in the practice of ceaseless criticism. Stoicism

sought to identify with an abstract ideal of thought which transcends individual consciousness. Skepticism knows that consciousness, through its negativity, is already that ideal in principle and as process. Self-certainty can't be sought outside ourselves or conferred a priori; it must be found in the immanent movement of consciousness itself. This is a watershed moment because dialectic is now fully internalized. Hegel's great maxim "To be aware of limitations is to be already beyond them" will now be lived out concretely. The skeptic's project is to comprehend the negativity defining subject by deconstructing all presences, especially the self-presence in thought that informed stoicism. Seeing through everything, however, skeptics will always have to see through one more thing—themselves.

Rather than launching a self-enriching process of determinate negation, the need to go beyond limitations may doom the skeptical subject to a ceaseless process of self-unraveling. Such, at any rate, will constitute the skeptic's experience, not because negativity is a bad thing, but because the skeptic's understanding of it remains far too abstract. Skepticism degenerates into logical binds and linguistic aporias because its understanding of negativity remains formalistic. This happens because skepticism performs the labor of the negative in bad faith, with its vast intellectual energetics deployed to protect itself from an experience it cannot face. Skepticism, like stoicism, is already unhappy consciousness, but tries to suppress a genuinely existential experience of that fact by turning absurdity and paralysis into facts of a purely logical or linguistic order. Thought, like the ouroboros, eats its own tail; the skeptics' task is to convict the self of its own impossibility. As a genuine but arrested dialectic, skepticism conceals through sheer intellectual brilliance its failure to confront the experiential sources of its discontent. That failure is then made foolproof through a deconstruction of the possibility of experience. As in stoicism, philosophizing is the act through which one conceals and later forgets one's roots. The pursuit of truth becomes a purely intellectual exercise, indeed a game, in which self-paralysis becomes the proof of one's superiority.

Because the dependency of objective being on human activity is here seized in the most abstract way—and separated from concrete labor—skepticism degenerates into the trivial game of proving that the external world does not exist. When its operation is extended to consciousness itself, however, truly exciting things happen. In annihilating the self one solves two problems at a stroke: one eliminates the problem of the other, and one becomes absolute master over oneself. Self-recognition becomes endless praxis: each position that arises is negated in an unending celebration of negativity as an end in itself. Skepticism is the content that accepts no content except as grist for its mill. The controlling need is to prove that intellectual daring—and the ability to embrace the most despairing position—is a substitute for experiential daring. The truth the posture hides is that the two are not equivalent and that the intellectual act suppresses psychological motives that keep breaking through. Experience can be controlled by reducing it to a conceptual bind or linguistic puzzle, but it cannot be done away with quite that easily. It keeps erupting on the margins, to use a fashionable term, of all efforts to eradicate it. The skeptical dissolution of the self will become the occasion for its richest recovery—as unhappy consciousness.

Skepticism's failure derives from the abstractness of its dialectics. In skepticism every problem becomes a logical game with an identical result: the inability to say anything or to escape the prison-house of language. Skepticism's denial is the denial of knowledge itself. There is no such thing as perception.[34] Trapped in language, which moves us where it lists, we are constantly adrift, lost in "the vertiginous possibilities of referential aberration."[35] There is no origin, center, structure, or end to either thought or discourse that is not thoroughly disrupted by the dispersive energies of free play. Such is the litany of skepticism in its contemporary realization. The skeptic's effort is to discover the binds that make discourse impossible and experience unattainable. The best we can attain is the knowledge that we, at least, are demystified where others remain blind. The strong reader is the one who knows, with Paul de Man, that reading is impossible. His own energy alone compels the skeptic's admiration, an energy that spends itself in constructing a formalism of pure linguistic and logical binds. The beauty of the prison-house is that it protects one from analyzing the "self" who inhabits it.

To prevent that operation, skepticism must dissolve the self. Trapped in a fundamental irony, skepticism is hoisted by its own petard. The unlimited expression of critique as an end in itself, unchecked by any reference to experience, must turn upon and cancel itself. Rather than issuing in a coherent self, the skeptical exercise of negativity ends, as Hegel says, in "total inner and outer disorder." Deconstructing the self is its finest flower—and its innermost necessity. Only so can the celebration of sheer energetics escape determination, which is the true enemy of abstract freedom. To attain that security, skepticism must void itself of content. The self must be reduced to a logical and linguistic puzzle: we are inserted in language which thinks us; the self is a logical and sociological impossibility, a fiction without reference, a category mistake. Through such operations, the existential unhappiness behind the desire to eliminate subject is put out of play. Deconstructing the subject absolves us of the need to take an in-depth look at our psychological motives. Assiduous abstraction puts existential issues on permanent reserve.[36]

Unfettered abstraction is essentially this: the need to resolve everything in experience into dichotomies of starkly opposed terms that are denied the possibility of any dialectical interaction. Adept at this operation, the skeptic thrives on the ability to generate "meaning" by taking the terms of a reigning discourse and simply inverting them. Showing how the marginalized term disrupts and overturns the "order" created by the primary term, one creates, through a purely formal operation, a discourse that is necessarily disruptive and comprehensive. This strategy enjoys a certain hegemony in contemporary criticism, but its source is as old as Plato. Whenever one divides the world, or any given problem, into two overarching terms and then explains experience by analogizing everything to one or the other side of the dichotomy, one has created a condition ripe for the skeptical inversion of the hierarchy thereby established. Abstraction is a wonderful thing because it produces a pseudo-content of sufficient largeness that studying the complexities of concrete human relations becomes unnecessary.

To probe skeptical inwardness, we must interrogate the skeptic's desire and the curious conditions of its satisfaction. Mastering the game of abstraction empowers one with an intellectual brilliance that can triumph over any situation. What is thereby exorcised? And what energies are thereby liberated? A psychological interrogation of skepticism begins with the recognition that skepticism is an angry reaction to the collapse of stoicism, to the failure of rationalist deliverance and the emptiness of all cogitos. The joy of self-deconstruction is that one thereby erects the perfect defense against any internalization of suffering. The sham is that beneath the self's disappearance lurks a pride which the skeptic can't help voicing: "I'm the one demystified being, forever safe because I've triumphed over existence itself." By exercising a critical energy too fine to suffer any determination, the skeptic forever holds experience at a safe distance. One is reminded of Hume, and his calm acceptance of a fundamental contradiction between thinking as a philosopher and living as a man. Through a purely linguistic endorsement of the absurd, contemporary skepticism achieves a similar state. Unless one sustains a dispassionate attitude toward one's demystifying activities, the contradiction between thought and life will surface and with it the need to adopt a new relationship to oneself.[37]

In struggling to suppress this contradiction, skepticism reveals its psychological subtext as an effort to ward off depression. The most interesting thing about Hegel's skeptic is the delight he takes in the untrammeled exercise of his power, the manic character of the whole project. One treasured idea after another falls before the withering force of an energy that ceaselessly celebrates itself. Just as stoicism may be seen as a form of schizoid withdrawal, skepticism might be seen as the perpetual dance of a turbulent existence that is afraid to stop, to risk closure and collect meanings, because halting the process means confronting oneself. Like Hamlet after the "play within the play," the skeptic has to keep the dance of wit going because its purpose is to delay death. That is why Hegel's skeptic stakes everything on freedom yet achieves a freedom of an abstract and wholly formal order. Freedom here is the rejection of all determination. The "self" it issues in—and deconstructions notwithstanding, the skeptic hugs this self—is like the Sartrean *pour-soi*, a self made permanently secure by the ceaseless canceling of each prior determination. Such freedom gives itself determinations only to blow them away, and the self resumes a spontaneity that cleanses and renews it by voiding experience.

As a consequence, skepticism arrests itself in the immediacy or first form of self-consciousness. It recognizes the unhappiness of all reflection only to deny rather than project upon that fact. All existential content is dissolved in a reflection that turns despair into a game. Such freedom plays it as it lays—"Why not?" being its response to all questions—whereas authentic freedom is the act of giving oneself determination. The skeptic cannot endure that process because it requires accepting the world as an equal partner in one's thought. With experience its suppressed term, skepticism remains mired in abstract reflection. And it forestalls a genuine interrogation of the rich psychological turmoil it harbors by keeping everything moving in the direction of a pure deconstructive mania. The skeptic can't be examined for he has already deconstructed any framework we would use to look at him.

Skepticism, like stoicism, is already a form of unhappy consciousness shaped by the effort to displace that awareness. Its manic flight from regarding suffering as significant, not unfortunate, experience is its most revealing moment because it confronts skepticism with the need for three in-depth examinations: of the experiential self; of the world as the scene of a fundamental situatedness that can't be denied; and of freedom as the act, not of rising above all determinations, but of giving oneself determination. The skeptic's demystified state is a mystification, and that is the blind spot skepticism represses. It deconstructs the self in order to avoid facing what emerges, through its failure, as the first cohesive self—unhappy consciousness.

Unhappy consciousness unlocks the fact that skepticism suppresses. Unhappiness is not a burden one can escape through thought, but a condition one must project upon by accepting experience, as that primary reality one can't deny, into the interiority of one's consciousness. Rather than an abstract problem before which one enacts a purely formal paralysis, experience must become the scene where one uncovers those contexts of self-mediation through which subject achieves concrete determination. To do so, subject must undertake an in-depth inquiry into its unhappiness, beginning with the recognition that ill will toward suffering is the basic tendency it must reverse.

It would be unwise to underestimate the staying power of skepticism. Skepticism is a permanent threat to dialectic—or a recurrent antidialectic within dialectic—because it offers such a richly satisfying expression of the critical energies that must fuel dialectic. Both live "the labor of the negative"—skepticism as the power that cancels all determinations, dialectic as the power through which one achieves self-determination. While the latter includes the former as a moment within a larger context, the former threatens to dissolve that context as an illusory progress. That is why dialectic and deconstruction are so easily confused and why reading recent intellectual history is such an ambiguous and seemingly circular pursuit. Recent advances in critical sophistication signal regressions to an earlier stage of dialectical development; yet the effort to restore that larger context appears foredoomed to deconstruction. With that contemporary dilemma in mind, the transition we now make to the unhappy consciousness entails two arguments: that structuralism and poststructuralism recapitulate the movement from stoicism to skepticism, and that our task today is to renew unhappy consciousness by situating deconstruction within a position that is scarcely mentioned any longer—existentialism.

Self-Consciousness as Unhappy Consciousness

The concept of unhappy consciousness is Hegel's richest contribution to the theory of subject. It is also his most frustrating discussion. Insights of great magnitude are buried in minute details about early Christian worship as if the former needed the latter for their embodiment. Nowhere else does Hegel's tendency to panlogicism—his need to intrude the *für uns* in order to assure us where the whole discussion is going, and his tendency to lose himself in particulars while arguing for the deductive and logical necessity of those very particulars—prove more intrusive. Extracting the kernel from the shell is a redoubtable labor because what Hegel gives us here is not simply a discussion of unhappy consciousness but a prime instance of philosophy as unhappy consciousness. The discussion mimics its subject matter; Hegel consistently uncovers major existential and psychological insights only to retreat into a contemplative meditation on their logical necessity and their eventual transcendence once one achieves the standpoint of *Geist*. The unhappiness of philosophy could not be better illustrated, nor could its struggle with itself produce more fruitful results.

To recapture the contribution this discussion makes to a theory of subjectivity, I will develop a series of interrogations which progressively probe and deepen the inwardness of the unhappy consciousness. As Dostoyevsky remarked of the soul, reading Hegel on unhappy consciousness is like peeling away the layers of an onion.

FIRST INTERROGATION: FROM LOGIC TO SUFFERING

Unhappy consciousness is the truth of skepticism because it brings together what skepticism split apart—the insight that consciousness is somehow the unity of self-identity and ceaseless change. Rather than identify with one of these functions or simply alternate between them, consciousness must mediate this contradiction. The impossibility of escaping this task is the first definition of unhappy consciousness.

The development of subject from stoicism to skepticism to unhappy consciousness might be recapitulated as follows. The stoic self is defined by the attempt to identify oneself with pure thought in order to escape the burden of existing. The desire is to achieve identity with and as an unchanging substance. The skeptical self is defined by the effort to ride out the sheer energetics of negativity in order to achieve oneness in utter contingency. The desire is purge the desire for identity in order to coincide with oneself as ceaseless flux. The unhappy consciousness brings together the terms—and the experiences—that the two hold apart. It thus constitutes their "truth" by revealing both as already instances of unhappy consciousness, the dialectic of each being an effort to escape this awareness.

The unhappy consciousness is a self radically divided within itself. The bad faith of the previous attitudes is the effort to employ one side of the self's division to get rid of the other. The unhappy consciousness disallows that escape route. Though it continually vacillates between the unchanging and the changing, it always experiences its opposite in whichever term it favors. This frustration is the key to its advance beyond the self-defeating strategies of stoicism and skepticism. For in holding together its extremes unhappy consciousness insists, in spite of itself, on a genuine self-mediation in which consciousness will no longer deny any part of itself but will take up its contradictions.

The refusal to escape proves that a genuine advance has taken place. Everything projected in the previous attitudes is now internalized; everything denied is experienced. Advance happens, not by reason of logic, but because of a new willingness to accept and project upon suffering. In stoicism and skepticism, unhappiness was externalized; misery and evil were seen as products of external situations. In unhappy consciousness, suffering is recognized as our lot; its source lies in the inwardness of the self. Unhappy consciousness is the recognition that we suffer prior to and beyond all worldly situations. Suffering has its source in consciousness. It is, in fact, the primary definition of consciousness. Suffering isn't something that befalls us, but an existential reality which confers upon us the possibility of a new order of inwardness. Seeing stoicism and skepticism as defenses against the experience of suffering, unhappy consciousness makes that reflection the basis for a total transformation of consciousness' relationship to itself. That act constitutes an irreversible advance beyond previous forms of consciousness because subject now grounds itself in the recognition that it is internally contradictory.

Hegel's great theme is the unhappiness of all reflection. That theme is here announced in its simplest terms. Self-consciousness is unhappy consciousness because the perpetual discovery of reflection is the same one that is lived immediately by desire—the inability of subject to coincide with itself. *Subject is the repeated experience of the impossibility of attaining the status of substance—and the impossibility of relinquishing that desire.*

Experientially, the unhappy consciousness suffers this recognition long before it becomes an explicit awareness. The gradual process whereby it gets from the former to the latter constitutes the dialectic of its experience. (Noting the gradualness of the development prevents a serious misunderstanding. Reflection occurs in many ways before it becomes a self-conscious imperative.) Forced back upon itself by the defeat of skepticism, unhappy consciousness accepts as its basic determination what skepticism tried to resolve abstractly: the unhappiness of existence cannot be denied but must inform the inwardness of consciousness. The existential world that skepticism tried to deny is thereby recovered; the brooding of consciousness finally has a content.

Unhappy consciousness is a decisive advance because it keeps its opposite alive in whatever stance it adopts. This circumstance compels it to reincarnate its inner dialectic in every turn. Contradictions are no longer resolved by extreme choices, but dramatized by a restlessness in which consciousness continually finds itself torn between the unchanging and the changing. A strictly rational account of this dichotomy cannot explain this movement because it abstracts from the primary fact: the dichotomy is lived and suffered not as a logical dilemma but as the self-reference defining the inwardness of consciousness. Hegel's conceptual language conceals an experience that is far more basic than logic.

A phenomenological description of unhappy consciousness will bring out that richer text. Consciousness has become the act of brooding over existence. Its mood combines infinte longing with a sense of defeat that has already gone the way of self-loathing. To be conscious is to fail repeatedly in the effort to coincide with oneself. This recognition, taken up into the inwardness of one's self-relation, produces a consciousness that is defined by anguish over the question "Who am I?" Longing for a self and the lack of assurance about ever achieving an identity have now become matters of infinite concern.[38] Nothing of this sort happens in stoicism and skepticism because those positions were fashioned to prevent an experience of the real disorders of subjectivity. Internally divided over its own value, the inwardness of unhappy consciousness is constituted by a brooding which is existential in the best sense of that term: the meaning of existence is questioned within an anguished consciousness that one's very being is at issue in that question. Skeptical unrest is no longer confined to logical games but bitterly directed on all the details of subject's concrete existence. What skepticism was as a pose is now the truth of inwardness: the need to deprive oneself of all inner and outer calm.

Unhappy consciousness is the first fully psychoanalytic moment in Hegel because here subject first begins to uncover the motives underlying its attitudes and actions. It is also the first coherent self because here the self has explicitly become a problem to itself. And, for all its vacillation, the unhappy consciousness can accept no cheap solutions. Taking issue with oneself has become one's primary self-reference. Subject will no longer abide any answer that doesn't address the depth of its unhappiness.

Experience is no longer a knowledge affair or an illusory phenomenon. The world reemerges as a realm of inescapable facticities which subject must take upon itself because projecting oneself in experience has become an inner imperative. Skepticism vanquished, subject confronts its situatedness in the search for those experiences that engage it in a way that allows the sublation of its contradictions. We stand at the origins of existential engagement, and the issue is necessarily one of extremity because the only experiences which matter are those which involve subject in a fundamental way. The distinguishing feature of unhappy consciousness is the centering of inwardness in a contradictory pressure: subject is defined by an infinite concern which may never be fulfilled but which cannot be renounced. To be a subject is to live a double bind.

With this description in mind, we will now attempt to define the basic laws of self-consciousness. Despite all efforts to escape, the recognition unhappy consciousness suffers is the impossibility yet inescapability of reflection within a recurrent experience that *nothing* can withstand reflection. It lives this condition through an unremitting critique of the very values it projects. Once referred to the brooding that defines unhappy consciousness, all projects not only fail to alleviate its state but actually make it worse.

Unhappy consciousness repeatedly inflicts this experience on itself because it relates everything to the one fact that is for it truly significant—death. The significance of death, first announced in the experience of the "sovereign master," is here renewed. The question "Who am I?" becomes the question "What can I do in response to the fact of death?" Death becomes the term to which all experiences are referred; it convicts most of our activities of utter insignificance. Death is the mother of inwardness, of that brooding that now defines subject. It is also the experiential reference that prevents any relapse into skepticism. For death establishes experience as the place where subject must project its unrest.

Death carries the question "Who am I?" into the world at large. Concrete experience is thereby reclaimed and charged with a universal responsibility. Once brooding is projected upon the particulars of experience, we see the inadequacy of everything we held dear. Subject now restlessly pursues coincidence with itself as if to say, "Stay, thou art so fair." But, like Faust, it journeys through the world only to increase its feelings of defeat and infinite longing. This is the moment when religious otherworldliness enters the picture. But to understand what is at work in religion—and why Hegel chooses it as the privileged example of unhappy consciousness—we must recapture all that festers beneath the deliverance it promises.[39]

Prior to the otherworldly projection of its infinite longing, unhappy consciousness is haunted by loss and emptiness. It mourns vanished hopes, and this mourning has already gone the way of a melancholia which masochistically turns its unhappiness back upon itself.[40] *That act, however, constitutes the sublation of desire.* The lack that defined desire has now become the effort, through mourning, to internalize the loss of all external supports for one's being. Brooding is the only possible response because this recognition of loss constitutes the first awareness of both one's total responsibility and one's utter failure to attain the status of substance. It is not surprising that the first effort of a subject harboring such an inwardness is to flee the world, nor that the project derives from a psychodynamics that Freud will later articulate.

God is the Idea in which unhappy consciousness projects both its longing for the parent as substance and the overestimation one accords that source precisely when one feels it slipping away. Subject is thus necessarily caught in the ambivalence that accompanies such a rendering of one's being to the other. Melancholia and masochistic self-criticism indirectly express aggression toward the sovereign other. They also thereby constitute the first step toward liberation. The death of God begins with his birth; this is the process which the development of unhappy consciousness will gradually trace. Unhappy consciousness' fate is that every attempt it makes to flee the world renews the need to overcome the psychological condition that motivated its flight. *Self-mastery* will come only with an acceptance of what religion flees. That irony constitutes the dialectic at work in Hegel's discussion of religion.

While unhappy consciousness only gradually comes to understand itself, Hegel's discussion provides an extended demonstration of that necessity, through the operation of basic laws, whereby self-consciousness remains constantly present as a force in the immediacy of consciousness. The constant imperative of reflection is that one must transform oneself totally, with a new plunge into experience as the only way one can undertake that task. Inwardness requires existence. And it is that process which gives the dialectics of subject a necessarily progressive direction.

Self-consciousness is an act of determinate experiential self-overcoming. Intrapsychic structure is the result of this process.

Such is the self-knowledge unhappy consciousness will attain, though at the beginning it knows naught of this. This knowledge is, rather, the subtext we must pry loose from Hegel's description of the progress of Christianity from Judaism to medieval asceticism if we are to recapture the secret religion hides—its meaning as a psychological phenomenon.

SECOND INTERROGATION: TOWARD A
PANTRAGIC UNDERSTANDING OF SUBJECT

The defining characteristic of unhappy consciousness is that it lives the unity of a contradiction. Any attitude it takes harbors its opposite. As in Dostoyevsky, when sunk in the sensual one longs for the eternal; when contritely religious one pines for the world. Hegel's discussion demonstrates why such conflicts must arise. As the unity of a contradiction, unhappy consciousness is necessarily driven out of each position it adopts and forced to incarnate its inner dialectic anew in each resolution it supposedly attains. The first instance of this process is dramatized in the opposition between the Unchanging and change because unhappy consciousness constructs this dichotomy both to punish itself and to express its pain. Since it regards its situation as meaningless, its effort is to separate the Unchanging from the world of change. It then seals its unhappiness by positing the former as wholly outside itself. Consciousness is thus confined to the unessential, trapped in contingency. Its task is to transcend itself.

Hegel's account of this development provides a fittingly ironic example of the inadequacy of panlogical explanation. He claims that the awareness of the contradiction between the Unchanging and the changeable forces consciousness to identify itself with the latter. That explanation is a priori, however, because it implies that consciousness regards experiencing contradiction as indicative of some defect in itself. Such a view washes only if contradiction and difference are already conceptualized as "evil," with perfection located in the abstract judgment of identity—*A* is *A*. The most dubious thing such an account requires is the assumption that the unhappy consciousness grasps its situation in such abstract terms.

An experiential explanation opens up a much richer possibility. The unhappy consciousness is a consciousness at war with itself, engaged in an effort both to belittle and to overcome itself. Exalting the Unchanging and overestimating one's distance from it serves both motives. The situational factor that warrants this reading introduces further motives which also have little to do with logic. Unless it seeks identification with the Unchanging, consciousness can't surmount skepticism, which took identification with the changing to the end of the line. Yet, unless it regards the project of otherworldliness as untenable, it will revert to stoicism. To achieve self-contradicting unity and sublation of those attitudes it must posit the Unchanging as wholly other yet refuse to remain indifferent to this otherness.

Logical reasons alone can't account for such a consciousness. Positing the Unchanging is an act of desire, and desire here reveals the new ambivalence that will come to characterize it. Desire is now the act of simultaneously positing a value and alienating oneself from that value. The object's unattainability creates its importance; our separation from it becomes the token of its power.

The opposition thus generates an impossible bind—of desire primarily and only secondarily of logic. Platonism and Christian otherworldliness are attempts to maintain a conceptual handle on the problem. The phenomenal world is sacrificed in order to keep the dichotomy intact in its initial and abstract form. Unhappiness is overcome by being denied any place in the order of being. Ironically, such a project succeeds only by a fit of abstraction, an insistence on purely conceptual solutions. Logic thereby reveals itself as a primary form of unhappiness: the desire to dissolve existence in abstract thought in order to transcend internal pain.

But Hegel knows that such abstraction is impossible because unhappy consciousness always produces its opposite afresh in each moment. (This insight plays havoc with every panlogical attempt Hegel makes to contain its implications.) The unhappiness at the core of consciousness exerts a constant pressure; both sides of the founding dichotomy thereby become haunted by absence. The Unchanging, empty, pines for worldly content; the unessential, lost, longs for deliverance. Unhappy consciousness is the origin (or what Derrida would call the nonorigin) of religious otherworldliness: the feeling of personal unworthiness is what posits the other world as alone possessing value. But that act gives no relief. Unhappy consciousness remains dissatisfied with its projections. Without this inner tension, God—or the movement of transcendence—would win. Such a solution works only if one can extinguish the unhappiness informing it. But unhappy consciousness preserves itself by constantly taking issue with itself. All its efforts to be rid of itself only underscore its need to overcome itself by mediating its contradictions in another way.

Although at this point in its progress passivity rules, unhappy consciousness remains blind to its underlying motives only to have them reemerge whenever it feels delivered from itself. This dilemma makes unhappiness, not logic, the principle of dialectical advance. Unhappy consciousness is distinguished from stoicism and skepticism by its internalization of what they dissembled. Unhappiness doesn't befall a consciousness otherwise at peace with itself, but coincides with the very inwardness of consciousness. Stoicism and skepticism tried to externalize this condition of ongoing self-mediation. Its internalization does not merely bring consciousness to a higher level of logical operations; it deepens and transforms consciousness' very relationship to itself. Suffering is not a logical but an existential advance, an internalization of the knowledge of what it means to be a subject. Accepting suffering is the sine qua non of subjective growth. That is why each development of unhappy consciousness uncovers more concrete experiential themes. The experiences that Hegel will shortly set down as necessary to subject's development —dread, shame, sin, guilt, and the problem of sexual identity—must be comprehended not as historical curiosities but as essential self-mediations.

Referring the unhappy consciousness to previous dialectical themes reinforces our argument for a tragic and psychoanalytic, rather than a logical, understanding of what happens when subject makes the Unchanging the privileged term. Unhappy consciousness is the internalized sublation of desire. It repeats, through relationship to itself, what desire hoped to realize through relationship to the world. Fulfillment in the object desired, the other, is now projected beyond the world. In God one can satisfy the desire to identify with a substantialized self, even if that self is wholly other. What desire suffered externally—the failure of the object, once had, to quench desire—is now experienced as subject's inner state. Desire sublated has become the desire for self-identity felt by a being who experiences inner reality as a ceaseless flux of feelings and impulses lacking all coherence. Without a center and, apparently, any power of self-centering, subject's noncoincidence is experienced as that repeated loss which cancels all efforts by unmasking the impossible desire at their source—the desire for a substantial identity. Bereft of experiential realization, that desire can sustain itself only by projecting identity as the property of another subject who would, in effect, be infinite subjectivity substantialized, centered, in full possession of itself. If God did not exist it would be necessary to invent him, for God is the adequate idea whereby we measure our pain.

The only meaningful sublation of desire for the object is the effort to have oneself as one's object. That project failed, the desire persists. Unable to see itself as ever attaining the status of substance, unhappy consciousness abases itself before that concept. It thus renews and internalizes the master-slave relationship. In defining the unchanging as wholly other and unreachable, it repeats, as its primary way of relating to itself, the initial relation of the awed slave to the sovereign master. This dialectic now takes place, however, within the inwardness of subject. In projecting God, the unhappy consciousness projects an ideal for itself. No matter how much it may subsequently whip itself for failing to reach that ideal, the projection implies the gradual reversal of the relationship. The desire for God is really the desire to achieve self-mastery. In projecting God consciousness indirectly posits an insight into its own powers.

Unhappy consciousness is the systematic recognition of the impossibility of all desired presences. Substantial self-presence is a myth because all of our moods, emotions, and thoughts are condemned to a reflection which deprives them of their supposed immediacy, transparency, and revelatory power. The double bind of unhappy consciousness anticipates and reinterprets Derridean "differance."[41] The desire for presence is not subsequent to consciousness; it is the original act through which consciousness takes issue with itself. Desire is divided, not because it lacks an origin, but because it destabilizes all apparent origins. Dissatisfaction is the fruit of critical reflection, not because reflection dissipates itself in tracking the trace, but because it is defined by the drive toward self-overcoming.[42]

Unhappy consciousness is unique because it raises this condition of division and dissatisfaction to the level of a self-feeling. Unhappiness is a weak term to describe the mood corresponding to such an act. The emotional state Hegel discusses here is not a passivity before unpleasant facts of life, but a rich recognition of one's internal self-division, which makes active and creative what was passively suffered and blindly resisted in stoicism and skepticism. Unhappy consciousness concretizes "the absolute dialectical unrest" that characterized skepticism. Manic diffusion and self-unraveling energetics are now referred to suffering, and to that inwardness centered in subject's awareness of its self-contradictory nature. Its mood or self-feeling is the most significant thing about any attitude because it inaugurates the self-reference struggling to be born. Hegel grasps what Heidegger will later brilliantly conceptualize: the ontologically revelatory power of certain basic moods. By turning "absolute dialectical unrest" into intellectual play, skepticism failed to internalize its psychological state. In what finally amounts to an angry attack on existence itself, free play displaces anxiety, giving one the heady sense of a freedom which outstrips nostalgia, since any mood that burdens signifies a failure to attain the intellectual transcendence of despair. But this position is rife with bad faith for it inverts the (true) relationship of consciousness to itself. Hegel "reads" Derrida and de Man in a way that will restore the proper sequence. Unhappiness is the only mood adequate to the dialectical unrest of subject. Internalizing one's unrest prevents the diffusion that characterizes skepticism by engendering a self-consciousness which stays focused on the central questions of experience. Brooding on suffering is the act that makes subject worthy of its knowledge. Analogous to Spinoza's adequate idea, one's mood is the proof of one's awareness and the initial form of one's self-consciousness.

All inauthentic responses to the burden of subjectivity entail an effort to escape that reality. Unhappy consciousness makes no definitive break with such inauthentic tendencies and will require a complex internal development before it earns the revolutionary turn it has taken. But proof of that turn consists of the fact that subject now has a guilty conscience about all efforts to escape itself. Unhappiness permeates all "solutions." The tragic introduces its credentials as the only adequate category for comprehending human existence.

THIRD INTERROGATION: TOWARD THE CASTLE—
HEGEL, A KAFKA OF THE SACRED

Unhappy consciousness sublates desire in an act of self-reflection that produces a total transformation of consciousness. Standing back from the world, consciousness now sees that it itself necessarily transcends all worldly objects and situations. Desire is thereby universalized. Consciousness also experiences its impossibility. To preserve itself, consciousness displaces both recognitions into the new form desire assumes: the quest for a transcendent object that will provide a satisfaction than can't be found in the world. This move is *a necessary mistake,* for it produces an unprecedented growth of inwardness that takes subject beyond all previous attitudes and forms. Desire, now experienced as that infinite longing which goes beyond all objects, totalizes itself as a dissatisfaction with life in general. That mood issues in a concept—the transcendent. Desire for that substance reveals the empty rationalism of stoic, Cartesian, and structuralist formalisms. For the transcendent is now charged with the task of fulfilling, not annulling, all of the desires at work in the subject.

Subject's experience of its nothingness concretizes the self-mediation implicit in desire. We thereby attain the great tragic formula defining the inwardness of the unhappy consciousness: desire, as the "consciousness of life in general," has become "an agonizing over one's existence and one's activity."[43] Subject passes the judgment of nada on the entire phenomenal world. This judgment is the motive behind the desire for the unchanging. The operations generating religious consciousness thus partake of the Kafkaesque. The changing and unchanging are set in such stark opposition that any chance of uniting ourselves with the unchanging is rendered impossible because it would import changeableness into it. Recognition from God, the supreme Other, would destroy the projection of infinite desire by suggesting that the Transcendent needs or takes any interest in our quest. To fulfill itself, the religious project must remain absurd. Its abjectness is manifested by the single-minded desire for an object that can have nothing whatsoever to do with the way we are. We crave recognition from this object, but giving it any qualities similar to those characterizing our consciousness destroys the project by suggesting that the desired object resembles us. Each attempt to unite with the unchanging thus produces a deeper unhappiness, which is the real purpose of the whole exercise. In religion, unhappy consciousness engages in the act of punishing itself for desiring to escape itself. Ironically, it is the process of backing itself into a corner which will leave it with no option but to take up its burdens.

The origin of religious consciousness is also the origin of a self-consciousness that will put an end to religion. Once subject sees religion as the project in which it alienates itself from itself by taking its own innermost power—self-consciousness—and setting that power outside itself as the property of another being, it will have no choice ultimately but to reclaim itself. This double movement is a direct result of the self-experience out of which religion arises. Religious consciousness knows the nothingness of both the world and itself without being able to raise that awareness to the level of a self-consciousness that could overcome that nothingness by giving itself, through self-mastery, the kind of being proper to a subject. Because it regards the ideal as a substance, it must posit it as outside itself and then use that act to reinforce the feeling of its own unworthiness.

Religion is the project in which unhappy consciousness both reveals and conceals its potential self-consciousness. Unhappy consciousness ex-acerbates the unhappiness that founds it by engaging in repeated exercises of bad faith. Subject gains an insight into its powers by simultaneously projecting the idea of a fully actualized self-consciousness and making that self-consciousness the property of another. To become adequate to itself it must reclaim and internalize what it has thereby externalized. Religious desire is essentially this: our own best image, our innermost possibility, projected as a state outside of and beyond ourselves. This displacement occurs because religion is an internalized repetition of the master-slave dialectic, with self-mastery projected as the property of a self-consciousness we desire but feel unable to attain. Implicit in the act, however, is the possibility that subject can now take action within itself.

Desire reflected back into itself universalizes itself as unhappy con-sciousness. This development proceeds from a deep and long-standing experience of a repeated failure to find "happiness." Unhappy conscious-ness is attained when one turns that experience into a charge against oneself. One is no longer Bellow's Henderson: "I want" is replaced by "I've failed." The psychological process known as identification with the aggressor is here revealed as a primary source of inwardness and of the tortured, indirect route necessary for its development. In turning against oneself one makes one's desire both the desire for self-consciousness and the act of an incipient self-consciousness. The former is the explicit text of religious otherworldliness, the latter its gradually evolving subtext. Be-cause consciousness sees loss and incessant change as the truth of "empiri-cal" experience, saving the ideal of self-consciousness requires projecting it outside oneself. Otherworldliness generates a psychological split within consciousness between quotidian experience and the autonomy it craves. Consciousness lives the gulf between the changing and the unchanging and tortures itself with the impossibility of bridging the gap. The secret it harbors is that self-consciousness requires change, but it will accept this truth only after a strenuous effort to deny it. For what Freud later terms primary masochism has here become the psychological position unhappy consciousness must mediate.

Dissatisfaction with life in general is turned back upon the self. Having failed to achieve the status of substance, subject passes unremitting judgment on itself. Self-torture is the underlying purpose behind the conceptual aporias it employs to maximize the unbridgeable distance between itself and the Transcendent. But masochism is a truly dialectical phenomenon, and it necessarily generates a restlessness that breaks out within each conceptual endeavor to sublimate it. While stoicism finds rest in the abstractness of an empty transcendence, the unhappy consciousness remains perpetually dissatisfied with its God.

A perfect example of this inner dialectic arises in Hegel's discussion of whether relationship to the unchanging can result from individual effort or must be God's gift.[44] Hegel's example (Moses and the burning bush) is weak because the dilemma he articulates will not receive its perfect representation until Franz Kafka. But the essential situation is that God, Master, the Father as wholly Other, totally secure in his power over us and unbending in his refusal to offer recognition, even of our abjectness, continues to convict a still fascinated subject of its unworthiness. Nothing can arise from such a dialectic but the deepening of subject's frustration.[45] Everything characterizing individual consciousness becomes doubly absurd. All talents must come from God's wholly gratuitous gifts; thus their exercise can in no way bring us into relationship with him. Deprived of authorship, we must nevertheless persist in acts which become self-punitive because they can only further our feeling of separation. In our inwardness we therefore suspect that the whole thing is a cruel joke: the Unchanging endows us with powers that can only frustrate us since neither they nor their development is our activity. One senses the source of Antonio Salieri's rage. It's all God's show. We are inert substances; gifts are simply implanted in us; all our efforts at creative self-realization are finally irrelevant. Hegel's cryptic text adumbrates a psychological condition that is one of the primary sources of inwardness.

Hegel's discussion also instances the two events through which self-alienation issues in a new inwardness: (1) the attempt at objectification and (2) its failure. In its internal discord, unhappy consciousness struggles to sustain the idea that an authentic self-consciousness exists somewhere. But it can sustain this idea only by the desperate move of positing self-consciousness as a principle wholly outside itself. That act, however, gives no relief. Every externalization turns back upon the unhappy consciousness, forcing a new inwardness. This process is the real "substance" of the discussion, but its recovery requires liberating it from Hegel's elliptical and forced allusions to specific details of early Judeo-Christian worship. The rich insights Hegel's discussion gives into the development of intrapsychic structure constantly exceed the frame in which he casts them. Seeing religion as a vast displacement is the key to recapturing its psychological text.

Unhappy consciousness desperately seeks some way to objectify itself; only by so doing can it preserve the power it senses beneath its discord, arrest its self-diffusion, and posit an image in which it might eventually remake and know itself. Objectification is a necessary release from inner pain; it prevents a suicidal enclosure of unhappy consciousness in its own inwardness. Unable to master itself, subject can still develop its possibilities by externalizing them. God provides the blank screen for projections in which unhappy consciousness meditates its inner possibilities, so that by the end of that process, through a sort of "cunning" of unreason, self-renunciation will become the means of empowerment through which subject puts itself above the deity before which it supposedly humbles itself. Methodologically, the process works as follows: self-alienation produces self-consciousness because reflection on subject's projections reveals them as the moment of *difference* required for self-consciousness' development.[46] Psychologically, that process amounts to the self-mediation whereby desire reclaims its projections as its own innermost possibilities. The psychological process is the concrete reality because it alone gives content to the methodological operation. In this sense, Hegel's discussion can be seen as an attempt to reveal the necessary intrapsychic developments we must go through in order to become authentic subjects. This is the reading we will now develop.

FOURTH INTERROGATION: IN THE DESTRUCTIVE ELEMENT IMMERSE

Devotion as Primary Masochism

The key to all feelings, for Hegel, is that they contain tensions and conflicts that must be liberated. Feeling is not a simple immediacy or self-expression but a conflicted position, an attempt by unhappy consciousness to mediate itself. Dialectical interrogation destroys its effort to cling to immediacy and lapse into self-mystification. Feeling, like mood in Heidegger, is a primordial form of inwardness but it legitimates itself only if it undertakes the struggle to develop the understanding of self and world to which it is attuned. Our primary duty toward our feelings is not to defend or indulge them but to undertake their critique. Hegel's discussion of devotion contains the model for such an effort.

The unhappy consciousness is a self-divided heart. Experiencing the impossibility of realizing desire for the transcendent, it falls back upon the experience of its wretchedness. The first issue of this process is the attitude Hegel terms devotion. By reconstructing its psychodynamics, we will uncover a Freudian subtext which goes far beyond archaic details of early Christian worship, revealing experiential self-mediations that are essential to the development of psychic structure.[47]

Mourning is the heart of devotion, whose true subject is a self disappointed in its effort to achieve independence. In mourning, the self turns back upon itself. Feelings of loss and unworthiness, directed at the self as if it were their cause, generate the intrapsychic condition of primary masochism. Subject cancels both its labor and its desire and sets them at naught. Pain is totalized, in a world that now appears to be no more than Hamlet's "foul and pestilent congregation of vapors." The masochist's desire is to undo desire itself.

The effort provides, however, the finest example of how "desire restrained and checked" is the primary law of dialectical and psychological development. In ceaselessly attacking the self, masochism constitutes the initial attempt of the unhappy consciousness to gain self-mastery through the exercise of critical reflection. The masochist wants to dredge up everything that disgusts him in himself, everything that a narcissistic estimation of self suppressed. As a dialectical phenomenon, masochism suffers the basic law of dialectical development: all efforts to get rid of one's subjectivity serve only to confirm and develop it. Masochism also establishes the primacy of experience over logic: subject lives out its dialectics long before it explicitly conceptualizes them. Understanding the dynamics of unhappy consciousness overturns the dichotomy between the conscious and the unconscious and the cherished notion that intentionality is the author of our actions. Subjectivity is not the transparency of a cogito but the dramatic living out of conflicts. Self-consciousness isn't rational self-presence but the struggle to uncover the conflicted motives that inform one's actions in order to subject them to critique. Such is the rich subtext at work in masochism.

But all dialectical possibilities also harbor an antidialectic; masochism finds, in its initial posture, the self-paralysis of the passive aggressive personality. Pride in the spectacle of one's suffering can easily trap the masochist in this self-reifying posture. Passive aggressive activity is the attempt to inflict one's suffering on others in order to win the struggle for recognition by becoming the victim. But victimage is trapped in a double bind which results in psychic undoing. The other still dominates;

passive aggressives are themselves victims of their underlying statement: "Look what you've done to me; look what loving you costs me." Such a subject reifies itself in an anger it steadfastly denies. The truth passive aggressives must deny is that their activity has only one aim—to provoke the other. The only recognition possible to receive is anger, because the controlling need is to accuse the other of this unforgivable sin in order to deny its overwhelming presence in oneself. This is the antidialectic which the dialectic of masochism must surmount.

In devotion, inwardness is experienced as infinite longing.[48] Projecting that feeling onto the absent other, devout consciousness experiences the depth of its subjectivity as the call for another self. A self-divided heart in its inward turning generates the dream of an unattainable object which would completely fulfill it. When this project fails, feeling collapses back into itself, experiencing a world defined by God's absence. The high romanticism of the devotional project does not blind Hegel to the reversal it will later receive at the hands of Samuel Beckett. Hegel finds both a significantly new subjectivity at work in religion and a self-mystifying vagueness of mind. With Kierkegaard he prizes the manifestation of subjectivity as infinite concern, but he also sees the danger of a flight beyond the bounds of any objectifying and experiential dialectic. That is why mourning is the dialectical moment: inwardness (like paradise) is defined by the object lost. Devotion projected a longing beyond all possible objectification; mourning experiences an equally disproportionate loss. Unhappy consciousness seeks determination in its desire for the object, but in both these experiences—mourning and devotion—the object is overshadowed by the depth of feeling projected upon it and slips away. Feeling is what matters. Retaining the object as the peg on which to secure itself, unhappy consciousness dissembles its fear that the infinite longing defining subjectivity can never be satisfied. God delivers us from solipsism and keeps us from dissolving in despair.

Mourning mourns the loss not of the object but of one's relationship to it. Its sorrow is over the failure of the desire for an impossible adequation with the other in mutual recognition or perfect love. That desire can be sustained only by internalizing it as the basis of one's self-relation. This is the labor of mourning, which is why psychoanalysts since Freud have seen mourning as the basis of psychic growth and the refusal to mourn as the basis of neurosis. Authentic mourning is not the Proustian quest to regain paradise by recapturing everything associated with those bodily sensations which restore contact with the original maternal love object. Nor is mourning a simple process of "reality testing" in which we extinguish the other by passing upon each memory connected with him the inflexible judgment of death. Mourning is a process of internalization which makes integral to our own internal structure what we previously projected into the other.[49] The other loved and lost is preserved as an ideal which establishes an internal psychological standard whereby subject measures itself. The possibility of self-consciousness depends on this operation; mourning can be regarded as its psychogenesis. Through mourning, subject develops the ability to regulate itself. We do it wrong when we identify the result solely with a malign and punishing superego. That internalization is a necessary first moment but also the beginning of a complex process.

In conventional wisdom, normal mourning relinquishes the object, whereas neurotic mourning passes into melancholia with the self punishing itself for crimes, real or imagined, that make it feel small and guilty by comparison with the lost object who has become, like Hamlet's father, a harsh internal judge and master. For Hegel, this melancholic response is a necessary stage of psychological development. Bent on convicting itself of a fundamental badness, masochistic consciousness assumes what Melanie Klein calls the depressive position.[50] Its dialectic holds the key to subject's further development.

At first glance it is not promising terrain. Yet masochism constitutes the first cohesive self. In primary masochism, infinite feeling, having lost the object, turns its longing back upon its source and "cathects" the subject. In contrast to the substantialism of ego psychology, where everything is built on the solid foundation of basic trust, self-punishment generates the first cohesive self in Hegel. Trust is not even in the picture, and its assertion blinds one to the permanently destabilizing psychodynamic in which the self originates.

Mourning derives its complexity from the hidden narcissistic dimension of all object love. The other as original object choice is a grandiose projection derived from the abyss of narcissism. Self-feeling, in its infinite emptiness, longs for an object that will guarantee all the heart's desires with fulfillment coming wholly from the other. As recent psychoanalytic studies have shown, narcissism is one of the primary modes of dependency. The most precarious thing in the narcissist's world is one's identity. The other must forever prop up a faltering sense of self. Feeling the self always slipping away, the narcissist projects the idealized other out of the need for constant reassurance of a phantom substantiality.[51]

Devotion's projection of the deity corresponds to these psychodynamics. The collapse of this projection is also a fortunate fall because narcissism becomes productive only when it experiences its emptiness. This happens when the unhappy consciousness blames itself for the loss of the object and turns the object's absence back upon itself. It thereby internalizes the dialectic it previously externalized, in a new experience of self-experience. We may term the experience existential pain—pain over oneself as foundationless lack.

This unhappiness is of a new order because experience now proceeds from a center. For the first time unhappy consciousness takes on the coherence we associate with *character*. Pain is no longer simply fled, but reflected upon. Experience takes on a meditative cast, and subject begins to see that its actions proceed from a self-reference which is not substantial but existential. Dialectic is no longer outside consciousness or suffered passively. Negativity remains in force, however, as a critique of those who would seize this moment to wax optimistic about ego stability: for the first issue of existential pain is unremitting self-criticism.

Masochistic critique is a necessary experience because the unhappy consciousness is far from having conquered the power of the other within the self. Masochism is the first step toward liberation because only through it can consciousness take up its unhappiness in an authentic manner. The relation of devout consciousness to the world offers a somewhat extreme proof of this necessity. Ideally, desire and labor should confirm our self-certainty, granting us the enjoyment of external existence. But for a consciousness in pain everything is set at naught. The very fact that one desires and labors is turned into a self-criticism.[52] The devout consciousness deprives these activities of the value they could have; life is viewed (as in traditional Christianity) as a vale of tears, with labor having no meaning beyond toil for subsistence, and desire reduced to the upsurge of base impulses we must spend our lives resisting. Unhappy consciousness incessantly totalizes. Projecting its pain into every aspect of experience, it establishes World as a comprehensive concept and encompasses totality by picturing everyday life as a cycle of senseless labors alternating with self-degrading pleasures, both having no meaning aside from the *tedium vitae* they engender. One casts one's eye over the whole of life, passing the verdict of nullity on everything.

The resentment thus engendered fuels the drive for otherworldliness. But the religious projection of masochism finds itself on the horns of a dilemma. Hegel formulates it in his discussion of "the broken world," a text that is rightly taken as one of the origins of modernity.[53] Consciousness and the world of its activity are seen as intrinsically null, absurd, without order or finality, yet as God's creation they must somehow be intrinsically sanctified. Seeing this contradiction as nullifying its activity, unhappy consciousness here repeats existentially the dilemmas it faced in its earlier effort to think or feel its way into a relationship with the unchanging. This is fine theological comedy, and seen with dialectical irony Hegel's text often prefigures Beckett.

In "the broken world," work is not only unnecessary but evil because it implies the creation is not complete. The only proper response to life is to do nothing. Unable to cease activity, we must find a way to justify it before the other by finding its source *in* the other. But this raises the second horn of the dilemma. Consciousness relates to reality by changing it, but to preserve the sacral we must *undo* our deed by regarding our "faculties and powers" as gratuitous "gifts" from an alien source.[54] We are resubstantialized precisely at the point where we could begin to existentialize ourselves. Everything enabling our activity derives from the other. The masochism could not be more complete.

The great recognition previously attained, that consciousness makes and transforms itself through its activity, is here undone. In reparation for imagined transgression we now picture our life—and our being as subjects—in substantialistic terms. We come on the scene already complete, fitted out with fixed faculties and powers which issue in actions that are not really ours but manifest the glory of their author. He is infinite and perfect Source; all our efforts merely witness a power which takes us as its medium. Unable to escape the orbit of the sovereign other, devout consciousness repeats the slave's initial relationship to the master. But repetition always involves both regression and the possibility that regression may prove finally creative. The master-slave dialectic, here internalized as the self-determination of our inwardness, takes on more extreme forms than ever before. In the slave, "desire restrained and checked" was a productive inwardness, whereas here inwardness falls completely under the Lacanian Law of the Father. We render everything that enters into our labor to an imaginary and voracious consumer. In reparation for the scandalous act of affirming our independence through labor, we restore the other to a position of internal dominance more total than before.

We seem to have reached a condition of almost complete psychic unraveling. But masochism is a genuinely dialectical phenomenon. As a sublation of "desire restrained and checked," it produces an equivalent state in the inwardness of consciousness. The truth of the matter is this: *the masochist has his pleasure*. As with Flannery O'Connor's misfit, it is the pleasure of finding that there is no pleasure in anything. Suffering makes one aristocratic, conferring the ability to nihilate all experiences by proclaiming their inadequacy. Bellow's Henderson becomes Kafka's Hunger Artist, the undefeated champion of self-denial. To sustain that project, the masochist must instill discontent into every moment of self-reference. What better way to do so than by installing God, the ultimate Other, as a principle of internal torture who passes eternal judgment on every facet of one's experience? Masochists empower themselves by a string of victories over each temptation to halt the drama of self-torture.

This dialectic is inescapable because masochism's source is in desire. "Desire restrained and checked" necessarily engenders the project of self-mastery. By exacerbating unhappiness, we eventually triumph over the desire for transcendence and deliverance. But abjectness has a double face. In debasing oneself before God, one performs an intensely self-dramatizing action. Dostoyevskian delight in making a spectacle of oneself is never far from the masochist's underground consciousness. All the rituals and ceremonies Hegel discusses are rife with an actor's pride in his performance. The strongest proof of the dialectical dimension, however, is its eventual issue—the disappearance of God.

Ridding oneself of that other who initially holds a position of total dominance within consciousness is the through-line of the drama. We master our desire for transcendence by giving it full scope only to see how empty God leaves us. We then return the compliment: God underscores the pain of the world only to reveal the abstract character of the paradise he offers. Masochism inaugurates the great reversal: the reclaiming as our own innermost power all we have alienated from ourselves in otherworldly projection.

This double movement is necessary because the dilemma Hegel here confronts is that consciousness recognizes but can't justify its negativity. As long as we long for substance we can't see complex subjective processes as anything but signs of separation from the stability we seek.

But all efforts to deny the significance of one's activity underscore the obvious: the unhappy consciousness is intensely active. Denying that fact requires a major new intrapsychic development—repression. And in its birth repression reveals its ironic law: we need to deny something only when its importance has already announced itself, yet all efforts to repress only increase the power of the repressed. The upshot of all attempts to deny the value of action is that activity is saved. Faced with a choice between passivity before an already complete and perfect creation and the scandal of individual activity, unhappy consciousness finds a way to preserve the latter by convicting itself of sinfulness. The attempt to cancel our activity by locating its source in God serves only to underscore the dignity of labor by investing it with transcendent significance.[55]

The basic contradiction between activity and its denial remains in force because consciousness regards the power it displays "in its action" as "the beyond of itself."[56] Its internal structure takes on a form Marx will later historically conceptualize as the condition of alienated labor. With God installed as absolute source of value, labor realizes not our "species-being" but his hypostatized essence. Labor becomes this ghostly thing: we do it we know not why, with everything our activity signifies placed forever outside us. We suffer alienation in the process of our labor because the individuality therein realized is not seen as our own. We are alienated from the product, which we offer up as a sacrifice. And we are alienated from one another, for each unhappy consciousness stands alone before God and the door of a Law which, as in Kafka, never opens. Primary masochism here sublates by internalizing the master-slave dialectic in a psychic structure that is ruled by a malign superego. Unhappiness becomes the act of living haunted by an internal judge who constantly demands greater efforts while telling us that nothing we do can alter our fundamental unworthiness. We bring this superego our gifts in reparation for having made the effort that went into their making. It, unmoved, passes on them the judgment of nonbeing. We thus "solidify" our internal division by making self-punishment a permanent intrapsychic condition. Once one does so, it is not hard to find the perfect metaphoric representation—religion, the Law of the Father.

In Hegel, as in Freud, internalization initially makes the self less powerful as an agent, more a product of "the discourse of the other." Yet in both cases self-alienation is necessary and makes possible a process in which subject makes its own what it has internalized by reclaiming the desire that underlies its empowering of the other. As in Freud, unhappy consciousness is a psychic structure in which repressed desire creates a superego which is a mirror image of the id. In Hegelian terms, self-punishment is an inverted expression of the very desire for independence it is designed to repress. Through the project of religious otherworldliness, "desire restrained and checked" engages in a subtle interchange of powers with the Godhead it posits. Through that process it gradually recaptures what it invests in the other. To liberate that self-consciousness, however, we must pay close attention to all the ways in which unhappy consciousness tries to repress and deny precisely what it is in the process of coming to affirm.

Initially, self-consciousness is virtually extinguished. It remains only in the desperate idea that through "reciprocal self-surrender" one gets a momentary feeling of oneness with the deity.[57] The deity's willingness so to extend itself must be posited as an article of faith, however, since there is no experiential warrant for implying any change in a transcendent and perfect being. The desperateness of the project signifies, in fact, that the desire fueling unhappy consciousness is hanging on by a thread. For what Hegel represents here is the religious equivalent of the feeling that characterizes children and unhappy lovers who want to believe that their suffering has the magical power to compel a sympathetic movement toward them on the part of the other. But, having made this obligatory gesture toward its regressive side, unhappy consciousness incarnates something fundamentally new. The act of thanksgiving is momentary and is already afflicted with self-division. No amount of self-abasement can deny the fact that through labor one has willed, acted, and enjoyed. Even abasing oneself is "one's own action." This is the pride that haunts the martyr and fuels T. S. Eliot's endless question whether one is doing the right thing for the wrong reason. As Hegel sees, through humility we meet the beneficence of God "with a like action."[58] Although, unhappy consciousness may resist, its relation to the deity is a self-empowering quest. Self-abasement always harbors this motive because the most powerful form of intersubjective dominance is not physical force but "spiritual" self-enhancement, with its triumphant "I suffer more than you do." No stranger to this motive, unhappy consciousness sees its surrender as an act greater than anything done by the deity. Whereas the deity sheds only the surface of its being, the unhappy consciousness gives up "its essential being."[59]

The dialectical irony is that subject's existential state is thereby confirmed. Renunciation of individuality is a sham. The internal opposition between the unchanging and the changing asserts itself more powerfully than ever before. Having acted, the unhappy consciousness can no longer deny its individuality. The changing consciousness is where mediation happens. With this recognition, further dependence on the unchanging becomes an act of bad faith, aware of its own dissembling. Dissembling still rules, but an irreversible development has taken place. The internal contest between renunciation and the desire for independent individuality has shifted decidedly in favor of the latter. While renunciation remains a powerful desire, it now bears the stigma of flight from the possibility implicit in subject. Unhappy consciousness now knows that establishing its own activity is the real significance of all processes in which it bows before the other. The dialectic of masochism thus completes itself by reversing the internalized master-slave relationship with which it began. The arduous and indirect way in which unhappy consciousness enacts this "labor of the negative" thereby emerges as a necessary stage in the development of subjectivity.

The Enemy: Sexuality and the Birth of the Body

Its gains come together in the new attack unhappy consciousness wages on itself. This attack is far more concrete than religious masochism, for it is waged on and in the body. The pages in which Hegel deals with the struggle with what he terms "the enemy" constitute one of the most powerful, veiled, and neglected discussions of sexuality ever penned.[60] Sex emerges as a psychological experience central to the development of subjectivity. The consciousness that appears here is markedly regressive, however, with the internalized master in charge and masochism again ascendant. For Hegel, as for Freud, all quests for liberation initially involve regression because psychological restructuring becomes possible only when one confronts the power of an internalized other who occupies a long-standing position of internal dominance. That is why the assertion of one's desires initially appears in the form of sheer animal instinct—what Hegel calls "the enemy."

But the subtext of the dialectic of subject's development undertakes an irreversible advance. Bad faith is now experienced at the level of self-consciousness. Inner conflict is replaced by inner struggle. Active reversal becomes a genuine possibility. Having created the superego, unhappy consciousness will now confront it as that internalization which necessarily externalizes itself by informing the experience we have of our body. Though intermittent, reflective awareness is now an irreducible moment because the unhappy consciousness knows that its true battleground is within. It has little idea how much internal territory it has to conquer, but it now lives the basic law of reflection: every consciousness contains a self-consciousness, and every self-consciousness adopts a negative attitude toward that consciousness.

As a halting, nascent recognition of the power of reflection, devotion prepares the way for a consciousness that will raise this possibility of active reversal to the level of an explicit principle. The intrapsychic structure of devotion is far from stable, however. Freedom and independence exist only at the level of thought. Liberation is private, secret, and purely internal. Content to worship God and keep secret its little knowledge, subject retains a public posture of self-emasculation. Rather than take issue with official religious observances, it contents itself with the fleeting awareness that "it's all a game." Reflection thus engenders a new rift between consciousness and self-consciousness. Content to preserve its supposed freedom solely in the order of thought, subject acquiesces in a sort of stoic obeisance toward rituals which it knows are effectively dead. *It doesn't constitute its self-consciousness, and therefore it loses it.* Realizing the great power reflection taps requires more than mere thought; it requires *praxis* and a pitilessly negative attitude toward the beliefs of ordinary, social consciousness. Self-consciousness is useless until it transforms the totality of one's way of living.

At this point, however, distrust of self-consciousness is still uppermost, reinforced by the fear that self-affirmation will forever remove us from reconciliation with the other. That is why the internalized master, the superego, takes on its characteristic double function, punishing us for transgression (real or imagined) and restoring us through guilt. In the first internalization, desire experienced itself as empty and powerless before the all-powerful other. Unhappy consciousness has now reclaimed that internalization by putting self-consciousness in a position of potential power over consciousness. But self-consciousness is not transparent rationality; it is itself internally divided. Every individual self-assertion thus confronts an internal regulatory power which satisfies the masochistic need for self-punishment by waging a minute attack on the body and every sign it sends forth indicating the possibility of individual liberation.

Self-consciousness always depends on defeating an otherness within. The desire that went into the constitution of the superego must be reclaimed and the superego's power made a property of self-consciousness. No purely rational dialectic can bring this about. Such a self-mediation requires a specific experience to make it possible. Sexuality is perfectly designed to fill this need.

To maintain its tie to the transcendent other, subject must negate everything that makes up the natural life of consciousness.[61] Unequal to such a task, unhappy consciousness initially feels only the pain and confusion of its increased distance from the unchanging. But the reaffirmation of its nullity leads to a new experience that is of the greatest importance for the development of inwardness—the discovery of *sin*. Sin is an excessively rich and ambiguous phenomenon, the consciousness of it a fundamental transformation of that brooding that was the origin of unhappy consciousness. Finding oneself in a state of sin, one now broods not abstractly but with a definite content: "O that this too, too sullied flesh . . ."

The unhappiness of consciousness is that it cannot cancel itself—and grows stronger each time it tries. Each new effort at self-destruction must do a thorough job by seeking out those areas of experience that really matter. With the achievement of self-consciousness, masochism faces a new task. However fleeting, self-consciousness puts one in a new relationship to one's experience. In sexuality the individual self experiences the value of individual existence in a peremptory and unforgettable way. This self-consciousness is the true origin of sexuality, and "the struggle with the enemy" an attempt to undo what first becomes possible in our experience of the body. For a self-conscious being, sexuality affirms existence and contingency in a way that presents a basic challenge to the transcendental designs of a rationalistic dialectic. That is why it is so dangerous and why its emergence is one with the effort to suppress it.

A double dialectic commences here because sexuality and its repression are equiprimordial and co-creative.[62] To regain union with the unchanging, unhappy consciousness must wage war on itself in its most intimate being. Contempt for pleasure must now focus on those experiences in which subject feels fully incarnated. A general distaste for life is no longer adequate. The war on pleasure must deny the significance of those pleasures that heighten bodily consciousness. Sexuality is the proper target because it is the true sublation of desire. Its object is another subject: in it, the body is experienced intersubjectively as incarnate subjectivity.

For sexuality to serve as the enemy, the self must have already announced itself there in a powerful and fundamental way. Initially, unhappy consciousness always dissembles, and what it dissembles here is a "transgression" it previously approved. Carnality can't be simply the fall into a base physical world (Saint Paul) or a mere instinct craving discharge (biologism). Such interpretations are judgments passed by unhappy consciousness after the battle has commenced, attempts to condemn pleasure by picturing it reductively as the lower side of a body-spirit dichotomy. By interrogating the experiential origin of sexuality, unhappy consciousness reveals the psychogenesis of the dualisms which have riddled Western thought. Paradise is always paradise lost; the denial of the body condemns us to the experience of living in two worlds, an incarnate one resisted and a transcendent one sought. To reaffirm the desire for the unchanging, unhappy consciousness must undo what binds it, in bliss, to the world. The inability to do so will anchor its dialectic to a deeper engagement in experience.

For unhappy consciousness, the power of sexuality and the effort to renounce it are experienced simultaneously: subject's project is to convict itself of sinfulness. The most intense experience of enjoyment must be turned into a feeling of wretchedness. The lived body must be riven with a contradiction that makes the experience of heightened feeling turn almost immediately into an experience of self-defeat, loss, and estrangement from the ideal. For a consciousness in sin, orgasm produces sadness and defeat. But there is also a rich dialectical possibility at work here. *The inwardness of unhappy consciousness here coincides with the experience of the body in its immediacy.* The natural no longer exists. The body is an immediate expression of one's psychosexual identity. Identity and sexuality are inextricable, with sex an immediate and unmistakable manifestation of one's basic conflicts. When we experience the body in its sexual being, the conflicting feelings that make up unhappy consciousness are felt in their greatest intensity, with dissembling no longer possible. Inwardness incarnates and alienates itself anew in the experience of the body; the body as a *spiritual* reality comes into being in the struggle each of us necessarily wages over this issue.

Sex becomes dialectical when, as Hegel puts it, the natural functions are "no longer performed naturally or without embarrassment."[63] Alienating oneself from pleasure at the very moment of pleasure enables unhappy consciousness to repeat internally the slave's act of rendering the product of his labor to the master. In making enjoyment coincide with a feeling of sinfulness, one lives the body in a way that begs forgiveness for the act in the very process of its commission. The new "gift" one gives the master is one's own body, "cleansed" through the disciplines of anhedonia and ascetic mortification. Obsessionalism becomes the new regulator of the psyche. Desire is "restrained and checked" anew by a regimen of endless concern with the most minute bodily manifestations. Inwardness thereby fixates and fetishizes the act of brooding. Longing is transformed into the three preeminent handmaids of the *spiritual*—shame, sin, and guilt.

But the dialectic of sex has another side. Experience has become interesting and dangerous. The possibility of genuine transgression now exists and has been given a most inviting abode. In making sex the barrier to otherworldliness, one makes it something it wasn't before—a problem. Thus the persistence of the dialectical tension between unhappy consciousness and its opposite is assured, not as a clever bit of logic, but as the experience of the flesh.

To convict oneself of nothingness before the unchanging, one must wage war on one's sexuality. But a negation that totalizes constantly uncovers new phenomena and occasions.[64] Obsessionalism makes the body a greater source of concern, and surprise, than ever before. All bodily functions now remind us of our estrangement and become matters of perpetual and intense concern. They can no longer be performed naturally but must become agents in a theater of self-conquest. Overcoming the body is a dialectical struggle because the effort identifies an area of resistance which it thereby solidifies as an abode of pleasure repressed and transgression foretold. For unhappy consciousness, a double movement is in progress: (1) Christian resentment in its dirty Pauline embodiment, that horror of sexuality which is the origin of asceticism; (2) beneath the surface, an effort to reclaim Eden by charting the many sites of transgression, suitably concealed beneath repressions which transform pleasure itself by establishing the conflicted feelings we now bring to the experience of it.

The self-division of unhappy consciousness has here taken on the form in which most of us in our culture first encounter it—the split between body and soul, sex and spirit, sin and self-discipline. The irony of the situation is this: the abstract dichotomy between sex and spirit asserts that the sexual can have no significance, yet also makes the sexual, in the drama of renunciation, repression, and transgression, the source of an unprecedented expansion of self-consciousness. It also engenders a condition that will eventually reverse the dialectic of renunciation. Sex as enemy is sex as permanent threat to the project of transcendence. Sex as sin is sex as pleasure denied. Sexuality repressed is sexuality forever erupting in new forms.

Preoccupation with controlling the sexual makes obsessionalism the new intrapsychic structure. We may define obsessionalism as that form of unhappy consciousness which is trapped in an effort to assert control over that which constantly escapes its grasp because the very effort produces the ubiquity of the contingencies opposing it. The obsessional knows no peace because the enemy is a brute facticity which is always breaking out because the obsessional constantly seeks it out. In saying that the enemy renews himself in his defeat,[65] Hegel is pointing not to a biological fact but to the dialectical law which necessarily defeats the obsessional project. Denying the body makes us more aware of it than ever before. We increase the realm and range of its possible excitations. But in spending our energies in the effort to reassert control, we shrink the personality and eventually succumb to that spirit of petty vindictiveness which reveals the obsessional's impotent anger before the recognition that all his efforts have served only to extend the scope and sway of the enemy. Obsessionalism reifies itself in abstract fixation on what it wishes to overcome. And fixation is unavoidable because the obsessional's quest is to affirm and deny an impossible desire—that for an absolute assurance that will free subject from contingency. The contradiction of that project requires that the obsessional continually find new sources of doubt, which he eliminates only to find new holes in his explanations.[66] It is necessarily an endless and self-defeating process. The only exit from it is a self-consciousness that internalizes the psychoanalytic insight that we endlessly go over the same ground yet deliberately find no conclusion only when we are refusing to admit something. Our anxiety is over our inability to impose rational control on experience. The idea we resist is that existence escapes intellectual control and always will. The obsessional's intense concern with getting all the facts down in just the right order and in just the right endlessly reiterated words ironically derives from a desire to deny facticity. The irony Hegel finds at work here is the same one Freud will later uncover: renunciation is a vast theater of desire which gains massive sexual satisfaction in mapping the immensity of its problems.

The study of devotion's conflict with the "enemy" contains a *methodological* insight of crucial importance for developing a dialectic rooted in experience. Every consciousness refers to a primary experience which it confronts as its basic burden. But this is also its blind spot because its goal, manifested in an attitude, is to eliminate all traces of the burden. In reconstituting what the rational presentation of attitudes conceals, we restore their experiential origins in a way that enables us to liberate their true content, the meanings which they suppress. Such a reading constitutes the active reversal of an attitude.

Attitudes like devotion arise as attempts to escape something disruptive in experience. All the talk about the enemy belies the truly significant fact: that sexuality has been transformed from a biological to an intersubjective process that concretely resumes the master-slave dialectic with new and surprising outcomes. Sexuality is an unavoidable problem for the unhappy consciousness because the struggle to preserve the dream of substance in the face of sexuality's assertion of our subjectivity necessarily sows the seeds of its own reversal.[67] This interpretation derives from a simple consideration. *The desire of devotion is to extinguish desire.* If one adopts this project, one necessarily confronts sexuality as the barrier, not because it is a stubborn biological force, but because the feelings of self-affirmation and mutual recognition found in sex make desire for it a peremptory and specifically human affair necessary to the search for identity and identity maintenance.[68]

The labor of renunciation, like reductive attempts to see sex scientifically as drive discharge or animal pleasure, always harbors a more disruptive and more significant prior experience, the traces of which it tries to remove. Prior to its moralistic interpretation, sexuality necessarily assumed a profound existential meaning for the unhappy consciousness. This is what the unhappy consciousness wants to exorcise. But in doing so one inevitably keeps that experience alive: witness the erotics of asceticism.

Every attempt to extinguish sexuality solidifies and extends its psychosexual meaning. When "the natural is no longer performed naturally," repression has already defeated itself. The search for absolute origins misses the point: unhappy consciousness gives birth to a doubling (and double reading) of phenomena because its internal division expresses itself with little concern for the principle of contradiction. If we need to posit an "origin" here, it must be the power of the orgasmic as bliss, as identity gained and lost, to pose a fundamental threat to a consciousness caught in the desire for substance. Because existence is seen as estrangement, that which produces the most heightened feeling of incarnate subjectivity must necessarily signal self-defeat.

The goal of the ascetic project is to deny the subjectivity affirmed in sex by turning the body into a thing. It is no accident that the entire dialectic of unhappy consciousness coalesces in concern over this phenomenon. A dialectic of experience necessarily turns on those *situations* where subject in its universality is faced with those conflicts which force an irreversible development of its being. The ascetic or devotional project is significant, above and beyond the antiquarian details of Hegel's discussion, because it identifies such a moment in the development of psychic structure: the attempt to attain the status of substance by denying the psychosexual significance of the body. Platonism and Christianity are not the only monuments to this desire. One finds it in Freud's economic point of view and in the unending effort of "academic" psychologists to find biochemical and physiological explanations for all sexual "dysfunctions." It also informs the way most people in our culture—including the "liberated"—relate to the body.

But just as the unconscious knows no negation, pleasure survives its apparent renunciation. To contain it, unhappy consciousness must carve out a new and intensely subtle inwardness. Renunciation has put it at odds with itself in a totally new way. To negate pleasure, subject must attack its subjective roots. The sexual manifestation of incarnate subjectivity must be dehumanized. Sex must be turned into a thing and made a source of shame. Pleasure threatens the desire for substance because it is more than a *promesse de bonheur;* it is a celebration of spirit in its contingency, a liberation of play, and an affirmation of existence as an end in itself. The desire for substance can remain dominant in consciousness only if it can deracinate the subjectivity which announces itself in sexual desire. In the contradiction unhappy consciousness now lives, sexuality is the voice of subject continuing its long battle with itself while still under the sway of substance. As such, that voice already constitutes a sublation of anxiety—and thus a major dialectical advance—because inwardness now focuses on a concrete experience that is an inescapable part of each subject's personal history.

In sexuality, otherworldliness confronts an otherness that it cannot sublate in any purely rational dialectic. Sexuality alters the very terms for understanding self, other, and what it means to live in the world by confronting the otherworldly drive of unhappy consciousness with a world the loss of which would constitute a genuine loss. To meet that challenge, masochism must become truly inventive, devising new mansions for itself within the inwardness of consciousness. These are the developments of intrapsychic structure we must now interrogate. In doing so, we will not leave sexuality behind. On the contrary, we will discover that it requires the long work of repression for its maturation.

Shame, Sin, and Guilt: The Origins of the Grand Inquisitor

Nothing serves as well as sex to nurture new forms of inwardness. The attempt by unhappy consciousness to abase itself, to convict itself of nothingness before the Universal, seizes upon sex as the sign of an untamable and alien otherness within the self which defeats all efforts to cleanse ourselves of existence. Pleasure is now experienced as that loss of innocence which marks the subject with an ineradicable stain. *Shame* is the first configuration of this inwardness. In shame one looks at oneself through the eyes of that other who assumes the position more of dismissive spectator than of harsh judge. One stands beneath a humiliating gaze which invades the core of what should be one's privacy. In shame we want to hide because we image ourselves caught and observed in the performance of all that is disgusting and mechanical in bodily functions. Shame is the worst feeling because in shame we unravel ourselves under the impersonal gaze of an other who does not partake of the imperfections that characterize our puny existence.[69]

Sin, in contrast, is the first movement toward active reversal. While the shameful are weak because they surrender to the otherness within themselves, the sinful proclaim the power of strong desires. While, in shame, subject passively deconstructs itself, sin is active because it internalizes the memory of a transgressive self. Transgression always has something Dostoyevskian and aristocratic about it; in the psychic economy of sin, one always imagines that daemonic energy exerts an attraction on the deity. In sin we give ourselves an identity which profoundly individualizes us and which can never be completely undone.

The two forms of inwardness arising out of the struggle of unhappy consciousness with sexuality mirror its self-division. Shame is the sad, nostalgic side; that passivity subject cannot surmount, the longing to reaffirm substance and return to a state prior to the fall into the body. Sin is the proud, active affirmation of a self that develops through transgression, outstripping both the law and the repentence it calls forth. No matter how strenuous the denial it later begets, in that great theater of masks and lip service known as repentance, sin remains liberating because it preserves the memory of the transgressive self.

Guilt "synthesizes" shame and sin. It is the intrapsychic struggle of the internalized other to reassert control over the transgressive self. As such, it is the most significant development of inwardness because in it everything previously externalized becomes part of an inner drama. The internalization of guilt is the cardinal moment in subject's development because it establishes distinct intrapsychic agencies, and with them, the possibility of self-mastery. Like all advances of the dialectic, however, it is an indirect one that proceeds from its opposite. The first product of guilt is the "priest"—the first great institutionalization of unhappy consciousness. Unhappy consciousness wants to undo itself by depriving sex of its annunciatory possibilities so that subject may again experience the body as a brute facticity to which it is condemned. But shame and sin bring masochism to the point of a psychic unraveling that threatens a collapse of the dialectic unless unhappy consciousness can find a way to mediate itself through the help of an intercessor who has risen above the Ixion of sexual bondage. Enter the priests, the first mental health professionals, and the most ambiguous avatar of the other.[70]

Initially, this dialectic looks like a solidification, rather than a new development, and a specious one at that. Hegel tortures out a deductive reason to account for a historical fact—the rise of the clergy. This is Hegelianism at its worst, history made the product of bloodless abstractions. But the discussion also constitutes a major advance in the articulation of principles of self-mediation that are essential to subject's development. Our task is to extract them from the mystifications in which they are embedded.

The priest's function is similar to that of Lacan's *points de caption;*[71] he halts the metonymic slippage of hysteric, masochistic, and obsessional processes and keeps the unhappy consciousness focused on its fundamental problems. Priesthood is the first institutionalization of the dialectic. As such, it points toward an understanding of the doubleness of all institutions. Institutions both solidify and reify; they preserve the gains of subjective development by anchoring them in objective forms (symbols, rituals, rules), but they also bar further development by attempting to arrest and fixate consciousness on these forms.[72]

To understand the psychodynamics at work in the priest—both in the consciousness that longs for the priest and in the subject who takes on this role—we must see priesthood as a reincarnation of the master-slave dialectic, which testifies both to the persistence of that dialectic and to a significant decline in its power. Initially, of course, one is tempted to say the exact opposite. Priesthood dazzles us with the invention of mystifications and forms of obeisance which trap and tranquilize unhappy consciousness in what we may term the confessional posture. The unhappy consciousness seeks out opportunities to throw itself at the feet of the spiritual father. Scrupulosity sublates obsessionalism, playing endless variations on that subtext in which nothing exceeds the masochistic eroticism of those saints who die "virgins and martyrs." Priesthood creates a vast externalization of master-slave rituals in ceremonies that bind subjects to its rule. But while institutionalization empowers, it is also haunted by an internal dialectic. For the purpose of institutionalization is to reinforce a power that is slipping away. Priesthood thus provides a rich instance of that process in which consciousness wins itself back, enriched and irreversibly changed, as a result of alienating itself.

The genesis of the priest is the desire of unhappy consciousness to give its will, its responsibility, and its thought over to another. The priest thus completes the process of masochistic emasculation. In the total surrender he commands, unhappy consciousness willingly becomes mindless. In blind obedience subject engages in religious practices that make no sense and which it makes no effort to comprehend. It is enough that the priests command them. Self-denial is the goal. Incoherence of thought is embraced as a principle. The flock takes delight in each mystification the priest concocts, for each new ritual gives it another way to capitulate to the will and word of the other. By refusing to question anything the priest tells it to do, subject successfully turns itself into a thing. Depriving itself of "all inner and outer freedom," it gains release from subjectivity.[73]

Dialectical development passes to the priest who attains the possibility of self-mastery by accepting the position of master while bringing to it a new kind of inwardness. The priest is not simply a cunning master who enslaves out of a lust for power. He is himself an unhappy consciousness and retains that awareness while in the position of master. His actions thereby give him a double insight into himself and his subjects, which is actually an insight into the two stances consciousness can adopt toward its subjectivity. (We are talking, of course, about the rare priest, the one condemned to see through it all.)

Understanding mastery from within liberates the priest from the servile motives that maintain it. The herd mentality of the servile consciousness becomes a fit object of scorn, and the priest casts it out of his consciousness by deliberately leaving the flock shackled to meaningless rituals which he devises solely in order to experience his freedom and power. He thereby undertakes a noble war on himself, enacting his hatred of what is weak and preserving what is best in unhappy consciousness. By isolating everything psychologically weak in unhappy consciousness, he herds the flock into a single mass consciousness, bound to him as its collective will, and frees himself to recapture everything powerful in unhappy consciousness. They believe through him; and their belief frees him from his own need to believe. God is dead.

Self-mastery has become possible because the priest gains an explicit understanding of the fact that consciousness is unhappy consciousness. He understands the logic of suffering and sees that its ineradicable source lies in consciousness itself. The unhappiness of consciousness thereby attains its proper category—the tragic. And since the priest is both the object and the subject of this reflection, he suffers this knowledge as the truth of his inwardness.

The priest is Hegel's metaphor for a consciousness that has internalized shame, sin, and guilt in a way that points toward self-overcoming. His is far from a secure freedom, however, and harbors contradictions that wed it to its opposite in a way that makes the discussion most significant as a contribution to understanding the intersubjective and intrapsychic developments subject must go through in order to attain a self-consciousness adequate to its internal dynamics. For here the two roles unhappy consciousness adopts represent the two positions it can take up toward itself. To bring out this layer of the discussion, we must trace the process that generates the priest, with careful attention to the activity of both participants.

Unable to work through guilt, the servile consciousness projects the priest in an effort to dissolve inwardness and become its other. The superego is reexternalized with the priest installed in the position of sovereign master. But in creating the priest, unhappy consciousness puts humanity in the place formerly held by God. Rather than remain in subjection to an absent other, it sets itself up as a principle of self-mediation. God gets the unessential relation—unintelligible, self-mystifying rites.[74] But the real object of worship is now humanity itself. In bowing before the priest the unhappy consciousness bows before an idealized image of itself.

Initially, this act looks like a regression to the worst kind of master-slave relationship. The inwardness found through sin has apparently prepared the subject not for liberation but for enslavement. Whereas, initially, unhappy consciousness desired substance, it now wants to escape subject. The sacrifice it attempts is the sacrifice of its very inwardness; the forgiveness it seeks is forgiveness for the sin of existence. This turn of events constitutes a major advance, however, because the underlying motive is the desire to flee the knowledge unhappy consciousness has gained of what being a subject involves. Finding that self-knowledge unendurable, it nevertheless finds a way to pass it on.

In bowing before the priest's dictates, unhappy consciousness honors itself and pays tribute to the possibility that there are some subjects who can aspire to a self-mastery that terrifies yet continues to haunt it. Sacrificing mind to the priest reclaims thought for subject. In craving absolution, consciousness makes another subject the lord of its very inwardness. It

empowers the priest by rendering unto him what was never given to
any previous master—recognition and the free gift of one's subjectivity.
The priest knows he receives far more than obedience and the fruits of
another's labor. To use Sartre's terms, a multitude of subjectivities congeal
as a group in fusion under his command.[75] As a subjectivity recognized
by other subjectivities, the priest is empowered to pursue a psychological
inquiry into this whole business of worship. As Nietzsche saw, priests are
the first psychologists.

The priest initiates this process by compelling unquestioning obedience to meaningless rituals and absurd doctrines. The goal is to force
the servile consciousness to a knowledge of its weakness. The aggression formerly invested in masochism is thereby turned back against that
masochism; it is now an aggression bent on rendering insignificant and
condemning to utter servitude all that is weak and self-destructive in
the subject. The priest thereby puts himself in an explicit master-slave
relationship to himself: his project is to overcome the weakness that characterizes his subjects. This effort liberates the desire trapped in those
weak behaviors and focuses everything within subject on the struggle
to achieve independence and self-conscious identity. The priest recognizes the seeds of corruption implicit in the position of master—the
self-reification that results whenever one accepts the outward show of
one's subjects rather than comprehending and taking on their inwardness. Internalizing that recognition produces a tragic understanding of
the entire dialectic that makes self-overcoming imperative. The human
being is unhappy consciousness, subject desiring substance, seeking and
avoiding a self-consciousness that condemns it to a freedom in which
it must undertake the endless surmounting of everything weak in itself.
This is the knowledge that constitutes the significance of the priest in the
development of subjectivity.

The priest's unhappy consciousness takes this form: like Dostoyevsky's Inquisitor, he realizes that he takes over the freedom of his subjects in order to establish his own and give them what they want—servility—while calling it something else. He alone knows that relief from
their misery has cost them the very possibility of their freedom.[76] The
result is a reinternalization of guilt: he takes the entire dialectic upon
himself as the self-consciousness that freedom requires people to overcome religious otherness and realize themselves totally in the world. In
seeing that the motive of religion is the desperate need of the weak to be

delivered from existence and a guilt they are unable to master, he attains an understanding that leaves him, the moment he fulfills their desire, in the tragic position of the Grand Inquisitor. In taking over the freely rendered freedom of others, he denies their humanity. "Miracle, mystery, and authority" are stand-ins that conceal the despair of both the flock and the shepherd.

The master consciousness has become a tragic consciousness, condemned to Nietzsche's "pessimism of strength," for it is constituted by the recognition that insight into weakness necessitates the effort of self-overcoming. The Hegelian maxim "To be aware of limitations is to be already beyond them" has become a tragic imperative. God is dead, but the agony of the Inquisitor is despair over humanity's inability to bear the consequence of that fact—the knowledge that the finality of death means total responsibility for one's existence. To grasp the priest's inwardness we must see the irony of his position. Having been given the very subjectivity of his subjects, he gets the recognition that defines our deepest desire, but it all turns to ashes in his mouth. The Grand Inquisitor's ideal, his impossible project, is to lead the flock to an understanding that the death of God is the truth that sets them free—of him. Success in his mission would mean his disappearance.

The Hegelian priest is a watershed moment in the development of subjectivity because, in canceling otherworldliness, he moves toward an explicit negation of the desire for substance which underlies it. God is that alienation whereby we project ideals for ourselves yet set them outside ourselves. Theology is the process whereby we gain an insight into self-consciousness by developing it under another name. The "trick" is to take the insight back and make it one's own. The priest, however, gains no more than the annunciation of this possibility; for, in him, the alienations that went into the projection of God have been reinternalized as a despairing consciousness about humanity. His unhappiness is signified by the fact that he remains a priest. He remains trapped in a role necessitated by the psychological needs he has transcended.

To give readers space for a reflection that will quicken the understanding of their inwardness, I have held back a question we must now ask. If Hegel's discussion of the priest constitutes an essential contribution to the theory of subject—and not just an archaic episode—it must serve as an especially clear and dramatic representation of an experience we all go through in becoming subjects. Only so can the discussion carry the shock of recognition that will bring its full weight to bear on our experience. What is the vital analogy, the true equivalent? An answer is not far to seek.

When, through love, someone bestows on us what we feel to be genuine recognition, we also face the greatest temptation. Flattered, empowered, made to feel self-sufficient, we are loath to see that the bestowal, and our courting of it, often derive from weakness, especially the weakness of those who give recognition in hopes that the other will take over responsibility for their being. If we love, our effort must be to lead both of us beyond the initial terms of the relationship. The sad fact of experience, however, is that most such efforts fail. Couples refuse to understand or alter their inwardness. Unable to transcend together, we must transcend alone by understanding the truth of the relationship. We take the inwardness of both positions upon ourselves, see through all the lies and failures of courage that sustain them, and constitute a new inwardness in the desire to conduct human relationships on a new and different plane. One might term such an effort the condition for attaining mature intersubjectivity; but one must also see it as the overture to isolation and a tragic understanding of the human comedy. In either case, if this experience is the true existential analogue to the priest's situation, then it wouldn't be going too far to say that the priestly position is the primary dialectic we must all go through in order to become authentic subjects.

"The Transition to Reason"

The best evidence that the priest—and his philosophic interpreter Hegel—remains an unhappy consciousness is provided by the transition to Reason that concludes the discussion. Here is a "leap of sentiment" if ever there was one. The series of universals Hegel proclaims in concluding the chapter can be seen as the triumphant assertion of a philosophic consciousness risen above the conflicts of unhappy consciousness, but it can also be seen as so much whistling in the dark. Rather than the move that frees us from unhappy consciousness—which can now be confined to a dim memory as we embark on the dialectic of dispassionate rationality —it is perhaps the crowning instance of unhappy consciousness and thus an inadvertent demonstration that unhappy consciousness is the perspective that cannot be transcended, even by Hegel. This is the reading we will now develop.

A close scrutiny of the steps leading to reason reveals the psychological conflicts that make it not the end but the beginning of a new and particularly regressive episode of unhappy consciousness. For all his immense gains, the priest harbors a contradiction that leads him to frame his achievement in alienated terms. The specific form this alienation takes is *hypostatization:* their locus displaced, Will, Action, and Reason are over-asserted in capitalized, impersonal, and wholly positive terms. A further sign of underlying psychological conflict is the need to adopt a stance—the attitude of observation—that places one safely outside conflict and then to use the defense mechanism termed splitting to vanquish servility and to aggrandize one's achievement by stating everything in suitably abstract and universal terms. To preserve the distance between thought and motives, subject here presents itself as a purified consciousness capable of adopting an impersonal objective standpoint that has risen above psychological turmoil and is now ready to gaze dispassionately at a larger world.

To prevent a relapse into the murky world of human unhappiness, the rationalistic subject deliberately overstates its case. The stance of observational reason is adopted in the hope of arresting any further dialectics. Reason constitutes subject's substantial being and lifts its "devout" observer above emotional turbulence. Rationality is that inner haven that protects subject from any further internal revolutions. The priest hypostatizes his achievement because he finds that he is not yet equal to sustaining the historical effort it implies. The assertion of reason frees him of that responsibility.

The priest's vital task is to reclaim all that has been projected in God by making subject that totalizing consciousness which has as its project the humanization of the entire world. As Marx will later show, this insight is the origin of historical praxis, but for Hegel the initial drive of totalizing consciousness moves in the opposite direction. Observational reason sees the universal as an existing state of affairs ontologically rooted in a subsistent order of being that simply awaits discovery. This standpoint is a positive achievement because it cancels otherworldliness, but it is also the weakest and most inauthentic way of conceiving of our presence in the world. No activity is necessary on our part. All we need do is passively observe nature to discover a stable order that guarantees us a substantial and privileged identity. We are delivered once again from the burden of subjectivity. And this "advance" necessarily leaves subject euphoric since it suppresses everything troubling in the psyche. We consolidate our gains and escape further inner struggle by reexternalizing the dialectic, this time placing it not in the hands of God but in a "Reason" that is in the world.

In this sense, the conclusion of the discussion both formulates subject's task and dramatizes its retreat from it. Psychologically it constitutes a series of refusals either to internalize or to relinquish the gains of the previous dialectic. Each concept advanced—Reason, Will, Action— invites a double reading which will articulate both the priest's implicit self-consciousness and his refusal to sustain that awareness. For example, the statement that the surrender of individual will by the worshiper posits the will of the other as universal can be interpreted in a nonmystified way[77] as an assertion of the universal will of the priest, not of some hypostatized *Geist*. In worship, the mass of unhappy individuals congeal in the desire that someone will for them. In taking that responsibility upon himself, the priest sees that willing must now become totalizing and refer to the world. The statement that "will in general must be the particular will of an individual" makes sense, moreover, only if the hypostatization of God's will is merely the ideological cover needed to empower the priest as the one who wills for all.

Will is the sublation of desire; its exercise is the development of power over oneself. Such is the possibility implicit in the priest and the reason why action emerges as the next major concept. A similar explanation demystifies the notion that the worshiper's act of "giving up its individual action" posits action as a universal value.[78] Action as the attempt to achieve the "unity of objectivity and being-for-itself" is the concretization of will. Its project is to master the external world by imposing subjectivity upon it. Nothing in this formula requires invoking *Geist* or the Absolute. The statement that the universal spiritualizing process becomes actual only in and through the action of individuals refers most directly, in fact, to the priest's knowledge that the worshiper has empowered him to make the dialectic a historical project. The master-slave relationship is thereby externalized and directed upon nature in a humanizing praxis that will operate to produce the good of all.

Such are the possibilities of action implicit in the consciousness of the priest. But in his enthusiasm he wants, like Macbeth, to catch the nearest way. Though it is usually seen as the capstone of the ascent to idealism, the idea of reason that concludes the chapter actually signals a regression to the simplest conception of how the possibilities formulated above will be realized. Reason is the priest's failure of nerve, his return to an unhappy consciousness in flight from its task. Reason's founding desire is to discover a universal mind that is already at work in the world and that operates independent of our activity. We fulfill ourselves as subjects by observing signs of its presence. In positing reason the unhappy consciousness sets up a new master; in bowing before the god of observation, it suffers a new alienation from itself. Unable to undertake the effort implicit in the concepts of will and action, it seeks convalescence by becoming a passive observer. Hoping to put an end to unhappiness, it sacrifices inwardness to the project of remaking itself in the image of science. It repeats before this new god all the gestures of obedience of the servile subject. This is the root of the ideology of science as savior which technological society draws on as its blank check.

It is ironic that most commentators have seen the transition to reason as a definitive move beyond unhappy consciousness rather than the inauguration of its longest episode, scientistic logocentrism. Reason is Hegel's most ambiguous "advance" because it inaugurates what will become the greatest quest for a substantialist guarantee—a priori rationality. But the secret of the dialectic is that detours and false turns fail to arrest it. It breaks out anew amid all efforts to contain it. Unhappy consciousness was authentic subjectivity because it kept its opposite alive in each moment. The shift to reason abandons this awareness; in that sense alone it can be regarded as a "transcendence" of unhappy consciousness. But ignoring internal contradiction is finally an impossible act; and a discovery of the bad faith hiding beneath the pose of reason will, in fact, constitute the dialectic of the next chapter of the *Phenomenology*. The truth of that chapter is the revelation of Science and Reason as among the subtlest and most internally mystified forms of unhappy consciousness.[79]

But the deepest dimension of reason as regression derives from its function in alleviating the priest's guilt toward both the subjectivities he has assumed and the God he has replaced. If all reality can now be pictured as an impersonal process, with truth self-evident to any rational observer, we can all wash our hands in the waters of science. Moreover, that standpoint offers an identity with which only the emotionally unstable can fail to coincide. The voice of guilt is silenced. Entry into the "academic" community of objective scientists and scholars frees us from everything disruptive in our subjectivity; it is the internalization that cancels all previous internalizations.

Lost in this process is the richer possibility that internalizing guilt is the primary experience needed for the development of intrapsychic structure. By internalizing guilt we become, in effect, priests to our own servility and bear the consciousness that the only forgiveness is self-mastery. Guilt over excusing one's weakness becomes a will toward self-overcoming. The priestly internalization of guilt is a metaphoric formulation of the ideal attitude subject can take toward itself. It thus brings to completion the process of psychic structuration the unhappy consciousness has been struggling toward in mediating its self-division. The transition to reason is not the overcoming of subjectivity but its ossification. With it, Hegel's contribution to our inquiry comes to an end. To make our own transition to a chapter that takes up that contribution and presses it to a further issue, we will attempt below to distill the basic conceptual structure of the theory of subjectivity we can derive from Hegel.

Toward a Dialectic of Situated Subjectivity

unhappy consciousness as a structure
of existential self-mediations

The discussion of unhappy consciousness has a three-part structure because it deals with the three basic conflicts through which subject achieves intrapsychic structure: (1) masochism or passive aggressive activity; (2) sexuality or dialectical doubling; and (3) priestly consciousness or the active reversal of guilt. From this perspective, the discussion constitutes a theory of subject analogous to Heidegger's existential analytic. For it articulates a comprehensive understanding of the contexts and ways in which subject's being is at issue. We may thus articulate the deepest layer of the discourse in a dialectical series of propositions about the nature and stages of inwardness.

The initial tension between the desire for the unchanging and the anguished experience of individuality is really a displaced expression of the internal conflict that defines subjectivity: the craving for identity within the repeated experience of one's noncoincidence with oneself. What was true of desire's relationship to its object is now true of subject's relationship to itself. Unhappy consciousness sublates the dialectic of desire, making it a quest for identity. *The object of one's desire is now oneself.* But one experiences oneself as irretrievably dispersed in a multiplicity of unstable feelings and changing relationships. Reflection produces the idea of the self only to open that idea to the charge of being an abstraction, empty of content and readily subjected to deconstruction as a fiction. Genuine subjectivity is born the moment we experience the contradiction between a plenitude of feelings in which we suffer random dispersal and a longed-for identity that is void of qualitative difference. Noncoincidence with oneself becomes now the source and theme of human experience. To be conscious is to suffer being conscious. Having made the self the object of desire, desire becomes the act of agonizing over oneself as being-in-the-world.

Through this experience subject is brought to earth. The abstract idea of self becomes a genuine self-feeling: subject broods on itself in its contingency. It is given over to existence within a consciousness not of its substantiality, but of its nothingness. Where before there was the abstract thought of identity, there is now the experience of thrownness, facticity, and ceaseless internal change. Powerlessness forces subject back on itself in a feeling of infinite defeated longing which is a displaced expression of subject's infinite Kierkegaardian concern to preserve its subjectivity. Defeat of the transcendental project forces subject to internalize the master-slave as its self-relation. Inwardness thereby attains an entirely new experience of noncoincidence. Under the dominance of the internalized other, subject's relationship to itself becomes one of primary masochism. But masochistic self-mediation is the ironic forerunner of genuine self-criticism, for in it subject takes up an active stance toward its internal division by attempting to root out everything that disgusts it in itself. Subject becomes the bearer of creative negativity.

The power of all "negative" emotions is that they protest our relationship to ourselves, demanding both internal and external change. The discipline of masochism makes subject aware that bad faith is not an unfortunate and occasional habit, but an unavoidable dimension of subject's self-relation. Bad faith exists whenever we live one knowledge within ourselves and another in the world. The truth that such a consciousness hides from itself is that we can't escape self-awareness. The self-reflexivity of subject condemns us to living our lies with strain, as bad actors aware we are playing a role, enacting our own *Verfremdungseffekt* in hopes the audience won't catch on. But subject lives condemned to reflection. The unhappiness at work in bad faith is potentially liberating because it doubles existence back on itself. In playing roles with strain one lifts them out of the realm of necessity and determinism and puts them in the arena of choice. Everything regarded as sociologically and behaviorally solid is lit up with the possibility of its negation. The possibility of freedom first arises when one knows one is living a lie. Bad faith sublates the feeling that one's being is at issue by showing that our being is implicated in a vast network of social interactions where the struggle for subjectivity is played out. As long as one remains content to manipulate public roles for private ends, one plays life as a comedy, preserving the illusion of a private freedom that is not dependent on concrete relations with others. For a dialectical struggle to take place, subject must discover its bad faith in an experience where the other bites deeper— where game playing becomes an act of depriving and being deprived of genuine possibilities. Interpersonal solipsism may guarantee a consciousness of narcissistic superiority, but the pursuit of masochism is limited by "love" and the experience of the body.

Masochism would prove inexhaustible were it not for the power of the sexually incarnate body to generate a new order of inwardness. This is the great neglected methodological and ontological significance of sex: it shows that limits aren't introduced by pure reflection but imposed by experience. Sexuality ties the dialectic to the flesh, making existence rather than pure inwardness its primary term. The body is not an extension of pure mind. Experience is originary; it, and not abstract thought, produces developments which take subject beyond anything that could be conjured by thought alone.

In sexuality, the contradictions of unhappy consciousness express themselves immediately and most powerfully. Dialectical doubling is doubled back upon itself. That is why the "struggle with the enemy" initiates the second major development of intrapsychic structure. Repression creates sexuality; and sexuality returns the favor by creating constant occasions for further repressions. The body and its "history" are the story of this doubling, a dialectic of discipline and transgression, renunciation and liberation. Unhappy consciousness is the unity which self-division engenders in the very act of trying to escape it. Sexuality develops this connection between unity and self-division by laying down a permanent threat to the very project which it engenders, that of otherworldliness. The great cultural secret is that the two are equiprimordial and exist in a tense dialectical relationship: when religious transcendence becomes subject's major project, sexuality takes on the complications that make it the most recalcitrant and variegated phenomenon. From an innocent pleasure, a natural part of life, sexuality becomes an experience fraught with danger and transgression. Otherworldliness feeds on the act of disciplining this other. Repression creates sexuality by giving it a new meaning that is necessarily a lived meaning. Subject has enacted an irreversible self-mediation. Sexuality has become psychosexual experience. We can't return to the state of nature, for the natural no longer exists. The body in its immediacy has "changed utterly." It has become the expression of a conflicted self-consciousness—the scene of fundamental, unavoidable conflicts one must go through in order to achieve "identity."

Sexuality cancels the dialectic of spiritual ascent or Platonic transcendence. It exposes the limits of rationalism and mocks all contemplative conceptions of identity. That is why the unhappy consciousness sees it, in anxiety, as fundamentally dangerous. The body laughs—and sometimes gently smiles—at all projects of transcendence. However momentarily, sexual pleasure takes us beyond nostalgia and the experience of life as a burden to the possibility of Lawrentian pentecost. Its annunciations are the phenomena repression must distort. The primary way of doing so is through the act of interpretation—the rereading of sex as shame and soma. Sex is not just a problem for the unhappy consciousness; it is the primary source of unhappy consciousness because it makes the effort to live in two worlds untenable. It thus contains the possibility of a genuine sublation of subject's noncoincidence.

Sexuality illustrates the primary truth of dialectic and concretizes— both intrapsychically and interpersonally—the law that was first formulated as the source of the slave's inwardness. Subjectivity develops only when "desire is restrained and checked," and that process produces new forms of consciousness and activity that are irreversible and irreducible. The irony of unhappy consciousness is that it continually produces the opposite of what it apparently seeks. In making sexuality the "enemy," one initiates the process that liberates its possibilities. The body repression creates is both more inhibited and more sexual than ever before. Conscious of the body, we live it in a completely new way and with a pregnant reversal. The exercise of obsessional preoccupation progressively robs the otherworldly of content while endowing the sexual world with a deepened meaning.

The body has become the sublation and internalization of a desire that necessarily externalizes itself. As incarnate subjects we stand in a mediate or dialectical relationship with ourselves. The body is our discipline and one of the most honest sources of self-knowledge because one can live it badly. It is not a given, biological constitution but a primary index of the extent to which subject is capable of realizing itself in the world. But once the sexual comes to bear the anguished desire for recognition that defines subjectivity, most relationships prove inadequate. We appear to live condemned to an endless Aristophanic search. Once erotic love has become the project in which subject attempts a full realization of itself, we suffer the repeated recognition that we have not achieved our goal. In sexuality, noncoincidence is not a logical impossibility but an existential experience. The project of radical human fulfillment in the world and the absence of any genuine satisfaction are born simultaneously. The struggle with the enemy may look like a dialectical comedy, but its true issue is a tragic understanding of our inwardness. The necessary sublation in which it issues, producing the third major development of intrapsychic structure, is guilt.

In guilt, one wages the struggle necessary for the attainment of psychic autonomy. The split that defines unhappy consciousness is now fully internalized and regulates one's self-reference: the pain of separation from ideals previously identified with and now lost is seen as the consequence of acts for which one is fully responsible. Thus, *everything now proceeds from within the interiority of the subject.* While transgression aimed at independence, guilt shows the inner territory one must conquer in order to achieve independence. Aiming for change through action alone, transgression pictured everything in externalized terms. Guilt reveals that the battle for oneself is an inner drama with no easy or quick solutions. Subject has now become the effort to mediate itself by confronting its internal core conflicts.

Conflict with the internalized other is now fully one's own, with the possibility of becoming an autonomous self the stake of the struggle. Discovering the power of the internalized other to dominate one's subjectivity, one also discovers how much one has made this other one's own through complex libidinal ties one has refused to face. The inner master or superego is now seen both as fully one's own and as a voice with which one is in conflict. Guilt often ends with self-collapse and the ascendance of the internalized other to a position of greater dominance than before. But that does not alter the dialectically significant fact that guilt mastered is the origin of the autonomous self. It is the pivotal experience in the development of inwardness because collapse or self-mastery is the only choice it offers, with the latter initiating the struggle which can totally transform subject's relationship to itself. There is no otherness left. Everything in one's subjectivity is now one's own—as one's problem. All conflicts previously externalized now reveal their subjective meaning. Master-slave has become the problem of attaining self-mastery by rooting out everything that binds one to the dream of substance. By forcing us to assume the burden of subjectivity as a discipline of *character,* guilt sublates the anguish that originated in the recognition that one's being is at issue.

More than any other experience, guilt reveals the dialectic of subject as a process of active reversal, of desire positing and binding itself to objects and ideals it will later surmount. Each attempt subject makes to get rid of itself, to arrest its dialectic, serves only to deepen the value of both subjectivity and experience. The real secret of the subject is that it doesn't want to get rid of itself; guilt is the struggle through which it comes to know this.

The alternative, though dominant, is not a pleasant picture. Guilt unmastered expresses itself as aggression turned inward. This may be the dominant human act, but it is also a reaction formation testifying to both the possibility it denies and the inability to discharge one's anger on the internalized other. Aggression toward the self is really the last resort and the final punishment one inflicts on oneself for harboring anger toward the internalized other and for refusing the challenge of freedom. That is why every suicide is a murder—of someone else—and why the walking dead outnumber the living. Aggression turned inward is aggression turned against inwardness: against the fact that subjectivity eternally disrupts the peace of substance. The death drive is an antidialectic in which the possibilities guilt gives rise to are inverted and parodied as the self unravels.

Genuine negativity, in contrast, cultivates itself through depression. The anger turned inward in depression becomes creative once internal otherness becomes its target. The fundamental conflict defining inwardness—the opposition between the desire for autonomy and the desire for recognition—is brought to a new issue. One strives to give oneself recognition by becoming the master of one's own house. If successful the depressive attempt to master guilt transforms the terms and possibilities of one's relation to the other; for it frees us from the power of the other to withhold recognition and from our own frequently desperate need to seek or compel recognition at any cost. We are no longer haunted by the Sartrean fear that the other has the power to turn us into a thing.

Guilt is the experience that first makes possible the fundamental changes which issue in that psychic integrity which alone deserves the names selfhood and identity. Contra substantialism, the condition of that possibility is struggle; its achieved "state" is character understood not as an unalterable ego identity but as one's way of acting in the face of those existential situations which compel us because they put us at risk and demand something fundamental of us. Psychic autonomy does not dissolve conflict in the harmony of an adaptational ego, but brings conflict to its ripest issue. Guilt mastered is the origin of the project because it brings us fully into the world with the recognition of our absolute responsibility for the determination of our being.

UNHAPPY CONSCIOUSNESS "FÜR UNS"

We are now in a position to summarize Hegel's contribution to the theory of subjectivity in a series of theses.

1. Subject is a hierarchy of integrations made possible by acts of self-overcoming in the face of the basic problems and contexts of human existence. This entire formula must be sustained or one lapses into idealism.

2. Reflection is inescapable and always produces an awareness which opens up a new context of experience in which one must undertake a further development of one's subjectivity. This entire formula must be sustained or one severs the connection of inwardness and existence. Reflection is the way all experiences are lived—even when the living of them is the attempt to arrest reflection—and its recurrent demand is the total transformation of oneself. The study of unhappy consciousness charts the ways in which reflection makes its presence felt from its initial appearance in anguish to its explicit understanding of self-overcoming as the principle defining the subjectivity of the subject. Jean Hyppolite terms unhappy consciousness the recognition of the unhappiness of all reflection. We might also call it a recognition of the irreversibility of all reflection. The deepest lesson of the discussion is that reflection produces the demand for a total transformation, not only of consciousness, but of reflection itself. Reflection provides the identical subject-object only insofar as it continually transcends its previous forms and limits. It is not a worldless act but the primary and most radical mode of our being-in-the-world, since it demands constant and irreversible change. Subject is what it becomes because reflection shows that its being is always at issue. If we simply reflected on our noncoincidence in an abstract way, the dialectic would become another hiding place for the dream of substance. But reflection stands in a dialectical relationship to itself: its development is both a progressive discovering of the contexts reflection must engage and a progressive transformation of the very nature and implications of the act of reflection. Reflection is not an essential form, forever repeating the same identical act, but an existential act.

3. Unhappy consciousness is not a state or a mood but a process of development. Reflection is always situated because it derives from the contradictions of a specific situation when that situation is experienced not as something to be endured but as something that must be surmounted. Suffering is always a potential birth pang because reflection is the imperative of self-overcoming that consciousness lays on itself whenever it is forced back upon itself. This process begins each time desire is "restrained and checked." For when that happens, subject is doubled back upon itself in a meditation that has the power to transform its self-reference. Inwardness develops not by escaping or resolving but by deepening the conflicts that define it. Reflection is neither a static nor a transitory thing, but the process through which consciousness enacts the total transformation of its relationship both to itself and to the world. Inwardness and existence are inseparable because the former develops only by progressively taking the latter upon itself. This process constitutes the dialectic of experience, which is not susceptible to reduction because its moments are not repetitions but irreversible developments of a subjectivity that puts itself fully at issue in the world. This is most true of the anguish which is its beginning; for in that act inwardness is not a worldless meditation or a *pathétique* of privacy, but the first moment of our effort, as existing beings, to project ourselves into the world.

4. No depth exists in subject until it is created. No a priori identity awaits us. Everything derives from experience. Inwardness is a process of becoming, a work, the labor of the negative. The self is not a substance one unearths by pealing away layers until one gets to the core, but an integrity one struggles to bring into existence. Inwardness is an emergent reality guaranteed by nothing outside its own possibility, and with its being residing wholly in the process of its coming to be. Experience is the author of its dialectic.

5. The paradox of subject is that it simultaneously desires to do away with subjectivity and to preserve it. It wants both to fulfill and to extinguish the feeling of unrest that defines it. Seeking the solidity of substance, it recurrently experiences the necessity to outstrip its previous forms. As surpassing, as the progressive transcendence of each limitation it imposes on itself, subject is condemned to enact, in a determinate and progressive manner, a repeated movement of perpetual dissatisfaction and renewed quest. Subject would like nothing better than to silence itself, to lose itself in the object, to achieve the bliss of an absorption containing no otherness. But subject is its own otherness, for being conscious necessarily

involves taking up attitudes toward one's situation. We are always questioning our experience, even if only in those passing, nihilating moods we flee. Discontent defines us because subject is a process of determinate negation in which one continually strives to outstrip one's previous forms in the effort to achieve an impossible adequation—an experience to which subject would say, "Stay, thou art so fair," because in it one would be substantialized by and in the object of desire.

6. Unhappy consciousness sublates and fully internalizes the pain of that perpetually failed project. It brings to experience a subjectivity that experiences its noncoincidence in the midst of the very activities in which it attempts to realize itself. We possess subjectivity to the extent to which we live such an awareness. Self-knowledge may, accordingly, be defined as follows: it is a self-consciousness that, having brooded on the failure of human relations and having discovered the cause to lie within subject in a fundamental and not accidental way, centers its inwardness in that awareness. The final question for us must be this: how can we, in our time, retrieve and live the knowledge Hegel offers, that we have inwardness only to the extent to which we suffer it—and project upon that suffering? A concrete answer to that question will be developed in the next chapter.

2 Existentialism: The Once and Future Philosophy

For herein is the evil of ignorance; that he who is neither good nor wise is nevertheless pleased with himself.   —Plato

Along with the sober anxiety which brings us face to face with our individualized potentiality-for-Being, there goes an unshakable joy in this possibility.

—Heidegger

THE EXPERIENCE OF THE EXISTENTIAL SUBJECT

Identifying Existence

The subject is that being whose very being is at issue. All that follows will be an attempt to articulate what this statement means for a theory of subjectivity.

We do many things, but we live as subjects only when involved in situations in which the meaning and value of our lives are at issue. Properly understood, the existential interrogation of subjectivity is not an attempt to construct a phenomenology of experience or of consciousness in general.[1] It is an effort to articulate in systematic terms the philosophic significance of a highly rarefied order of experience, that which arises out of those situations in which we ask ourselves "Who am I?" or "What does it mean to be alive?" Most of our relationships to ourselves are not of this order. Experience is of existential significance only when it brings us before the imperative of making choices that will not be incidental but will in some way irreversibly determine our very being.

Existential subjectivity has its origin in such experiences. There is nothing abstract or a priori about it. The self-reference involved when one's humanity has become a question, however vague or intermittent, is the core of existential subjectivity because all specific choices are defined by reference to certain fundamental and inescapable problems which life invariably presents. These problems—death, the dilemma of choice, the relationship to others, the struggle to give integrity to one's character—form the universal context of all our activities. The choices we live out in the face of them determine our being as subjects.

The existential subject may be defined initially as a self-relationship in recognition of the primacy of certain problems. In so relating to itself, subject both experiences its being as at issue and actively makes it so. Internalizing an awareness of what it means to be alive is the self-mediation that produces the first coherent *self-feeling*. Subjectivity is the process of deepening one's relationship to oneself—as a question, a "who" rather than a "what." Inwardness is not a substance with some sort of fixed nature one can discover through the less exacting exercises of traditional reflection. From its inception, reflection, if existential, is not a Kantian or Cartesian process with fixed a priori guidelines and rational limits, but an opening up of holes in one's being, gaps in one's experience, questions of peremptory force which lack any apparent answer.

Part of the difficulty of conceptualizing existence is that reflection on the self has rarely been conducted or conceived along such lines. Two circumstances have combined to channel it in another direction. (1) The metaphysical tradition, dominated by a logic of substance or self-presence, so inhabits thought that it is hard for any reflection to break out of its controlling assumptions. (2) The radical openness of existential experience so disrupts ordinary patterns of living that sustaining it requires uncommon anxiety tolerance. Reflection, as traditionally conceived, bears these factors as the scars that control both its self-understanding and its practice. One reflects up to that point where reflection discovers the substantiality or stability of something that is already there—behavior, rationality, the defense ego, social consensus—and that puts an end to reflection. Reflection, so conceived, has strict limits because its goal is cessation in the discovery (and contemplation) of a substantialized being.

Existential reflection, in contrast, is a going into the dark with no idea what one will come up with aside from the knowledge that one's very self is caught up in the act. The self-mediation which this process engenders consistently forces one beyond previous, supposedly fixed determinations and into a self-relationship in which one's being becomes progressively more, not less, unstable. The self engaged in existential reflection achieves through that act a fundamental alteration of its very subjectivity. Such a subjectivity cannot be comprehended, along traditional lines, as the maintenance of the same (a fixed identity or "identity theme"), the adaptation to an external reality (normalcy, society), or the discovery of a rational core capable of producing the eventual elimination of everything not congruent with reason. Nor can existential subjectivity be conceived romantically as the search for that core experience—infantile memory or an analogous deeply affective Proustian self-presence—one must spend one's whole life endeavoring to recover. There is no core, no prior self-presence for us to plumb. Subjectivity exists caught up in a process of becoming in which everything is at issue.

Such a fundamentally new understanding of subjectivity remains the untapped legacy of existential thought. In the hope of rescuing that legacy from the popular views that have done more than any opponent could to render existentialism passé, I will begin by advancing a series of theses. The dialectical connection of these theses and their concrete development will be the burden of subsequent sections.

1. Subjectivity is the relationship one lives to oneself as that being whose very being is at issue. This relationship is the origin and "theme" of all authentic self-awareness. Other states of consciousness and modes of self-reference derive from it as particular determinations that reveal, as their deepest meaning, whether the question of one's being has been genuinely posed.

2. The degree to which one's existence is at issue underlies and determines all one's relationships to others. The existential relationship subject lives to itself inhabits consciousness as the subtext and horizon of all perceptions and activities: it thus forms the dialectic of any act, attitude, or positionality of consciousness.

3. Subjectivity originates in the questions "Who am I?" and "What shall I do?" These questions are inseparable, and any posing of either apart from their mutual complication indicates that neither has been properly appropriated.

4. As a "who" rather than a "what," one experiences oneself not as an essence with a fixed nature but as the projecting of possibilities— with the result that it is necessary to submit oneself to experience for determination. Possibility is not the romantic experience of a world that is "all before us" like a limitless dream. Possibility bites into the very being of subject; one exists only when one chooses in a finite world, fully bound to all the consequences of one's choice. Understanding oneself as being-possible does not imply an inner freedom defined by the pure projection of either the heart's desires or reason's dictates. Rather, it delivers us

over to our situatedness. Possibility is not the way one communes with a pure self, but the way one inhabits the world—and is inhabited by it. Possibility strips subject bare of guarantees, plunging it into the world while maintaining the questions "Who am I?" and "What shall I do?" as measures of each particular choice. Such an understanding of possibility transforms subjectivity because it reveals a disquietude that is at the center of our being and that haunts experience. I don't *have* possibilities, I *am* the possibilities I project. To be is to act: subjectivity is totally in the world; it exists as the way we live out the attitudes we take toward our situations.

5. The understanding of one's humanity—of what it means to be a human being—is the basis of all activities and is lived as their subtext and their ultimate term of reference. Just as in Hegel, this context is the self-consciousness, harbored in each consciousness, that haunts both our understanding of the world and our activity in it. As such, it is the source both of the general attitude we take toward possibility, whether eager or indifferent, and of the kind of possibilities we project. Intensity is a function of awareness. The understanding one has of the duties involved in being human determines the demand one places on life and the dynamism of one's experience. Awareness of "what it means to be alive" is the ground phenomenon that shapes and quickens perceptions or deadens them. It is both the self-feeling that lights up the significance of certain situations and experiences, and the slumbering principle of instability that comes to disrupt so many of the relationships in which we seek rest. The questions "who" and "why" may be intermittent, but they never fail to exact their price. While this dimension of subjectivity becomes explicit only in experiences like anxiety, it is with us, even when we flee it, as a permanent threat and appeal. Boredom is a revelatory mood, for example, because it reveals my situation as a compromise, a loss, a waste of my being. Though we generally flee such moods through new distractions, our need to do so reveals our boredom as a momentary annunciation of the need to take up a cleaner relationship toward our being.

6. All intentional activities entail some intending of *oneself* and include an implicit reference to the potential self-consciousness that acts as their interrogation. The burden of existence is not just that we can't get away from ourselves, but that we are always, even in flight, living out that fact. Reflection isn't a private or occasional act, a room divorced from experience that we enter from time to time, but a constant force of

self-interrogation that is lived out immediately in the moods and attitudes we take up toward our projects. In this way, reflection is constant with experience. I am always, though usually without knowing it, engaged in a critical relationship to myself.

This consideration helps us to redefine reflection. When I rise to reflection I have not taken wing beyond experience or entered into a realm of pure essences that I can contemplate disinterestedly, delivered from the taint of existence. The first and proper act of reflection is the effort to grasp the world as it is revealed to a heart made alive to itself in passion, to develop, not extinguish, the questions of the "who" and "why" of subject by taking the problem of being a subject upon oneself. For that reason, reflection can never satisfy itself with an analytic or phenomenological description of existence. It must project upon that description, for its implicit call is to quicken the act of existing. "To be or not to be" remains the question.

7. As a process of self-reference defined by the simultaneous deepening of an inwardness that destabilizes the self and the projection of possibilities that are submitted to the world, the existential subject makes a clear break with a logic based on substance or self-presence. Subject cannot be defined as an a priori identity within the order of thought (i.e., human beings are rational animals), or as a thing among things determined by external behavioral processes which fix its nature. When used to establish the logic that will control the question of self-identity, both frameworks are equally guilty of abstraction from experience. The first never gets into the world of concrete striving except by superimposing abstract preconceptions upon it, whereas the second labels as anomalous and interprets reductively everything disruptive in experience.

Who Am I . . . What Shall I Do?: Understanding the Question

Subjectivity is determined by the relationship one lives to the question "Who am I . . . What shall I do?" This question is the origin of subjectivity because, through it, one first comes to live a relationship to oneself. Self-identity is the project one forms on the understanding one has of what is involved in the question.

Obviously, this question is not first in the order of experience. Its primacy is strictly ontological. In fact, we can term humanity a "self-caused" or unmotivated upsurge in the order of being precisely because this question need not happen and, for many people, apparently never does. Whenever it occurs, however, subject's relationship to itself is fundamentally altered—and experience takes on a new meaning and direction.

Naturalistic attempts to provide a causal account of the origin of this question are not without merit, since certain experiences are necessary to bring one to this point. Part of the precariousness of our humanity is the possibility that modern society will succeed in eliminating these experiences. But when it is deployed reductively, the naturalistic standpoint ends up dissolving the question. The question's significance is not where it comes from, but what it inaugurates. The irreducible fact is that it puts the one who asks it into question.

There are, of course, many ways of understanding and resolving the question. We are trained, in fact, to think of understanding as a sort of prescientific operation, the clearing away of prejudices and emotions and the movement toward clear and distinct ideas. The dominance of this way of understanding suppresses the richer dialectic from which it derives. All understanding derives from some prior experience, the comprehension of which suggests a direction for inquiry and the methods that are appropriate to it.[2] We are always brought back to what it means to understand the question—as a question. The "answer" derives, in turn, from the degree to which one finds oneself involved in the question as a subject. If one responds to "Who am I . . . What shall I do?" as a nagging confusion one wishes to be rid of or as that vague shudder of discontent before the rush to fulfillment in the goods offered by one's society, one "naturally" finds certain methods, disciplines, and ways of discussing the matter compelling while dismissing others as signs of "neurotic" confusion and philosophic unintelligibility. A response such as Hamlet's inverts that alignment: one finds that in taking up the question one has taken on a critical relationship to most of the traditions of Western thought. The beauty of the question is that it puts all our ways of thinking on trial.

The question, then, becomes this: what is a proper understanding of the question? While subjectivity may be inappropriate when dealing with other kinds of questions, it is essential here. The only response adequate to the question is one that opens up the questioner in a radical way, with the recognition that the question must be kept alive and lived out so that its stakes may be raised and its issues developed. The response that engages most deeply in the question is the one most appropriate to it—its adequacy deriving precisely from the degree of its passion. That response is, as we shall see, anxiety.

Whenever passion is invoked as a principle of cognition, objections are sure to arise. To clear the air we must, however, raise the stakes by noting that passion as used here refers, not to a biological disposition or confused perception, but to an existential act. One has passion to the extent to which one grasps the question of existence and commits oneself to its imperatives. The differences in the amount and force of passion that distinguish people are not a function of natural endowment or neurotic instability but an "objectively" discernible result of their response to existential issues. One has passion to the extent to which one comprehends what it means to exist. Passion is a function of imperatives that the world imposes on us, and that is why it can be regarded as a prime agent of cognition. Those lacking it don't lack some natural biological endowment; they lack engagement in themselves as subjects. We here glimpse one of the ways in which our subjectivity is not "subjective" but measured and judged by the depth and adequacy of our response to the "objective" problems of existence.

Subjectivity transcends both the pleasure and reality principles. It is the deepening and self-transformation of one's inwardness through the discovery of experiential complications that continually force subject beyond its previous forms. The proper response to the question "Who am I?" is to hold oneself open in an anxious effort to engage and complicate the question. In anxiously appropriating the question that it is, subject mediates itself by overcoming itself. The deepening of inwardness that characterizes subjectivity has been persistently misinterpreted and mystified as a retreat into an ineffable privacy of the self. The truth of the matter is the exact opposite. Life forces the question of the "who" on us. Subjectivity hurts.

Once the primacy of passion is grasped, the long reign of traditional epistemology and its conception of experience as a knowledge affair is at an end. Consciousness is not at base the act of perceiving or knowing the external world. It is, rather, an ethical self-relationship that is immediate and that informs all my dealings with the world. The task of self-consciousness is to bring to the surface the existential understanding that one's being is always at issue so that its disruptive force might come to fruition. Subjectivity is the "ethical" relationship one is living toward oneself. Ethics so understood is not something derivative or tacked on after rationalist and scientific understanding has been formed. It is the primary relationship which underlies all the positions and attitudes one adopts toward the world.[3]

By refusing to separate the questions "Who am I?" and "What shall I do?" we establish their existential connection as the circumstance which prevents both a contemplative view of thought and a rationalistic view of ethics. The "who" is not a question that can be resolved simply by thinking about it. This is so not only because the self of pure thought is empty but also because the weight of the question lies in the pressure it puts on us to do something about it in a world that hardly corresponds to the dictates of reason. The question reveals its terms, in fact, only when seen as calling for an ethic of action, with ethics problematized in a new way. A conflict of goods can no longer be ruled out a priori, nor can we derive ethics either from natural law or from a priori rational identity. The logic of harmony that has ruled the history of ethics, and that has served as a criterion in eliminating positions that don't fulfill that requirement, loses its primacy. We must act, but action must be adequate to the "who" that defines us and the contingent world into which we are thrown.

The question "who" not only defines the emergence of subject. What one does in living out a response to it determines and measures one's subjectivity. The self is its project because the project is not something attached to an already substantial self, but the very way in which the self exists. Even in its most private and passive moments, subject is already outside itself, referring to a world upon which it has either failed to project itself or wishes to do so. The whole question of what it means to be a subject can be posed and focused in terms of how one responds to that primordial experience from which subjectivity derives—the experience of anxiety. But that experience, as we'll see, has been subjected to an almost total loss of meaning.

Toward Anxiety: The Other and the Value of Fear

We begin to understand anxiety only when we know what precedes and is perhaps more basic than it. Rather than being an absolute, transparent, primary experience, anxiety initially finds itself in a secondary position. It constitutes a rupture with a long-standing opacity and fallenness of subject. Anxiety arrests us and turns us around only because we have lived for a long time undisturbed by its force,[4] safe in the comforts of that which delivers us from it, the other. As we shall see, the emergence of the other as the before and about of anxiety does not condemn us to privacy but reveals the self's implication in an unavoidable dialectic of intersubjectivity.[5]

The problem of bringing a solipsistic self into relationship with other minds is significant primarily as a false beginning that shows one hasn't reached down deeply enough into the internal constitution of the subject.[6] Our relationship to the other is a fundamental determination of our being because the other is already present in the initial constitution of inwardness. Subjectivity is intersubjective: in reflecting on myself the first thing I confront is the massive presence of the other. We live in the midst of others with their beliefs and values, fears and conflicts already so deeply embedded in us that the initial experience of reflection is the shock of discovering how utterly the voice of the other comes pouring forth whenever I, the sovereign individual, speak, feel, think, or act. Initially, I find myself no better than a thing, the tablet upon which the other's messages have been writ. The other is prior to the self—and in most cases remains so. The power of the other is such, in fact, that it is sociologically inviting simply to eliminate the self, since at this point in the analysis of experience it has no basis in being. The lure of all apriorisms is that they offer us a way of avoiding this reduction. Supplanting them will require a radically different conception of the self based on a demonstration of its experiential emergence. But, that possibility aside, for the most part individuality is a fallacy of misplaced concreteness beneath which lurks the generalized other of consensual validations and reflected appraisals that keep "other people" firmly in charge as the sovereign authors of our being.

It would be hard to imagine a more abstract view of how one becomes self-conscious and independent than the traditional humanist attempt to conceive this process along quasi-rationalist lines: individuals, tapping reason, freely deliberate about the values society has tried to persuade them to accept before deciding, on the basis of a rational autonomy (innate or acquired), which of them to make their own. The other strikes far more deeply than this into the life of subject; and as long as we pose the problem of the self in the old ways, we have no way of grasping the struggle which identity and liberation entail.

Existential integrity isn't a starting point, but an achievement dependent on reversing processes long since begun. When the other comes before us it is not to meet an already formed subject which may or may not choose to enter into relationships from which it can always subsequently detach itself. Relationships have "always already" begun. From the beginning I am already tied so deeply to the other that everything I do—even when most alone—is relational. Intersubjectivity is one dimension of its being that subject never transcends. Even the most private moods are conversations; the most abject passivities have the character of a "look what you've done to me." Emotions are interpersonal and reflect actions one wants or fears to take in situations defined by relationships with definite others (who may have long since passed from the earth). Even suicide has the character of a dialogue, though hardly a Platonic one.

Heidegger's description of the structure of everyday life articulates the ways in which the other inhabits our being as the subtext that is constantly at work in a vast array of activities that make up the busy business of the day. The purpose of Heidegger's description is to lay bare the motive that sustains our fitful preoccupations precisely because they deflect attention from the deeper problem to which they nonetheless constantly refer. The other is a primary force in structuring consciousness because being with others is both a flight from existential anxiety and its primary cause. Being with and like the others, we are one in the comforts of the commonplace, the already thought, which is not outside us but within, already at work producing an "identity" which is prior to all subjectivity.

In conceptualizing the "they" (*das Man*), Heidegger's achievement is to have situated subjectivity in terms of an initial loss of self that can't even be termed a loss since it is prior to any subject whatsoever.[7] On one level, the discussion contributes to the "death of subject"; on another, it points to a new concept of subject. Otherness is not something we can strip away to regain a pristine or ideal identity, but something we must take up and surmount in order to become subjects in the first place.

The "they" is always busy. A phenomenological description of the structure of everyday life attempts to conceptualize the basic processes (idle talk, curiosity, ambiguity, and fear) that shape our eternally vigilant endeavor to be like one another so that we may live our lives, "distracted from distraction by distraction."[8]

Talk is *idle* when there is something in the background that must remain unspoken. We talk on incessantly lest it surface—in the interstices, the Pinter pause. Together we "make conversation." We chatter on about one thing after another, displacing our concern among diverse topics, "deferring and differing,"[9] until we run out of things to say. We talk on, even when silent, in an obsession to put the tissue of language between ourselves and the anxiety that surfaces whenever that vast edifice grounds to a halt.

Curiosity gives idle talk its themes, thereby assuring that it will remain in a world of known and manageable realities. "The world is so full of a number of things," and we are curious about all of them for curiosity protects us. We never have to go deeply into anything and can always move on to the next affair. Curiosity also takes issues that could prove internally disruptive and puts us at the proper distance from them: thus we live in the confidence that science will one day explain everything, especially those psychological realities that will continue to trouble us until we find the key to their biochemical resolution. An encyclopedic gaze fastened firmly on fact moves securely through the world assured that it will never be arrested and challenged by anything. Curiosity is the mood of the surface and has its appeal because it engages subject least. It might, in fact, be taken as the mood in which subject successfully externalizes itself. We are curious—and endeavor to remain so—because there is much we don't want to know.

Ambiguity is the capstone that keeps the two previous structures in place whenever they begin to totter. It assures that whenever things get out of hand—whenever embarrassing questions arise—there is a foolproof way of bringing them back into line. Ambiguity is that systematic intellectual vagueness we maintain in the face of fundamental issues. Unlike the other structures, which are constant, ambiguity is called in only when one is burdened by the upsurge of something one must exorcise through the exercise of "intelligence." There is, indeed, something deliberate—and often perverse—about the exercise of ambiguity: the insistent demand that one define one's terms; the quick perception, especially by academics, of any semantic vagary; the endless tergiversations about our lack of knowledge and our need to remain humble in the face of things we are not meant to understand. Such practices have a remarkable power to defuse any question. Unlike the first two structures, ambiguity is an internalized attitude of mind one cultivates to secure one against difficulties. The most interesting thing about these structures is that they function as displacements that just miss and thereby highlight the more basic disruptions underlying our need to be relieved—together.

Fear is the glue that binds these structures. And, as Heidegger discovers, fear is also our greatest need because fear is a successful and publicly accepted displacement of anxiety. We are constantly preoccupied with fear over this or that contingency because fear has a wonderful way of attaching us to the world. Fear is always remarkably particularized, eminently pragmatic, rooted in the this, here, and now. In fact, fear gives us an "identity," constituted by the ceaseless effort to fortify our "piece of the rock." Fear is that public-private state of mind that holds us all together in common investments that require for their sustenance a constant production of fear.[10]

But the fact that fear exorcises a more disruptive subtext is the reason why Heidegger can say that fear, though "sociologically" primary, is a derivative phenomenon and that the structures of everyday life are grounded in flight from anxiety. This understanding is one of Heidegger's greatest achievements, and the logic behind it is of central importance for a theory of subject.[11] To grasp it we must note at the beginning what Heidegger doesn't mean. At no point in the discussion does he assume that there was an original experience of anxiety from which one fled into the "they."[12] The "they" is primary. *We* don't fall into it from a prior self-presence, but are in it and delivered over to it long before any question of independence arises. The "they" does not require a conscious experience of anxiety to motivate the flight which empowers it: its structures are already in place and operate independent of any awareness of their underlying rationale. Conscious awareness and choice have little to do with the processes in which we live and move and have our being. The effort to relieve anxiety is at work long before anxiety arises. Genuine anxiety, in fact, always refers to something we didn't know which we now come back to. In comprehending fear and the structures of everyday life as flights from anxiety, we grasp not what fear knows about itself but what it doesn't know about itself. In calling us back from our lostness in the "they," anxiety doesn't renew our contact with a pristine self. It brings the possibility of an existential self into being for the first time.

We are social subjects before we are any other kind of subject, and finding ourselves comfortably ensconced in the structures of inauthenticity, most of us contrive to remain there. The "they" is that which is most primordial and hardest to overcome because it reaches down deepest into the original constitution of our subjectivity. It is, in effect, that which is most personal. The source of its power is the desire to be relieved of existence. This desire is coincident with the initial appearance of the subject. That is why subject is a problem and a precarious achievement. The only thing present before the "they" is the motive that gives birth to and sustains it: the desire to be delivered from anxiety, to be one among others, like them and liked by them. In the struggle for liberation, the main battle subject must fight is always with itself, with that otherness already firmly planted within its internal constitution.

Inauthenticity, the effort to relieve one another of existence, constitutes our primary relationship both to ourselves and to others. This is the mutual deception which coalesces in and sustains the "they." Inauthenticity is not something that befalls social relations when they go sour, but the original motive behind their constitution. The tyrannies we inflict on one another in enforcing conformity to this process make it truly vertiginous. We mature, fleeing existence, among others engaged in like pursuit.

Anxiety and inauthenticity need not compete for logical or temporal priority—as is the case when existentialism is opposed to sociology or marxism—because their secret is that they are experientially equiprimordial. Chicken-egg thinking always distorts the logic of existential conceptualization. Anxiety, unmastered and already fled, is the unattended experience that makes the other an inordinately sought source of comfort and support. The "they" is the most immediate issue of anxiety because anxiety and inauthenticity are virtually indistinguishable at the "origin" of experience.

Existential subjectivity is a triumph against the odds, a rare effort requiring the surmounting of a prior "identity" to which we are deeply committed. Nothing in subject guarantees the emergence of existential self-reference. The recognition of inauthenticity in existentialism is so strong, in fact, that the real problem is to account for the possibility of anything else. Existentialism isn't opposed to sociology. On the contrary, it lays bare the bases of this discipline by showing why human beings are so correctly characterized by sociology and what that characterization means. Contra Lukács, existentialism isn't opposed to ideological understanding, but constitutes one of the most powerful arguments for the primacy of ideology in the formation of the subject. Existentialism adds the factor that prevents reductionism, however, by establishing tensions where other sociological perspectives locate inert, positivistic givens. In doing so, its larger concern is to underscore the precariousness of the very possibility it introduces. Becoming a subject is always a question of overcoming heavy odds which have their primary seat within. Experience alone can introduce the need, and an experience of a special order is required. This is the issue we will now take up.

TOWARD ANXIETY: LOVE AS EXISTENTIAL EXPERIENCE

We don't yet have an adequate theory of subjectivity because we have not yet comprehended the philosophic implications of love. Love is the perfect example to help us attain an existential understanding of the fact that relating to oneself in depth is the key to subjectivity and the sine qua non for its development. For love amends Heidegger's great formula—the human being is "that being whose very being is at issue" —in and through the act of loving. My purpose, in developing this idea, is somewhat abstract. Rather than describe love in detail, I will try in this section to articulate the concepts of subjectivity and of experience that can be derived from an ontological reflection upon it.[13]

When Descartes carries out his famous meditation he ironically places himself in a position in which he cannot know himself. When I consider myself purely, objectively, bracketing my passions and the noisy business of the world in an effort to establish self-identity through a purely cognitive self-relation, I embrace a myth, however well-intentioned or defensive my motives. Such a concept and practice of self-reflection (which have been favored in philosophy) don't involve me in the way I become engaged when I take up the density of my relations with others. The primary function of such a concept and practice may, in fact, be to keep subjectivity at a safe distance so that a substantial identity via the purity and precision of the scientific cogito can be established. It is then but a short step to relegating the life of passion to the status of a confused and derivative phenomenon which the rule of reason must marginalize. In doing so, however, we deny interpersonal experience the ontological significance it could assume.

Diotima's secret is that in teaching Socrates about love she puts him on the road he must follow if he is to fulfill the oracle's command, "Know thyself." To know myself I must do so through the other because the other delivers me over to myself in a way that is more primordial and revelatory than that of any purely cognitive relationship. To comprehend, as philosopher, the laws and dynamics of subjectivity one must plumb the tortured dialectics of human loving. Far more concretely than Heidegger's *Befindlichkeit*, love fits the description "more basic than cognition and volition and beyond their range of disclosure."[14] In knowing myself as cogito or rational animal, I know myself protectively and superficially; while the other encountered in love reaches down into the depth and quick of my being as a subject.

Love is dangerous because when we love we give the other the power to inflict the wound that can kill the spirit. One of the primary facts about us is that we often die in our being long before the physical fact. The power to love is not a limitless capacity, and the day may come when we find the disposition no longer at our disposal. But even in loss there is an ontological yield. The fact that we can lose the ability to love reveals that our very being is at issue in the business of human loving. If I weren't already bound up with the other in a fundamental way I could scarcely find myself in peril, nor, to put it in more romantic terms, could we account for the value human beings have attached to love.

"The other is my original sin" not because he or she comes to disrupt or threaten an already complete and composed subjectivity, but because my being is already implicated in the other, so much so, in fact, that the entire history of our previous relationships and conflicts is revived whenever through love we open and extend our being toward another. "Hell is other people" not because I am threatened from without but because I am haunted from within. At the center of our inwardness we are already captured by others in intersubjective relationships defined by unavoidable conflict and infinite concern. The other has the power to destroy because the other already has a place in our heart. Our deepest concern about ourselves is always bound up with a concern about a possible relationship with the other. Love is a primary source of anxiety because the other doesn't simply hold out the promise of completing us. The other tests the adequacy of our inwardness to its projection in intersubjective experience. This is the primary thing lovers do unto one another.

"Falling in love," one experiences oneself as a being fundamentally incomplete and at issue, not in some solipsistic isolation or private anxiety, but precisely as a result of the radical implication of one's subjectivity in that of the other. Being-in-the-world is being with the other. Love engages us in a way that is fundamental because it reveals the other as the term that existentializes our entire relationship to the world. Falling in love quickens our attention to everything aesthetically compelling in the natural world because it reawakens our sense of the world as a place of wonder, with existence sufficient as an end in itself. Suddenly heaven pales, and having a fixed, substantial identity isn't such an attractive idea. We become aware that we are our bodies and exist, as subjects, in the desire to incarnate ourselves.[15]

If anything deserves to be talked about in terms of "being called back from one's lostness in the 'they,'"[16] it is love. Love involves a rupture, however transitory, with all the modalities of tranquilized existence —the meek adjustments, the long-standing defenses. Love challenges us to root out everything false in our being. It also asks us to reopen all of our basic wounds and unresolved conflicts. That is why the great yes of thanksgiving we utter whenever we love is one with the upsurge of an anxiety that is both intense and specific. That anxiety is the initial appearance of the recognition that one can fail at love and actually lose oneself. Romantic lovers deny this feeling through mania, while the discourse of more "mature" lovers displaces it into fears about career, money, compatible "life-styles," etc. The subtext in both manners of loving is the deeper anxiety that keeps breaking through. In love, one is in a situation in which one can lose something that has no stable or substantial foundation in the order of being but is fully submitted to the world. That something is one's being as a subject.

One feels alive yet in peril when one falls in love because in love the subject is fully given over to its acts. We are bound up with the other in an experience that allows no separation between the self, its "emotional" condition, and its activity. Unlike other stances we take toward the world, love makes us coincide with ourselves in the anxious knowledge that we are our project. Called back from other activities, we reexperience the deeper claims that it is possible for us to make on our being.

Romantic commonplaces call attention to the significance of love only to deflect attention from the exacting process that is at work in it. The anxiety hidden in the bloom of love is the voice that constitutes its just and challenging truth. When authentic, loving is an irreversible self-determination. It delivers us over to ourselves as subjects, not only because it shows how deeply we can become engaged, but because it reveals how utterly we are determined by the issue of our engagement. Fail here and loss becomes an indelible, fully internalized determination of one's self. Love is a fundamental risk because the power to love is precisely what it puts at stake. If one is not so engaged, one is not really in love, no matter what one says or feels. Existential experiences are what they produce: events in an irreversible history which is, at its deepest layer, the history of our loves.[17]

Norman Mailer makes an interesting statement in his book on Marilyn Monroe: "The logic of our emotional life is such that our next love must be greater than our last." For all its "romantic readiness," the first thing Mailer's statement calls attention to is why there must be long arid stretches between our loves despite the ready availability of numerous "object choices." Because love takes us beyond the biological, we need considerable supplies of the latter to salve and disguise the true nature of our wound whenever love fails. But the more disruptive implication of Mailer's statement is that in the matter of loving we can only go forward. If love is genuinely existential, one keeps nothing in reserve. One projects one's total being in a way that is irreversible. Because we are determined by the conduct of our loving, we cannot, with time, return to a prior identity. We can love only a limited number of times in our lives, and each time we must "make it new," not in the popular sense of the term, but by making it an act in which we take up our entire history, resuming our core conflicts in an effort to surpass our previous limits.

Love thus provides the best evidence of the primacy of the future in existential time and the connection of that primacy with the accumulated weight of the past.[18] As such, it is one of the best refutations of the notion that we can always begin again (and thus of the popular identification of existentialism with gratuitous choices made out of nothing but our eternal *disponibilité*). Love reactivates the past that mattered and endeavors to project it into a future defined, necessarily, by the impossibility of discarding one's past. What love teaches (usually through repeated failures) is that to reverse the past we must discover the cause of our previous failure in ourselves and make that (strenuously resisted) self-knowledge the basis of the effort to project ourselves anew.

One doesn't lose the ability to love the way one eventually loses one's muscular dexterity; one loses it because of what one has done with it. And in losing it one loses, to a great degree, one's ability to be as a subject. None of these reflections alters the fact that most of us conduct our business in this matter self-protectively or as Proustians engaged in the endless, and progressively more pathetic, repetition of the same infantile needs. But such sad facts only underscore the possibility, to be seized gladly, that one can embrace love in the category of necessity, seeing it as the project in which we risk ourselves as subjects condemned to an irreversible history. Perhaps this is what it means to be an adult: to will irreversibility over repetition, to live forward, without resentment, bearing the full weight of all one has done. Love reveals us as historical beings with a historicity that is not an accident we can escape or forget but the only "essence" we shall have. The identity of the self is the history of its loves.

If genuine, the knowledge one gains in confronting a failed love liberates in a way that has nothing to do with denial or any naive conception of beginning over. In contrast, the refusal to work through failure leaves one with nothing but the seeds of future defeat: the experience of oneself as victim, jealous monster, desperate child, core of indifference. We prove ourselves worthy to love again only by taking our failure upon ourselves and using it to plumb everything inauthentic in our being. In that necessarily incomplete project, love offers an existential and psychological redefinition of the categorical imperative.

It would be nice if we could work everything out through reason alone and become transparent to ourselves "between the acts." But we can never have reliable self-knowledge in the privacy of reflection, because in the other's absence the defining condition of our subjectivity is missing. We can't know what we've learned from experience until the upsurge of the other puts everything we've worked toward on trial. The best we can do is submit ourselves to the risk, knowing that we necessarily live without guarantees. If self-critical reflection on loss has done its work, when we again extend our being toward the other, we bring, in place of defenses and lies, a willingness to engage one another in an effort of mutual self-overcoming. Change requires no less. An intersubjective being can achieve genuine change only through the act of relating to another intersubjective being. That is why one must always love again. Until then, we have no way of knowing who we've become.

The truth Mailer's formulation just misses, owing to its romantic fixation on the object, is this: our next love must be greater because we must be. We love again only when we are able to ask more of ourselves. Loving is a question not of finding the right person but of becoming the right person. Perhaps the most exciting thing about loving is that it is the act through which we put ourselves on trial.

The missing link that adds bite to this discussion is, of course, the other. The "beauty" of love is that the ante goes up in every direction. The riper one becomes, the more one diminishes the field of suitable others, since what one now demands of the other is the willingness to engage in a sort of mutual war in which we vow to root out all the inauthenticities in one another's being. Conflict—not mutual dependency, narcissistic merging, romantic blindness, obsessional reassurance (I'm OK—you're OK), or the mutual nurturing of one another's neuroses—is the only worthy goal for human loving. It is also the "logic" whereby lovers either come together or eventually discover they are apart.

Love's finest issue, however, is an inescapable self-knowledge. Love brings us before ourselves more radically than all other means of disclosure. We can hold all sorts of nice views about our humanity, but love reveals what our real relationship to the other is: whether conquest, flight, dependency, manipulation, withdrawal, or that rare possibility of regarding the other as other self. As cogito, I may know myself in my rationality, but as lover I know myself in terms of my character, with the "self" fully situational and in process. For the exacting reality is that the self-mediation one undertakes in loving constitutes the truth about one's character, no matter how artfully that truth may be dissimulated in other exercises and concepts of reflection.

Let us now attempt to uncover the ontological yield of these reflections. Love clarifies the concept of "relating to oneself in depth" that we have set down as the requirement for each development of inwardness. In contrast to rationalist self-mediation, which always returns us to the repetition of the same set forms and stable functions, the logic of existential reflexivity puts subject fully into the world by engaging the innermost resources of our being in situations to which we are given over without reserve. Subject is the irreversible issue of this engagement. Naturally, this seldom happens, but that's an unessential point. We exist as lovers to the degree to which we become engaged. This, if anything, measures "how much" we love. Love shows that projection, not habit or necessity, is the only self-relationship that matters. Fail though it may, love retains the power to reawaken the need for living a discipline toward our being. Revealing subject as defined by the possibility of such an integrity is its primary significance for a theory of subjectivity. Love reveals subject as a process rather than a substance and existence as an effort at surpassing. Inwardness is that self-reflection which issues in the upsurge of possibilities that plunge us ever more deeply into the world. The distinctively human phenomenon we call love is noble when it moves within the medium of that self-reference.

Love is one of the places where the connection between existentialism, Marxism, and psychoanalysis becomes apparent.[19] One of love's greatest challenges is that it forces us to confront an otherness and an inauthenticity that are there long before we become subjects and that usually stay in control long after. If love asks us to root out our inauthenticities, it also shows us how powerfully they are already implanted, not as external forces, but as integral to the core of our self-relation. In the most painful ways, love shows me how much my subjectivity is not mine; how little of my parents' conflicts I've worked through; how much my "individuality" is bound up with socio-economic "values" that capitalize most, perhaps, on what they do to limit, if not destroy, our ability to love. Our relations with the other are marked by a fundamental "falling" because "proximally and for the most part" we seek out one another in order to avoid anxiety. Love may be inaugural, but the more basic fact is that, in most cases, it proves too taxing because it requires too great a rupture with all the ways in which we have contrived together to gain deliverance from existence. Nevertheless, love always puts us, however briefly, into a dialectical relationship with ourselves because it forces us to experience inauthenticity, not as an accident from which we can readily detach ourselves, but as one of the essential terms of our inwardness. If love puts us on a collision course with the "they," if it puts us in conflict with all the ways in which, as docile subjects, we have internalized the logic of capitalism, and if it forces us to renew our struggle with the conflicts that formed the familial "birth" of the psyche, it is because love reveals these relations as prior to and of greater force in the constitution of subject than the authentic possibilities that arise only upon their reversal. In bringing us back to the primacy of inauthenticity, however, love reveals inauthenticity for what it is: flight from anxiety and existence. In this sense love is always an act of incipient protest, however abbreviated. Love grants the inauthentic life of the "they" its primacy but lays bare the fear at its core. At the same time it shows that the "they" is so basic that the primary truth of human relations may be the inevitable loss of subjectivity rather than its slow emergence. The test love always faces is the choice between the austerity of existence and the comforts of inauthenticity. In loving one another we don't embark on a glorious career of mutual recognition, but run a collision course with inauthenticity which can prove the more powerful force, in one or both of us, determinative in the last instance, if not in the first. Capitalism, in interpellating us as subjects, sets down all the conditions whereby love will prove too costly, the family all the ways in which the psyche will be unable to escape its net, while everyday life forms a vast semiosis that so tranquilizes us that we suffer without knowing it the loss and forgetting of our being. The "they" is the primary form of subjectivity, love no more than its possible dialectical modification. Love and anxiety make perfect bedfellows because, as the next section will show, they are dialectically related and concretize one another.

Anxiety: In and for Itself

The attitude we take toward anxiety is the constitutive act determining our humanity. If anxiety has the most to tell us about ourselves, it is also the last and least understood of our moods. Its phenomenological character is so vague, so lacking in concrete reference to specific matters at hand, and at the same time so overwhelming, that we flee it like automatons. Most of us become so good at this that we no longer know we're doing it. Sullivan's theory of the "self" as a system designed to avoid anxiety derives its power from this primary fact. Initially, anxiety is that fitful experience which makes no sense, yet which we must of necessity flee because it is unbearable. We need no reminder from Heidegger to proclaim, once anxiety is past, the verbally ironic judgment "It was nothing."[20] In one sense, it's easy to claim that all other emotions derive from anxiety because anxiety necessarily puts us on the move, plunging us into activities. Apparently, there's nothing else we can do with anxiety or about it.

But, as mood, anxiety opens up an emptiness in subject that reveals the body in a fundamental way. Anxiety is unendurable because it brings us before that fundamental panic which we are. Our coincidence with ourselves here is physical and total: in anxiety there is no way to distinguish oneself from the nauseous feeling that one lives *in* and *as* one's body. Anxiety is always first an affair of the body; it is, in fact, one of the ways in which the existential body refutes Platonic and Cartesian dualisms. In anxiety, existence assaults us in the body: one experiences it in the pores long before one does in the head. As in love, the body is foregrounded and revealed in anxiety in a compelling way. Burdened by a facticity that is claustrophobic, anxiety cancels everything we are doing in order to infect us with ourselves. In anxiety, one literally cannot sit still. We have nothing to do because everything has dropped away, yet we have to do something. We pace, we wring our hands, tighten our facial muscles, feel the viscera constrict as they try to contain a panic that must out, or else we will feel that chill that is like death and makes us sweat even when we remain motionless. In anxiety, the body is one vast disruption. All the physical "symptoms" that accompany the mood mandate the flight that constitutes our initial response to it.

The prevalence of flight should not be underestimated, as so often happens in pop existentialism where anxiety is praised (and thereby tamed) as the transparent source of an existential attitude we readily assume. For the primacy of flight reveals existence as a burden which most of us refuse. If accepting anxiety defines the possibility of authenticity, it is a gambit most successfully avoid. Perhaps flight is all that most of us ever know of our existence, which is no more than a tremor long since forgotten in our rush to the business of everyday life.

The founding moment of existential thought rests on an experience and a "concept" that many regard as philosophically unintelligible—a "scandal" both to common sense and to the terms of meaningful discourse. But more than a scandalous intrusion into the house of philosophy, anxiety is a fundamental challenge to traditional modes of conceptualization. It is so hard to think through because it asks us to alter most of the ways we have traditionally gone about the business of thinking. For those positively rooted in a world of facts and simples, those concerned to uncover the wisdom at work in the ordinary ways we use language, or those seeking to give order to thought through the attainment of clear and distinct ideas, anxiety will always remain the uninvited and incomprehensible guest.

The verdict against the existential valuation of anxiety has taken a variety of forms. That which we cannot talk about meaningfully we must consign to silence. Fleeting experiences confined to an ineffable privacy of the self and lacking all intentional reference are inconsequential except perhaps as signs of a correctable biochemical disorder. Human beings, as Aristotelian problem solvers, live among things and pragmatically take up relations with concrete matters at hand; they are so particularized in their being that the only "emotions" worth talking about derive from and refer to such involvements. With the attainment of rationality or a knowledge of how the mind works, one leaves childish things such as anxiety behind. Anxiety may, as Heidegger claims, "bring us back from our lostness" in the "they," but for most people that is the primary proof of its insignificance.

These views receive support from their psychological corollaries. Anxiety doesn't simply give me nothing to do; it indicates that something is wrong with me. And whenever there is something wrong, the American branch of ego psychology steps in to fill the breach by offering us new ways to learn how to "feel good about ourselves." Anxiety derives from a low "self-image," an arrested development resulting in failure to free oneself from punishing parental introjects, a failure at adaptation, a retreat from life, an inability to accept one's limitations and embrace one's position in a triumphant capitalist order. There is not a concept, value, or practice in psychology that isn't defined by reference to anxiety, but for the most part psychology recognizes anxiety only to exorcise it. It thus carries out its social function, making us ashamed of our anxiety by teaching us to interpret it as evidence that we haven't "made it" yet. Once anxiety has been deprived of any other significance, its elimination becomes the only relationship we can live to it.

The power of Heidegger's phenomenological description of anxiety is that it welcomes all of this in order to stand it on its head. The negative characteristics that are pointed at to debunk anxiety conceal another, and eminently positive, meaning. In giving us nothing to do, anxiety calls us back from our involvement in practical matters to a deeper and prior concern. In anxiety my experience of myself is totally different from the self-relationship I have when pragmatically engaged in this or that affair. In telling us nothing definite about ourselves, anxiety restores our contact with that which is indefinite.

Anxiety strips bare the lie of substance: it disrupts our involvement in particular roles, sets at nought the rationalist and consensual identities we have established for ourselves, and throws into question those psychological theories that base everything on the maintenance of a fixed identity. "Basic trust or mistrust" is subjected to something more fundamental— our ability to throw ourselves into question in a fundamental way. The key to reinterpreting the complaints against anxiety is to see how anxiety undercuts them by delivering us over to a self-relationship of a radically different order which they are unable to comprehend. In wrenching me out of my everyday life, anxiety brings me face to face with a "self" that is radically empty—but is so in a novel way. The emptiness opened up by anxiety is totally active. It is not a bottomless pit into which I passively descend but a vital tension that drives me forth into the world. Unlike the cancer that sits there like a dull and impersonal thing slowly accumulating its dead weight, *anxiety is a visceral mania of the self.* In anxiety we are active because anxiety brings us before the fact that, at bottom, we are nothing else.

Anxiety constitutes the first appearance of that process of *taking action within oneself* that defines existential reflection. It is the first appearance of inwardness as a project that is fully at issue in existence. The phenomenological description of anxiety—that all anxiety is anxiety over oneself as "that being whose very being is at issue"—takes on its proper bite only if we see that anxiety throws into question the assumptions concerning thought, knowledge, and experience that make up "the metaphysical tradition." In initiating the process of taking action within oneself, anxiety reveals an order of inwardness that cannot be comprehended substantialistically. The first coherent self-feeling is an inwardness that exists as a question to itself—in the imperative mood. In giving me no specific information about "myself," anxiety delivers me over to a far more basic self-relation, revealing me as that pure possibility that must choose and that has being only through the radical projection of itself into its choices. Anxiety thus establishes situatedness in a way that brings the world as a totality under the sign of the question. Anxiety always sets at nought whatever we are busy with because it puts us in contact with a self-reference that is paradoxically both prior to any situation and radically situational.

Anxiety is always situational but dialectically so. It reveals the situation one is in as lacking in terms of the deeper demand one puts on oneself. It thus "calls us back from our lostness in the 'they,'" not by returning us to a prior and essential self, possessed with a substantial stability independent of the world, but by revealing a self that is fully implicated in its situations. Anxiety arises when we are aware of possibilities we want but fear to project yet realize we will lose unless we take action. It thereby reveals situatedness as both dense with the facticity of the already lived and pregnant with the emergence of the new.

An understanding of anxiety enables us to make a first attempt at articulating a specifically existential concept of the self as possibility. Anxiety is the negation of all contemplative views of self-realization. By delivering us over to the imperative of having to make specific choices in concrete situations, anxiety reveals possibility as the imperative of having to choose now in a world characterized by irreversibility and finitude. Anxiety doesn't offer a self that can picture a world of pure possibilities spread out before it as a theater for limitless desire. Anxiety drives us with urgency into a finite world; even when we flee anxiety, it reveals us to ourselves as the possibility we thereby enact.

Possibilities are possible by reason of their very precariousness. They are first known as possibilities only when seen as being in danger of slipping away, and when there is nothing guaranteed about their projection. Yet they retain their power to measure us even when we flee them. For flight is one of the possibilities we enact. In one way or another we are "always already" engaged. There never was a moment of pure possibility held in suspension before the gaze of an a priori, contemplative self. We have already involved ourselves in countless determinations; the only possibilities we have are those that outstrip the given by initiating some effort to transform our situation. Part of the bite of anxiety is, indeed, the revelation of contingency and a past it is impossible ever simply to cast off.

What is anxiety anxious over? Again the negative characteristics of the phenomenon contain a positive insight. Anxiety puts me in touch with my subjectivity as "something" over which I am anxious. To say that anxiety makes us anxious is not an empty statement but a genuine clue to the reflexivity of the existential subject. In anxiety I am anxious over myself as a being who is at issue: anxiety is the way such a being experiences its being. Anxiety is the first self-feeling given to a subjectivity that has transcended the lie of substance. Its impact derives from the fact that it is the inaugural moment of the struggle to assume our being as subjects. The order of inwardness it incarnates can be termed, as in Kierkegaard, "infinite concern over one's very subjectivity," if we understand such inwardness, not as the discovery of an essence we can preserve and cultivate in spite of the world, but as a panic that is already fully outside itself, caught up in a world into which it is utterly delivered. We become "infinitely concerned" only when we realize that the self is fully, irretrievably at issue. You can lose yourself; that is your innermost possibility. The meaning of meaning is that "only *Dasein* can be meaningless"[21]—and usually is. Existence commences only when we know there is no stable identity to which we can retreat "when the going gets rough" and no transcendent source that will one day come to enfold us in its arms with the comforting assurance that we were never really at risk. Anxiety reveals my subjectivity as something that is fully at issue and for which I am totally responsible.

Anxiety is "anxiety over oneself as being in the world." Anything short of this understanding fails to appropriate the situatedness of both the concept and the experience. Anxiety remains the permanent judge of all situations, the one possibility we can never exorcise. However tranquilized we may be, anxiety has the power to tell us how things stand with respect to a humanity from which we are never delivered. That condition brings us to the final question: what is an authentic appropriation of anxiety?

The deepest lesson anxiety teaches us is not that we exist, but that we must act. This is the secret Heidegger cunningly kept from himself. One always has to take action in the face of anxiety—even if that action be only flight—because anxiety reveals the self as action through and through. Deprived of any contemplative stance toward either itself or its possibilities, subject is driven into the world in a way that makes action the source and the locus of whatever qualities of character the subject wants to give itself.

The primary significance of anxiety for a theory of subjectivity is that it deprives subject of all substantiality while revealing the primacy of action in the constitution of our being. Methodologically, this conclusion teaches phenomenology an important lesson, which applies most tellingly, perhaps, to Heidegger himself. Phenomenological description is good when we take it to the point where it issues in a dialectic, where it completes itself by establishing the imperative of an existential act. The main difference between my discussion of anxiety and the Heideggerian text to which it is indebted is that I proceed in an unabashedly experiential (*existentiell*) direction whereas Heidegger separates his analytic of existence (*existentiale*) from any concrete decisions in order to preserve its quasi-Kantian and formalistic purity from the taint of existential complexities which would admittedly lead him far afield—into ethics, philosophic anthropology, psychoanalysis, sociology, etc. My argument is that the distinction cannot be maintained. If mood is existentially revelatory, and if understanding is the project one forms upon its appropriation, then there is no way to maintain the analogy of an a priori analytic of *Dasein* to the methodology of the Kantian critiques.[22] The key to anxiety is that it cannot be understood formalistically. The only adequate idea we can have of anxiety is one that makes us anxious about ourselves. This realization leads to an important clarification regarding the nature of the existential a priori. The existential a priori is not one more a priori that we can comfortably line up alongside those of Kant, Cassirer, Chomsky, and Lévi-Strauss (or, for that matter, Jung and Frye) as a contribution to some new essentialism. The distinctive quality of the existential a priori is that it is caught up in its issue and totally passes over into what it becomes. It is not a static cognitive form or "subjective state" into which a wealth of phenomena can be resolved in terms of the universality of their content or mental operation. Were that the case, Lukács's criticism would be valid: the existential a priori would be only the cloak for a new essentialism—this time one of worldless solipsistic despair.[23] But the distinctive character of this a priori is that it exists—and is caught up, without reserve, in its issue. As in Hegel, there is no point of stability in any of the categories of existential thought. All are thrown into the world and implicated in an effort at surpassing. This is so because these "categories" are forms of possible self-overcoming each of which defines ways in which subject is in and given over to the world.

In delivering us over to our existence, anxiety delivers us over to something that cannot be transcended. If one internalizes this awareness, one no longer experiences anxiety passively or impersonally. It becomes, instead, the basis for choices made in the readiness to open oneself to a renewed experience of anxiety. Anxiety thus becomes the basis for determining possibilities and the term of reference for judging the adequacy of their projection. The question of how one's action stands with respect to anxiety becomes the new imperative for willing.[24] It would be incorrect to say that by so appropriating anxiety one simply gives oneself more anxiety, for what one does is progressively give oneself anxiety of a new kind. One's anxiety becomes one's own and is made concrete and specific. One now knows that when one has anxiety one is in a situation in which one's being is at issue in some definite way. When one vows to take that reality upon oneself, authentic anxiety isn't resolved, it is deepened. In the development of existential subjectivity, anxiety is replaced only through its sublation. We may thus set down the following as the contribution of anxiety to the definition of subject: *Subject is the ability to open oneself to anxiety and project upon it by fully internalizing all that it reveals about the world as the context in which one must act.* Our duty toward anxiety is not to get rid of it, but to maximize it and make it existence-specific. For all anxiety is ultimately anxiety over oneself as a situated subject. Anxiety is both the ground phenomenon from which other moods and activities derive and the ultimate term of reference for their evaluation. Its overpowering character derives from the fact that it reveals our utter responsibility for ourselves and the inescapability of taking up that task. *Anxiety is the one self-feeling we cannot not act upon.* It must be lived, but as an act that is one with the project in which it completes and sublates itself.

Taking one's anxiety upon oneself means having the will to sustain the world it opens up as "the one most worth having." It is the attempt to live Nietzsche's recognition that "the reconquest of one's humanity is [our] daily task." Our being as subjects is determined by the project we form on the basis of our appropriation of anxiety. This connection leads, in fact, to a more concrete concept of the project. Anxiety isn't a passive state to be endured until it passes but an active self-relation in which one attempts, however momentarily and in the face of some definite situation, to take up the burden of one's existence. Anxiety is not something we suffer but something we do. Like all existential realities, it is what we do with it. To uncover its truth, one must stay with anxiety in the way Hegel had in mind when he said that subject does not retreat from death but abides with it, thereby turning the negative into a positive power. The concepts of project and possibility can easily be misinterpreted if one forgets their rootedness in anxiety. When this connection is maintained, relativism receives no comfort. Everything we do is measured dialectically by its adequacy to the world opened up by anxiety. Possibilities are genuine only when they arise from anxiety, and the project is significant only when anxiety has been made the basis for actions that attempt to totalize one's responsibility. So defined, little we do deserves the name of the project.

To pursue the specifically ontological implications of this line of thought, we must give one further turn to the wheel of anxiety. There is no such thing as a pure self-reference. Anxiety is a response to the world and a primary index of the world's character. Were the world not what it is, anxiety would not define us. To gain an existential concept of the world, we must turn accordingly to the original source of anxiety. We will find it in death, the mother of beauty and prime agent of that unique order of inwardness that defines the existential subject. It is often said that death has a remarkable power to concentrate the attention; as we shall see, this is so because death is the reason why there is consciousness in the first place.

THE MOTHER OF BEAUTY

Death is the origin of subjectivity; our inwardness is touched to the quick by the fact that we must die. From this perspective, death is not an event that befalls us at the end of life but a constantly lived relationship to our eventual nonbeing. Death informs life because it enlivens our response to the value of everything in the world. Through the awareness of death, subjectivity achieves a new depth which transforms it utterly. Death is the end of childhood, the abrupt termination of all romanticisms of unfettered desire. The limitless prospect in which one projects all of the heart's desires, with world enough and time to realize literally everything, is canceled. Death delivers us over with urgency to the reality of choice and the task of choosing. Genuine choice first becomes possible when death introduces limit and finality into all our deliberations. Deliberation itself changes from a contemplative to an impassioned process. While death initially paralyzes the will, it also creates it; and while this thought makes cowards of us all, it also creates the terms of courage. Enter Hamlet, thinking for the first time, in a reflection that ceaselessly circles back upon itself, "To be or not to be / That is the question." The most profound change wrought by death is in subject's relationship to itself. In the face of death, to be isn't to think, but to affirm in passion the act of existing, the utter contingency of the "I am." We know our existence with certainty only when we comprehend the possibility of the utter extinction—or worse, the meaninglessness—of that which we hold most dear. We don't even know how dearly we hold existence until we internalize this threat. The value of life—its meaning as ours, as an existential and not a biological category—is given only when we see the sand rushing through our hands. Through death the "I am" is transformed; the self-reference of inwardness becomes the urgency of doing something in the face of death. Time is transfixed and transformed. Every moment becomes a moment of choice measured by reference to this fact.

The need to make a meaningful response to death is the source and underlying theme of anxiety. Death is more than a threat to particular wishes, dreams, and possessions. It is the threat of the utter cessation of consciousness itself. Death blows a cold wind through our desperate attempts to exalt the petty world of our concerns, concerns which, in turn, conceal and reveal its presence. The denial of death is the deepest subtext at work in the anesthetization that structures everyday life. It is right to honor death as a source of human nobility; but we must also see it as a primary cause of our pettiness, our mendacity, and our greed. Death measures most of us because it makes us small, perpetual infants, huddled together, denying the dark by hoarding money.

But inauthentic responses to death only give further evidence of its centrality to subjectivity. Our primary need with regard to death is to do something in the face of it. Like anxiety, death puts us on the move; attempts to cancel its force serve only to underscore the need for a response that will allow us to take the fact of death upon ourselves and make it our own. Heidegger's distinction between authenticity and inauthenticity derives from the reality of death. It is neither a relativistic nor a formalistic distinction, but one that issues directly from the perception of death as the ultimate context for subject's self-determination. The possibility of authenticity—of making existence one's own—is given by death. The great novelistic meditation on this connection is Thomas Mann's *The Magic Mountain*. It reveals fascination with death as the origin of self-consciousness. If successfully internalized, concern with death transforms my relationship both to myself and to the world. Stripped bare of all particular matters at hand, we experience a more basic contingency. As Hans Castorp learns, all our business plans are set at nought. We are delivered over to ourselves in an experience that we may term a cogito only if we see that such a cogito is incapable of the precision of clear and distinct ideas because *its being is anguish over its eventual nonbeing*. Death is the source of human time because it quickens our awareness of everything. It creates the moment and its value as well as the bitter, unshakable regret over opportunities not seized or harmful things done to others.

Death delivers me over to the world because through it I experience myself as a being who bears definite duties toward myself. There is a "categorical" imperative at work in death: the responsibility to give my being determination through concrete choices that are fully submitted to the world. Death as our limit is also the source of our freedom. Through death, the radical self-love implicit in the "I am" is "restrained and checked"; desire for the first time becomes concrete possibility.[25] Self-reference is no longer a limitless calculus of possibilities determined solely by the absolute value of one's self-regard, but the anxious need to project oneself without reserve in finite situations. Choice first becomes authentic when one no longer hoards a private self or finds some other way to stay at a safe distance from one's choices. Death transforms subject's relationship to itself by offering it an inwardness that, like all other authentic self-mediations, is fully out in the world. The deepening of inwardness is always no more and no less than a suffered transformation of subject's relationship to itself. If subject is equal to death, it has canceled all contemplative stances toward the world. There is nothing private about the self-feeling which results. Existence is subject's impassioned response to death.

The deepest meaning of death is the challenge it lays down. What is an authentic appropriation of death? Since death is the supreme insult, the only adequate response is to make it the standard whereby all choices are evaluated. We are humanized by death because death gives us our humanity as infinite concern fully projected in the world. Death has been fully internalized only when grasped as an ethical experience, as, in fact, the origin of ethics. Our basic task in life is to throw something up against death.

Death thus becomes the term that measures the authenticity of our projects. In fact, it makes the project, for the first time, something with which subject can coincide. For death doesn't release choice into a relativistic universe, but makes choice ontological, burdening it with a totalizing responsibility. In this way, death comes to inhabit the center of consciousness as the ground of the ethical relationship we live to ourselves.

As its ultimate source, death gives us an understanding of anxiety that was not possible before. Anxiety over death is the first coalescence of subject's self-reference. As such, it establishes self-criticism as our innermost possibility while exposing the lie of all self-protective theories of identity. Its revelation is that all genuine reflection is an attempt (like Hamlet's) to discover what thinking is in the face of death. Because it is defined by concern about death, the existential dialectic of subject supplements and concretizes Hegelian phenomenology. Anxiety is the mood whereby we tell ourselves that our present desire is an inadequate response to the reality of our death. The reason that consciousness feels threatened by anxiety is that anxiety is that immediacy of self-consciousness which reveals how we stand with respect to the fact of death.

This conclusion concretizes the conclusion we reached in trying to define an authentic appropriation of anxiety, because it establishes a context that deprives subject of all assurances and submits it totally to the world. In many ways the Heideggerian meditation on anxiety and death constitutes an extended gloss on Hegel's notion that by not turning away from death, consciousness makes the negative a force in our being. Death humanizes us when it makes us Nietzschean. Rather than creatures of weariness, resignation, or petty hedonistic willing, death makes us metaphysical, philosophic animals because it forces us to totalize the "who" and "why" of subject by referring that question to "the whole of things." Death causes the world to rise up, not as an ensemble of knowable entities, but as an abode with which subject is already one in an inseparable and reciprocal determination. World is an existential rather than a cosmological category, a way of being of the subject. All existential concepts have that context as their reference. Such a perspective is generally described as an attempt to develop a philosophic anthropology that would also be a dialectical ontology. Everything we've said thus far about subject points to this attempt. Its development will, in fact, deepen and transform the meaning of the entire previous discussion.

DIALECTICAL ONTOLOGY OF THE EXISTENTIAL SUBJECT

Two Misunderstood Concepts

NOTHINGNESS

Our goal is to develop an existential concept of dialectic. A preliminary clarification of two widely misunderstood concepts will facilitate that effort.

The existential subject introduces nothingness into being. Subject gives the negative an ontological status and locus. The act of questioning reveals that lack, absence, emptiness, loss, and longing are not vague quasi-theological themes but primary characteristics of experience. Once anxiety passes we gladly say, "It was nothing": existentialism uncovers the "positive" meanings we conceal when we classify as unimportant, transitory, or meaningless experiences that have the power to alter all our habits of thinking. We have been trained to ask questions as if they were merely the transition points to answers that remove all doubt, leaving us with full positivity. From Aristotle through Wittgenstein the general assumption has been that if there is no answer it isn't a question. Existentialism argues, in contrast, that the "correct" relationship to the fundamental questions is to keep them alive and deepen our relationship to them as questions. A question is a great hole in being, a rupture with positivity, an experience of nothing as prior to and more profound than something. Nothing can, indeed, come from nothing because from its initial appearance nothingness has a double meaning and points in two directions. Subject as existence is the nothing that is, that instability who introduces negativity into matters previously thought solid, self-evident, beyond question. As that open question who recurrently experiences itself "as what it is not and not what it is," and who determines itself only by assuming responsibility for the absences its questions uncover, subject lives and is defined by "the labor of the negative." Through subject, lack becomes a reality of far greater importance than the positivities it outstrips.

So understood, the experience of nonbeing gives a new insight into the nature of possibility. Possibilities are projections in the face of lacks and absences which we must take up. A positivistic world is a static one, as is one in which all deliberations are determined by an order of ontologically subsistent goods. When possibility is conceived of as the actualization of metaphysically assured potencies, as in Aristotle,[26] subject is reified precisely at the point where it first resists reification. In such a world, action is in effect contemplation. Existential possibility arises in contrast, because there is an absence of meaning both in the world and in the subject. Recognition of the fact that nothing substantial supports our being is thus one with the discovery of contingency in all areas of human concern.

Negativity and nothingness are not vague metaphysical concepts but existential realities that come into being as determinate moments in the self-mediation of subject. As a subject, one is estranged as long as one lives a relationship to oneself that is defined by questions whose answers are not fixed in external reality or provided by a subsistent order of being. The negativities in the previous sentence give a capsule summary of the determinate meaning of nothingness as an existential concept, i.e., as a lived relationship implicit in the "fact" of existence. They also reveal negativity as the first moment of possibility; for every part of the statement reveals a dimension of existence which subject must take upon itself.

Subject can be defined as "the coming to be of nothingness" if by this we mean the determinate, dialectical assumption by the subject of the absences it introduces into the world. We experience a conversation, an institution, a relationship, or one of our own actions, emotions, and choices as lacking because they are, in fact, lacking; they fail to fulfill the demand it is possible for us to place upon ourselves. Such an understanding of nothingness has nothing to do with a *pathétique* of mourning in a world haunted by the absence of God. Nor is it the projection of a private or cultural malaise onto realities that exist independent of our activity. It is the eminently positive recovery of the ontological dependency of being on us. This idea of ontological dependency has always encountered strenuous opposition for two obvious reasons: it deprives reality of substantiality, and it delivers us over to an exacting responsibility. The existential focus on nothingness suggests, in fact, that our responsibility extends to being in general or "the whole of things."

THE WHOLE OF THINGS

Kant's critique gave the quietus to any further attempt to conceive dialectic along epistemological or rationalist lines. But it also inadvertently put an end to the assumption that knowing the world (or knowing how the mind operates when occupied with that act) is the privileged standpoint from which concepts such as the whole, totality, and world must derive their meaning. To develop a post-Kantian concept of dialectic we must rethink such concepts from a radically different perspective and establish their distinct meaning as existentials. In a mood such as anxiety, subject relates to a totality that is of a fundamentally different order than the world of science. We experience the world as a whole and attain a specifically modern idea of dialectic when we leave the stance of perception and scientific understanding and take up the problems of action and history. We then think from the perspective of a subject who is one with the world as the place one inhabits. World is not a boundary of cognition but the essential term of conduct. It is an existential category rather than a cognitive one because it is the concretization of what it means to have one's being at issue. It is only in the world, and not in Cartesian space or Kant's extended manifold, that subject can relate to itself as a "who." The world is a relationship we live long before and long after it is something we know. Objects stand before me forever waiting to be seen, but the world is something I experience primarily in terms of temporal urgencies and the necessity of taking action. I perceive objects, but the world, including nature, is a social and historical category. That is why Hiroshima weighs like a nightmare on the brains of the living. It established the horizon that must inhabit any contemporary concept of totality and of what it means to be in the world. Dialectic will never be rehabilitated as long as we remain within a context of scientific knowing; but Hiroshima made totalization a categorical imperative. Today we know the world as a totality because we know that someday soon we may all be blown up. Knowing this we live a new relationship to the world.

The lesson of any analytic of existence, however abbreviated, is that the context in which one's existence is at issue is not particular or private but comprehensive and total. Existential inquiry is a study of the necessary connections among such contexts and experiences. Its concern is never with isolated themes or unique acts, but with a comprehensive structure. Experience has a dialectical structure because the process of existential self-mediation is such that each experience that brings subject before itself necessarily produces a deeper and more complex relationship with the world. The totality of self-mediations whereby our being becomes an issue for us in a concrete and determinate way precipitates the discovery of our duty to assume responsibility for our existence within an englobing context.[27] An analytic of existence cannot remain a formalism of pure phenomenological descriptions because existential self-mediation is an act of surpassing which incessantly totalizes by discovering and creating connections. It thus resumes the insight Hegel began to move toward: dialectic is not a preexisting reality awaiting cognition, but a human possibility awaiting construction.

THE EXISTENTIAL A PRIORI

It often looks as if existentialism is walking both sides of the street on the question of the a priori. It attempts to derive everything from experience and is unremitting in tracking down all the ways in which the Kantian tradition fails to attain the *Lebenswelt*. But to assure that experience won't be reduced to a behavioristic or narrowly pragmatic process, it is equally intent on endowing subject with a power to transform the given. That effort opens it to the charge of being little more than a remnant of German idealism. The difference between the existential a priori and the a priori of the neo-Kantian tradition is considerable, however, and provides one of the clearest examples of the distinctive nature of existential thought. The neo-Kantian a priori is a fixed principle of cognition imposed upon experience to give it the form required for the maintenance of an identity defined by our correspondence with a priori rationality. Such an a priori consists of universal and unchanging forms of knowing (or cognitive sets) which are imposed upon phenomena and which remain identical before and after their use. Such forms are not submitted to experience; experience is submitted to them.

In contrast, the unique character of the existential a priori—and of the categories, or existentials, that constitute its analytic (i.e., situation, world, project, etc.)—lies in its being a form of change that is immanent in experience and that has its being wholly in its becoming. From the start, it is irreversibly outside and beyond itself, submitted for its determination to the world it opens up. The analytic of such structures articulates *forms* of the world as it is lived and suffered, not as it is cognized. Such forms are not ways of knowing, but modes of engagement which are fully implicated in their issue. Existential categories light up phenomena by establishing ways in which we are necessarily engaged in the world and must live out this relationship as an emerging process. Rather than establishing universal forms of cognitive intelligibility, the existential a priori describes the universal context that makes experience a process in which our being is at issue. The only stability such "forms" provide is the assurance that one is condemned to live them.

The function of the existential a priori is not to assure that experience will take on a definite and rational order—as is the case in all other theories of the a priori—but to guarantee that everything, subject uppermost, remains on trial. The inwardness that existentialism posits as an irreducible condition for experience is not a content, nor a clever way to recycle the old beliefs and values of traditional humanism in modern dress. Nor does this a priori offer us a privileged insight into an unchanging essential humanity that awaits us with the set of immutable values we can use to free experience of ambiguity and contingency. Existential categories are questions and have no content beyond their power to affirm the importance of the questions they establish. Each is best understood as an attempt to put in the interrogative something that was previously conceived of substantialistically.

In affirming inwardness as an irreducible and unmotivated first principle, existentialism is never guilty of that kind of a priori that delivers the world into the arms of some immutable and rigid belief structure disguised as a phenomenology of "the acting person."[28] The only inwardness the existential subject has is that which plunges it into the world; an inwardness thrown and initially lost and ever only as good as its labor. Posit such an a priori and one has a world in which drama becomes possible; eradicate it and the reification of subject is a foregone conclusion.

Rather than originating in pure mind or in some set of rationalistic-discursive requirements, the existential a priori arises only when subject experiences itself as a "who." Nothing motivates or causes that experience. The truth of the matter is that it rarely occurs. Yet once it does, one sees that it was "always already" there, not in a chronological sense, but as the origin of human experience proper through the upsurge of that inescapable self-relation which we are no matter how long we have tried to keep the fact a secret from ourselves. The a priori status of such a principle of self-reference derives not from a preestablished cognitive or categorical function, but from its power to give experience a direction it would not otherwise assume.

The subject as "who" already has anxiety as the innermost possibility that coincides with its very existence. In this sense, anxiety is the original and originating existential a priori. Its a priori status, however, is not the repetition of a fitful mood, but the upsurge of the project into which an authentic appropriation of the mood necessarily translates itself. Anxiety may be the primary truth of experience, but it is not an abstract truth. It is a situational one because it always arises out of and directs itself upon specific situations. Unless this connection is maintained, it becomes that truly inauthentic thing—angst as life-style, as the abstract pose of a reified personality. The existential war on abstraction is never more important than when directed on its own speculative tendencies. Existentialism loses itself whenever it arrests itself in a lyric meditation on certain abstract themes (angst, the absurd, being, etc.) as a substitute for taking up the concrete experiential development of its categories.

The larger issue this distinction introduces is the nature of existential universals. The key to avoiding formalism is to see that existential categories, like Hegel's phenomenological concepts, have their being in their becoming. Their universality is one with the concrete actions in which they issue. Such a universal is not forever the same, with an identity secured outside experience or rooted in "human nature," but a principle which attains its universality, and its explanatory power, through the process of sublating itself. Such a universality does not reside in an essence but arises out of experience. Its universality derives solely from subject's effort to develop the imperatives implicit in its existence. Rather than fixed forms in which one can find stability, guaranteed meaning, or contemplative peace, the categories that make up the analytic of existence give us a comprehensive insight into those principles that make life unintelligible except as drama. The "content" of such categories is no more and no less than an articulation of the principles that prime us to understand drama as that primary truth of human experience that philosophy has not yet comprehended. To recapture this possibility, a rather thorough reversal of Heidegger is required. We will carry this out concretely in the next section. But as preface to that effort, we here offer the necessary methodological clarifications.

The existential analytic of *Being and Time* is an arrested dialectic, a formalistic description of the series of *reflective experiences* through which subject's being becomes a concrete issue for it. When Heidegger sustains this reflective dimension, his inquiry moves toward the concrete: thus, anxiety points to death, which delivers us over to time. Each phenomenological investigation, in completing itself, leads to the next as its necessary development. Thanks to that movement, phenomenology in Heidegger's hands is no longer a descriptive discipline with isolated topics, but a dialectical study of experience. It is the reflective dimension of Heidegger's inquiry that produces this development. Each experience Heidegger describes is one in which subject can mediate itself by confronting one of the fundamental determinations and contexts of its existence. Self-reflection thereby becomes the principle that informs the immediacy of lived experience. Hegel alone presents an equally compelling picture of reflection's rootedness in experience.

But there is also something curiously abstract, static, and formalistic about Heidegger's descriptions. Part of the difficulty results from Heidegger's recognition that experience can't be pictured in Hegel's consecutive, cumulative, and quasi-evolutionary manner because the most significant moments are those ruptures which give density and a certain "all at once" character to experiences such as anxiety. Probing the depths of such realities is the source of Heidegger's unique insights into subject.

The unfortunate consequence of adopting a purely descriptive procedure, however, is that it confines Heidegger to a methodological Kantianism which prevents him from following up the dialectical implications of his inquiries. Thus the great meditation on time completes our understanding of the existential structure of projection without giving us anything concrete to do. Anxiety remains anxious about itself abstractly,[29] and all Heidegger can do at the end of the inquiry is invoke "joy" and proclaim *Dasein*'s vow to keep repeating itself,[30] as if this wholly formal repetition constituted some sort of existential courage when what it really signifies is the refusal to violate a canon of methodological purity which here "ontologizes" itself. Formalism always ends in a circle. Heidegger is forced to a fit of abstraction whenever existence gets too close because his refusal to contaminate his "existential analytic" with specific or "*existentiell*" decisions mandates precisely such a procedure.[31]

Being and Time thus repeatedly splits itself in two on the horns of a dilemma. As each of its inquiries moves toward concrete experience, Heidegger reverts to analytic formalism. Yet the implication of each description is the impossibility of this separation. As with Hegel, we read Heidegger best when we read against the grain, not toward a deconstruction of the text, but toward the discovery of a central contradiction that makes it possible to liberate a determinate meaning from his text that is other than the one its conceptual limitations dictate.

The only authentic understanding of existential concepts is one that projects upon them. As Rilke knew, understanding any part of existence requires changing one's life.[32] Ironically, Heidegger is the one most entitled to this conclusion because his reconceptualization of understanding —as the projection of possibilities—cancels any pure Kantian analytic. The ontological reality of the structures Heidegger studies is that they have their being in their existence. Unless one formalizes oneself out of existence, one must accordingly stick with their issue. The existential analytic calls for a dialectic that has as its task an estimation of specific projects in terms of their adequacy to an englobing existential situation. Heidegger notwithstanding, if we are looking for the critical relationship of existentialism to Kant, it is ethical: the analytic of existence performs a function analogous to Kant's categorical imperative because it enables us to evaluate all projects in terms of their adequacy to certain unavoidable questions and responsibilities. Any project that is inadequate in these terms convicts itself of bad faith. Contra Heidegger, the analytic of existence is not a circle but a progressively concretizing dialectic which can't be arrested because it never has a purely analytic moment. The inwardness of the existential subject is totally unlike the a priori categorical identity of Kantian understanding. The existential a priori presents our existence to us as a burden we must project upon. This is the key to discovering which structures of lived experience are of existential significance. Such structures have the character of ethical imperatives requiring action rather than sufferance. Heidegger's dependence on the Kantian analogy risks concealing everything distinctive about these structures. The search of neo-Kantian thinkers is for those a priori elements that have the status of fixed forms and unchanging cognitive functions of universal applicability. To establish both their essence and the substantial identity of the know-ing subject,[33] experiences need only be subsumed under these a priori forms. As Lévi-Strauss, the current champion of this way of thinking, continually reminds us: the structures of mind await us and predetermine the intelligibility of experience, whether or not they are being used. Exis-tential structures, in contrast, offer no point of rest or of identity; they are always in process and are given over to experience for their determi-nation. Existence isn't something we have but something we do. It is an imperative that is situational rather than categorical. Its attainment does not derive from pure thought but arises directly out of an effort to be which is one with the immediacy of lived experience.

This understanding of the existential a priori drives a final nail in the coffin of formalism. The categories that make up the existential analytic are necessarily empty because they point to structures that are lived and that take on content only through that process. To conceive of thrownness or historicity or anxiety otherwise—as, say, abstract pessimistic themes or blank checks for relativism—reifies what is no more than a beginning. Pop existentialism is a catalogue of such errors, with the absurd elevated to a quasi-Platonic status and freedom turned into a bit of whimsy.[34]

In his desire to keep his analytic separate from specific disciplines, Heidegger unfortunately contributes to such developments, for he traps himself in a formalism that is merely the opposite side of the pessimism of abstract content since both comprehend the existential analytic ab-stractly. Heidegger's Kantian legacy led him to an untenable distinction between the analytic of existence and the study of specific existential acts. For methodological purposes this distinction may be useful. But the more one understands the "existentials"—and what they reveal about the na-ture of understanding—the more questionable it becomes. As Heidegger shows, understanding is genuine only when it increases one's power to be. It completes itself only through a deepened engagement in the world. Lacking that development, "the analytic of existence" becomes a repetitive thematic arrested in the lyric evocation of certain moods. When such is the case one can be pretty sure that real human engagement has been sacrificed to the pleasure of abstraction. Endless meditation on the absurdity of existence deflects attention from those concrete anxieties one does not want to face directly. Formalism is its finest flower. But having one's existence at issue is neither without content nor possessed of determinate content. It is the dynamic one carries into particular situations and relationships that makes them dramatic by giving them the driving force of questions they would not otherwise contain.

Existential Categories as Principles of Drama

Existentialism's concern is with those experiences that make a difference, those experiences that open up a new configuration of one's humanity and that require a new dimension of awareness and activity. By bringing emergence and surpassing to the fore as the primary ontological categories for understanding experience, existentialism entails a reversal of the traditional ontological focus on natural continuity from fixed origins and on the typical, repeatable characteristics of "human nature." The existential perspective rests on the recognition that certain things need never occur for their primacy to be established. With the emergence of existential self-mediation, all that went before loses its supposedly solid ontological and experiential moorings.

Subject, experience, and being are locked in an inexorable dialectic. Subject is defined by the deepening of its own inwardness, and this process is one with the emergence of new contexts and problems that alter the course of experience. Each new relation to oneself, as a result of experience, produces a new relationship to the world. That is why anxiety is a watershed moment, not just psychologically, but ontologically. The world of the "they" is laid bare, stripped of its apparent foundations and made part of an emerging and comprehensive ontology of the subject. What seemed solid is now seen in terms of what it is not; what appeared anomalous and meaningless announces its primacy.

Existential experience has a retrospective structure and doubles back upon itself. Its focus is the emergence of that which is, in effect, unmotivated or uncaused. Reflection, the origin of subjectivity, is the unmotivated act which places experience under the sign of self-questioning. The "why," in its upsurge, alters everything, giving experience a direction it did not and could not have before. It inaugurates a drama of self-mediation that gives birth to new and unprecedented activities. Rather than pursue a fruitless search for origins, existential understanding focuses on those experiences in which something emerges that alters the meaning and structure of what went before. It thus transcends that contradictory movement of the retreat and return of the origin which Foucault describes.[35] Existential experience cannot be accounted for along the lines of causal continuities but must be conceived in terms of breaks and leaps. Rather than constructing experience step by step we must conceive it as a *hierarchy of integrations:*[36] subject's act of surpassing itself establishes englobing contexts that can't be lined up pluralistically in some encyclopedic picture of the world but must be comprehended dialectically in terms of their essential connections. Experience is not an empirical record of all that happens in our lives, but the system of self-mediations determined by a developing awareness of what it means to have our being at issue. Dialectically, experience must be conceived not in terms of its initial or quotidian forms but in terms of its eventual issue. *Subject is the act of experiential self-mediation through which one surpasses the given by inaugurating possibilities.* Experience is not the accumulation of knowledge or the gradual fixing of habits but the emergence of that flawed, intermittent understanding of the problems and contexts subject must assume in order to be equal to the duties implicit in its humanity. Experience must be rethought in terms of subject's recognition of its own deepest needs.

Hegel's model of dialectic as a continuous ascent with a series of necessary transitions is misleading because it suggests that the origin and moving principle of experience is already in some way fully formed or self-present at the beginning of the process and in complete control throughout its development. Hegel's mistake—a product of his adherence to what Derrida terms the metaphysical tradition—was to seek a continuity and center for experience that would issue directly from a single first principle. Derrida's antithetical vision—endless free play forever proliferating new energies in constant deviation and fragmentation—is its abstract inversion. The existential process we are attempting to conceptualize cuts between these alternatives: it is much more open than Hegel's to the contingent without, however, making experience a matter of chance or "free play." Nothing, strictly speaking, causes or guarantees the act in which subject transforms both itself and experience by asking the question implicit in its being. Yet once that question arises, subject, experience, and the world have undergone a fundamental transformation.

Existential subjectivity is an achievement, dependent on a fundamental *reversal*. It need not and usually does not occur.

As long as we continue to conceive subject along the lines of naturalistic determination or in terms of some a priori essential humanity, the distinctive thrust of existential thinking will continue to elude us. A theory of human nature modeled on those activities that characterize human beings in general inevitably compromises the life of subjectivity. The failure of such a theory is a failure to face the basic fact: subjectivity is a matter of extremity—of lawful, rigorous extremity. The effort to be sets the standard that measures ordinary, normal behavior, rather than the other way around. Questioning oneself is our noblest self-relation. Subjectivity isn't a quasi-evolutionary process with maturation guaranteed,[37] but a process of self-overcoming in which the rare rather than the typical is the measure of experience. The only genuine relationship subject has to itself is that deepening of its problems which both maximizes and concretizes them. Subjectivity transcends both the pleasure and the reality principle. Our subjectivity is ours not as a burden to be resolved but as a possibility to be developed; that process bars all forms of complacency because the deepening of subjectivity, by definition, always opens us up and engages us further. Having one's being at issue means making it so in a progressively determinate way. *This is the law and logic of subjective growth.* Growth in subjectivity requires that one discover and project oneself upon those contexts where the basic conflicts of one's being are sure to be dramatized. Knowing that one's being is at issue is already a fundamental transformation of one's subjectivity because such knowledge totally alters one's relationship to everything. Endless formal repetition of the vow to keep repeating oneself is not really an option open to us. We know our being is at issue only through our relationships with others, and knowing that fact already involves living these relationships in a new way.

What is the subjectivity of the subject? In posing this question, the first thing to note is how the issue is leveled off whenever it is treated in substantialistic terms. Kant, who first probed this dimension of subjectivity,[38] provides a perfect example of such leveling off through his assumption of a priori rationality and his effort to fix the identity of the subject and the intelligibility of experience in this image. The trouble with such explanations is that they deliver us into the arms of an essence rather than keeping us in active relationship to the question that defines the original emergence of subjectivity. To preserve this question, our effort throughout has been to conceive "the subjectivity of the sub-ject" without substantializing. Each definition of subject we have offered attempts to show ways in which our being remains at issue in experience in such a way that subject deepens its self-relation only by maximizing and concretizing its openness to the question it remains. We maintain ourselves as subjects by a constant willingness to throw our very being and all our values into question. Heidegger's formalistic understanding of repetition, and the popular ideas of absurdity and gratuitous spontaneity, are equally abstract retreats from the concrete life of subject.

The deepening of subjectivity must be a determinate process or it is nothing. Overcoming substance doesn't mean keeping oneself perpetually empty; it means giving oneself the kind of determination that is proper to a subject. To grasp subjectivity, one must avoid both the Kantian trap of resubstantializing subject and the deconstructive trap of random dispersal. One must root out the desire that ironically sustains both efforts—the desire to be delivered from existence and made secure in a single determination, even if abyssal. Both views arrest the true life of subjectivity. To live out Kierkegaard's notion that subjectivity is defined by an "infinite concern to preserve one's subjectivity," one must dissolve all escape routes. The only way to do so is to focus thought on those experiences that burden us with ourselves. We don't live the anguish of subjectivity in abstract repetition, forever differing and deferring, or as exiles forever moving in nostalgia toward the future harmony of a fixed identity. We live it as a discipline of progressive concretization in which we always remain at risk. The one possibility we never escape is that we can lose ourselves, totally and irretrievably.

Every existential category thus requires a double reading: one that shows our total submission to the world and another that reveals that fact as the condition for the emergence of concrete possibilities. The key to an existential understanding is not to separate these moments but to maintain their dialectical connection. My submission to the world gives me myself as possibility; and only when I abandon myself to the world do I experience possibility as such—as that which has no assurance and could just as well not be.

Thrownness and projection are always equiprimordial.[39] Inwardness and existence are mediated from the start and remain reciprocally deter-mining throughout existential inquiry because its organizing purpose is to articulate the necessary connections that make these seemingly opposed terms reinforcing and mutually defining. This understanding avoids both reductionism and idealism, for both errors arise when one gives either term priority or causal primacy. The best example of necessary connection, in fact, is the relationship between situatedness and the project. While the concept of situation points to our submission to contexts outside our control, the project prevents the reductive interpretations of naturalism, behaviorism, and determinism. A situation doesn't exist until the upsurge of a project reveals our opposition to that situation—and its opposition to us. Situatedness is both the first surpassing of the given along the way toward our freedom and the first revelation of the limiting of our freedom by opacity and an inescapable "coefficient of adversity."[40] Situatedness forces us to be there by revealing a world we aren't simply in but already up against. Before projection there is no situation, only a scene we have inhabited in a vague passivity. Situatedness is always mine: it is a way of being of the subject. Being in a situation means that one has carved out from that constant displacement of attention that characterizes the "they" a place for projecting possibilities. Situatedness thus inaugurates drama. It is both the condition for choice and a discovery of the context that opposes and limits choice. Nothing in this formulation encourages philosophic idealism. The main thing situatedness reveals is our thrownness into facticities that exert their effects on us long before and long after we take up the effort to make them ours. One side of situatedness is always the revelation of how utterly we are delivered over to contingencies we did not choose, but which nonetheless have a chilling impact on our possibilities. But this circumstance is precisely what makes the effort to alter things a unique act, markedly different from idealistic conceptions of freedom. The defining character of the existential subject is the ability to take over determinations of long standing and reverse them by projecting a new direction for situations that nevertheless continue to exert an opposing power.

The concept of existence establishes *emergence* and *surpassing* as the primary characteristics of experience. The logic of these categories supplants both reductionism and apriorism. The projection of possibilities is not the translation of reason into temporal terms. Possibilities arise out of the world and are submitted to it. They are always in and of our situation, but never its naturalistic replication. Subject is already beyond its situation by the act of making it its own. The projection of possibilities takes over the thrownness of situations and galvanizes it. Existentialism does not repeat the idealistic error of deriving "reality" from an autonomous subject, but it does share with idealism the recognition of the ontological possibility—that things are what they become and are bound up, in basic ways, with the development of the subject. The autonomous, rationalistic subject of the idealist tradition is an aprioristic and protected version of this possibility; existentialism is its anguished realization.

Surpassing isn't a Faustian stance, but a concrete act. I am my world by projecting possibilities upon it. In forcing that necessity upon me, the world drives into the very heart of my inwardness. In surpassing the given, I always remain delivered over to the world in a continued effort that has no inner guarantee. Surpassing is the exception, a triumph against the odds, because it depends on surmounting forces most of us find too great to bear.

Surpassing depends on *self-overcoming*. Subjectivity isn't a fixed form or function but an irreversible movement into expanding contexts that are defined by the continual emergence of new problems and activities. Reflection isn't an identical act with fixed laws of rational operation. It is most genuine when it does not know where it will lead or what will be required of it. Subject thereby becomes one with the act of deepening itself. Each change in subject's relationship to itself alters its being— and all its operations. The deepening of inwardness is not the movement toward an unchanging identity but the act of putting oneself further at risk. The problems one uncovers as one takes a situation upon oneself are the defining facts in the deepening of subjectivity. And problems are determined not by the rationality of a prearranged solution, but by the complexity of the relationship one sustains to them as problems. *Engagement* is originary because it forces reflection to discover all the ways in which it has not yet reflected and is not yet determined. *Surpassing* has its origin when situations are experienced in terms of what they are not, when possibilities not guaranteed by the situation are brought to bear upon it. But that act becomes possible only when we fully assume our situatedness. The completion of this circle brings us home to the recognition that dramatic agency, not substance, constitutes the identity of the existential subject.

DRAMA: THE LAW/LURE OF THE CONCRETE

CONFLICT AND CRISIS

Conflict and *crisis* rather than the study of ordinary behavior are the key to understanding our internal constitution. We know the truth of our character only when we are tested by situations in which something basic to our humanity is at stake. It is easy to convince ourselves that we are all good people when all is said and done. But the way one behaves in a situation of crisis is the only legitimate source of self-knowledge.[41] Existentialism is an attempt to think through the ontological implications of these commonplaces.

To put the issue in quasi-Kantian terms: "What must subject be like for crisis to be possible?" One of the most revealing aspects of crisis is its after-the-fact character. Crisis befalls us when we have become sloppy in our being and have let ourselves drift along the channels of complacency. In arresting us, crisis reveals the double temporality of experience by forcing us to see that we have "ta'en too little care" of the questions that now assault us. We face the loss of what we have already compromised —usually without knowing it or wanting to do so—and the question of whether or not we can take up a more demanding relationship to our existence. Calling us to account, crisis measures us by forcing us to attempt the reversal of ourselves. It shows how utterly our being is determined by certain situations and relations, whether we wish it or not, since values aren't assured in a fixed ego identity or stable life-style but sustained only through our actions—or inaction, which is the primary form of action for most of us.

Subjectivity is the acceptance of crisis as one's lot, the welcoming of it—even in the midst of depression—as a genuine occasion. The cost of lapsing as a subject is to have our world come back on us as more burdensome and entangled than it was before we opted for the easy responses. Crisis shows that we are never delivered from existence. In crisis anxiety outstrips all the "identities" we have tried to put in its place. We relate to ourselves in depth in a way that brings our entire history before us. The primary significance of crisis for a theory of the self lies in its power to show that we sustain such a continuous relationship to ourselves despite the long stretches of tranquil and wasted time in which we remain relatively unburdened.

Through crisis we know our past not as an empirical record, but as the system of choices that has brought us to this present. The past is presented, not as a spectacle for some ideal summing up, but as existential hamartia—the accumulated burden of interconnected mistakes and actions we must now attempt to *reverse*. Crisis is invaluable for an understanding of subjectivity because it shows that we exist fully only when we are in situations in which we can either lose ourselves irretrievably or discover our freedom as that rare and always subsequent act which has as its defining character the possibility that we may fail to live up to its demands. Crisis thus reveals the unity of existential time.[42] In bringing our entire life before us as something for which we remain responsible, it brings us back to the inescapability and hidden continuity of that self-relation which we are condemned to live. Crisis is also the origin of reversal and surpassing because the self-knowledge it offers is necessarily negative and self-critical. In crisis one suffers oneself not in passivity but in terms of the need to inaugurate a project that will respond to the situation. As long as one can suffer oneself one remains capable of existence. The negative attitude toward suffering that underlies most theories of identity here receives a just rebuke. Crisis reveals that ripeness is all because identity lacks substantialistic supports: it has never been anything but the basic choices one has lived out, whether consciously or not, in that long acting of one's being that constitutes the true locus of one's character.

Crisis points to a concept of identity that circumvents the current deconstructions of the "self." The identity of the existential subject is not a cogito but an activity of decision and living through in which we "carry ourselves along" toward an issue that brings everything to fruition. The "self-presence" suffered in crisis is the knowledge of ourselves as dramatic agents living an open-ended but thoroughly determinate relationship to the meaning of our entire past. This process of living is neither self-present nor discontinuous, but cumulative.[43] If deconstructing the self means the rejection of the autonomous individual of bourgeois thought and its conceptual supports—traditional humanism and a priori, essentialistic theories of identity—then existentialism is deconstruction *avant la lettre*. Its critique of these concepts does not, however, proceed under the sign of free play or the infinite dispersal of subject along linguistic chains in which one remains forever lost. The alternative existentialism offers to both deconstruction and self-presence is a recovery of a self as a determinate process of self-mediation that arises from and remains utterly submitted to existence.

DECISION AND LIVING THROUGH

For an existing being, *decision* is a constant pressure at the center of consciousness. We are always in some way making decisions about the meaning of our being. That ongoing act forms the existential unity of consciousness and is the key to understanding the dialectical direction of moods, emotions, and other reflective processes. We are at issue in a situation only when we face the necessity of fundamental, ontological choices.[44]

We seldom live, however, with the transparency implied by such a formula. Decision is a process of *living through*. In fact, we generally realize only long after the fact that the choice we made or didn't make was a turning point. Consequences only gradually announce themselves. The hardening of the heart is a slow subterranean process. Finding that one is no longer able to love or even to care about one's indifference is not the result of a single transparent decision but the conclusion of a process built on a series of imperceptible "decisions." To feel open or to feel protective; to strive for some basic integrity in one's dealings with others or to consider only one's immediate advantage; to run risks or to dance only on protected turf are existential processes. They are never constituted once and for all through a single privileged act, but lived out over time. The major dramas happen, but they always find us with our roles already carefully prepared by the little choices and habits of being that now reveal themselves as a vast facticity resisting change. As we drag ourselves along we bear a historical density that is constituted by all the ways we have returned the ticket of our existence.

Just as we are never without a mood, we are always making some sort of decision about ourselves. The existential is the subtext of everyday life. In certain moments, experience comes together—whether in action or in soliloquy—but this happens only because such events bring the recognition that our life is the series of choices that have produced the self-determination that now burdens us. The significance of such experiences for a theory of subject lies in their doubleness: the existential continuity of our life is presented as a loss we can't deny and as a problem we must address. The bill comes in, but with it we experience that upsurge of possibility that arises whenever we are delivered to ourselves. Our life is submitted to the possibility of a new decision. There is nothing abstract or Sartrean about this moment. In recognizing the density of all one has chosen, one accepts the undeniable facticity one must take upon oneself. Deprived of Sartrean spontaneity and the comforting supposition that one can annihilate the past at a stroke, one grasps the desire to change one's life as the concrete need to reverse oneself by struggling with one's whole life. The truth Sartre grasps is that freedom is always possible. But its possibility depends on taking up the full burden of one's history. The possibility of freedom arises only on the basis of facticity, of prior choices and determinations that were made by and for us and which we may find ourselves powerless to reverse. Our failures and our habits weigh on us, often insurmountably. Freedom inaugurates possibility, not by casting off the past, but by concretely surmounting it. It arises only when prior choices reveal their consequences. We then find how difficult it is to reverse their force yet how necessary the effort. Contra Sartre, freedom is no more than a possibility with the stakes already stacked against it.

The other side of living through reinforces this recognition. Existence is a challenge that presents itself to us primarily in terms of its difficulty. Existentialism never denies our passivity, our temporizing, our meek adjustments and convenient lies. What it asserts is that these "behaviors" are ours and remain so. Mediocrity is everywhere, but that does not absolve us. In losing ourselves we always retain a mute awareness that we are doing so. Things never simply happen. Life doesn't simply pass us by. The pain of failure is that in losing my possibilities, I retain the awareness that they were once mine. Judgment is a constant of experience that is lived long before it becomes an abstract ethical concept.

Subject is always living out some kind of decision about itself and is always in some way burdened by this fact. This is the ontological reason why we always have a mood. Though inauthenticity, flight, and anesthetization characterize the greater part of our lives, the ruptures in our complacencies reveal the heavy toll they exact. The intermittent call of existence is sounded in the very midst of our strenuous vigilance to keep it silenced. Ethics is not a problem we arrive at after perception, cognition, and language are firmly in place, but the unity of the relationship subject lives to itself throughout the range of activities that make up everyday life. Subjectivity is the pressure existence exerts in the midst of our flight from existence; the depth of subjectivity is in strict proportion to the degree to which I let myself be burdened with myself. The self-consciousness which forms the horizon and reference of every act of consciousness is the recognition that our being is always at issue. That is why the existential relationship one has to oneself is the basis of every situation one is in and every action one performs. It is the inescapable self-mediation that volatizes all situations. The decision one is now living out about oneself bears steadily accumulating consequences for which one remains fully responsible.

A subject is its *project* because the project is the sublation of decision and living through. Our relationship to our subjectivity is not a matter of fitful and evanescent psychological states, but a question of taking determinate actions in specific situations that always find us already involved in the world. The deepening of inwardness is neither a contemplative process nor the descent into a bottomless pit of anguish and nausea. It is the effort to change the nature and scope of one's activity by changing one's self-relation. Whenever we deepen ourselves as pure self-contemplating subjectivity, we can be sure some form of bad faith is afoot no matter how intense the feelings that accompany our meditation. The only genuine relationship we have to our emotions is projective because inner feelings are not private but mirror our engagement. There is no such thing as pure inwardness. Inner turmoil, however involuted, always refers to the world. Pure subjectivity is an unreal abstraction which reduces engagement to a *pathétique*. Situatedness is not the loss of subject but its recovery, for subject is not the reflex of its situation but its Socratic conscience.

Situated Subjectivity: The Ethos of Inwardness

Situatedness is ontologically primary in the constitution of our being: the original upsurge of subjectivity is a function of situatedness. Situatedness delivers us over to ourselves because the primary lesson it teaches is that our humanity is not an inner state or a secure possession but a task; we are no more than a possibility that arises and develops in the face of definite contexts which we are powerless to transcend. Consciousness perpetually entertains complex views of the world and adopts a variety of attitudes toward things, but such processes lack reality apart from the act of projection. It is in action alone that desires complete and submit themselves. Values, as self-determinations of subject, are authentic only if they form an integrity of "character," a consistent way of acting in the face of whatever the world throws up at us. Subjectivity, as a discipline of character, is the willingness to put oneself at issue whenever experience imposes this demand. When faced with the prospect of suffering, its logic in not to bewail the fact or seek deliverance but to accept the opportunity in the knowledge that suffering is the source of consciousness. As Nietzsche said, "Spirit is the life that cuts back into life; with its suffering it increases its knowledge."

Reflection necessarily partakes of the anguish of existence: only anguish disposes the act of reflecting on existence in a way that maximizes our responsibility. Reflection emerges in its most legitimate form when the "who" radically poses its being as a question that it must extend comprehensively to all its dealings with the world.

Subject is at base an ethical self-reference. From its inception, our subjectivity is defined by the imperative of making choices in the face of those situations where our being is at issue. Ethics isn't something tacked on later, after we've done the serious business of scientific cognition. It forms the immediate unity of consciousness because it coincides with the "who" of subject. The question we need to ask, in fact, is why ethics has been so persistently marginalized and treated as a derivative phenomenon, with its problems resolved by reference to some prior order of mental operations. Ethics thereby becomes another tidy affair, deprived of the danger that gives it a uniquely revelatory power. Situatedness subverts the possibility of ethical formalism—and of its cunning post-Kantian reassertion, Christian personalism. There is no moral order of subsistent transhistorical values waiting for me to attain rationality so that I can identify with them, thereby giving myself the human identity or personhood I already possess, according to this view, however often I may have fallen from it. Nor does the Sartrean idea that in choosing I choose for everyone offer some easy "existential" equivalent of the categorical imperative. The personalist position inverts the picture: with all values known ahead of time, the only question becomes whether I'll make the proper choice. It is comforting to be delivered over to one's existence when thus assured. For then one's existence is never really at issue.

Attention to the phenomenology of choice shows that values are a good deal less assured and the risks we run a good deal more substantial. Choice is a matter not of doing or not doing the right thing but of projecting values in a situation so as to inhabit it fully. When the choice involves matters of genuine concern, anguish necessarily defines this experience for a number of reasons. There is always a transgressive dimension to existential choice because it entails a psychological battle with the ethical and religious traditions that have provided more secure and absolute views of conduct. It also puts us at odds with the social and familial internalizations that bind us to those traditions in ways we scarcely know until we find ourselves engaged in the struggle to outstrip them. Traditional ethics is by and large a matter of hedging our bets before the fact of existence, whereas existential choice is always a question of conflict among duties in a world defined by contingency and by an ambiguity that gives ethics both its urgency and its lack of finality. Willing is not simply a matter of translating rational deliberations into temporal terms. It is more a matter of throwing oneself into a situation one sustains by sticking with the complexities that emerge the more one enters it. Nothing is set down finally because the values we project are given over to the world for their veracity; they remain bound to the new situation they create no matter where it leads. Drama is the law and logic whereby ethical values develop because existence leads only to more existence.

Ethical thought is further complicated by the circumstance that subjectivity emerges only when one puts oneself at odds with the "they." This proposition naturally encounters strenuous opposition since it reverses all the ways in which we ordinarily distinguish between the normal and the neurotic. Because of the value it places on extremity, the concept of emergence enables us to avoid two traps that have persistently frustrated attempts to think through the relationship between the social and the individual. The first is the trap of causal, naturalistic reasoning from behavior, especially the kind of reasoning found in the brand of sociology that denies the possibility of anything other than that which is shared, consensual, and socially determined. The most conspicuous extension of this way of thinking is the dissolution of subject in the semiotic and structural rules inhabiting "linguistic" and social communities. The second trap is the abstract mirror image of the first: the attempt to posit a totally free individuality, prior to the social, endowed a priori with the power of free deliberation on social beliefs and values.

The existential problematic enables us to begin thinking about subject in a way that displaces both alternatives. By conceiving subject as an emergence that need not and usually does not occur, existentialism breaks with the fixation on metaphysical origins that underlies both frameworks. One of the most challenging things about the existential turn is the idea that humanity is at ontological risk. The two positions outlined above protect us from this possibility, whereas existentialism puts this disruptive implication at the center of thought. The common criticism that existentialism can't establish naturalistic and causal origins for its view of humanity misses the point. The significance of the emergent is that it alters the ontological status of all that goes before.

Our humanity is circular and, at best, subsequent. The "they" is our common origin, but its social dominance confers no ontological stability upon it. Authenticity, in turn, does not offer a clear and distinct "cogito." The existential may be ontologically prior, as Heidegger argues, but its initial appearance lies in a panic we flee. That flight creates and empowers the "they." Neither a logic of sociological explanation nor one committed to the notion of an autonomous individual is able to comprehend the logic of this connection. The ontological primacy of the existential subject resides in an anxiety one has "always already" fled. Subject originates experience not in a cogito or self-presence of any kind but in a feeling of dread so powerful and so intimate that one's initial way of coinciding with oneself in it is flight. That flight may stamp the "they" as derivative; it also makes the effects of the "they" well-nigh impossible to reverse. We may be measured by the ability to open ourselves to anxiety, but anxiety would not be what it is were we not initially overwhelmed by it. The call of one's humanity is always at first a call one does not answer. Subjectivity might be seen, in fact, as an effort to earn—to make one's own for the first time—emotions and experiences that were once overwhelming. We become worthy of our experience only when we master what we once suffered in a way that brings about genuine change in the "structure" of our personality. And the proof of that effort is attested only by the way we subsequently act.

Such is the logic of subjective growth. Existentialism is often criticized for its preoccupation with extreme states and crisis situations at the expense of ordinary and typical processes of psychological maturation. But this is another case where extremity may be the point and normalcy the derivative and questionable phenomenon. Crisis is revelatory because it alone contains the conditions for the possibility of genuine self-knowledge. Engaged in a situation in which there are no longer any guarantees into which I can retreat to protect or absolve myself, I exist fully in the act of suffering my way toward a choice that will irreversibly determine my being. Subjectivity is never given to a calm, objective, rationally disposed consciousness; to get in touch with ourselves we must be fully engaged in the issue. We are so only when we find ourselves *thrown*. But though suffering may be what makes consciousness possible, before one is "heightened" by it one *suffers*. Self-mastery always requires an act of self-overcoming that has the character of resuming a long-neglected dialogue with oneself that is now all the more difficult because we come to it with the weight of experience passively lived in hopes of avoiding the task that now announces its primacy.

The question of subject is always a question about the nature of inwardness and its relationship to existence. If existentialism is "pragmatism with a sense of inwardness," the inwardness makes all the difference. For inwardness is neither a content (the old humanistic values in modern dress), nor a quality (the idiosyncratic, Germanic gloss on our pragmatic dealings), but an act. And that act has as its sole logic responsibility for one's existence. The only inwardness that is authentic is that in which I am now at issue. Subject sustains and deepens itself by increasing the ways in which it keeps itself open as a problem. Inwardness isn't the deepening of an emotional dilemma, the *pathétique* of a Proustian paradise lost, nor is it a fixed state of mind such as worldless angst. It is the quickening of one's involvement in the unavoidable problems and duties implicit in one's humanity. Genuine inwardness always revolves around the ground question of ethics: "What shall I do?" There is nothing worldless, contemplative, or private about it. Subjectivity develops only through a willingness to open oneself to suffering. In the life of spirit, suffering is the "privileged moment" because one can master it only by self-overcoming.

The theory of existential subjectivity charts the terrain between two popular positions: the relativism of those who regard their subjectivity as a refuge in which they are "free" to indulge themselves, and the supposedly hardheaded objectivism of those who would confine our dealings with the world to pragmatic calculations over narrowly pragmatic affairs. Existential inwardness is not the fleeting, affective by-product of experience nor the storing of regrets as food for future nostalgia. It is that process of assessing the meaning of experience which completes itself only when it quickens our readiness to act. The key to that process is the will to unremitting self-criticism—the will to discover all one does not want to know about oneself. The resentful person is never done with anything because that person is incapable of this kind of self-reference. Existential inwardness is a discipline that derives from a single question: What does my experience mean in terms of my being being at issue? *Character* is the most concrete term we can use to identify the "self" that issues from this process.

SUBJECT IN ITS IMMEDIACY: SKETCH FOR AN
EXISTENTIAL PSYCHOLOGY

Recognizing the primacy of ethical self-reference brings us back to the beginning, but in a way that enables us to know it for the first time. Existence is the act that shapes the unity of mental "faculties" and the reference in which the various processes constituting the stream of consciousness achieve completion. Subject isn't a multiplicity of distinct psychological acts (perception, feeling, cognition, deliberation, will, etc.) that can be described in separate phenomenologies, but the unity of such activities in their effort to effect a single dialectic. That dialectic is defined by the contribution each makes to an overarching self-consciousness of the ways in which our being is at issue in the world. There is nothing automatic about the achievement of psychic unity, however. It is an effort, and every mental state potentially arrests its dialectic. That is why it is possible to take up a purely contemplative attitude toward oneself or to regard knowing the world as the only proper stance toward experience. The most powerful motive sustaining the "dissociation of sensibility" is not a cultural-historical situation of alienation and fragmentation, but the anxiety attendant upon the recognition that a unified sensibility must center itself in the act of existence. Once split, the psyche finds innumerable ways to hide from this imperative, philosophy being one of the best. The effort to unify one's consciousness is a triumph against the odds because it requires an act of what might be termed psychological authenticity. This possibility announces itself in each moment and act of consciousness, but it just as constantly finds itself assaulted by anxiety and then deflected from following where its dictates lead. The psyche dear to academic psychology provides a perfect model of such an arrested dialectic, frozen in the vast anarchy of commotions and unrelated behaviors that generate a continual displacement both of mind and of experience.

An existential psychology must attempt to restore the connections it severs. All psychological dispositions and functions express, as moments, the full reality of the subject. They must be understood, accordingly, as attempts to effect the subsequent "act" of consciousness in which they are sublated. As existentials, all are caught up in the process of their becoming and reveal distinct ways in which subject relates to its existence. All intend the world, and that reference is the key to their dialectical movement. There is never a moment of privacy, never a moment in which we are not out in the world. This point is crucial, especially with respect to psychology's traditional starting point—the consideration of feeling— where misunderstanding has the worst consequences. One of Heidegger's great achievements is the demonstration that *mood* is not a passing state or a privacy of the subject but the initial form that awareness both of the world and of our existence takes. Mood is that which first gives us to ourselves as subjects. It is both a revelation of our thrownness and our initial effort to surmount that fact. Moods aren't passively suffered and then discarded in a constant metonymic displacement of self along chains of association; they are developed into feelings and emotions. These, in turn, aren't private dispositions lacking reference but incipient actions that sustain and refer to the entire context of a situation. Emotions aren't private dilemmas, but stances we adopt toward the problems and contexts of existence.[45] Even the most protective emotions—obsessional control, schizoid withdrawal, disavowal, and the absence of affect—derive from and continue to refer to situations one was unable to master. In fact, it is in our emotions that we first pass judgment on ourselves.

Emotions are also the first form the project takes. The basic emotions one takes up toward oneself and the world are the clearest index of one's understanding of what it means to be a subject. The key to understanding emotions—and to rehabilitating many a discredited emotion, anger uppermost—is to see them as attempts to mediate those conflicts that are central to our understanding of existence. *Understanding* is not a matter of knowing the world but the act of projecting possibilities upon it.[46] Its goal is not the overcoming of mood in the direction of a proper cognitive or scientific standpoint, freed of affective confusions, but a development of the awareness that feelings first uncover.

In this sense, understanding is already a form of volition. The assertion that existentialism, like romanticism, unites thought, feeling, and will expresses in popular form an important consideration. Just as the existential subject strives to reverse the passivity of the ordinary subject, existentialism as a psychology attempts to apprehend the integrity of subject by thinking through the categories that constitute the philosophy of mind from the standpoint of engagement. This is the dialectical dimension that galvanizes what would otherwise be merely phenomenological descriptions. The aim of such descriptions is to apprehend the phenomenon under investigation—waiting, willing, anger, love, perception—in terms of its contribution to subject's understanding of existence. There are no separate phenomenologies.

The charge that the emphasis on precognitive awareness puts existentialism in opposition to reason, opening it to irrationalism, is mistaken because it derives from a dichotomy which existential awareness continually transcends. The existential effort is to situate reason, not dissolve it, to rethink thinking from the perspective of engagement. The charge that existentialism values feeling over thought is wide of the mark because it depends on the old rationalist and Cartesian dichotomy between logical thinking and confused feeling. The charge of voluntarism proceeds from similar assumptions, leading to the reductive picture of existential ethics as a matter of gratuitousness and relativism. The sorriest consequence of these readings is that they blind us to existentialism's main achievement: the development of a concept of thinking that is fully as rigorous as rationalism and science yet radically different in its logic and its operations as a result of the situatedness out of which it emerges and the distinctly human experiences to which it refers.

Little wonder that the "most thought-provoking thing about our most thought-provoking age is that we are still not thinking." *Thinking*, as a way of being in the world, is a discipline of passion. *Intelligence* is not a logical power measured by one's ability to perform abstract calculations, but a question of courage determined by one's ability to sustain fundamental questions by deepening one's engagement in their existential roots. The primary act and proof of intelligence is not reflection on abstract logical dilemmas and relations but reflection on existence. The goal, moreover, is not the removal of contradictions but their discovery. Thought has no contemplative end, nor is it the free exercise of a disinterested power to know, be delighted by, or find peace in eternal forms, essences, and those "things" that are ends in themselves. Reason is the cutting edge of passion, our most precise and lucid way of deepening the terms of our existence. "The most thought-provoking thing" may indeed be "that we are still not thinking" because thinking, so conceived, is an act of will and will a moral effort. Will is not an obscure ontological force (Schopenhauer) or a relativistic power (Nietzsche misread). It is the imperative we set down for ourselves so as to focus our thought —and our actions—on those situations which measure our humanity. Power of will is the direct and immediate issue of a thinking which has being-in-the-world as its subject.

POSSIBILITY, PROJECT, SITUATION, WORLD

Project and *world* are inseparable determinations of subject. Maintaining their connection is the key to attaining the concrete. In developing this line of thought, I will emphasize project, somewhat at the expense of world, in order to underscore the fact that the world is already surpassed whenever subject is. This argument does not deny either the reality or the primacy of the world, nor does it open existentialism to the charge of idealism. We are in the world long before we take it up, and it remains the context and limit of all our projections, so much so that any attempt to transcend it bears the mark of inauthenticity. But taking up the world is the act that first makes it world; and, in this sense, world and its corollary terms (situation, thrownness, facticity, etc.) must be seen not as external opacities but as existential determinations of the subject.

The world is not an ensemble of entities outside us but the encompassing scene we inhabit whenever we project possibilities. Its unshakable reality lies in the fact that until we do so, we have no possibilities. The richest ontological implication of this circumstance is expressed in one of Heidegger's finest formulations: *"Dasein* is not the basis of its *[Dasein's]* being, but the being of its basis."⁴⁷ Subject is the act of surpassing whereby the world in which we are thrown is sublated through the emergence of possibilities which are themselves wholly submitted to the world out of which they arise.

Subject *is* the projection of possibilities. Its being is caught up totally in this act. Possibility isn't something added on to perception but the final and most concrete form perception takes. We grasp what is by seizing it as a situation for us. Consciousness is not the disinterested perception of objects with which we later enter into relations, but the organization of our surrounding environment into situations toward which we adopt attitudes. In this way, existence underlies and informs everyday life. The primacy of possibility shows that our "cognitive" relationship to the world is already appetitive. No behavioral or positivistic formation is needed to get us into the world, nor is possibility the application of a deliberative, rational calculus to a fixed order of external goods awaiting our approval. We are caught up in the world long before we know it. We don't have to pass through an elaborate set of cognitive stages in order to comprehend the world, nor are possibilities the function of prior socialization processes. Possibility is the original act whereby we inhabit the world in an upsurge of desire which is as peremptory as it is opaque to itself. Possibilities are not like fully formed potencies awaiting the occasion to actualize themselves. Possibilities are so much a thing of the world, in fact, that they are initially imposed upon us; they announce themselves in conflicts we had not foreseen, moments seized or forever lost, and challenges in which, lacking guarantees, we still must summon that courage which is already a rejoinder to regret. Such circumstances indicate why possibilities exist only in their projection. Possibility is our way of living out the recognition that we are delivered over to our situations. We don't move from potency to act with the guaranteed and permanent security of a substance. We exist wholly in the world because the act of projection plunges us further into it. The metaphysic of potency assures us before we enter the world; possibility hurts because it puts us fully at risk there. Possibility isn't the translation of a rational identity into temporal terms in a plastic world eagerly awaiting the idealistic determination we will give it. It is our situations, in their harshness and their precariousness, that give us our possibilities. The world is always first, and it is always first as limit and as threat. The opposition of contingency to desire is what first concentrates the attention. We seize possibilities only when we see the danger of their slipping away. We are in a situation only when threatened with the loss of the very values the situation gives us the chance of realizing. Possibility reveals value as that which has no locus apart from our actions; and possibility submits value to a world characterized by precariousness, facticity, finitude, and loss.

Its rootedness in the world notwithstanding, possibility is also the world surpassed. Its origin lies in dissatisfaction with ourselves and our situation. Self-criticism, as always, is the force that galvanizes experience. Possibility is the initial form of the recognition that being depends on us, not in the manner dictated by philosophic idealism, but as a result of the power of the project to transform situations into which we are irretrievably thrown. Possibility sublates both self and world. And the ante always goes up because possibilities don't take us beyond our situatedness, but plunge us more deeply into it. Possibilities are not fantasies or noble ideals one conjures up out of thin air to flatter one's self-esteem. They are attempts to bring oneself fully into the world. Possibility is the first concrete fusion of inwardness and existence in a dialectic that stays wholly within the world.

If possibility plunges me into the world, it is because I don't enter my possibilities from some secured identity which now attaches itself, in a harmonious relationship, to a preexisting order of goods. I am my possibilities because they reveal me as an emptiness that is one with the desire that propels it forth. Subject is verbal, the act of its own projection. Possibility is the first concrete self-mediation of the subject because it is an innerness that is always already outside itself.

Situation and possibility stand in a dialectical relationship that keeps both terms fully in the world. That connection severed, possibility becomes abstract self-indulgence and situatedness a deterministic reduction to the given. Both positions dissolve the concrete. Situations rise up before us with their undeniable facticity, but this opposition is what first creates possibilities. Thrown into situations, we find we don't have limitless choices but are touched to the quick by contingency. Possibility is the act which volatilizes this recognition. Contingency announces itself in its most meaningful form: it is *our* contingency. In sublating that fact through the projection of possibility, we don't magically transform the world by imposing pure mind upon it. Every projection entails a coefficient of adversity. At best, projection creates a new situation. Thus are we forever driven further into the world. Prior to this drama we don't have a situation, we have no more than a scene. Situatedness is an existential, a self-determination of subject. We don't have situations from time to time. We *are* our situations. Situatedness is part of the internal constitution of subject, an essential moment in its experiential self-mediation.

The unity of possibility and situatedness gives us the existential concept of the world. The world is first given, not through the impossible Kantian dialectic of the cosmological ideal, but through the revelatory power of basic moods such as anxiety to render a comprehensive and totalizing experience of both the range and the limits of our situatedness. Being-in-the-world isn't a cosmological idea, a lyric experience, or an abstract pessimistic theme. The key to defining the concept is to understand world not as an externality that surrounds us, but as the furthest reach of our responsibility for being. It is the encompassing framework we are already in and must take over as the ultimate term and context of our choices. Worldliness is an existential self-determination that is part of subject's internal constitution. The moment subject is, world is also. The world, like death, is an end and a limit that bring us back from pure contemplàtion. It is defined by realities I keep running up against (thrownness, facticity, absence) and must internalize since there is no way to transcend them. These limits are my limits and deliver me over to myself as subject.

In an attempt to deny our situatedness, we try to project beyond this context. World is the concept that brings us back to the concrete. It is the negation of the metaphysical desire for deliverance. World offers neither closure nor substantiality because it signifies the recognition that there is no preestablished order of being waiting for me to correspond to it, and thereby coincide with myself and be freed of the burden of existence. Worldliness is the awareness that there are no metaphysical supports. It is the furthest reach I can make in that search for deliverance that brings me back to my responsibility. This is the deepest meaning it has as an existential self-mediation. Its characteristics are not negative qualities we must bewail in "guilty, Rousseauistic nostalgia" over the loss of origin, center, and structure, but a call to a responsibility we must assume. To claim that being-in-the-world means finding oneself abandoned in an absurd, impersonal, and menacing realm lacking any haven means not that I'm lost but that I'm found. What is lost is the illusion that I can project beyond the world or impose a priori ideals upon it. When delivered over to utter contingency, the world is for the first time mine—and I am for the first time wholly in and of it. Authentic projection is now possible because I have discovered the standard which measures all possibilities and the context which they must assume as their burden. *World and existence are corollary concepts, the former being the fullest articulation of what is implicit in the latter.*

The notion that the concept of world first arises from certain basic moods is not an overture to poetic self-indulgence. Nor is it the improper attribution to being in general of a questionable psychological state. It derives, rather, from the demand that one totalize the understanding that mood first makes possible. Mood is not a passing state, but a cognitive awareness; it earns itself only through a complete articulation of the "reality" it puts us in touch with. Thus, boredom totalized gives me the world lost in inauthentic living. Boredom totalized is not an improper generalization but an articulation of the scope and force in everyday life of that flight from existence to which my boredom attunes me. Anxiety totalized gives me the world regained as responsibility for projecting myself in the comprehensive context such totalization reveals. Anxiety totalized is not a fitful hiatus disruptive of normal living, but the negation of that negation. Its power lies in its ability to call the normal into question. Our responsibility to primary moods is not to displace but to develop them. Our moods derive from and intend the world; they contain the possibility of giving us the broadest and the most concrete understanding we can have of our situatedness.

World is the sublation of situatedness, and project the sublation of possibility. The world, as a concept and as an awareness, is not derived from an abstract philosophic meditation on situatedness, but arises directly from the way situations are lived. In taking up my mood, I progressively uncover its scope and its complexities. A situation becomes mine as I discover the multiple determinations that have created it. And possibilities become authentic only insofar as I take this developing context upon myself. World thus signifies the totality of contexts and contingencies I must take over in order to make my existence mine.[48] That is why the proper reference of the term is to social, cultural, and historical forces and not to the cosmological preoccupations of traditional philosophy. World is misunderstood as long as we think of it in terms of physics and the natural world. Like all existential concepts, it refers to the being of the subject. As such, it has for existentialism a function similar to that of *Bildung* in Hegel: one becomes a subject only by assimilating the entire historical-cultural context of one's existence.

Historicity is the sublation and concretization of world. Just as world undoes the dream of transcendence, historicity undoes the dream of substance. Nothing protects us from history because subject is historical to the core of its being. There is nothing we can posit for the subject (i.e., rationality, language, sexuality, etc.) that is not derived from and submitted to history as to a destiny. Historicity is an existential, a self-mediation that we must internalize because history is already inside us forming the framework and the internalizations which constitute that "precious individuality" we think of as the product of autonomous choices. History is more personal than anything else in the constitution of the "personality."

Historicity has two meanings, one personal, the other cultural. Discussing them separately will bring us to a recognition of their necessary dialectical convergence. Each of us has a personal history: I am a member of this class, race, and gender; I am the child of these particular parents, bound together, usually, in conflicts not met and thus passed on in the most insidious ways; my family is mediated, in turn, by its position in a particular socio-economic complex. I internalize a heavy weight of values long before I come to any question of choice, and my beliefs are deeply ingrained in conflicted affections and loyalties. The abstract idea of freedom is brought up short by the recognition that most of my possibilities have already been chosen for me. It is the act of projection, however, that alone uncovers the force of this fact. Only by running up against an internalized parental value, for example, does one discover its perhaps irreversible force in one's internal constitution. The past is my past, which I carry with me now as the burden of choices, made by and for me, which create the present I strive to outstrip by projecting myself into the future. This is the self-reference which concretizes existential time by giving its *extases* their content. In some way, we always experience our life as a whole—and as given over to the world—because it is impossible to understand oneself except in terms of living out a relationship to a personal history that one cannot escape. Our true relationship to ourselves is narrative. And it is as narrative beings that we unify our relationship to any mode of experience; memory is, for example, not the empirical recollection of all that happened in one's life, but the conscience of what mattered. Historicity doesn't attach to subject like an accident one can remove in order to resume one's essential being. It is the one self-mediation we are condemned to be, even applying retroactively to our thrownness into circumstances we can take over only subsequently.

The broader cultural meaning of historicity is the dialectical corollary of the personal one. Our personal history is necessarily bound up with the history of our time, not only because possibilities are first determined there, but because it is there that they may well disappear. History is a destiny because it is the yet unfinished work to which all possibilities —including our very existence as "being possible"—are submitted. It weighs like a nightmare on the brains of the living because there can be no separate peace. When history cancels something, it is gone. The prospect we now face, with the advent of "the last man," is that the happiness of humankind will be achieved: we will no longer relate to ourselves as subjects. Perhaps the bomb's already gone off. That possibility measures our thought because we now face history without theological and "metaphysical" presuppositions. History has no center, progressive structure, or determinate closure. There are no a priori structures of mind we can impose upon it to keep it moving in the right direction or give the assurance of an eventual triumph of Absolute Spirit, of Liberty, or of an identical subject-object that we can locate at the level either of culture or of class. There are no guarantees. Nothing protects us from irretrievable loss. We are delivered over to history as the ultimate horizon of a worldliness to which we must respond, without reservation, knowing that its possibilities are our possibilities. Whatever may be "repeatable" from the "rich" cultural past must submit its credentials to the historical present.

The internalization of historicity situates projection in a world-historical context. The dialectical connection between the personal and the sociocultural concepts of historicity constitutes an existential rewriting of the idea of *Bildung*. History is defined by a universal problematic. To make this problematic concrete we must carry the question "How stands it with humankind?" into every aspect of everyday life. As historical beings, our task is to become what Hegel, Lukács, and Mann term "world-historical individuals": those who appropriate the entire context of contemporary historical existence as the framework in which all their possibilities must be located and projected.[49] Only so does worldliness become an authentic self-mediation of the subject. This understanding entails a dialectical redefinition of the project.

Descriptively, the term *project* simply calls attention to the pragmatic dimension of experience: we are constantly making and carrying out plans. Dialectically, the term introduces the possibility that a hierarchy is at work here. This idea brings not peace but a sword because it implies that the question of our humanity keeps coming up with persistent force out of the way projects are lived. Even the most solipsistic of us does not succeed in living forever the relativism of the moment. All activities relate to life goals since we organize our various affairs in terms of certain basic plans that promise the fulfillment we seek. Dialectical interpretation ontologizes this relation by placing all particular projects before the bar of anxiety and the responsibility it implies. Before that standard, most projects reveal themselves as, in effect, antiprojects, designed to arrest and defend us against the imperatives of existence. This interpretation is not a humanistic or idealistic imposition, but arises directly out of experience. Although one comes to existence only retrospectively, there is an important sense in which our most pragmatic possibilities are never simply random projections. We are always living some kind of relationship to ourselves. Possibilities derive from that fact. They thus bear the question of the "who" of subject as their underlying dynamic. In this sense, anxiety doesn't come to assault our projects from outside, but is already gnawing at them from within. We first know authenticity, in fact, as a problem we struggle to escape only to be brought back to it.

Anxiety is mastered not when it is fled or successfully defended against, but when it is made the basis of actions that take what anxiety reveals about existence upon themselves. To make the point through a deliberately difficult grammatical construction, an authentic project projects upon anxiety; it is the way anxiety sublates itself. In so doing it establishes the possibility that experience has a dialectical unity. The project is the first true coalescence of the existential subject—the act in which everything we have said about subject achieves completion. The self does not have a project; nor does it have an identity from which it descends, from time to time, to toy with this possibility or that. The self is its own project. Until there is a project there is no self.

We are so much the creatures of our actions that we have no qualities of character prior to or outside them. That is why all projects, however trivial or base, are totalizations of the self and carry that burden as their underlying dialectic. The significance of the haunting which defines subject is that our life, however fallen, remains perpetually referred to what Heidegger terms our "ownmost" and "innermost" possibility—the appropriation of our existence. Existence thus remains the ground and the horizon that measure everything we think, feel, and do. If appropriated abstractly, this recognition ends in Heideggerian formalism—the vow of *Dasein* to keep repeating itself. Understood existentially it means that one's project must take on, in a totalizing way, the Nietzschean task of giving a meaning to life on the earth.

The dialectical reference of particular projects to our innermost possibility is not something we live out explicitly. It is an understanding we come to only as our understanding of experience develops. One doesn't assume one's being at the start, in transparent self-consciousness; self-consciousness comes only through the progressive negation of inadequate projects. This process constitutes the dialectic of experience. The relation of particular possibilities—which are initially pretty much a matter of catch-as-catch-can—to my innermost possibility is mostly a silent discourse heard only in that retrospective moment when I find that I've lost what I never really tried to achieve or what I kidded myself into thinking I'd already secured as a permanent possession. Anxiety assaults us intermittently and usually after the fact. But however and whenever it arises, anxiety carries a dynamic capable of calling our entire life into question. Our innermost possibility always remains with us as a term of judgment, if in no other way. Though the project may be last in the order of experience, it is first ontologically because it has the power to reverse all that has gone before. It thus completes the conceptual reorientation that is existentialism: experience is not a cumulative, continuous, or chronological process, but a matter of reversal and recognition. Accepting existence is the act through which we first assume the duties of our being.

We can best summarize the project by relating it explicitly to the concept of subject we are developing. Human beings live a dialectical, destabilizing relationship to themselves. Because that is so, experience must be conceived of as a hierarchy of possible self-mediations which progressively bring together initially separate contexts and realities. One has subjectivity to the degree to which one internalizes, suffers, and lives out a relationship to the fundamental questions. Subject is not merely a psychological but an ontological reality because it is defined by the universal problems which existence imposes on us. This recognition puts an end to all subjectivisms and formalisms. Existence is always outside and beyond itself, en route, committed utterly to the new situation in which it issues. And it is so, not as a pure spontaneity (Sartre) or an abstract thematic (Heidegger), but in a dialectically determinate way. That is why the recognition of historicity does not provide a new theme for a purely analytic meditation which will end in the same abstract and finally worldless angst. It establishes a new context into which we must pour our being totally and concretely as a result of having discovered that our being is already at issue there in precisely that way.

The project reveals *action* as the being of the subject. The self is its actions, not some substance outside, prior to, or above them. This understanding of action brings the entire existential examination to completion.

We are delivered over to action utterly because it is only in and through action that we can give ourselves being. We miss the thrust of the existential attempt to renew the life of feeling and to establish the cognitive credentials of our lonely confrontations with ourselves as long as we fail to see that existentialism's central assertion is a rebuke of subjectivism and the myth of a private, contemplative identity. Even in those moods that seem evanescent, subject is fully out in the world, already engaged in the effort to act. Inwardness is always a response to one's situation. Our identity is the character we give ourselves through those values we live out in our deeds. Every other conception of the self is an exercise in bad faith, an attempt to hedge our bets, to preserve ourselves at some safe remove from the world.

The existential subject is so constituted that every "psychological" operation of consciousness is pointed to the primacy and necessity of action. That constitution is the key to the correct understanding of every existential concept. Anxiety over oneself isn't a worldless malaise or a self-indulgent privacy; such interpretations constitute inauthentic responses to what anxiety reveals. Authentic anxiety is the recognition that one is totally responsible and must act in a world that offers no guarantees. Action defines us because our being is at issue, not as a problem we can contemplate dispassionately, but as an inwardness urging us to take those actions in ourselves that will issue in actions in the world. Existential inwardness is the internalization of this recognition as the imperative one uses to measure one's subjectivity. As such, it exerts a constant pressure that constitutes the ongoing drama of our feelings and moods. Feeling is not a privacy of subject, nor is it a simple reflex of external situations. It is the initial *act* in which we assess a situation in terms of the burden to exist it puts upon us.

All the operations that characterize the inwardness of the existential subject not only point to action, but complete themselves in action or consume themselves in futility. Action is our only way of giving ourselves being. This is the concept the next two chapters will concretize.

3 Subject in a Marxism without Guarantees

I have never found anybody without a sense of humour who could understand dialectics. —BRECHT

The desert grows . . . woe to him who harbors deserts within. —NIETZSCHE

THE DIALECTIC OF SUBJECT WITHIN MARXISM

TAKING STOCK

THE PROBLEMATIC STATUS OF REFLECTION IN MARXISM

Marxism is currently in the midst of one of its most creative and conflicted periods. Every idea in the tradition is under interrogation, and a new understanding, quite different from Marx's in many ways, is struggling to be born. With Marx, as with Freud, our problem is not to fix, once and for all, the one true interpretation of certain canonical texts, but to conceptualize the history of an understanding that has developed as it has opened itself both to other currents of thought and to the necessity of undertaking its own internal critique.[1] After reflecting on that history, Stuart Hall called for a "marxism without guarantees."[2] That call goes to the center of contradictions endemic to marxism by calling into question such notions as economic determinism (whether in the first or last instance), class reductionism as an explanation of the nature of consciousness, and the base-superstructure theory of ideology (especially when used to explain thought and culture). It also exposes both the progressive historicism and the covert utopianism that has controlled the marxist understanding of history. For all its emphasis on history, marxism has found many ways to put on shields before that Medusa.

Hall's project also entails reopening questions that many contemporary marxists have gladly left behind—foremost among them the question of the subject. For perhaps the grandest function of the guarantees enumerated above is that they eliminate or short-circuit the need for an in-depth consideration of subject. But reopening that question cuts two ways. The critique of particular theories of subject and of the general ideological function of that concept is widely regarded as one of the most solid achievements of marxism. In fact, showing the ways in which theories of subject blind us to our situatedness constitutes the primary value of marxism for our larger project. Like Freud, Marx doesn't simply relate to the surface of our consciousness, but reaches down into the depths of everything we think of as most deeply and personally "ours." It would be convenient if we could distinguish the public from the private and restrict Marx's critique of "consciousness" to a concern with public beliefs about political affairs. We could then find innumerable ways to limit his impact on our subjectivity. But the distinction itself, and the motives for making it, beg the question Marx poses. Marxism is concerned with the entire range of practices and institutions that attempt to guarantee the reproduction of a given historical situation (i.e., relations of production) by producing the internalizations that lead subjects to acquiesce in those relations. It offers us a systematic insight into the ways in which our thoughts, feelings, beliefs, and values are not eternal or natural but historical. They derive from the social process and attempt to mask its contradictions.

In Marx, the traditional concept of autonomous individuality reveals itself as an archaic abstraction. It becomes an open question whether any concept of self-identity can survive once the exercise of sociological suspicion has done its work. Marxism disrupts and challenges the very idea of subject that has been an essential prop of traditional humanisms. It asserts that there is nothing prior to the social: nothing free from the impact of history. The very idea of subject is rendered suspect because theories of subject have functioned by and large to limit or control the consciousness of contingency.

Marxism's primary lesson for a theory of subject lies in the discovery of the social and the historical where we thought to find the natural and the universal. Marxism charges traditional concepts of subject both with a fallacy of misplaced concreteness and with an ideological role in covering up what emerges once they are eliminated. The methodological value of current proclamations of "the death of subject" lies in revealing all the ways we have tried to limit the impact of the sociohistorical on the formation and regulation of consciousness.

While endorsing this line of thought, my purpose will be to reintroduce the dialectical dimension in order to construct a theory of subject for marxism. The main idea I will develop derives somewhat ironically from Althusser's great insight that the formation or "interpellation" of the subject is the primary task of ideology.[3] Whereas Althusser deploys this idea to eliminate the category of the subject altogether, in favor of what Spivak terms his "scientific anti-humanism,"[4] I will show how it points to a marxist theory of situated subjectivity.

Ideology is the primary category for this reflection because marxism shows us that when we talk about the subject we are "proximally and for the most part" talking about ideology. We are what we are as a function of a continual series of messages that are secreted by the practices and institutions that make the social process our true *Lebenswelt*. It produces us rather than the other way around. When one enters into reflection,[5] ideology is the text one finds already writ large both in the "immediacy" of consciousness and in its laws of operation/exclusion. We are "always already" within ideology. It doesn't come to disrupt or attach itself to a prior self-presence which we can establish or regain by stripping away its encrustations. There is no "prior to ideology," no origin outside it, and no cogito protects us from its force by providing the standards of truth and correct consciousness with which to measure or oppose it. We are first and foremost products of the thought, language, and beliefs of others.

To attain a concept of subject that will be more than pseudoconcrete and epiphenomenal—and thus a genuine alternative to current deconstructions and semiotic dissolutions—we can no longer rely either on an a priori identity (rationalism) or on some natural, utopian spontaneity outside, prior to, or beyond the ideological (romanticism). Subject must emerge and must do so because "we" are able to do something with and within our ideological situatedness, not because we have some identity prior to or outside it. Subject must be conceived of as something that arises in the course of experience, not as something we begin with. To constitute this possibility, we must face experience in the knowledge that subjectivity does not provide us with a substantial identity we can never lose. For only then are we *in* the world.[6]

Given the difficulties of this task, it is not surprising that many contemporary marxists have chosen to eliminate subject. While that decision is strategically inviting it ignores the new task Marx set for our humanity. This task is as complex as the one set by Freud, and its necessary complement. That task is to become a subject by rooting out and reversing the capitalist internalizations that structure our inwardness in ways we have scarcely begun to realize. The marxist "exercise of suspicion"[7] doesn't simply relate to our political beliefs, but reaches down into the depth of our subjectivity, calling into question the very meaning of relating to oneself in depth. Reflection itself is brought to a crisis because marxism reveals all the ways in which inwardness replicates, both in its contents and in its limits or structuring principles, the contradictions of the social order it claims to comprehend. Marxism thus offers us endless discoveries of the various ways in which our being is not our own. As such, it fully implicates us—as subjects—in the inquiry. (This is why marxist theoreticians, whether they like it or not, move in a hermeneutic circle of engagement in which their being as subjects is at issue and is determined by the understanding of marxism they develop.) Until one sees the radical and personal challenge marxism implies, one has not really taken the sociological turn or experienced the power of marxist texts to perform a function similar to that Beckett claimed for *Endgame*: "the power of the text to claw."

Marx asks us to undertake a double interrogation and discipline of reflection: first, to discover all the ways in which the social order produces the subject; then, to make those discoveries the basis for a radical transformation of one's subjectivity. It is possible to object, of course, that the process is endless and endlessly disruptive, a process not of progressive advance but of ceaseless self-unraveling or deconstruction.[8] As we've noted in previous chapters, reflection is always subject to this somewhat formalistic critique since it depends on what can be made to look like a grammatical or logical impossibility. What Nietzsche said about language—"How can the instrument criticize itself?"—can be used to argue the impossibility of reflection's ever escaping the vicious circle of using some unreflected content or principle to criticize another only to discover at a subsequent moment the dubiousness of the concept or assumption that made the critique possible. There is merit to this objection, and it applies to many things that traditional, humanistic practitioners of the hermeneutic circle thought they had placed beyond doubt. One can never be sure that a new development (feminism, say) won't uncover neglected phenomena that call into question all that a supposedly complete, transparent, and self-critical exercise of reflection has established. Such is the service that each new philosophic development pays its immediate past, overturning it by finding the controlling presence of the assumption/fallacy it has failed to reflect on. *This fact does not refute reflection but calls attention to a necessary limit that it must take up into itself.*[9] Reflection's limit invalidates it only for those who remain locked in the curious notion that they will one day achieve the one true starting point by taking a definitive step outside all previous thought.

The life of authentic reflection is such that I can never be assured that I have reflected enough or that a new reflection won't require a major rethinking of my entire framework. Complication doesn't necessitate cancellation, however, nor does the incompleteness of reflection invalidate it. Reflection may be endless, but one of its finest flowers is the recognition that discoveries don't cancel one another. Events are overdetermined. Motives intersect not to force a choice (feminism or marxism, say) but to complicate our awareness by revealing the need to establish necessary dialectical connections. Reflection finds no privileged starting point, no one cause, no single context or principle of explanation—be it economics or patriarchy—which underlies and determines all others. It discovers instead a multiplicity of factors and contexts that have necessary and intricate connections to one another. Reflection is not embarrassed by this fact, because it is precisely the discovery it seeks. It welcomes the demonstration that there are a wealth of things it has not reflected on, because the chance to do so is precisely the experience that sustains and renews it.

Marxism adds the consideration that concretizes and solidifies this understanding of reflection. The primacy of action is marxism's greatest thought. This thought determines a basic direction for reflection. Discovering social determinations in which we cannot acquiesce is not enough. The only way we can actually overcome them is by acting in new ways in precisely the situations where those determinations function to deprive us of our historicity.

Until we become "socialists in our instincts," with that act transforming all our relationships with others, we're just playing an academic game. Self-overcoming through reflection requires and only completes itself in praxis. At a level that has not yet been articulated, marxism, like psychoanalysis, makes sense only as a theory of drama: its deepest imperative is that we transform our activity as actors in those institutions (the university, say) and social arrangements (scholarly discourse) that function to maintain the self-evident status of the capitalist order. Brecht and Burke alone, perhaps, understood this imperative.

The human being is a social being. Whether or not that recognition spells the dissolution of subject is a complex question, but one thing is certain: any theory of subject that ignores social formation convicts itself of abstraction. For, by and large, we are subjects by rote. Entering ourselves we find the objective, social world replicated at a safe remove from critical understanding. The discipline of sociology is a primary text for any theory of subject precisely because it clears the ground by helping us dispose of a whole series of naive and abstract beliefs about individual autonomy, personal choice, and self-identity—beliefs which have not only a clear function in the legitimation of questionable social arrangements, but a devastating effect on the practice of self-criticism. Believing that one's belief is one's own autonomous product makes one more ardent in its defense and less likely to see where it's really coming from. Sociological awareness is a healthy antidote to our alleged autonomy and an essential moment in the quest for self-knowledge because it reveals the ways in which many of our most cherished beliefs and attitudes, as well as the behaviors that sustain them, don't arise from individual choice but are socially determined.

Marxism is the most systematic and critical attempt to think through the implications of a shift far more radical than Kant's Copernican revolution in epistemology: the sociological turn. Marx's effort as sociologist is to grasp the ways in which everything—ranging from philosophic thought to the beliefs, attitudes, and feelings that make up the contents of everyday consciousness—is socially determined in order to convince us that the total system not only can be comprehended but must be overthrown. This double effort makes Marx's social theorizing a challenge to our subjectivity where other social theories tend to confirm it. We may be a product of social consensus, but the consensus is rotten to the core.[10]

Marxism complements and concretizes the previous chapters by situating subject in history in a way that enables us to uncover the historical and motivational conditions behind those theories of subject we have thus far interrogated primarily in conceptual terms. In most discourses, the concept of subject functions to deny or check the ways in which we are delivered over to history. "Human nature" is a way of keeping something in reserve, out of play, free of taint; it is an escape hatch, a separate peace. The autonomous individual, disinterested a priori rationality, the Cartesian cogito, the inward voice, the privacy of feeling, and the romantic self are among the most powerful ideas we have developed to prevent the dissolution of the subject. Yet it is doubtful if any of them can withstand Marx's demonstration that ideology reaches into the core of the "self." Where other theories find subject, ideology relentlessly uncovers object; where they find essences, it finds history; where they find nature, it finds the force of circumstances. The natural, the essential, and the universal become questionable concepts, as does any logic based on privileging being over becoming. Nothing we initially hold about ourselves escapes reflection on how utterly socialized we are. Consciousness is exposed as false consciousness, and all the supposed immediacies it takes as solid experiential beginnings dissolve in the revelation of vast and thoroughly historical connections and contingencies. If subject equals the attempt to establish a principle of identity or of an essential human nature that can be used to control or center our situatedness in a field of social forces, the primary lesson of marxism is that such a concept is a myth.

Under the scrutiny of ideology, the whole notion of essences and universals becomes suspect. Ideologically, essence functions to sustain questionable historical realities by giving them the stamp of that which is unalterable and/or good. It is hard to untangle the logic implicit in the concept of essence from the many ways the concept is employed to provide guarantees against contingency, and hard to resist the suspicion that there are important connections among these uses. The idea that capitalism corresponds to the inherent selfishness that is an essential fact of human nature is a case in point. But it merely performs for one audience a function similar to what the vast edifice of a priori Kantian rationality does for another. The later idea may, in fact, be of greater, though subtler, ideological force. Post-Kantian formalism is the most proficient, essentializing cogito yet invented since it is infinitely extendable. It has, accordingly, given birth to a predictable imperialism of discourses all dedicated to demonstrating that a number of distinct disciplines (and phenomena) can be subsumed under the grand idea that rationality is found everywhere. The larger assumption, of course, is that the identity of the self and the intelligibility of experience lie in correspondence to "reason." Thus we have cultural (Cassirer), historical (Dilthey), linguistic (Chomsky), mythological (Frye), ethical (Kohler), psychological (Piaget), and political (Habermas) extensions of the Kantian project. Though it is frequently content with less speculative rationales, traditional *humanism* (Aristotelian, Christian, secular Enlightenment liberal) also constitutes a monument to the desire to posit an essential human identity and dignity that are untouched by historical contingency and that we can always recover, whatever our circumstances. The same "metaphysical" desire is still present in more recent theories of subject that "begin" with "experience" (pragmatism and phenomenology) or that ground themselves in an awareness that explicitly breaks with Kantian and humanistic models (Sartre). As Derrida has shown, the notion of self-presence in self-consciousness is implicated in a subtle Cartesianism that suppresses those disruptive linguistic and unconscious forces that would turn reflection into the endless process of deferral and delay (differance) in which all notions of self and identity unravel.[11] Anyone who thinks the move from substance to subject is secured once we make existence and experience the themes of reflection would do well to reflect on all the ways in which we arrest/halt reflection as soon as it has given us an identity in which we can acquiesce. Althusser's scientific antihumanism and Derrida's antiscientific antihumanism contribute to the systematic "exercise of suspicion" by alerting us to the possibility that all languages of subject conceal essentialisms that can't stand up to either historical or grammatical scrutiny.

Shifting back to the more immediate social formations through which capitalism takes root, we can apply the same critique to what we might, paraphrasing Adorno,[12] call the "subject industry"—the manufacture, through the media, of popular conceptions of subjectivity and the therapies and programs of "self-help" whereby these notions are disseminated and inculcated. Thanks to the operation of such forces, when we go inside, we replicate what is outside. In fact, getting us to go "inside," incessantly, in precisely the right ways and with just the right results, is the crowning achievement of such formations. We thereby defend as our personal voice, our unalterable identity, a collectively shared acquiescence in objective conditions. For the most part, consciousness is not only false consciousness but no consciousness.

From this perspective, knowing oneself means becoming aware of all the ways in which one's existence is not one's own. Unless we experience this idea as a challenge that goes to the "core" of our subjectivity, we haven't understood it. But taking up the challenge may entail endless aporias. The most closely guarded secret of self-knowledge may be that there is no self. The very notion of the "core" may assume an insupportable logic of self-presence that is complicit, in spite of itself, with the substantialisms and essentialisms it hopes to overcome. The marxist understanding of ideology leads, as we shall see, to a crisis in reason itself. Reflection finds itself fully implicated in that crisis.

It is hard to read Marx and come away with the notion that any of our traditional humanistic beliefs about human identity or human nature can survive—either as commonsense postulates or recycled under some suitable a priori guise. In fact, as Marx shows, one has recourse to the a priori only when it has become difficult to sustain certain ideas historically.[13] The primary function of the idea of human nature is that it sets limits to certain inquiries, puts certain things beyond question, and thereby provides assurance that reflection will not become too disruptive. Ultimately, all such operations deny or limit the effect of history—especially the unthinkable notion that we may be given over to it without reserve. The historical or empirical corollary to the philosophic critique of the concept of human nature is the demonstration that these supposed universals are actually produced by and function to sustain institutions —such as the patriarchal family—which are historical to the core. The thoroughness with which Marx reveals such connections raises the question of how much of the baby must be thrown out with the bath water. Trying to untangle reason or human nature from the sins committed in its name, one may find oneself left with nothing but a gigantic tautology or, what actually amounts to the same thing, a historical predicament.

Another way of posing the question is to ask if the concept of ideology hoists marxism by its own petard. Once ideological scrutiny has done its work, are we left with any alternative to the relativistic way in which the term "ideology" is currently deployed in academe? There it does double and ambiguous duty. Applied to oneself ideology constitutes permission; applied to one's opponent, it constitutes refutation. Ideology thus serves both (1) as a term interchangeable with theory, and preferable to it as a sign that one recognizes the necessary yet unalterable limitation of one's position (i.e., "our ideology requires that we make an intervention . . . express our rage . . ."); and (2) as a pejorative label applied to characterize or refute other, especially opposed, positions (i.e., "the ideology of the patriarchy demands . . ."; "modernist ideology blinds its followers to . . ."). Ideology is a concept caught in incipient crisis because it enables beliefs to be proclaimed without self-criticism and without any real demonstration aside from the presumed truth of certain feelings and "experiences" that constitute the solidarity of the ideological group. Such practices are then reinforced by using the term ideology in a second sense as the all-purpose label that refutes opponents' arguments by imputing concealed and illegitimate motives to them.

Rhetorically efficacious as such practices may be, they entail a concep-

tual dilemma. Is there something other than ideology? Or are we trapped
in a situation where each ideology simply misinterprets and "refutes"
other ideologies, empowered to do so, and powerless to do otherwise, by
the necessary limit of self-understanding that the concept of ideology has
brought to our attention? Is there an alternative to ideology, or is belief
in such an alternative itself an ideology? Are "pluralists" deluding themselves when they try to understand positions other than their own? Are
ideologies refuted only by other ideologies, or is there a position *within*
our ideological situatedness that provides something analogous to traditional standards of truth and verification? The possibility we will develop
is that the alternative to relativism is not a rejection of ideology but a
development, through its study, of a distinctly marxist concept of critical
reflection.

In terms of our larger concern, the question posed by that inquiry
will be whether it leads to a distinct marxist theory of subject or whether
it drives the final nail in the coffin of such a theory. Marx would be the
first to point out that these questions are historical. They may, in fact,
hold the key to understanding our current historical situation, but we can
pose that possibility only after a historical consideration of ideology. To
understand where we stand today we must trace the concept of ideology
from its beginnings to the crisis which its perhaps inevitable dialectical
expansion has spawned. Such a consideration must be both a conceptual
reflection and an attempt, by tracing a history, to break into history.

Ideology and the Dissolution of the Rational Self

The history of marxism can be seen as a progressive broadening of
the concept of ideology as it comes to refer, not only or even primarily
to political ideas and our public frame of mind, but to the production
of consciousness in general. As this understanding develops, it becomes
impossible to find a correct marxist consciousness that can be attained
through the exercise of science or disinterested rationality, as opposed to a
false ideological consciousness. This is the crisis in reason to which marxism leads: ideological suspicion calls into question every attempt to posit
the autonomy of science or reason. Reason may, in fact, be the prime agent
and cloak of ideology. Nevertheless, the two dominant movements in
marxism today—Althusser's scientism and Habermas' neo-Kantian rationalism—define themselves by an attempt to limit the impact of ideology
on "reason itself."[14]

But the history of marxism raises serious questions about the effort of marxists to place anything outside ideology. Lukács's seminal demonstration of the ways in which the contradictions—or limits—of Kantian philosophy (the a priori rational subject and the unknowable *Ding-an-sich*) correspond to the contradictions of bourgeois society constitutes a thorough challenge to the most developed concept of "rationality" we possess.[15] But rather than providing an alternative rationality, Lukács's solution extends the problem. To escape relativism and "existentialism," Lukács invokes the proletariat as the identical subject-object of history that necessarily possesses a correct consciousness since its "privileged" position in history, and its very survival as a class, depend on attaining that understanding. One could not ask for a better example of what Gramsci calls *class reductionism,* marxism's characteristic flight into its own brand of Hegelian historical necessity.[16] The balmy or desperate days of Lukács's historical moment prevented him from placing this article of faith under ideological scrutiny. Gramsci's critique of class reductionism and Althusser's later critique of "efficient causality" will perform that service. But once they remove the guarantee of class consciousness, the crisis of reason implicit in marxism will have come a cropper.

Critiques of "reason" usually try to keep a rationality in reserve because if we go too far with "the poverty of philosophy," we appear to eat our own tail. Following Lukács's lead, Marcuse, Adorno, Meszaros, and others drive a series of brilliant nails into rationalism, scientism, positivism, and analytic philosophy by showing how each of these movements of thought corresponds to a particular historical "stage" of bourgeois capitalist society. From such studies, the true significance of philosophy emerges: it gives us the clearest picture of the contradictions of its historical moment. Reading philosophy reveals, not what sovereign reason discovers as universally true, but where we stand in history. However, having used philosophy to mount this critique against itself, these thinkers find themselves inside the coffin they have so brilliantly constructed. It should come as no shock to those who have followed such developments to see Derrida take the step that appears to be implicit in all of them by arguing that philosophy itself—i.e., the whole "history" of logocentric metaphysics or, more recently, phallogocentrism—is ideology incarnate.

Though reason may prove rotten to the core—and I will offer much in support of this consideration—taking a step outside it may amount to little more than a regression to the worst form of abstract dialectics in which all the old utopian guarantees resurface, with the Lukácsian identical subject-object of history recycled under a new guise. Thus recent "marxists" claim that phallogocentrism is part of our prehistory and that by developing *écriture féminine* or schizoanalysis we can untangle ourselves from its coils and regain a pristine identity.[17] The key assumption, of course, is that until we do so our *consciousness* and our *experience* are completely controlled by the "other." Such arguments are a good example of the self-destructive gesture the left repeatedly makes against its own history by finding the fatal fallacy which confines everything in its intellectual tradition to the flames.

The attractions of such projects notwithstanding, it is possible to see them as degenerations of radical consciousness that are inevitable, even mandated, by the thoroughness of the marxist critique of reason. For it needs no triumphant bourgeois ideologue to remind us, with Mannheim, that marxism is itself an ideology and cannot escape the limitation entailed by its fundamental discovery. But the threat of that charge is apparently such that Althusser will go to great lengths to torture out a distinction between marxist science and ideology, while in another quarter Habermas will sacrifice everything genuinely self-critical and tragic in the Frankfurt school in order to reaffirm the very Kantianism that Adorno and Lukács strove to overcome. What makes Habermas' endorsement of a priori rationality particularly distressing is the wholesale and noncritical appropriation of everything stabilizing in bourgeois thought: ego identity, the maturational order, reality testing, communicative competence.[18] Habermas talks as if it is comparatively easy to detach these ideas from the social order that produces them and that they serve to legitimate and institutionalize. It should not surprise those of a more critical disposition to learn that the most mature, competent, rational, and reality-tested ego is found in the academic servant class, which has as its mission the scientific discovery of the utter rationality of the system and the world. In Habermas' "formalistic" idea of a rational speech community, the simultaneous expansion of and resistance to ideology within marxism comes full circle. We are left, perhaps, with a vast tautology.

The point of this abbreviated survey of recent "developments within Western marxism" is not to torture out yet another exit from the charge that *marxism is just another ideology,* but to suggest that we embrace it. The aporias of current marxist understanding suggest that marxism may no longer be able to "advance" as intellectual history until it recovers forgotten chapters in its past. Like the hermeneutic circle, our ideological situatedness may contain a positive possibility that we cannot constitute as long as we bewail ideology or try to recover a rationality outside it.

That possibility is the reconstruction of an immanent dialectic of experience capable of transcending the opposition between rationalism and relativism. But if that possibility reintroduces the problem of subject, it does so in full recognition that the recent comprehensive extension of the concept of ideology has begotten a crisis in the very idea and experience of subject. As deconstructors argue, the most striking thing about the extension of ideological suspicion to every aspect of experience is the suggestion that one can no longer use "experience" as a term in thought because there is nothing left to which it can refer. It is no longer possible to posit anything outside ideology so as to limit its force or assure an eventual liberation from it. Our task is not to situate or recover the subject, but to dissolve it.[19] But in echoing Lévi-Strauss's scientific ideal one can no longer find refuge in the a priori hypostatization of reason Lévi-Strauss used to formalize and recenter a thought freed of subject. Society is always issuing messages, which I have bought into long before there was any "I" to do the buying. The subject is a language effect, produced by discourse, trapped in the differential and binary logic that dictates our dispersal in a system of signs from which we can never extricate ourselves, that system being itself a product of structures of political and social domination from which there is no exit. Purged of rationalism, self-reflection still appears fatally contaminated by a logic of the proper, or self-presence, and of interpretive closure. The language of the subject and of ego identity may signify no more than nostalgia—or the metaphysical desire to limit and center the impact of experience and history by exorcising the specter of subject's irretrievable abandonment within a field of unconscious forces and linguistic differences. We are the sport of their play rather than the other way around.

If this line of thought sounds too Gallic and "metaphysical," one can find abundant sociological evidence for similar conclusions. Empirical study suggests that when we enter the privacy of consciousness we merely testify to the ubiquity and depth of our social situatedness. And one can supplement this idea by reflecting on all the things that rationalist theories of subject make it impossible for us to consider in any genuinely critical way, all the experiences that the recourse to "subjectivity" protects from scrutiny, and all the complexities that concepts such as ego identity, reality testing, the maturational process, and the achievement of stable object relations suppress while insidiously urging our identification with the social structures they sustain. If Lacan does nothing else, he enables us to see all the ways in which the idea of the ego constitutes a vast system of the imaginary that domesticates Freud's more disruptive discoveries in order to reify our position in the social structure.[20] The language of the self functions, by and large, as a vast defense mechanism that displaces and paralyzes our attention by giving the stamp of self-evidence to those assumptions and beliefs that are most in need of critique. Marx's impact on the question of our being as subjects is thereby held at bay. Rather than take that question upon ourselves, the easier course is to equate the term subject with the bourgeois epoch and find any use of it evidence of archaism or nostalgia.

There is much in this line of thought that I find worthwhile. A preliminary bracketing of subject has strategic value as a methodological, if not ontological, imperative since it focuses our attention on all we tend to ignore about the social determination and positionality of consciousness precisely because the function of theories of subject is to conceal these factors or mitigate their force. Moreover, once we bracket subject we can no longer escape or limit the power of capitalism to dehumanize. No essential humanity, a priori rationality, or personal ego identity comes to deliver us from its force. Bracketing the personal also enhances the practice of self-criticism in many valuable and dialectically connected ways. It is much easier to cast a cold eye on beliefs we stubbornly defended as long as we thought of them as truths of the inner voice or products of self-consciousness. We can now take them as the objects, and not the eternal veracities, of inner struggle. Of even greater importance, it is possible to see their necessary connection with the social structure they sustain. The true nature of that structure, deprived of its most covert and most powerful means of support, begins to emerge. It is possible, in effect, to become pure phenomenologists for the first time—content to describe every cell in the "prison-house."

But once we've carried our work this far, we come again to marxism's endemic crisis. We have canceled ourselves so thoroughly that the struggle for liberation through reflection may no longer have any meaning. With no subject left, we regress, of necessity, to the worst forms of vulgar marxism. Either we await deliverance from above by reinvoking our own form of voodoo economics, reinforced by the notion that we will become free "subjects" only with the collapse of the entire system in which we are so thoroughly enmeshed that our thought corresponds either to its most advanced form (i.e., structuralism) or to the abstract negation of same (poststructuralism). Or we seek out some new utopian principle that will enable us to overturn the whole system through a new practice, such as *écriture féminine*. The faces of contemporary marxism enact a battle for hegemony which has become purely speculative. Abstraction drives us to the necessity of constructing a discourse that is totally outside everything that characterizes the system (logic, language, etc.) because we have regressed, whether we know it or not, to the worst form of speculative idealism—the notion that the revolution can be made within thought alone. We have no choice but to move in this direction because, lacking a subject who is actually engaged in self-critical struggle with the totality of his or her experience, the battle for hegemony can have no other meaning. Nor can the struggle for liberation reach down into the self with the suggestion that self-disgust and a painful confrontation with all one does not want to know about oneself are the sine qua non for self-knowledge and authentic political change.

No doubt the elimination of subject appeals to many precisely because it eliminates the need to look into oneself. Instead, one can simply chart all the ways in which we've been victimized, confident that collective rage (and the refusal to be seduced into self-scrutiny or dialogue) is the new inner voice revealing a romantic self-presence of prodigious utopian powers. Self-knowledge then becomes little more than the battle cry of a "class" trapped in the rhetorically indulgent moment of its initial formation: the abstract need to make everything good the natural property of one's once and future consciousness and to identify everything one hates with the enemy. To complete the process, one need only argue that once consciousness is cleansed and purified of the Fall and its prehistory it will embark, for the first time, on the making of "human" history—or herstory.[21]

Maxim: Liberation always involves the discovery of painful facts about oneself—not simply about one's tormentor. Abstract dialectics are psychologically and aesthetically compelling because they enable us to slough off everything we don't like about ourselves as the product and voice of the enemy. Ideological purity, marxism's shibboleth, is never more inviting than when it delivers us from the need for an in-depth struggle with the minute particulars of our experience. In delivering us from that task, poststructural marxism may, however, have canceled the possibility of genuine liberation.

Marxism uncovers the depth and ubiquity of our historical situatedness. But none of its discoveries need spell the death of subject. What they establish, instead, is a task that is as complex and as personally anguishing as the psychoanalytic task of comprehending and reversing one's relationship to the core conflicts of one's personal history. Like Nietzsche, Marx plays the dangerous game because he challenges us to reflect on all the ways in which our consciousness is socially produced to guarantee our acquiescence in a system of fundamental injustice which we must, on reflection, find intolerable. In doing so, Marx asks us to discover all the ways in which we must find ourselves intolerable. In this sense, existential anxiety is the primary reading effect he produces. As with Nietzsche, one has not begun to read him until one "is profoundly wounded" by everything he says. Whether one is also "profoundly consoled" remains an open question. For the fundamental challenge he sets down is this: can "the instrument"—here the subject—"criticize itself" and reconstitute itself through that act? [22]

The problem Marx poses for a theory of subject and the challenge he poses for the effort any individual must undertake in order to become a subject are the same. The task in both cases is to track down and root out the effects of capitalist ideology in structuring the very inwardness of the subject. This is both the most concrete and the most *totalizing* perspective we can adopt within marxism because a discovery of the ways in which we are socially determined always refers concretely both to the institutions and practices producing that determination and to the actions one must take to reverse the process. It thus identifies both the terms for reflection and the arena of struggle. It also offers an idea we can take as Vergilian guide on our journey: every site of determination is also a site of possible liberation.

While such a perspective on ideology brings it all home, it would be unwise to underestimate the immensity of the task. Ideological formation is a matter of form as much as of content; a determination of the logic structuring thought as much as of the beliefs in which such logic issues. Capitalism triumphs as much in the problems we pose and the ways we pose them as in the kinds of answers we inevitably come up with by following established methodologies. Rooting out capitalism doesn't involve simply checking certain economic imperatives. It requires an exhaustive inquiry into the ways in which, in Foucault's words, individuals are subjected to an array of disciplines and incitements to discourse that complete themselves only when we become subjects and experience ourselves as such along certain definite lines.[23] Our ways of thinking and talking, especially about ourselves, are perhaps so many modes of power and subjection in which we produce an illusion of freedom that shows only how completely we are enchained.

The reconstitution of subject or its dissolution is the basic issue facing marxism today because marxism is necessarily situated within the problem I have been tracing throughout these chapters. My attempt to recapture a theory of subject for marxism is thus an extension of the effort to construct a position that cuts between the "humanist" and deconstructive alternatives. What I hope to show is that the choice is not between Derrida and Habermas, as Perry Anderson makes it appear in an otherwise fine discussion of contemporary marxism.[24] For subject is neither the transcendental architect nor the uninvited guest that must be banished to secure the house of marxism for science, but the situated inhabitant who has not yet found his or her proper home there because we have not yet developed a marxist understanding of situated subjectivity.

THE CONCEPT OF IDEOLOGY: A DIALECTICAL HISTORY

Our goal is to comprehend ideology as the totalization in which we live and move and have our being, to see it as the process that makes the existing social order secure by eliminating all sources of otherness within its subjects. The gradual expansion of the term *ideology* within marxism, so that it now signifies how all areas of everyday life contribute to the production and control of consciousness, constitutes a necessary development of marxism's concern to comprehend the social nature of consciousness and discover the ways in which every aspect of our awareness and our experience is socially determined. There is nothing prior to ideology, no other to the social-rhetorical subject. The ideological process is a totality forming a seamless web of necessary connections which can and must be comprehended as a whole. In the following five sections we will trace the developments that bring the marxist understanding of ideology to this pass.

MARX: IDEOLOGY AS PUBLIC, POLITICAL FRAME OF MIND

Because ideology totalizes itself through practices and institutions that are situated throughout the social order, to understand its working one must transcend the public-private dichotomy. To that end, it may help to imagine the following situation. Picture a society in which ideology is all powerful, but only in the sphere of public political beliefs, a society in which individuals would be free to develop themselves in whatever ways they wished in all other areas of life, constrained only—but with necessity —in this one realm. They would be free to entertain unlimited desires and realize universal human values in their sovereign privacy and in those activities, like art, that have no bearing on politics. We need not look far to find such a view of things; it corresponds to the set of dichotomies dear to those who believe in the autonomous individual, the bourgeois subject. This is why that concept and the methodological framework sustaining it deserve to be called the ideological formation par excellence, and why it is the main thing marxism must undermine. To do so, however, we must go far beyond Marx's understanding of ideology. We can best measure the distance by seeing just where a rigorous interpretation of Marx's canonical texts on ideology leaves us.

Such an interpretation has recently been offered by James McMurtry in *The Structure of Marx's World-View*.[25] McMurtry defines ideology as a "public frame of mind" composed of that set of core assumptions, beliefs, and commonplaces that structure thought about our sociopolitical world in a way that both validates the established social order and invalidates whatever challenges it in any fundamental way. Ideology concerns public conceptions about the nature of human affairs that are publicly formulated and subject to state control. Accordingly, Marx's thought about ideology focuses on relations among the economy, the state, and the use of legal right as a stand-in for power. Ideology shapes the understanding of our political-social world in a way that leads us to see it, and our place in it, as a result of unalterable ahistorical truths grounded in human nature. Ideological concepts function as empty generalities that shift attention from specific to general issues. These generalities are then selectively employed to legitimize the established social order and invalidate alternatives. By referring to the past and to unalterable universals of human nature, these generalities mystify the present state of affairs and give it an attractive, affirmative guise. The basic function of all such operations is to deflect attention from the actual character of the ruling economic order. Ideology thus relates more to inaction than to action; its function is to protect the ruling order from change either by concealing it or by making it appear eternal and unchangeable, a direct result of unalterable human nature. All essentialistic concepts of human nature have this as their underlying purpose.

After discussing this general concept, McMurtry shows that Marx's special concern is with that part of ideology that controls and determines social consciousness. He terms it "the public frame of mind."[26] In the bourgeois-capitalist period this consciousness is constituted by the following "beliefs": (1) the existing social order is morally good; (2) it cannot be qualitatively altered; (3) what promotes it is good; (4) what does not comply with it is bad; (5) the rank held by individuals in the social order represents their intrinsic worth; (6) the social order represents the interests of all in the society; (7) a part of society must always represent the whole of society (i.e., there must be a ruling class); (8) the social property of the ruling class is an independent, self-moving power (i.e., capital creates jobs, etc.); and, as capstone to the whole thing, (9) ultimate social agency resides in a nonhuman entity—God/Gold, the Invisible Hand—which sets the limit that puts an end to all inquiries.

Such beliefs are rarely articulated, but they form the deep structure determining the more colorful opinions that circulate in public forums (barrooms, town meetings, the media). There is nothing in the concept of ideology that assumes people must be conscious of such basic beliefs for them to determine their attitudes or activities; nor is it suggested that subjects arrive at such structures of living as a result of some quasi-deliberative process that necessarily takes place in consciousness.[27] On the contrary, ideology is the thought that structures our thought without passing through our consciousness. It works as tacit assumptions that simply operate everywhere with the status, more or less, of that which goes without saying. The underlying assumption set in place by the totality of operations constituting ideology is that the existing social order is both good and unchangeable: if one of these characteristics is attacked the other comes into play.

McMurtry gives us a powerful conception of ideology, and if the marxist exercise of suspicion had achieved no more than this critique, it would constitute a major force in destabilizing traditional conceptions of consciousness. But keeping ideology so focused is also convenient because it leaves many things off the agenda. Keeping them off generates, in turn, the series of contradictions that structure the history of marxist thought on ideology. Invited to imagine all the things that are not part of ideology, one can posit an order of thought outside it (reason, philosophy, science)[28] or find innumerable sites where consciousness and experience are free of it (the class consciousness of the proletariat, art and culture, the natural relations of the family, the humanistic subject).[29] The base-superstructure distinction, or some variant, can then be used to blow away the whole edifice of ideology by invoking the marxist equivalent of magical thinking: economic determinism. False bourgeois consciousness can be opposed to a correct marxist consciousness, the latter identified with a priori reason, universal pragmatics, or autonomous science.[30] Or class reductionism can be used to argue and guarantee that the consciousness of the proletariat (or some other group) is necessarily liberated.[31] If none of these operations work, one can rise above ideology entirely by discovering that utopian force in our midst that is pristine and forever free, in principle, from ideological taint: the law of the heart, the orgasm, schizophrenic desire, *écriture féminine,* etc.[32] As the above indicates, the contradictions that structure the tangled history of marxism derive from a desire to limit or transcend Marx's most basic discovery—ideology.

There is, of course, an important sense in which the political dimension of ideology on which Marx focused will always remain the most important, since the overall function of ideology is to produce acquiescence in the status quo—or paralysis before history. But political formation has no autonomy because it can't be separated from the production of consciousness in general. If it could, we could easily place ourselves outside it or find the otherness enabling us to oppose it. Consensus and legitimation would remain precarious rather than being what they now are—virtually automatic.

LUKÁCS: PHILOSOPHY AS/OF IDEOLOGY—IDEOLOGY AS CRITIQUE OF REASON

There is no way the concept of ideology can be developed without calling into question the assumptions one uses to limit or control the range of its reference. The development of the concept thus leads inevitably to a crisis in which philosophy is implicated. One of the most significant expansions of ideological understanding took place, in fact, when Lukács made the critique of Kantian philosophy the center of *History and Class Consciousness.* In doing so, Lukács recaptured all that was most vital in Hegel's convoluted effort to establish a correspondence between the contradictions in attitudes and worldviews (stoicism, the law of the heart, virtue and the course of the world, the community of animals, etc.) and the contradictions in the historical situation they "reflect."[33] (I cannot here recapitulate the details of Lukács's consistently brilliant discussion. My concern is simply to formulate its methodological implications for an ideological understanding of philosophy and for the attempt to preserve, for marxism, a nonideological conception of critical thought.)

As Lukács sees, the study of ideology is, in a sense, the marxist substitute for philosophy; one of its richest implications is to bring philosophy down from its traditional self-image as pure, objective, disinterested, ahistorical speculation by demonstrating the thoroughness of its connection with particular sociohistorical situations. Lukács is not out to show just that philosophy is a species of apologetics. His effort is to show that philosophy has motives—many of which it has carefully concealed from itself—and that these motives tie it much more intimately to historical situations than has been apparent. Concealing one's motives may, in fact, be *the* philosophic motive.

The reason this connection escapes us is that in philosophy motives generally take the form of contradictions and conceptual dilemmas. But no matter how rarefied, the philosopher thinks within a certain experience of the world, and the structure of his thought corresponds to certain definite features of his sociohistorical situation. Though uncanny, the connections are often striking, as Lukács shows in demonstrating how the paralogisms and antinomies of Kantian Reason correspond to the inability of the capitalist subject to resist commodification, while the unknowability of the *Ding-an-sich* plays in Kant's system a capping function similar to the invisible hand of classical economics. In presenting as eternal what is really historical (as do Plato and Adam Smith), or in setting the limits beyond which thought cannot go (and this, since Kant, has been the primary philosophic act), philosophy supplements the primary function of ideology by leading us to adopt a passive and contemplative view of the given. The stamp of the actual, the necessary, the categorical has a wonderful way of putting an end both to thought and to praxis.

To grasp the full significance of these operations, we need to take a further step that is only implicit in Lukács. The basic function philosophy performs is to determine subject's relationship to itself. It does so by establishing the concept subjects form of their identity which, in turn, organizes their relationship to their experience. Offering such a concept is perhaps the cardinal motive behind any philosophy and the source of its deepest appeal. In fixing a self-image for us, a philosophy establishes the basic "set" we bring to all activities and perceptions. It thereby determines not only the assumptions whereby we can know certain things but, more important, the rules of exclusion that blind us to others. Further down the line, it thereby also sets the assumptions that control what gets institutionalized as meaningful activity in the pedagogies and lines of research that organize different disciplines. The point, I hasten to add, is not that philosophy is on the throne directing abstract Hegelian history, but that it's implicated in sociohistorical affairs from which it cannot extricate itself.

Any philosophy sends forth as perhaps its most significant message a conception of the nature of our subjectivity. This is so because every philosophy expresses some particular relationship it is possible for us to live toward our subjectivity. That expression, in turn, reflects a particular historical situation. As we'll see, the contradictions of the former correspond to and mirror the contradictions of the latter.

Concepts of subject, in fact, give us one of the clearest pictures of a historical situation because of the purity with which they express its contradictory imperatives. Philosophy is not simply the poverty of false consciousness, but the contradictory and self-revelatory effort of an unhappy consciousness to identify itself with one self-image in order to marginalize or control another. Insofar as it remains contemplative, philosophy is implicated in this contradiction. By offering us a concept of subjectivity that substantializes us, it carries that contradiction into the realm of self-reification. Accordingly, the marxist task becomes one of reading philosophy so as to liberate its repressed content. The goal is not to see what a philosophy enables us to say about our experience, but what it makes it impossible for us to say and know. Such a reading of philosophic texts forces the motives behind a particular philosophic self-image to reveal themselves and the underlying anxieties and contradictions that image is designed to exorcise. Its motive is present in the philosophic text as a scar in the center of the very concepts formulated to repress it. The purpose of such a reading is to uncover history as it exists for a conflicted subject engaged in the effort to mediate historical contradiction through recourse to thought. Tracing this circle reveals philosophy's roots in the social process, and that is where the ideological formations philosophy "reflects" have their objective correlative in historical situations that the philosopher wants to protect, avoid, or overcome.

Once a philosophic framework is firmly in place, the connections between it and the social practices directly formative of consciousness become pervasive because philosophy establishes an image of what is intelligible, proper, normal, "that which goes without saying." This image controls what can be thought in certain institutions (the university, jurisprudence in the climate of legal positivism, etc.) as well as what filters down through the ministrations of other institutions (the mental health professions) to form the way in which people make sense of their lives and police their experience in order to bring it into line with the ruling order. Formed by such practices, subjects attain maturity through systematic education in how to misinterpret or lie about their experience. For ideology to work, everything must be internalized; the total system of internalizations constitutes both the possibility and the limits of subject's experience. Whether philosophy is the capstone or merely one of the planks in the process isn't finally that important—since this will be largely a question of its importance for different "individuals."

What is important is to see that the connections ideological investigation uncovers are central to the practice and the reception of philosophy. That recognition not only eliminates philosophy's pretensions to transcendence; it restores philosophy as a genuine area of ideological struggle. Moreover, since philosophy is the glue, the deep structure, that holds so many things together, its critique has ramifications that open up numerous areas of struggle. Each time one exposes the contradictions in a particular concept of subject, one regains countless experiential possibilities. For critique shows how the discredited concept has structured situations that could be interpreted and lived quite differently. Since ideology primarily determines what won't be thought or experienced, critique always entails the possibility of experiential recoveries. Leaving that prospect aside for the moment, we can conclude this phase of the investigation with a recognition that may be even more liberating. Philosophic struggle is not a waste of time on ghostly movements within an epiphenomenal "superstructure." It is an essential act and enables us to overcome a dichotomy that has been the source of some of the sorriest developments in the marxist study of ideology—the base-superstructure distinction. Once that dichotomy and the economic reductionism that underlies it are gone, marxism moves, of necessity, to a much richer and broader understanding of ideology than Marx was able to achieve. Gramsci's concept of hegemony provides the best articulation of that movement.

GRAMSCI: IDEOLOGY AS THE FORMATION OF CONSCIOUSNESS

Hegemony

The concept of hegemony interrelates the battles for political, cultural, and popular dominance by bringing together ideology and the task of historical struggle in a way that refuses to limit the arena of struggle or import any of the old guarantees. Much that was thought insignificant and epiphenomenal by a more dogmatic and reductive marxism reveals itself from the perspective of hegemony as essential. This is especially true of cultural struggle and the battle for control of the institutions disseminating education (family, church, school, etc.). As Gramsci sees it, the task of any ruling order, required if it is to create the conditions necessary for its reproduction, is to create a "popular religion" and a "collective will." These terms may suggest too much of the idealist tradition, but Gramsci's effort in using them to define hegemony is to get us beyond three reductions that have dogged marxism: (1) economism as sole cause; (2) the base-superstructure distinction used reductively to explain away thought and culture; and (3) class reductionism as the sole principle used to account for both the formation of consciousness and the entire process of social living. Economics may be determinative in the last instance, and class consciousness may be the most important awareness we can work to produce, but neither is automatic or guaranteed, except for abstract deductive Hegelians.

Class consciousness is a wonderful thing. But it is not necessary, nor does it account for either the immediate unity or the totality of consciousness. Lukács made it all these things so that it could become the deus ex machina for his progressive theory of history with its imminent *parousia,* in proletarian consciousness, of the identical subject-object. Preserving that guarantee of the imminence of the subject-object forced Lukács to exclude from his account of consciousness everything not readily assimilable to the subject-object; i.e., psychoanalysis, existentialism, modern writers.

According to Gramsci, until we wage the battle for cultural hegemony, economic crises will remain temporary (i.e., the staying power of late capitalism will remain a puzzle) and the call for revolution sporadic, because until we create a much broader kind of revolutionary consciousness, real change cannot occur. To do so, we need to reformulate Marx's notion that circumstances make consciousness. Circumstances impose their imperatives upon us only after we have overcome the ideological formations that blind us to them—or that persuade us to sacrifice our "economic" awareness to our ideological need. (This is why those who should know at some level of their "class" consciousness that Reagan is not in their best interests remain hot for the glut of "superstructural" celebration he offers.) Economism and class reductionism have had a deleterious effect on marxist praxis because their deterministic invocation blinds us to the concrete circumstances that must be supplanted before they can come into being as genuine forces. Class-consciousness is an achievement because the "perception" of one's economic interests remains fitful until one roots out the internalized formations that prevent one from constituting oneself a member of a vanguard or emergent class.

The concept of hegemony attempts the substantial revision in the concept of class consciousness required to articulate that struggle. Hegemony refers to the process whereby any "class" (ruling or still in formation) tries to become universal by creating a union of political, intellectual, and moral leadership.[34] This union is complete only when it attains the status of a "popular religion" that both animates the individual consciousness and holds the allegiance of all "groups" in the society. The consensus thus established is not a sullen obedience to force (police power), but has the status of a "collective will." The struggle for hegemony might be regarded as the creation of the conditions whereby one and all say "Yes" to the society.

There are problematic traces of idealism, romanticism, and nationalism in this concept, but one of its first implications is that Reagan, Falwell, and the liberal press really matter. They aren't engaged in some "superstructural" game we can regard with comparative indifference because we know it will all be swept away, leaving nary a trace in consciousness, when economics presents the bill. They are engaged in an absolutely essential process: the formation of mass consciousness. The secret they know—and it is high time marxism learned and theorized it—is that in order to win, one must descend to the rhetoric of the tribe and fill "hearts" as well as minds, not with political commonplaces, but with symbols and "myths" and a narrative paradigm capable of guiding and interpreting individual and collective experience.[35] One of Gramsci's most challenging assertions is that we will never seize or maintain power until we have *won* the "ideological" battle for hegemony.

For Gramsci, hegemony is a concept that applies both to the practices of the ruling class and to the task of those laboring to create the consciousness of the oppressed. And, for Gramsci, both processes are constant because ideology isn't free-floating, but has an institutional, material existence. It comes to be through definite practices, each of which has a relative autonomy.[36] That is why each arena of ideological formation can and must be made the site of a distinct form of struggle. This line of thought is liberating because it legitimates and dignifies all struggles, even the struggles of us who labor in the groves of academe. Economics isn't the whole ballgame, and we have no excuse to wait around for it to resolve everything. What we do or fail to do really matters. That bracing recognition has as its correlative an imperative—that we take on that struggle in every aspect of our daily professional existence. Struggle is constant because, as Gramsci shows, ideology is realized in practices that are literally everywhere, systematic and superfluous. Once we get beyond intellectualist conceptions of what socialization entails, we face the prospect of an endless uncovering of assumptions and practices we must challenge because we now see their function in sustaining the social order. Like Salieri's mediocrity, ideology is everywhere because social formation creates the unreflected "yes" of beliefs and perceptions that can't be questioned because they form the lived assumptions or *Lebenswelt* that prestructures everyday life. When their coincidence with the socialized subject becomes total, reification takes command.

Because ideology is everywhere, a new understanding of totalization is necessary. Particular struggles within any one of the "relatively autonomous" sites of ideological formation must lead to an understanding of how that arena relates to the social process as a whole since that is the final object both of study and of struggle. Marxism is a dialectical philosophy, and its object must always be the discovery of totalizing connections. Without lapsing into formalism, idealism, or what Althusser calls "expressive causality," [37] we must, to achieve hegemony, coordinate our understanding of different sites in a way that enables us to see the common direction that informs their contribution to the formation of consciousness. Developing this line of thought constitutes for social theory a modern equivalent of the Platonic notion that the dialectician is he who discovers the necessary connections among things. Thus, the more specific one makes the study of a particular site—educational practices, say—the more apparent it becomes that the educational system functions as a whole to prepare our insertion as docile subjects into what Lefevbre terms a "bureaucratic [and technocratic] society of controlled consumption." [38] Hegemony is the true struggle for power, because power, for Gramsci (anticipating Foucault), is not localized in repressive state apparatuses but diffused throughout society. It operates as much in the "incitement to discourse" and the ways we are taught to talk (about literature, philosophy, experience, etc.) as in the general drudgery enforced to anesthetize us in our leisure.

If we are to get what Gramsci is driving at, his work needs the kind of supplement Kenneth Burke provides. Gramsci's discussion of collective consciousness remains vague, romantic, and at times dangerously close to fascist formations. Burke offers a far more concrete theory of the self as a product of social interaction because he turns quite explicitly to literature for his sociological categories. The self for Burke is a system of attitudes and motives, not ideas. Attitudes and motives are tied, in turn, to the symbols and symbolic actions that establish the dramatic paradigms through which we interpret experience. Changing people's minds—and actions—is largely a matter of changing the a prioris of their dramatic agency.[39] The main reason marxism has failed to move in this direction is its persistence in its own version of the rationalist tradition. In studying ideology we have made ideas and commonplaces the primary forces in consciousness, when in most cases ideas are merely the afterimage of far more primary processes. This error also accounts for the failure of our praxis. Gains made by addressing the pragmatic intelligence and interests of the oppressed so often prove temporary because our rhetoric doesn't reach down into the roots of consciousness. Once the immediate issue is past—Vietnam, say—"radical" consciousness lapses, and everything that was left untouched reasserts control. We end up, not surprisingly, where we began—with the apathy of the 1950s now secured as the key to yuppie success.

The Social Self

Hegemony is the process through which a ruling class *totalizes* itself by producing its image, and the conditions of its replication, everywhere as that which is immediate, self-evident, natural, orderly, good, and intelligible in both inner and external reality. Its proudest product is the inwardness of subjects.

To comprehend the social nature of the self, the main ideological formation we must break down is the opposition between atomistic individualism and social determinism. Perhaps the primary act of capitalist ideology in structuring the logic of thought is to keep us trapped in this dichotomy. On the one hand, we are offered a self that is both prior to the social and always in some way independent of it, with individuality seen as a unique center of personal choice, and as such, an ultimate value. On the other hand, we are taught that failure to maintain such a self will leave us with nothing but the collective "they," the generalized other, the *Massenmensch* powerless to be anything else. The irony is that the two concepts stand in perfect abstract correspondence, a result of their hidden identity and complicity in mirroring the "truth" of modern society.

The dialectical transcendence of such dichotomies depends on referring concepts of subject to the social structure to which they correspond. The way we conceive and experience our subjectivity is not an isolated matter but a prime index of the social structure that has produced this particular form of self-reference as the one most conducive to its functioning. Solipsistic American individualism thus serves as one of the clearest signs of an advanced form of collectivism, its pseudopermissiveness revealing how completely an impersonal and valueless society of controlled consumption has succeeded in totalizing itself. That social order is now so solidly in place that the experience of subjectivity as self-indulgence in random opinions, needing no defense and beyond any possibility of self-criticism, has become the *dominant* way in which people relate to themselves. A subjectivity that so conceals the public, shared, and wholly derivate nature of its inwardness is powerless to experience itself except in terms of the greatest self-complacency. The secret it must hide from itself is its absolute correspondence to the reifications of the social order that has produced it. If a society must reproduce the relations of production in order to sustain itself, the subjectivizing of experience is capitalism's innermost need. Its proudest product is the modern mass subject that experiences its precious individuality as a totally arbitrary principle which it lives and loves, consumerlike, but is powerless to change or understand in any depth. Incited to opinions and kept at a certain blind emotional pitch about them, such a subject is prevented from any genuine alienation and from any discovery of inner otherness as an opacity it must overcome. Atomistic individuality is, indeed, one end of the dialectic, its cardiac arrest. The modern experience of individuality corresponds to a historical situation in which the social order has taken on the character of what Hegel calls "a community of animals."[40] Each atom is out for number one, with nothing binding it to other atoms beyond naked self-interest. The relationships we live to ourselves (self-indulgent whim) and to the other (immediate advantage) stand in perfect correspondence with the social order and offer a demystified understanding of it. Once we start making such connections, the dichotomy of individualism-collectivism collapses, for we see both concepts as opposite sides of a common paralysis.

But to recapture the concrete life of subject, far more than tinkering with binaries is needed. As many readers have no doubt been itching to remind me, the scope of socialization calls the very idea of the subject into question. Once we see ideology as the process through which one acquires consciousness in the first place—and is disciplined in it ever afterward —it is hard to think of subject as anything but a fallacy of misplaced concreteness.

Though this reminder reintroduces pessimistic prospects well worth preserving, the value of Gramsci for our inquiry is that he points toward the possibility of conceiving subject without either humanistic guarantees or sociological reductionism.[41] With Gramsci, the distinction between false, or ideological, consciousness and correct, or scientific, consciousness starts to dissolve. On the one hand, Gramsci shows that we are not somehow already liberated, needing only to commune with rationality, communicative universals, or our true feelings in order to shed the husk of ideology as the shell covering a pristine self. On the other hand, Gramsci does not eliminate the subject or see it as a mere effect of the social structure. Instead, he conceives subject wholly within the terms of its situatedness. He thereby offers the possibility of developing a specifically marxist contribution to the understanding of situated subjectivity.

To develop this theory we need, once again, to transcend the framework which traps us in false alternatives. Because ideology refers to the production of consciousness in general—and not just to political ideas or a public frame of mind—one can no longer oppose false consciousness to a correct consciousness that can be identified with rationality or attained by simply thinking. Nor is it possible to sustain the equally abstract, though more romantic, notion that we are free in the privacy of our feelings and can attain liberation through an inner colloquy with our true self. Ideology is the process of social formation in general, prior to which consciousness simply is not.

To avoid sociological reductionism, however, we must resist blanket endorsements of the popular conclusion that has been derived from such perceptions. Rather than eliminate subject, we must rethink it. In doing so, it isn't enough just to show the ways in which traditional theories of subject are ideologically determined. We also need to confront a possible aporia of reflection. For our task is not simply to root out ideology. We also need to root out the ways in which rooting out is an ideologically controlled practice. Does this complication entail an impossible situation? Will not each corridor we open through reflection merely show us another way in which we are already imprisoned? Is the act of reflection itself perhaps the main sign and exercise of our imprisonment? It is inviting to seize the obvious—the reflection that should put an end to reflection—by proclaiming that any and every language of reflection is fatally contaminated with assumptions that make it little more than the metaphysical apologetics of capitalist ideology. Though this deconstruction of subject has a somewhat formalistic smell—the game of employing ideology as the garbage can into which one throws everything that has been thought and felt prior to the grand moment of one's own utterance —it also has the look of an irresistible operation that will persist until the language of subjectivity reconstitutes itself by undertaking its own critique. The beginning of that effort must lie in the recognition that ideological thrownness is primary and may be irreversible. Consciousness

contains no principle of independent thought assuring it of subjective autonomy. Social situatedness is prior to everything else and totalizing in
its effects. The question, in fact, is whether self-consciousness is possible
at all.

Developing that possibility depends on establishing the conditions
for subject's experiential emergence. It requires, in short, a specifically
marxist theory of existent reflection that will situate self-consciousness by
showing that it is no more than a particular modification of our historical situatedness, utterly defined by that to which it refers. Recognizing
the priority of the social in subject's internal constitution yet establishing
the possibility of subject's experiential liberation entails, within a marxist
framework, the notion that self-consciousness is that particular awareness or modification of the social that is constituted by negativity; it is
the moment in which society submits to critical reflection on itself. That
act does not derive from some a priori autonomy of reflection, but requires disorder within the social for its emergence. Reflection comes into
being when one is arrested by conflicts and contradictions that cannot be
resolved without a transformation both of oneself and of one's relation
to the given. Without conflict and contradiction, there is no motive for
reflection. And reflection, so understood, is the initial way in which struggle is waged. Negativity within the concrete reference of its situatedness
defines it.

ALTHUSSER AND BARTHES: IDEOLOGY AS THE
INTERPELLATION OF SUBJECTS

But positing existent reflection as a power implicit in consciousness
that cannot be eradicated may be the ultimate act of self-mystification.
The greatest triumph of ideology may lie in producing and predetermin-
ing what goes on when we engage in reflection. Any attempt to affirm
reflection is complicated by the fact that there is a language and grammar
of reflection which structures that process along certain channels from
which we can perhaps never extricate ourselves yet which make reflection's conclusions so many examples of either self-mystification or aporia.
Reproducing in reflection the conditions of one's reification while thinking oneself engaged in producing one's autonomy may be the deepest bite
ideology takes into the subject.

But, if this is so, it is because reflection is the crucial formation
ideology needs in order to complete and secure a regulation that will
extend from everyday consciousness through the ultimate reaches of self-

consciousness. Reflection controlled, the reification of subject is assured. Self-consciousness becomes an ironic and unconscious parody of the very struggle for liberation it takes as its goal. Yet it is at precisely this extreme that a dialectical turn of the coin suggests the possibility of a striking reversal. Just as each site of determination reveals a potential source of resistance, the final site where all determinations complete themselves remains contested terrain. Ideology must conquer reflection because reflection poses the greatest threat to the apparent solidity of the practices regulating all the other sites.

Althusser provides the richest framework within marxism for posing this possibility because he mounts the strongest attack on it. In eliminating subject entirely, he identifies all we must overcome in order to reconstitute it. Althusser's willingness to take the line of thought on ideology we've been developing to its experiential and logical conclusion generates his most challenging concept: ideology, for Althusser, forms "the natural attitude" and constitutes the very inwardness of subjects who are interpellated and produced qua subjects as the end result of its operations.[42] Ideology comprehends the totality of "representations" that, as *Lebenswelt,* shape everyday life and determine the phenomenology of perception. There is no unmediated moment in experience. Ideology is not something that befalls a subject, but the originary process that produces subjectivity itself. Our ideological subjection is, in fact, overdetermined because ideology is constantly at work in a superfluity of practices and institutions, each with a relative autonomy as a distinct site of formation and struggle, yet composing, with all the others, a total system that produces and inhabits us rather than the other way around.

Developing this perspective enables Althusser to unmask the ideological factors underlying a number of conceptions of subject. Among his favorite targets are the autonomous subject, the humanist theory of man, and the discourse of the imaginary. Althusser holds that the primary act of ideological interpellation is to fix "individuals" in place as subjects for a certain "meaning."[43] The creation of subject in and through discourse (i.e., in philosophic systems, literary representations, psychological theories, etc.) produces a subjectivity subjected to certain meanings and explanatory paradigms which control the relationship individuals form to their experience. This is the most significant ideological operation because its function is to close the subject off from the perception and movement of contradictions.

For Althusser, the goal of ideology is to produce the consciousness of the human subject. There is nothing free-floating about this process because ideology requires and has a real material existence.[44] It is located in those rituals[45] and institutions of communication that have as their common task the production of consciousness, such as the church, the family, the educational system, and the communications media. As Marx teaches —and this *is* dogma—a social order survives only if it reproduces its economic conditions. The function of ideology is to secure this reproduction by inducing those who are subjected to the system to adopt an *imaginary* or false relationship to the actual historical conditions of their existence.[46] Ideology thereby supplements state power and the agencies that enforce it (police, law, asylums, etc.). In fact, it would be more accurate to say that the institutions that secure power through force are the supplements, since their function is to fill the breach whenever or wherever ideological consensus breaks down.[47]

Althusser was not simply imitating Lacan when he made his most famous statement: "Ideology has no history."[48] For the statement refers to far more than the fact that ideology blinds us to history in order to preserve the status quo and the relations of production from revolutionary change. The larger reference is to how this function is secured by the traditional conception of philosophy and culture as the search for those ahistorical universals which alone provide the true object and content of thought. Ideology (as philosophy, literature, cultural theory) universalizes beliefs, ideas, feelings, and commonplaces that are actually historical by presenting as unchanging essences, rooted in nature, what are really the products of contingent historical situations. Ideology thereby carries out its grandest function, which is not simply to arrest history but to deny the subject's radical situatedness in it. In developing this insight, Althusser takes the political dimension of ideology that McMurtry conceptualized and shows that in order to secure it ideology must undertake the larger tasks McMurtry excludes from it. No public political frame of mind exists until the privacy proper to it has been formed.

That is why the primary operation of ideology consists in the organization of "individuals" into "subjects." The key to understanding any ideological phenomenon, from the rankest advertisement to the subtlest conceptualization, is to see that all ideology is subject-centered. The purpose of any and all ideological operations is to create both the content and the operations that will determine the inwardness, identity, and self-consciousness of those who are hailed or interpellated by them. As Kenneth Burke argues, ideology must be conceptualized as a vast rhetorical system. The attitudes, beliefs, feelings, and especially the literary paradigms, that I discover when I reflect on myself are so many myths and commonplaces, which regulate my consciousness by leading me to regard as true, originary, and self-present what is no more than an *imaginary* relationship to my experience. Personal identity is largely a product of following the conventions and rules of discourse I have been taught to employ in constituting myself as a subject.

Ideology may thus be most meaningfully defined as a representation of the imaginary relationship of individuals to their real conditions of existence. Among its most important cultural formations are the discursive protocols of philosophy and the narrative paradigms of literature. The primary object of a marxist reading of such texts must accordingly be to produce what they suppress; history being the "absent cause" which these structures reveal in their very effort to conceal.[49] Once ideology has done its work, our situatedness takes this form: assumed as "true," the imaginary constitutes the way people live their lives and how they reflect on them. The Althusserian "subject" is a rigorous equivalent of Marcuse's one-dimensionality. It presents the system of late capitalism as entirely self-contained and totalizing in its effects.

But if Althusser's expansion of the concept expresses the contemporary truth of ideology, it is not because Althusser comes at the end of some purely theoretical history. On the contrary, the conceptual expansion we have traced is *necessary* because it reflects a historical process and direction which will attain completion only when ideology has secured its totalizing power over the life of subject. The history of ideology is thus the palimpsest in which we read the history of the modern world. This is what the Grand Inquisitor already knew and why an ahistorical formalism proclaiming the "death of subject" finds itself in such perfect correspondence to the contemporary world.

Through the study of this topic, Roland Barthes supplements Althusser in a way that makes ideological investigation the necessary propaedeutic to any attempt to rehabilitate reflection. Barthes is an important figure because he historicizes structuralism's contribution to "the exercise of suspicion" by applying its ahistorical methods to everyday life. His semiotic investigations debunk the myth that immediacy and everyday life are realms impervious to the force of ideology from which a liberated or autonomous consciousness could be derived.[50] As Barthes shows, *the situatedness of everyday life is a situatedness in ideology*. That demonstration revitalizes, rather than refutes, phenomenology and existentialism by

purging them of the residual romanticism lurking in the desire for pure
descriptions and unmediated experience. Everyday life is a dense and vast
forest of signs which position us rather than the other way around. We
are continually bathed in ideology, and, finding ourselves in the midst
of messages/massages, most of us never escape Lotusland. As Barthes
shows, the beach to which we flee is dense with social signs. The surface
of everyday life is, in fact, a primary field of ideological formation, for,
as Barthes shows, the secret of ideology (or what he calls myth) is that
it lacks depth. Ideology is constituted by taking the commonplace, the
already thought, and extending it by superimposing it on new instances.
The historical thereby takes on the appearance of the natural, and everything is seen as so self-evidently true that "it goes without saying." The
function of such processes is to reduce everything to the surface while
convincing us that the surface has depth. Ideology isn't a deep meaning
but a surface meaning—or nonmeaning. Its function is to map the ways
we think so that no thinking can occur.

Barthes saw that the value of structuralism and semiotics for marxism lay in enabling us to describe the ways in which ideology is everywhere, forming our hearts and minds totally *without ever passing through
our consciousness.* This insight is one of the sources of "the death of subject" argument, but its implications may be a good deal more complex.
Barthes's semiotic displacement of the rational, autonomous, deliberative
subject gives us another major insight into the nature of our situatedness.
Reflection can no longer be conceived of as a process in which we stand
back and rationally assess the ideas, beliefs, and commonplaces society
presents for our free deliberation. To get anywhere, reflection must direct
itself to the logic of the structure. Its new object is the understanding
of that which controls thought without ever having been thought, without ever having passed through or presented itself to consciousness. We
must delve into our inwardness in search of an otherness we didn't know
was there because its way of being there was not as a content or belief
but as the structure constituting what we took as the immediacy of our
experience.[51]

In terms of our inquiry, the most significant way in which such a
"structural unconscious" operates is by establishing the formal principles
that control the logic of thinking. As the "deep structure" of mind, this
framework underlies and determines the rules and procedures one has
internalized in order to produce both the idea and the experience of one's
identity as a subject. The battle with ideology would be fairly simple if

we internalized only contents. But we don't. We internalize structures and rules, which control our thought and our experience without ever having been articulated or requiring articulation. Getting at them is, in fact, as difficult as getting at the personal, Freudian unconscious; and in many ways the resistance is both stronger and subtler.

While Lévi-Strauss ends with the Kantian formalization of such structures as universal a prioris of language and mind, Barthes's concrete studies suggest the possibility of developing a genuinely poststructural concept of reflection. Structure isn't what is unthought finally, but what is unthought initially. Its articulation is the first order of business—a sine qua non for reflection—because only through that act does the "structuralist unconscious" become an object accessible to critique. As with the Freudian unconscious, the fact that it is initially unconscious does not mean it must remain so. Becoming the self-consciousness of this structure depends, however, on taking the history of ideology a final step by constituting the concept of existent reflection implicit in it.

RETRIEVING SUBJECT: IDEOLOGY AND EXISTENT REFLECTION

Althusser's refutation of Hegelian expressive causality creates the possibility of studying the relatively autonomous sites of ideological interpellation as distinct arenas of contradiction and potential resistance. Gramsci's rejection of economism and the reductive use of class consciousness to provide a total account of the formation of consciousness points in the same direction. Different sites must be comprehended in terms of both the contradictions specific to them and the kind of struggles those contradictions make possible. Discovering the different places where consciousness is determined reveals the experiential contexts where the contradictions of that situatedness can be felt, articulated, and resisted.

The great and inadvertent value of Althusser's attack on expressive causality is that it clears the way for an independent and in-depth study of many neglected phenomena. It does so by putting an end to all reductionism, whether of mind or of matter. It is no longer possible to posit one principle—the economic, class, *Geist*—and use it to explain everything. Vulgar marxism is seen for what it is: dogmatic, a priori, deductive reasoning from abstract dichotomies. But Althusser no sooner opens things up than he formalizes and closes them down through his scientistic concept of structural causality, unless, that is, we develop the "structuralist" idea of "a cause that is immanent in its effects" quite differently than Althusser does.

Contradiction remains the forgotten category that liberates Althusser's richer possibilities. Once "expressive causality" is rejected, the true complexities of a historical situation stand forth because there is no longer any way to limit contradictions or to coordinate them deductively in terms of a single dominant one. Contradiction, not spirit, becomes the main category for comprehending our social situatedness because it directs attention to conflicts and experiences that cannot be sublated in any purely speculative dialectic. There are many different kinds and sites of contradiction; and though contradictions are related, their relationship is not one of simple coordination, nor does one subsume all others.

One of the things implied by the concept of relative autonomy is that many different "needs" have to be met in order to produce the interpellation of subjects. That is one of the reasons why ideology cannot be free-floating but must be realized in numerous practices and institutions. Independent examination of the different ideological state apparatuses is important both for developing a "pluralistic" understanding of how ideology operates and for establishing the tactics and possibilities of struggle in distinct arenas. The mistake of all dogmatic marxisms is the notion that there is only one proper or primary arena of struggle. This view is sustained by the reductive belief in a single *cause* of history; its most deleterious effect is the belief that there is only one way—organizing the workers—to constitute one's marxism.

What Gramsci, Althusser, Burke, and others enable us to see is that struggle is everywhere and that all struggles matter. The sites of potential liberation—or of irretrievable loss—are many. Totality—and a totalizing consciousness—is the last thing we get to, not the first.[52] The interpellation of subjects is a ubiquitous process because ideology is a pressure constantly at work in all the ways we think, perceive the world, and struggle through the heart's intermittencies. Getting at ideology requires no extensive search. The problem, rather, is that ideology is everywhere.

Thus, all our struggles bring us home to our primary one. If the task of ideology is to create the very inwardness of subjects, then it in our own inwardness that we must track ideology down and root it out. But we cannot even begin to do so as long as we continue to think, with Althusser, that "science" is the other to ideology and offers a definitive way to overcome any further need for a concept of subject.

The unintended legacy of Althusser's understanding of ideology is not the death of subject but its recovery as a major issue on the agenda of marxism. The fact that the ideological bathing of consciousness produces effects that are ubiquitous and control thought even though they never pass directly through a deliberative consciousness does not mean that such processes can't be made the object of reflection. To think so prematurely arrests the dialectic of one's thought. To paraphrase Barthes's notion that a little structuralism leads one away from history but a lot leads one back, we can say that a little sociology leads one away from subject but a lot leads one back because it brings home our social situatedness, the otherness of the "self" to itself, as an experience of imprisonment that must be resisted.

My effort is to restore this dimension to marxism by mapping those sites and possibilities of contradiction and negation that can be located in the subject, given the way subject experiences itself under capitalism. Recovering contradictions reopens many things, even perhaps the possibility that the term "individual" in Althusser's formula is not simply a ghostly abstraction or linguistic concession that is erased in the movement from subject to predicate, person to group. It may also imply a concept we have not yet constituted because doing so requires establishing what has not yet been thought—the possibility of a dialectical movement within our ideological situatedness.

Contradiction within the subject is not the only kind of contradiction, nor does its recovery entail belief in the presence within consciousness of an autonomous principle of necessary liberation. The study of economic contradictions must remain the primary marxist focus. But without the struggle for subject, none of what we discover about "consumer capitalism" finally matters. The whole point in trying to recover an understanding of situated subjectivity is to place the subject in history, thereby dialecticizing both terms.

The trouble with the humanistic reading of Marx which Althusser criticizes (and with the 1844 Manuscripts for that matter) is that it is insufficiently dialectical.[53] In retrospect, it is embarrassing to see the lack of conceptual sophistication that informed efforts to celebrate the early "humanistic" Marx and to make alienation the primary category for marxist social science. After Stalin, it was salutary and rhetorically desirable to discover that Marx had humanistic sentiments. But without the heavy Hegelian glossing few scholars have been in a position to give Marx's early writings, sentiments are about all they offer. "Liberal," "humanistic" commentators are not the only ones at fault here. While the 1844 Manuscripts brilliantly situate the Hegelian concepts of master-slave, alienation, and unhappy consciousness in the historical situation and everyday life of the proletariat, Marx maintains a basic and systematic vagueness about the category that grounds the entire discussion—that of our "species-being."[54] Without the Hegelian grounding Marx never gets around to providing, there is no way this concept can escape the eminently marxist charge of being an essentialistic and ahistorical imposition. What does consciousness have to be like for alienation to be possible? One finds no answer to this quasi-Kantian question in the 1844 Manuscripts or in the essentialistic approaches of followers of the early Marx. Both sides of the humanist-scientist debate thus collapse in hypostatizations—the one of science, the other of a romantic humanism. One grounds everything in a principle outside subject (structure, *écriture*); the other embraces the specter of a suprahistorical humanity.

The more concrete perspective I have tried to develop shifts to another order of conceptualization. The social subject is still a potentially unhappy consciousness because capitalist society requires the sacrifice of any residual, oppositional inwardness. The dialectic between inwardness and capitalism is unavoidable precisely because inwardness is not an a priori property but a possibility that arises directly out of those experiences in which capitalism confronts its own "coefficient of adversity." Capitalism may be triumphant, but the *cost* is the fundamental dissatisfaction that it both produces and exacerbates.

In advancing this thesis, my goal is to renew the dialectical and Hegelian dimensions in marxism, against the taxonomic abstractness of structuralist sociology, by offering a way to conceptualize our social and ideological situatedness in a double way: as sites of determination and of struggle. Such a method must take as its task a description of modern society that simultaneously reveals the ways in which, as subjects, we are determined and the ways in which we suffer this fact—whether consciously or not. Throwing subject up against those formations it cannot ignore constitutes this method's contribution to a nonessentialistic theory of situated subjectivity as a hierarchy of integrations made possible through (and only through) acts of experiential self-overcoming.

If we want to retain as orthodox marxism the belief that dialectical materialism means that everything in history is finally determined by economic factors (i.e., by the forces and relations of production), we still must rethink this article of faith along contemporary lines. For a theory of situated subjectivity, economic determinism in the last instance must mean this: "late" or consumer capitalism is defined by the subtle insinuation of the economic profit motive into areas of life where other residual motives are still given lip service, though they're in the process of disappearing from history. The capitalist subject is a totalization still in process, but it is now clear that the goal of this totalization is the extinction of inwardness, of any internal otherness opposing the great capitalist "Yea." In order for the vast capitalist effort of interpellating subjects to complete and perfect itself, everything must be remade in terms of its sole imperative: greed. While that process assaults us daily, it also gives us a new understanding of the terms and nature of struggle.

No "essential humanity" protects us from what is at stake in our time. The concern with culture and with residual "structures of feeling"[55] and experience must become an effort to produce a massive feeling of alienation by locating human possibilities at the precise experiential sites where they are currently being deracinated by the capitalist imperative. The task is to track down capitalism in the places where one still necessarily suffers it. In seeking out such sites, however, our hermeneutic is engaged only if it questions and risks itself at every step, because the compelling truth of capitalist ideology is its ability to annex and incorporate other values. Ideological imperialism is capitalism's categorical imperative; it naturally and necessarily finds humanistic and religious ideas one of the most serviceable ways to gloss its operations. That is why discovery of residual values or liberating experiences can never rest in contemplation but must proceed to praxis. There is no slumbering eternal human essence buried under the capitalist detritus. The hard lesson of history is that any hermeneutic dedicated to recovering humanistic universals is kidding itself. When they are felt or contemplated in consciousness alone, possibilities are sure to vanish without a trace. Ideology may not be the whole story, but in order to make a "difference" we must constitute possibilities of resistance in experiential sites it has not yet conquered. We must, that is, seize possibility by acting in a new way in the situations in which it is precarious and at issue. For praxis to happen, each discovery must regain its proper pain and become a struggle to root out the ideological concretely by constituting, through action, an oppositional self. The next section will assess the chances for such a project.

CAPITALIZING ON INWARDNESS: A NONDIALECTICAL COMEDY

The Belly of the Beast

We thus arrive at the great challenge and possibility marxism poses for subjectivity: to become a subject by rooting out and reversing the capitalist internalization. The study of ideology offers a systematic insight into the ways in which we are subjects by rote, with our inner life replicating structures that have an objective, public, historical existence. By stripping away all the protective and illusory conceptions of self that prevent a recognition of how thoroughly we are delivered over to the social—and to internalizations that are made long before there is a subject to make them —ideological awareness makes the existential question of subject as that being whose being is at issue authentically historical.

Becoming a subject requires a dialectical reversal and reconstitution of one's social situatedness. As we conceptualize this possibility, our guiding idea will be this: wherever one locates an area of ideological interpellation, one also identifies a site of struggle and of potential liberation. For ideology operates only where there is a potential source of conflict or contradiction that must be contained. It has no other rationale. Within marxism, becoming a subject accordingly requires taking over the full complexity of one's social situatedness as the essential term of one's struggle. The idea of situated subjectivity depends here on the possibility of reversing the initial ideological determination of one's being. Rather than a *Bildung* we might think of such a reversal as an anti-*Bildung*. Its maxim: subject is not the sociologically given, but its negation. This project is the equivalent, in a marxism without guarantees, of the Hegelian concept of subject as an act of self-overcoming through the determinate negativity of reflection. Such a project is unlike essentialist and humanistic conceptions of subject in that nothing guarantees its emergence or success. Existent reflection, grounded in social situatedness, is a possibility that need never occur. Nor does its upsurge provide any assurance of its continuance, the determinacy of its content, or its progress toward a tidy and necessary end. Like anxiety, it may be no more than an evanescent moment; and, historically, our time may be witnessing its last gasp.

Reflection constitutes itself within marxism through a systematic discovery of the ways in which one's "subjectivity" is initially the field of the capitalist other. Given the nature of reflection, that discovery can't be recorded passively, but must activate, however briefly, the beginnings of internal transformation. The common human response, the attempt to extinguish reflection, serves only to establish its ontological primacy. Marxism concretizes the idea that reflection as the labor of the negative is the act whereby one becomes a subject by demonstrating that social situatedness is the very thing that establishes both the possibility of critical reflection and the achievement, through its practice, of authentic freedom. By mapping the extent of our imprisonment, we establish the terms and the possibility of our liberation. Once social situatedness becomes reflection's primary object, the rooting out of capitalism becomes the act through which subjectivity is constituted.

Marxism's distinct focus helps resolve a difficulty that has often been raised about the negativity of Hegelian reflection. The negativity of reflection derives not from a psychological disposition or disorder, but from the fact that an active consciousness keeps running up against situations that are intolerable. The basis of negativity is not some abstract, Sartrean, ontological exigency, but the contradictions of thought's historical moment. Reflection discovers inauthenticity everywhere because it is everywhere. To be true to its inaugural moment, it must live out that awareness through the labor of the negative.

The problem we face here is analogous to that of the previous chapters: to account for subject's emergence without positing subject as prior to the operations of something else, in this case, ideology. Semantic and grammatical ambiguities are such that two distinct conclusions can be drawn from our ideological situatedness. Bemoaning it, we can seek evidence for an essential humanity or a priori identity from which social determination alienates us but which we can regain by removing its effects. Romanticism and rationalism share this pathos. The dialectical response, in contrast, welcomes each new insight into our ideological thrownness, seeing it as the recovery of a site for constituting an emergent possibility, which can come into being only if we surmount an otherness we have already internalized. The concreteness of such a dialectic derives from the fact that everything remains firmly rooted in experience. To develop this possibility, I will here advance, in a deliberately aphoristic and rhetorical voice, a series of propositions about inwardness and everyday life under capitalism.

A Last "Dialectic of Enlightenment"

As Gatsby knows, the secret of Daisy's voice is the sound of money. Being social subjects, we reproduce and internalize as our self-reference and self-regulation the ruling principles and ideals of our society. As the depth of our inwardness and the quick of our desire we thus experience, under capitalism, this relationship to ourselves: capitalism is the agent; we are its products. This is perhaps the most compelling way in which economics makes itself "determinative in the last instance": it is determinative in the first. We live capitalism as the law structuring our deepest relationship to ourselves and to the other.

We choke on the almighty buck, not because it comes first in all our pragmatic affairs, but because everything else gets remade in terms of money. From the cradle, every "talent" is managed as a bit of capital, or every intellectual interest is reinterpreted in terms of its capitalist usefulness. The very *worth* of each "person" is weighed in terms of exchange value. This has become the source of attraction and the new condition of what psychoanalysis calls object choice. When the logic of capitalism rules, every relationship, especially love, must be managed as an investment. That is why when we tally up our experience, we inevitably find ourselves balancing the books. The most insidious result is the breeding of that attitude Nietzsche conceptualized when he saw that the root trouble with the man and woman of resentment is that they can never be finished with anything. A capitalist's reflection on experience is necessarily trapped in resentment. The only meaningful response to loss is to get tough and live out from the beginning, coldly, what one formerly experienced at the end, bitterly, as victim. Bitterness sublated sets down, as the deep structure controlling one's experience, the need to conduct all relations solely in terms of a calculus of investments and debts. A relationship ended becomes the need to review one's efforts to "give" in terms of debts which the other has incurred and now refuses to pay. Disappointment can no longer bring vital, painful self-knowledge or liberate new possibilities because we have installed, as our new "superego," the defeated capitalist who can interpret loss only as a sign that he or she has not yet mastered the rules of the game. Reflection isn't the step toward freedom; it's the jailer who forever turns the key locking the door. Through it we reify ourselves, forging the inwardness suited to the imperatives of the capitalist order.

Just as capitalism gobbles up new markets in its inexorable imperialist drive, the capitalist social order incessantly annexes to its logos all other forms and possibilities of human inwardness. Just as its economic "logic" eventually dictates that there be only one giant capitalist (i.e., the corporation), its ideological logic mandates that eventually there be only one kind of human being. The true genius of capitalism, however, is that it always annexes without apparently subtracting anything.[56] Capitalism promises all good things. That is its innermost need and its suppressed contradiction. All the "qualities" that have been ascribed to the human being must attain their fulfillment in the capitalist. Capitalism doesn't simply make us come to resemble Goneril and Regan in our behavior; it makes any other way of acting unintelligible, while preventing us from seeing that behavior for what it is. People today are ashamed if they haven't achieved hardness of heart because they can no longer see it as such.

In turning the heart to stone, capitalism proceeds, as its logic dictates, by a necessary incorporation of all otherness. The process is essentially one of reinterpreting all ideals, values, and qualities so that they can have only one meaning: that corresponding to their capitalist form. A double mystification results: what's really going on can no longer be understood, yet nothing outside the system can be found to oppose it.[57] (The process is analogous to the way in which capitalism annexes older economic structures by preserving, whenever necessary, their values as a convenient husk.)[58] Once the process whereby all meanings become their capitalist meaning is completed, no oppositional possibilities outside the system will any longer exist because everything good will have been realized within it.[59]

To secure the conditions for its reproduction, capitalism must create subjects who regard themselves as the triumphant representatives of all the values that have evolved in the long march of culture and history— to the capitalist. It is a mistake to picture the capitalist as a cynic; the real rot lies in the need to think well of oneself. Capitalism can't work simply by cloaking itself in the veneer of traditional values; it must regard itself as the definitive *Aufhebung* of the entire cultural past.

The formula structuring life under capitalism is this: subjects reify themselves by repeating—as both the content and the self-reference of their inwardness—the operating laws of capitalism. We are capable, structuralist beasts; the ability to abstract and then mimic the laws of our society may be the defining human act. Perhaps that's why our emotional life under capitalism has come to resemble the law of the falling rate of profit. Profit is the concrete universal, and self-interest its priest. But acquisitiveness derives its power from the need to prove oneself better than others by possessing and consuming more than they. Ontological insecurity may be the threat all this is meant to allay, but the disruptive force of anxiety is rapidly becoming no more than a vague and receding memory. Reason is now purely operational, its function quantification and calculus along the lines of the most degenerate form of pragmatism—immediate material interest, security, comfort. The self-reference of subject becomes the banishment of anxiety, the abolition of feelings in favor of roles. Deception is universalized. Other people are tools, objects to be used. Capitalizing on all relations becomes a moral imperative. Conformity is a powerful motive, but competition is the subtext that makes all social occasions ones of snobbery and mutual envy. Money provides the universal standard whereby we evaluate everything. All valuable human qualities —intelligence, attractiveness, responsibility, good character, psychological health, ego stability, and "moral" integrity—derive from one's connection to money. Desire in capitalism is boundless and must be satisfied because capitalism must annex *all good things* to itself in a wholly positive dialectic.

But the need "to complete the happiness" of humanity bequeaths a double burden: capitalism must eliminate any negative consciousness about itself while demonstrating that it actualizes all values. Kant said that a conflict of moral goods and duties was a priori impossible. Capitalism is the parody realization of that idea in the material world. Capitalist subjects stand in perfect correspondence with their world because "the Good" is always to have, never to be. Money is the "substance" one gives oneself by adding property to the "I know not what supposed support" of these sensible indications of a phantom identity. The empty circularity of the process creates the need to make reflection the stilling of any questions or activities that might challenge the *harmony* of the whole enterprise. In that whole, there can be no contradictions. Capitalism and Christianity thus make perfect bedfellows because our heavenly father put us on earth to have all good things before getting even richer rewards in heaven. A less acquisitive response to life involves lack of respect for the Creation.

True to its logic, capitalism can contain otherness only by claiming to accommodate it. That is why capitalists love the arts. The truth of annexation, however, is a progressive degeneration of meaning. Everything in culture must be deprived of danger, reduced to a "subjective" matter of taste. The capitalist's relationship to art is either proprietary (another proud possession of the capitalist community) or private (one likes whatever one likes one knows not why, but inarticulate "feeling" remains absolute.) The anarchy of privacy and the privilege of privacy are here identical. To find a place in such a psychic economy, literature, art, and other works of thought must be "democratized" and relativized in the Cuisinart of public opinion. Whatever most people like is good. There is no other standard. Culture can never have the value of something that measures us. Whenever threatened with the Socratic prospect of giving an account, we retreat into the solipsism of "feeling" so that we can be absolved of the need to understand or interrogate our experience. We like it, in fact, when we find that we really have nothing to say about the book we've just read or the film we've just seen. Absence of thought is a sure sign one is progressing toward tranquillity.

The ruling principle that makes the whole thing work is the desire for surplus security. This is the darker, less stable side of consumer capitalism. The display of wealth is merely the external sign of a fundamental ontological impoverishment, another way of acting out what has become a collective obsession: "There can never be enough money." [60] The fetishism of commodities referred initially to the economic fact that in capitalism relations between people assume the impersonal character of relations between things. Capitalist subjects internalize this truth of their world by making it the truth of their inwardness. In commodifying oneself one achieves the adequate idea: relations within oneself become like the relations among things. We replicate the social order by turning ourselves into its mirror. The irony behind the preoccupation with the "self" that is the "psychological" capstone of late capitalism is that the goal of this vast therapeutic effort is to extinguish the very reality that preoccupies us. Feeling good about oneself is a collective obsession, and the labor to produce it the one thing that is a matter of constant concern. We are still a problem to ourselves, but the problem is how to tailor oneself, through private "happy talk," to a public conception of mental health as bovine complacency. Ego identity is maintained through a bottomless insecurity about one's lack of substance and an obsessional need to prove the contrary.

Total inner disorder thus creates the compulsion to speak incessantly about oneself, saying only good things. To foster that process, a vast network of "educational" institutions (the family, the school, the media, the mental health establishment) work together, from the beginning, to establish the content of the terms that will define identity. One thus becomes healthy, mature, responsible—a suitable partner, potential parent, and representative of the community—insofar as one finds a monetary place in the capitalist order, with the specter of being labeled neurotic, immature, and undesirable for failing to do so serving to grease the wheels of one's incorporation. The mature capacity for reality testing of the integrated, stable ego is but another name for capitalist subjectivity triumphant, seated on the throne, engaged in our highest occupation: the need to set ourselves up as the universal standard of beauty, goodness, and intelligence so that we may think well of ourselves within the terms of our infinite condescension toward everything we are unable to understand.

The key to the capitalist subject is the need to feel good about oneself—absolutely. That feeling is the capitalist equivalent of Absolute Knowledge. The one thing the capitalist can't stand is the threat of an otherness that possesses value. Indeed, the one way left to give capitalists anxiety is to suggest some value they haven't incorporated. The capitalist must *have* all good things, even at the cost of reducing all values to their most degraded parody. Such is the perfected inwardness of the capitalist subject.

But is it possible that the basic imperative of capitalism—the need to annex "all good things" in a purely additive process, intolerant of subtraction—is also the weight that could dissolve the "puny, inexhaustible" voice of capitalism in sheer noise, make it collapse under the superfluity of its incessant affirmations? Might capitalist inwardness dissolve in the babble of tongues it must incessantly invoke in applauding itself? One end of the dialectic would be at hand. But, though we may envision capitalists straining under the glut of all they must represent, we must do so with the sad realization that no possibility of Socratic reversal is in the offing here. Residual meanings cannot be opposed or even juxtaposed with their capitalist "realization" because the inwardness in which such a contradiction could be felt no longer exists. At the depth of its inwardness capitalist subjectivity stands perpetually prepared to give a speech before the chamber of commerce.

EVERYDAY LIFE UNDER CAPITALISM: THE WORKINGS OF AN ANTIDIALECTIC

LOVE AND SEXUALITY

Marxism introduces the crucial concretization that complicates our entire theory of subject: to understand oneself one must grasp the ways in which one's immediacy—one's feelings, opinions, experience, one's so-called privacy—is a function of the contradictions of one's time. To gauge the proper pain of this discovery, sexuality offers a privileged site. Let me introduce this idea through an aphorism, writ November 7, 1984. With Reagan, sexuality regresses to its pure capitalist form: we become excessively delicate, even obsessional, about the conditions under which we will "give" ourselves; our body is our property and must return a profit with each investment.

Sexuality in late capitalism has become its own parody and a privileged site for showing us how utterly historical we are. The key to capitalism's "human" appeal is that it offers its subjects a way to reduce the complexities of the human to the conditions of commodity circulation. If we sell and buy ourselves in the marketplace of love it is because we have already internalized a commodified way of relating both to ourselves and to the other. In capitalism, being is having. I am what I can buy—with my looks, by flashing my checkbook, by attaching my person to certain places and things. I am what I can get from the other in exchange for my worth as a representative of success in the economic order. Power derives from the degree to which I enact that position without internal conflict. The return of all investments is the mutual experience of one another as inert pieces of property, frozen in roles, deceptions, and that calculated contempt that permanently arrests the struggle for recognition. One is neither master nor slave here, but a being eternally calculating debts, balancing the books, and presenting the bill.

A statement by the young Marx on money still provides one of the best introductions to how internalizing capitalism alters sexuality. "I am 'ugly' but I can buy the most beautiful women for myself, consequently, I am not 'ugly,' for the effect of ugliness, its power to repel, is annulled by money. . . . I am a detestable, dishonorable, unscrupulous and stupid man, but money is honored and so also is its possessor. Money is the highest good and so its possessor is good."[61] The fetishization of one's entire psychological life vanquishes the possibility of bad faith; eventually we all become whores by eradicating the residual inwardness that would enable us to describe ourselves by precisely that term. Through the acquisition of a language that systematically blurs consciousness, one learns to describe one's actions in the appropriately positive terms. Successful self-marketing depends on self-mystification. Every experience that could engender unhappy consciousness, and thus the possibility of change, must become an occasion for self-reification. Everything must be made into a matter of individual life-styles, with all "ethical" questions relativized. Loving money and those who have it is a sign of maturity and mental health. Any questioning of this set of identifications must be turned back against the questioner, made a proof of failure, envy, or shame for not having "made it." To "complete the happiness" of humanity, bad faith and unhappy consciousness must be vanquished and their dialectic extinguished. The goal of capitalism is to eliminate any inwardness other than that which says "Yes" to the system.

But it is precisely at this point that capitalism may engender a dialectical turn. Erotic love is never simply a reflection, but a potential source of trouble—a site of resistance and potential liberation. Late capitalism won't have secured its hegemony until it assures its reproduction within the order of pleasure by eliminating any otherness that could emerge there. Pleasure must become a commodity, as incessant, disposable, and lacking in qualitative difference as a McDonald's hamburger; only so does it become an object that can be manipulated for the maximization of consumption and profits. While making us constantly desire sex, capitalism must progressively rob us of sexuality.

Today the sexual is largely conquered turf, and if we regain its power, it will be through an experience of the frustrations and absences of contemporary sexuality rather than through the body's subtler annunciations. The body in late capitalism is like Chaplin's in *Modern Times*: mechanization has taken command. Liberating the body is a matter not of tapping an erotic self-presence that is always lying in wait for us,[62] but of cutting out a cancer that is in an advanced stage. Just as the five senses are the work of all previous history (and the malleable subject of all future advertisements), their reconquest is a long struggle to root out those counterfeits of pleasure we initially take as the true article. Eros has become the pornography industry, sex the great technological performance agon where the real pleasure is mutual avoidance, manipulation, and denial. If we can still be surprised sexually, if the touch remains an act of incipient protest, it is also for most people an occasion of anxiety. The coming into being of a relatedness that can't be assimilated to the dominant order is experienced as a loss of control rather than as the incarnation of a possibility that must be explored, nontechnically, by entering its flow. The true hysterics today are the technicians of sex.

To avoid lapsing into its own brand of romantic a priorism, the recognition of historical thrownness must take as its first moment a contemporary assessment of whether a dialectic of sex is still possible or whether it is now just another piece of nostalgia. In the ideological formation of subjects, the body is of necessity one of the primary targets. By getting us to live it in a certain way—as an object performing scientifically established techniques—ideology makes pleasure a matter of calculation, as it must for the all-encompassing advertising industry to perform its function. Sexuality is a perfect example of Foucault's notion that the power to subject is diffused at all points in the social system and operates by inciting us to a certain kind of talk about and experience of the body. If one wants to know the force of the political and the difficulties of liberation, one can find few better places to begin than with the genitals. There is no pure, unmediated experience of the body. We live our bodies along definite and prescribed lines, according to mass-produced images and fantasies and with the appropriate results: we swoon in cadence, moan, our own voyeurs, in imitation of the picture of pleasure implanted in our heads, and celebrate our eroticism in a catalogue of banalities worthy of Flaubert. The obsessional nature of pleasure in late capitalism is one of the best proofs of how thoroughly we've turned ourselves into things.

If love remains the bad conscience of capitalist society, it is also today a residual experience in danger of losing its oppositional character. For, by and large, we love today on the capitalist model, reducing what could be the most dangerous and meaningful game to a matter of exchange. Disruptive possibilities are thereby domesticated along definite commodity lines. The history of love is not the history of an identical Platonic essence, immune to time, but the history of what happens to emerging erotic possibilities as those possibilities are submitted to the larger socio-economic forces lovers follow when, even in the garden of delight, they delicately try to nudge one another into line with the dominant social order.

WORK AND LEISURE

A neglected aspect of Marx's economic thought is the study of how contradictions within the relations of production are lived by those subjected to them. The still unrealized promise of the phenomenology of labor that Marx first began to develop in the 1844 Manuscripts derives from its least developed proposition: the notion that labor should realize our "species-being."[63] The smell of essentializing apriorism clings to this concept because the oppressive conditions of work under industrial capitalism—alienation from oneself and one's fellow workers in the very process of one's labor—did not permit Marx to develop it. The dialectical idea that remained buried in the horrifying descriptions of *Capital* is that labor can be the existential source of possibilities that are discovered in and through experience. The values thereby created are wholly historical and reside within the product of one's labor. Labor should be not only the freest but the most ennobling thing, the act that gives value to life upon the earth. This is what Hegel meant by labor as "universal formative activity," a joyful freedom, which makes one of its last, ghostly appearances in the sense of human relatedness that momentarily comes into being as the prisoners build the wall in Solzhenitsyn's *One Day in the Life of Ivan Denisovich*. Labor contains such possibilities, not because there is a preexistent human essence which we impose upon matter, but because in and through labor there emerges a creative, expressive, and playful relationship both to oneself and to others.

But what should be the site of emergent possibilities has today become the scene of losses that aren't any longer even experienced as such. The cooptation of the labor movement is merely the most conspicuous sign of an advanced process in which work is now no more than a way station one endures as the price of incorporation into capitalist society. Drudgery is only the surface. The primary alienation now suffered in work is inward. Our occupation is to strip our labor of any meaning other than the price one pays for something else.

The notion that we endure the drudgery of work so that we can resume our freedom and realize ourselves in our leisure is the crowning mystification. Leisure is the most managed, manufactured, and ideologically dense area of everyday life. In leisure, we live, as the innermost desire of consciousness, the needs required to reproduce the relations of production of the ruling economic order. In consumer society, the ceaseless production of superfluous goods requires an absolute need for them on the part of consumers. The vast expanse of our desires—have we ever desired more?—thus repeats with a monotonous and shoddy regularity the same basic message. To be is to have and to consume so that one can start the process anew. Leisure is the site where this reduction of the human being circulates as a behavioral and psychological imperative. In attaining the consumer "ethic" one replicates M—C—M$'$ as the deep structure of one's consciousness—the message upon which one *must* act. Consumers aren't created by rhetorical appeal to a freely deliberative consciousness. No such appeal is necessary because no such subject exists. The management of leisure strikes far more deeply into the "integrity" of consciousness than this traditional model suggests. Determining the way we experience our leisure is the most significant interpellation, in fact, because it fixes our basic relationship to ourselves as desiring subjects. All that is required is the production of the next new need—the subject follows of necessity. The cruelest part of this hoax is that we've been trained to think of our purchases as the free choices of autonomous beings.

The marxist understanding of leisure gives a materialist concretization to Heidegger's concept of the "they." Idle talk, curiosity, and ambiguity are the means through which idle purchases prepare and sustain themselves: everything we talk about functions to ready us for the moment of consumption. Anything hindering that end becomes truly idle, and thus we consign it to silence. Hoping to uncover sites of resistance, this section has tried to rub raw the sores of discontent. Its pessimistic faith is that sores can still be found. But if we have uncovered any possibilities here, they are the barest ones, having the status only of questions.

To develop them we must turn to those larger institutional sites that claim to nurture "human" possibilities but which may actually be the scene of their primary reification—culture and the family.

Anti-*Bildung*: Retrieving the Contradictions of "Objective Spirit"

Contrary to Kierkegaard and traditional commentators, Hegel does not dispense with subject in the second half of the *Phenomenology of Mind*, but situates it. Hegel knows that culture (his general term for all aspects of our social being) is not external, but makes up the very life and immediacy of the subject. He also knows what we are today most in danger of forgetting—that subject remains the unquiet life of culture.

Hegel's discussion of Objective Spirit provides the basic categories —the family, alienation, *Bildung*, modernity, historicity, and the world-historical individual—that we need in order to think through the dialectics of subject's social situatedness. To establish their contemporary relevance, however, we must break every one of these concepts back against itself. Everything Chapter 1 established about unhappy consciousness remains alive as the disruptive subtext in Hegel's consideration of Objective Spirit. Historical complacency prevented Hegel from sustaining the destabilizing implication of that fact. My purpose is to recapture it for marxism by conceiving of the categories of Objective Spirit as sites of conflict, contradiction, and tension: to think them through in a way that breaks with the movement toward Absolute Knowledge structuring Hegel's understanding of our social being. The great value of Hegel's thought—a value that exists in spite of him—is that all his categories are replete with tensions he imperfectly sublates and sublimates. Objective Spirit isn't the holy ghost come to deliver us; *it's the public being of unhappy consciousness.* The desire for recognition is the great need that remains alive in all social formations; it is also the desire most in danger of reification in late capitalism. By reading Hegel against the grain, we can recapture these suppressed insights.

THE FAMILY: NOSTALGIA AND ITS SECRETS

The approach we've taken to ideology makes its study the act preparatory to subject's reconstitution. But for that to happen we can't rest with a sociological description of work and leisure. We must open up those formations that strike deepest, the ones where scrutiny really hurts. To know oneself through the study of ideology, one must begin with that site where we sucked it as our mother's milk. To establish an ontological basis for subject's emergence, we must confront the primary institutional site where its social determination first takes shape. The route to the concrete goes through the family. The family is the primary agent of ideological interpellation because it catches and addresses the "full" subject in the initial moment of its formation. The determinations it imprints sustain all other social practices. They are also the hardest to detect because the family shapes subject in a way that is deepest, most immediate, yet hardest to identify and oppose because the otherness it instills in subject cannot be uprooted without tearing out one's own heart in the process.

The family is the crucial formation to study for a marxist theory of subject because it is the social institution where the "private" and the "public" are most intimately joined.[64] As such, its study provides a concrete negation of the public-private dichotomy that sustains so much of capitalist ideology. The family is also one of the most significant formations for the larger theory of subject we are constructing because its understanding requires a genuinely existential synthesis of marxist and psychoanalytic theory.[65]

Subject is familial. Because the family is its origin, the internal structure of subjectivity is inherently interpersonal and social. The family is the originary determination that shapes the intrapsychic relationship subject lives to itself, the interpersonal conflicts that structure concrete relations with others, and the dominant attitudes that characterize our general social behaviors. When we "go inside" we inevitably find ourselves in conversation with our parents—and this "dialogue" is always a discourse with our society. The discourse is reactivated whenever we meet "the significant other" or seek/accept our place in society. Because everything coalesces in the family—and because, in a sense, we never leave it—interrogating the family is the starting point for any attempt to reconceptualize objective spirit. But the key to such a study is to see the family as a nest of contradictions that can't be resolved and are necessarily passed on. The beauty of this idea for the marxist lies in its irony: in the family, capitalist society tries to contain its historicity and universalize its forms only to exacerbate its contradictions.

The family is the primary agent of socialization. Its members are assigned their roles as bearers of social identities and imperatives. The task of the family is to create the kind of subject mandated by the society. Father and mother, son and daughter, gender itself, are social assignments, reflecting socio-economic imperatives. In the family, our deepest identifications and the seeds of their discontents are sown simultaneously. For the family is never simply a representative of society, but a theater for staging the resentments it breeds. The family is the place where we bring it all home. It is the helpless animal onto whom we displace the objective, socio-economic anger we are forbidden to express. Powerless to tell off the boss, a man abuses his wife or beats his son; the son internalizes the whole thing as his founding confusion. The violence of the family—the rape, the incest, the mutual cruelty, the metonymic chain of displaced anger inflicted on each less powerful "subject"—represents and enacts the repressed truth of the objective social structure. The family may thus be defined as the first *Aufhebung* of unhappy consciousness as a social reality and an objective social institution.[66] No invocation of *Geist* is needed to sustain this proposition. Nor does it deny the reality of the individual subject. On the contrary, it preserves and concretizes the latter by revealing that subject's familial situatedness is a dramatic, conflicted awareness, demanding action, and not a simple reflection of social reifications.

The family is a conflicted representative because it is the place where subjects struggle to engender relationships denied by the society at large. As Aristotle observed, tragic drama focuses on the family because the "unnatural" is most painful when we find it where there should be love. The family necessarily sees itself as the test and proof of our ability to love one another. That is why failure there is experienced in a unique way that has a special significance for a theory of subject. It is in the family that a certain truth about oneself—which reflects a larger social truth— is enacted and suffered in ways that make self-knowledge hard to avoid, even though the primary way in which one comes to this self-knowledge in "the happy family" is by exhausting the possibilities of "shifting the blame." (As O'Neill shows, blame is the primary structure of everyday life that moves the family along its journey into night.)

The untruth of the family is that it tries to suppress its drama and deny the connection of that drama to the objective social order. The answer to the question Michael Corleone asks his mother—"Is it possible for a man to lose his family?"—is that one "always already" has. The family is not the last bastion of universal and natural ethical relations that are opposed in principle to the economic imperatives of one's society. It is, rather, the site in which the possibility of such values faces its historical destiny. The suppressed truth of the family is that it is a historical institution; the values it proclaims are not secured in human nature, but fully submitted to history. Conservative nostalgia for the family as a permanent haven of human values corresponds, in fact, to a historical situation in which the family is the disciplinary school inculcating the rules and roles demanded by the social order.

The family thus brings into the open the "human meaning" of the contradictions and imperatives of the society at large. But it does so by enacting a mutual unhappiness it is forced to displace and deny. The ravaged psyche of psychoanalysis is its gross national product. The haven where we can supposedly treasure humane relationships denied in the society at large has become the torture chamber in which we inflict on those huddled with us the very laws of our dehumanization. There is no essential human nature we can rely on to protect us from this depressing line of thought. The family, like everything else, is given over to history. Psychoanalysis is an implicit and abbreviated politics because it grasps the family at the point where its internal contradictions reveal their connections to the social structure that produces and sustains them.

CULTURE AND OTHER CRYPTS

The critical study of ideology is the modern equivalent of the *Bildungsroman*. It is also analogous to the process of an authentic psychoanalysis. All three are, as we'll see, complementary acts. Classical *Bildung* referred to the process of acculturation in those social values an initially empty and naive subject needs in order to take up a responsible position in the world. The concept of *Bildung* we will develop for late capitalism reverses that process and negates the philosophic assumptions underlying its view of experience. For our purposes, *Bildung* is the discovery and rooting out of all the formations that are already impressed upon us. It is the act of stripping away those contents and determinations that rule our inner and outer life prior to reflection. The tracking of ideology thus becomes the act through which the reflective subject strives to become free and the inquiry preparatory to the very possibility of freedom. Like psychoanalytic reflection, ideological scrutiny is a double process: one constitutes oneself as a subject through a reflection that tries, of necessity, to effect an act of reversal. So understood, ideological reflection is the process through which the marxist subject comes into being. For it to be so, however, ideological detective work must produce more than "self-knowledge." It must form a will and issue in a praxis with which, as subject, one strives to coincide. The "categorical" imperative informing such a concern with ideology is the determination to root out capitalism wherever one finds it, especially within oneself.

If alienation concretizes the recognition that one is already thrown into a sociohistorical situation that has writ its message large in every dimension of one's being, culture (the arts) is the search for terms of opposition. Without the discipline of culture, and its implicit call for subject to constitute itself, alienation remains a private malaise destined to pass without issue. But like everything else, culture is no utopia, no realm of transparent universal meanings and values. It and its study (criticism) constitute one of the densest fields of ideological mystification and historical struggle. To approach it with the proper reverence, one must come to it with Benjamin's great statement in mind: "There is not a monument of culture which is not a monument of barbarism."[67] Unless one thinks culture along such lines, one lapses into "idealism": the notion that culture represents some universal, atemporal humanity, and the corollary belief that one can turn to it for aesthetic refuge and escape from history. The fact of the matter is that there is nothing necessarily oppositional about culture. Dense with the subtlest mystifications, its primary function has been to smooth over rifts in ideology by cloaking reality (often in the name of realism) with the veils of illusion, order, fantasy, and pleasure. Culture could, with some justice, be regarded as the most insidious and resistant ideological formation, in fact, because it gets us to embrace and identify with self-reifying "structures of feeling." These are the hardest formations to detect and reverse because they both name and attempt to fill subject's deepest needs.

The study of culture can't seek a Reason that is already in the world so that one can overcome alienation by identifying with the objective order;[68] nor can it remain content with that romantic aestheticism that posits art as a transideological or utopian force that is necessarily liberating.[69] Macherey's somewhat different view of culture as "the internal distancing of ideology" that enables us to detect its operations moves toward a more dialectical position.[70] Like the family, culture holds the possibility of liberation only if we are prepared to approach it with the proper suspicion, realizing that the artist is not only just as mystified as we are but often the prime agent of mystification, the great sublimator of tensions that can be "resolved" in art because its forms offer an apparent freedom from historical contingency.[71] To explore a richer possibility, writing and other cultural practices must break forms back against themselves. Critical interpretation, in turn, must become an anti-*Bildung* which desublimates aesthetic "forms" in order to recover the historical contradictions they are meant to conceal. In seeking out oppositional possibilities, the critical act must take the form of a struggle to liberate the work of art (or philosophy) from its inherent limitations.

Culture has been a preoccupation of the major marxist thinkers of this century. This concern has been essential because culture is not a mere "superstructure" that must be debunked so that everything can be reduced to economics and class motives. It is, rather, the site where the full complexity of motives, contradictions, and possibilities make themselves "felt" in a way that can't be denied. As such, its study has been the unacknowledged source of the slow conceptual movement toward a marxism without guarantees. To carry forward this project, the study of culture must take a further step: it must become an explicit attempt to complicate our understanding of every concept in marxism through a recovery of the concrete subjectivity that dissolves every guarantee marxism falsely claims for itself.

For the study of culture to become such a fully dialectical process, both critics and their objects of study must be brought into a mutually destabilizing relationship. Only then would "history hurt" at both ends of marxism's realization of and contribution to a hermeneutics of engagement. The contours of that project can be schematized in a series of propositions.

1. As deconstructors know, the task of interpretation is to produce the contradictions of the text: to show the ways it both represents and "exceeds" ideology. Culture is often the site of our reification in structures of feeling that are insidious; but it is also the site of struggles for liberation that are uniquely revelatory. The trick is not to see it as solely one or the other. Every text potentially involves both things, in unstable relationship. The goal of marxist criticism is to halt the consumption of the text,[72] to discover its contradictions and bend the text back against itself, not in order to debunk it, but to situate it and liberate its secrets.

2. Culture is a battleground between dominant, residual, and emergent ideological forces.[73] This formulation, from Raymond Williams, cuts through the opposition between reductive and utopian conceptions of culture. We don't know ahead of time what the text will be or how it will situate itself within ideology. Culture always stands in possible otherness to the socially given. The battle of ideological forces is not an abstract thematic one, but a matter of attitudes and motives. In literature, it is generally played out as a conflict between dominant, residual, and emergent genres, forms, and "structures of feeling."

3. Literature is the ideological form par excellence for a theory of situated subjectivity because literature claims to represent reality (inner and outer) in all its variety and concreteness. In doing so, it addresses three basic questions and fulfills three basic desires. (1) It represents the structures of everyday life (including fantasies) as structures of feeling. (2) It represents the subject as a being whose fate has a meaning realized in experience. One of the primary motives for reading has always been to find out what human beings are like. Literature offers its answer as the unity of apperception which underlies and shapes the representation of character. The question it thus treats, in a concrete and continuous way, is that of subject as an integrity realized in action. (3) Finally, literature presents a narrative or dramatic paradigm of the order—or lack of order —that constitutes the course of experience. "Plot" emplots both a concept and a critique of the category of purposiveness. In so doing, it speaks to our desire to gain a coherent and comprehensive knowledge of experience and of our place in it. In addressing these three questions or desires, literature attempts to represent the "truth" of subject in a way that is both immediate and comprehensive. It thus offers an experiential answer to the three questions Kant took as the ineradicable and unanswerable concerns of Pure Reason: How can the self be seen as centered and "free?" How can everyday life in the world be grasped as a coherent totality? How can both these realities be grounded in a purposive order? Literature reestablishes the credentials of dialectic and offers a genuine response to Kant's critique because it forces the three grand ideals of thought and desire to test and earn themselves through the representation of a concrete manifold. Any ideas which fail this test are banished, by the dialectical writer, from the republic of letters.

4. Form is content. The ideology of form resides in its power to realize/reify desire in a genre and a narrative ordering of experience.[74] The appeal of form is not an incidental added to some abstract thematic content. Form is the true content of the literary work and the source of its primary ideological effects. Kenneth Burke's theory of symbolic action remains the finest attempt within marxism to develop such an understanding. Burke shows that ideological formation in literature is a matter of feelings, attitudes, and motives (not ideas) as they are enacted in roles and dramatized in conflicts that "plot" a symbolic action that has the power to shape (or misshape) the social self. Literature is the most concrete manifestation of ideology's fundamental operation because

it directly represents the primary process that forms us as social subjects. A work of literature is the making or unmaking of the audience as a community.

5. The limits of a form are the limits of the ideology implicit in it. In discovering a form's limits, the writer or critic discovers the contradictions of its historical moment. Often the most significant works for a marxist understanding occur, however, when a writer tries to use a form that is no longer appropriate—or when the form breaks under the burden of pressures it can no longer contain, revealing, in the process, some of its inherently regressive, sentimental, and nostalgic tendencies. Arthur Miller's staging of the contradictions of "bourgeois tragedy" is a conspicuous example. If modernity (and postmodernity) equals the breaking with forms in an effort to evolve new ones, the explanation for this practice cannot be found in some autonomous aesthetic motive, but must be seen as part of a cognitive effort to become adequate to inner and outer "reality" by evolving forms that "reflect" its complexity. The development of new forms and the clash of genres, forms, and styles in Dostoyevsky, Joyce, Faulkner, etc., constitute an attempt to evolve a new awareness through a demonstration of the inadequacy of received genres and forms to a historical understanding struggling to be born.[75] The interest of marxists in literature has always been primarily an interest in form. But, in contrast to "formalism," which prematurely arrests its understanding of the very thing it supposedly values, marxist understanding aims to articulate the vast system of interpellations that coalesce in the achievement of form.

6. Reading and interpretation accordingly become attempts to retard the moment of consumption, to produce the breaks, gaps, and binds in the text in order to reveal them as sites of historical contradictions which the text has not overcome but is exploring, often in spite of itself.[76] We must read all texts the way Brechtian actors speak their lines. But the main text that stands in the way of doing so is criticism itself. Before we can recover the complexities of the literary work, we must undertake a criticism of critical theories in an effort to uncover and explode their repressed ideological meanings. Criticism is far more deeply imbued with ideology than it would have us believe. The current fixation on "the profession" as the "epistemological" answer to all our questions is a last-ditch effort to maintain control by keeping the larger issue of ideology both on and off the agenda.[77] The "truth" it ironically reveals is that capitalism, in its relativistic authoritarian stage, no longer needs residual "humanistic"

values for its legitimation—and is no longer capable of making them do the work they once did. A "legitimation crisis" over this issue could, therefore, have profound ramifications. That is why, as marxists, we must welcome every opportunity to expose the impoverished foundation of academe, even if this means provoking the professional community into an explicit proclamation of the terrorism that sustains it.

4 *The Drama of the Psychoanalytic Subject*

I could be bounded in a nutshell and count myself a king of infinite space were it not that I have bad dreams. —HAMLET

I am an excellent patient of the soul. —DIMITRI KARAMAZOV

ON CATCHING UP WITH ONESELF

POINT OF ENTRY: THE PROBLEM OF BEGINNINGS

Psychoanalysis gives us the richest understanding of the self as a dramatic agent and of experience as a dramatic process. The subject matter of psychoanalysis is the conflicted agent and the hidden dramatic pattern of that agent's activity. This formulation takes us to the core of psychoanalytic theory because it describes what goes on in the analytic process. From the opening moves in that elaborate chess game the intelligent analyst is after one thing, and that quarry is the basis of all the analyst's questions and inferences. The task of the therapeutic encounter is reconstruction, and its object is to uncover the pattern and unity of a life history in terms of the *core conflicts* that have shaped it. Analysis is a quest in which, through the progressive uncovering of layers of defenses, resistances, and counterfeit emotions, one gets back to the "unconscious" and "repressed" *motives* that have been *actively* at work throughout a person's life and which, on recovery, reveal that life to have the unity and structure of a drama that can be described in rigorous terms. Everything said and done in the analytic process contributes to this reconstruction, and all of the concepts developed in psychoanalytic theory make sense only when seen from this perspective.

This view of the analytic process enables us to proceed directly to a number of methodological clarifications that will situate our interpretation of psychoanalysis as a critical reflection on its conflicted history. The one thing we can be sure of in studying psychoanalysis is that there is no canonical text or innocent interpretation. There is Freud who went through from three to five discernible paradigm shifts in his never completely successful effort to articulate a theory that would account for his discoveries. Then there are the many developments, revisions, and competing theories that make up the internally conflicted history of the discipline he founded. Finally, everything in that history is subject to competing interpretations, each of which claims the correct hermeneutic or scientific standpoint. It would be an endless and thankless task to attempt a critical survey of the history of psychoanalysis because such a survey could hope to do little more than bring us to the point we attain once we realize that psychoanalysis has not yet found the model that will offer the best theoretical articulation of what is today a compelling fact, namely, that the considerable developments in psychoanalysis since Freud call for a new theoretical paradigm that will discard what is outmoded and preserve what is sound in psychoanalysis.[1] To keep that focus, I have bracketed psychobiographical issues: Freud's resistance to his discoveries, the ways in which psychoanalysis is dominated by the figure of Freud, and the conflict of the sons/daughters with the father. I also leave aside an even headier issue: the way in which Freud's texts as instances of writing necessarily imitate what they are about, thus producing a textual unconscious that awaits discovery.[2] As long as we think that the one correct interpretation of Freud's texts is our main task, we remain caught in a maze we have deliberately constructed for ourselves. It is also a convenient one. Determined to expose Freud's dogmatism or his sexism, many commentators spend all their time refuting certain "statements" under the comforting illusion that one thereby escapes the assault of psychoanalysis.[3] Such exercises are fine but also finally pointless since many of Freud's dated dogmas and outmoded clinical practices have been cast off. When used to obfuscate larger issues they become pernicious: Freud's sexism, for example, does not invalidate his discovery of the unconscious or give us a warrant for denying the reality of repression. Psychoanalysis needs a radical rethinking, but we can't undertake it simply by washing the slate clean. Nor, finally, can we appeal to a new authority or father figure —whether Lacan, Kohut, Fairbairn, Schafer, or Irigaray—to straighten things out. Overcoming the need for an authority figure might, in fact, be the first sign that one has begun to think psychoanalytically.

There is no privileged text, no authority figure, no absolute beginning for the study of psychoanalysis. One should not be surprised by this since beginnings have always been a clinical and theoretical problem in psychoanalysis. It is easy to get lost in a misguided effort to reconstruct the first three years of life or spend inordinate time probing dreams and paraphraxes in search of vanished memories that supposedly hold the key to self-understanding. The effort to make a beginning becomes its own parody. Psychoanalytic theory provides numerous conceptual analogues of such efforts: the axiom of psychological determinism, the belief that someday all our conjectures will be put on a firm biochemical foundation, the economic point of view, the hydraulic model, the drive-discharge mechanism, etc. The fallacy of such constructs lies not just in their "scientistic" reductionism, but in their complicity in the dream of origins.

Our opening paragraph, in contrast, deliberately begins in medias res. Its lesson is that psychoanalysis always begins there and is wise when it stays there. We make a beginning only when we have the full complexity of the subject under view. Heidegger's notion that the only way we can begin to understand *Dasein* is by describing those experiences (anxiety, death) that enable us to get a perspective on it as a whole has an untapped significance for psychoanalysis. We need something analogous to situate our reinterpretation of psychoanalytic theory. We need to find a concrete situation that will take us to the center of psychoanalytic understanding, an experience of such power, density, and centrality that its comprehension provides a privileged experiential and hermeneutic entry into the reinterpretation of psychoanalytic theory. Trauma is the experience that plays this role: probing its significance will enable us to reconstruct the core of psychoanalytic theory.[4]

BEGINNING IN MEDIAS RES: TRAUMA AS INAUGURAL EXPERIENCE

What is a trauma, and what must the psyche be like for it to be possible? This quasi-Kantian question takes us to the center of both psychoanalytic theory and its clinical practice. A phenomenological answer will show why psychoanalysis must reconstitute itself as a theory of drama.[5]

A repeated discovery of Freud's was that an external trauma (an affair, a death, an accident) has the power to bring on a neurosis only if it "reactivates" a latent internal conflict that has been steadily accumulating force and now seizes the day. The closer one studies the connection between the two, in fact, the more apparent it becomes that the external event is often relatively insignificant but is given force, indeed "chosen," as if one had been eagerly awaiting the occasion. The precipitating event may be relatively circumscribed but won't stay so because one attaches a litany of other issues to it in a concerted effort to dredge up everything that has ever happened in one's life. Trauma is an event that is carefully prepared, readily seized on, and then exploited for all it is worth. One is flooded with the entire past. One pours all the buried conflicts of the psyche into the traumatic situation in the dim recognition that the trauma is one's own, one's chance, the thing one has been waiting for.

From one perspective trauma looks inflicted, from another created. That doubleness is the key to its understanding and, as we'll see, to the interpretation of all psychoanalytic concepts. The rationale behind this doubleness is the carefully concealed fact that all of one's life prior to the trauma has been a movement toward it. This, the circumstance most strenuously denied in the initial reaction to trauma, is also the recognition that is invariably present at a deeper level of consciousness. It must be resisted because otherwise one must assume full responsibility for one's situation, including the recognition that one loves one's suffering.

It has often been observed that a crisis brings back all of the past in a way that mandates a painful review of our entire life. The past thereby regained is not a set of facts, but a "system" of frustrated desires and recurrent conflicts. Trauma revives and collects not an empirical past, recorded on some slate of memory,[6] but a past that is already present because it consists in the core conflicts one has failed to deal with throughout one's life. Trauma thereby restores our contact with a subjectivity that operates by distinctly nonbehavioral and nonsubstantialistic principles.[7]

It is comforting to think of trauma as an abrupt reversal, as something that assaults us from the outside as a result of actions taken by others which we passively suffer. We are off the hook. But closer inspection always shows that there are no abrupt reversals and that the other is always the partner in a drama we have constructed together. Reversal, as a dramatic and psychological category, points not to an external event but to the central Shakespearean fact that one "has ta'en too little care" in the business of knowing oneself. Reversal is always the reversal of oneself; it dashes a self-image one sustained only by not paying attention to the real direction of one's actions. In fact, trauma can most profitably be thought of as the "act" in which everything comes together precisely because we've finally found the situation that will force us to call ourselves to account. Freud's idea of "the choice of trauma" is an attempt to show that in many ways life can be seen as a process of falling ill.[8] Psychological breakdown has a double face and harbors a positive possibility. For the person in trauma, anxiety supersedes defense because repression is no longer working. The drama of the "self" has finally reached its turning point. Recognition emerges as a dramatic and psychological category because one must face oneself and find a new way of acting or remain, even when "coping" or "cured," in a state of collapse.

I now want to underscore some of the concepts that can be derived from this description. Psychoanalysis gives a new meaning to the biblical saying "In order to save your life you must lose it," and to the Socratic command "Know thyself." The possibility of self-knowledge depends on trauma. Only then are all the parts of the puzzle in place, with the subtext of one's life revealing its power of authorship by presenting the bill. Everything significant that has happened in one's life leads to this point. It is also the experience in which the mental and emotional functions defining the psyche operate in a particularly revelatory way. We know what we really think and feel—and what kind of character we have—only when faced with an event that brings us before everything we've refused to confess about our lives.

Trauma is the point from which one can begin to reconstruct the past because it reveals the conflicts that have shaped the past. It is also the only point from which one can proceed into a future that will be more than a repetition, under disguised and increasingly paralyzed forms, of the past. Trauma makes both temporalities possible because it collects all the conflicts that have to be confronted if there is to be genuine change. Though trauma is initially experienced (and too often theoretically conceived) as the call for deliverance of a fractured subject flooded with an anxiety it is unable to face, this passive posture conceals the truth of the phenomenon: passivity (victimage etc.) is a sign of the vastness of the task trauma identifies and the inadequacy one feels when finally faced with the depth of one's self-deceit—and one's responsibility. Life is littered with those who have proven unequal to the challenge, and psychoanalysis is guilty of complicity in minimizing the problem, especially when it responds to trauma by offering new defenses or the panacea of social normalcy as the standard of health. Such conceptualizations blind us to the philosophic significance of trauma in revealing the experiential unity of subject.

Trauma collects the past that matters because trauma is its finest product. Trauma brings to fruition conflicts that have been deferred and thereby exacerbated. Trauma collects what we've failed to mediate in the apparent mediation of our conflicts. The belief in social maturation and the adaptational normalcy of the "reality-tested" ego gives way before the recovery of a deeper drama of subject.[9] An event has the power to traumatize not because it calls up something one has forgotten or never considered, but because it brings to a head conflicts one has been consistently preoccupied with but unwilling to face.

Trauma brings to the surface a buried history—and reveals it as one's true history. As analytic inspection invariably shows, trauma is never the result of an isolated event but always the outcome of a series of prior events and conflicts. Trauma thus supplants the reductive and genetic tendency in psychoanalytic explanation by calling for a dramatistic mode of conceptualization. When one uses trauma as one's lever in reconstructing the past, the search is not for a privileged event or set of events in infancy that will confer a deterministic stamp on all that follows. The task, rather, is to reconstruct a history in which conflicts are what they become. The main thing one discovers, in fact, is that all the events of one's personal history make a vital and progressive contribution to the production of the trauma. Such a history follows a dramatic, not a genetic or causal, structure: conflict unmastered or deferred begets conflict anew in a more developed form. Wherever one "begins," this is the story analysis must reconstruct. No matter how much data one collects, none of it makes sense until it finds its proper place in such a narrative pattern. Such a reconstruction is impossible, however, if one reifies the genetic moment and then abstractly superimposes it on all that follows. For what one thereby loses *is* the primary fact—experiential emergence, the primacy of conflict, and the inescapability of drama in the life of the psyche. Trauma is the moment of reversal, and, as tragedy teaches, reversal is not the unexpected but the moment of truth when everything comes to the surface. The self is its conflicts: that is the key to using the logic of drama to rethink psychoanalysis. Conflict forms an irreducible and rigorous structure of self-mediations, even when the effort of a life is perpetual deferral. The alternative to reductiveness in psychoanalysis is not simply the development of an action language,[10] but a full-scale application of the logic of tragic drama to a rethinking of the core of psychoanalytic theory. (This is the structure of concepts the next section will articulate.)

Trauma underscores the contribution of psychoanalysis to the larger theory of subject we are constructing because it highlights the problem of identity in a unique way: as a burden that arises only when our subtext catches up with us, demanding no less than a reversal of the entire pattern of living we have constructed to hide us from ourselves. In trauma the issue of identity is suffered in a way that makes the recovery of a genuinely existential relationship to oneself possible. It also brings psychoanalytic theory to a crisis that has still not been addressed, especially by those who make self and identity the cornerstones of their revisions of Freud.[11]

Trauma foregrounds an essential consideration that is conveniently overlooked as long as we focus on dreams, paraphraxes, and jokes, or confine psychoanalysis to the classification of a panoply of disorders (hysterical symptoms, obsessional rituals, phobias, sexual dysfunctions). All neuroses are character neuroses. The real disorder is not one's symptom but one's life. This recognition has the power to strip away the complacencies that enable ordinary, healthy people to proclaim the irrelevance of psychoanalysis to an account of their lives. Freud never systematically developed the concept of character neuroses. But in a little essay called "Some Character Types Met with in Psychoanalytic Work," he describes a personal favorite, which he terms "those wrecked by success."[12] Such is the familiar story of those who know how to snatch defeat from the jaws of victory while making it look as if the world is inflicting on them a destiny they repeatedly bring upon themselves. Their neurosis is their life. By comparison, hysterics and obsessionals are lucky. They have apparently managed to locate and localize their psychic disorder in a symptom. Most of us are not as fortunate. Our neurosis lies in our ability to structure experience for payoffs that constitute a misery far greater than hypochondria, agoraphobia, or some other quasi-physical disorder, relief from which magically cleanses the psyche of all its problems. The point of the contrast, of course, is that the hysterics are kidding themselves too; the symptom is merely the stand-in for a whole pattern of disorder they do not want to face.

Such a recognition motivated Freud's shift from the cathartic to an interpretive method in his attempt to reconstruct the history that symptoms arrest and symbolize. In effect, Freud tried to show all his patients that their real neurosis was their life and that it was to it, rather than to their symptoms, that they needed to direct their attention. Character neurosis is not one disorder among others, but the unacknowledged basis for any classification of psychic disorders.[13] Moreover, this concept breaks down the distinction between the normal and the neurotic and eliminates any way of limiting the impact of psychoanalysis on everyday life. Hysterics are useful because they help us hide the fact that the normal neurotic is the functional one who has found a way to act out and inflict his or her disorder on others. Psychoanalysis challenges each of us to such an

account of the structure of our lives. It is valuable—and intelligible—
only when we let it impinge on us in this way.

THE CORE THEORY OF PSYCHOANALYSIS AS A STRUCTURE OF THESES

The strange relationship in trauma between the loud yet passive
suffering of one's "fate" and the silent recognition of one's authorship
holds the key to the task of psychoanalysis: to reverse that relationship
by articulating the knowledge contained in the marginalized or repressed
term.

The discussion of trauma gives a number of methodological leads for
an attempt to outline the core of psychoanalytic theory: (1) the doubleness
of all psychoanalytic phenomena and the impossibility of explaining that
fact apart from a dramatistic interpretation; (2) the need to establish connections aimed at the narration of patients' histories as unified totalities;
(3) the demystification of immediacy and the need to recognize that the
psyche always expresses itself as a whole and stages its entire drama, in different guises, in each of its enactments; (4) *Nachträglichkeit* (delayed effect)
and the need to break with linear time and linear causality in accounting
for the formation of the psyche and the effect of events on it; (5) the impossibility of understanding sexuality—or psychosexual identity—apart
from such connections. Properly understood, psychoanalysis is the most
eloquent refutation of the reductionism it has so often encouraged.

Such principles obviously have a much broader application than to
the analysis of "the person on the couch." Their true impact may lie,
in fact, in putting much of psychoanalytic theory on trial. Psychoanalysis
will be adequate to its subject only when it applies its discoveries to its
own modes of understanding. What that means, ultimately, is that all
of its concepts must be reinterpreted and take their place in a theory of
drama. This is the dialectic of concepts we will now set forth. It will
necessarily involve a critique of existing psychoanalytic theory and should
enable us to show how different psychoanalytic "schools" arrest the dialectic of their subject. This will enable us to transcend oppositions such
as the one currently controlling discussion—that between the substantialistic framework of ego psychology and the French dissolution of subject
in the play of linguistic signifiers and metonymies of desire. Like the previous one, this chapter is an effort to supplant the conceptual framework
that establishes such alternatives by recapturing an experience of subject
that transcends both ways of thinking. Psychoanalysis thereby becomes a
major part of the theory of subject we are developing.

To begin at the beginning, *the subject of psychoanalysis is the conflicted agent and the dramatic pattern of that agent's activity*. The repressed is the missing term not in the discovery of the underlying but in the description of the phenomenal. By breaking down defenses, resistances, and lies, the analytic process recovers the repressed motives and desires that have been actively at work throughout a person's life, giving that life the unity of a drama that can be described in rigorous terms. Psychoanalysis isn't a return to the vanished past, but a narrative of the hidden unity that brings one to the conflicted present. Appropriately, the first concept this perspective enables us to rethink is the unconscious.

The unconscious is not a hidden substance anterior to the subject and existing like an impersonal thing controlling our acts. It is, rather, the missing link to the most complete description that can be given of the conflicted "intentions," motives, and desires we have constantly acted on while just as persistently refusing to recognize the fact. Freud's cardinal insight was not the existence of the unconscious, but the fact that the unconscious remains active throughout our experience. The unconscious is not an alien otherness in the subject, but an otherness that subject gives birth to and sustains—often desperately. Born through the act of repression, the unconscious remains active because, contrary to popular opinion, repression is not a way of getting rid of a conflict but the act that gives the conflict greater force and extended sway, making it the primary organizer of the psyche.[14] We have a way of running into what we fear, for example, because we constantly project our fears and interpret events in terms of them. Repression doesn't bury a desire, but empowers it. The unconscious is never out of play. Those who think they can spend their lives sitting on Pandora's box don't know that the box is "always already" open: it contains the image of someone in the act of sitting on himself, oozing betrayal in every direction. The unconscious isn't impersonal or thinglike. But the desire to so conceive it becomes an understandable defense once one begins to suspect that it is one's deepest personal truth. For that truth reveals the primacy of psychic disorder in the very pattern of those events we'd like to set outside the unconscious.[15]

Conflict isn't something that happens to the psyche from time to time; it forms the very essence and "origin" of the psyche. Conflict is the distinctive fact that makes us human because the human psyche is born through the originary act of primary repression,[16] which is not a simple process of forgetting and should not be confused with ordinary loss of memory. Repression is an act; it grows out of a particular kind of situation and requires a particular kind of effort. Contra the scientistic Freud, we don't repress instincts; we repress conflicts, charged interpersonal relations replete with complex desires we are unable to deal with or renounce. This is why every repression requires and creates a defense.

One of the contributions of both the object-relations and the interpersonal (Sullivanian) schools has been to dethrone "instinct" and the "economic point of view" from its traditional and reifying place in psychoanalysis. A language of force is needed to account for the power and the peremptory character of the desires and conflicts psychoanalysis uncovers, but the mistake has been to think that only a theory of instincts, "our mythology" as Freud put it, placed on a firm, natural science foundation (biology, organic chemistry, etc.), can provide what a theory of drama offers in far less reductive terms. Instinct is a derivative phenomenon— and its language a flight into impersonality, which is of course one of the best defenses in the face of psychological reality. The person who claims to be ruled by instincts is really ruled by the need not to understand his or her actions and motives. As long as psychoanalytic theory stays fixated on the theory of instincts, it lends complicity to this desire.[17]

These recognitions spell the end of one version of the libido theory.[18] As Fairbairn has argued, "Libido seeks not pleasure but the object"[19] (or, better, a relationship with the other), and as Schafer says, we inhibit actions, and instincts are the result. Classical libido theory arrests this dialectic and reduces it to a mechanism. Once we begin with the interpersonal "origins" of the psyche—rather than with a bundle of biochemical processes which, dammed up, produce those Blakean reptiles of the mind termed "repressed instincts craving discharge"—we discover that what we repress, first and foremost, are interpersonal conflicts, affect-charged relationships we are not able to understand or deal with, usually because they involve some mixture of desire and prohibition connected with a double message we are getting from some other person—most often, initially, the mothering one.

This much can be said without any risk of adultomorphism.[20] When one is talking about the early stages of psychic formation, one is obviously not talking about fully conscious processes. But one is not talking about biological reflex-arc mechanisms either. The virtue of the former language is that it at least provides the right analogy and enables one to make the qualifications that preserve the distinctive character of psychological phenomena. This perspective also cuts through another of Freud's ambiguous terminological legacies: for just as it is incorrect to say that we repress "instincts," it is equally incorrect to say that we repress "ideas." Consider the incredulous reader of Freud who asks, "Do you mean to tell me I once knew I wanted to have a penis or sleep with my mother and later chose to banish this idea from my consciousness through some act of will?" Such a reading is a convenient defense, and psychoanalysis is partly responsible for fueling it. But experience shows that as children, adolescents, and even as "adults" we seldom operate along such conveniently conscious and intentional lines. The notion that we repress desires, conflicts, and affect-charged relationships that we cannot deal with because we have never articulated the bases of our actions takes us a lot closer to the way we operate as dramatic agents throughout our lives, when faced with situations of genuine and deep concern. In restoring the continuity of that kind of agency as the key to conceptualizing "self-identity," psychoanalysis contains the possibility of moving us beyond both reductive and rationalistic models of behavior. There is, however, an ironic sense in which the neurotic process can be seen as a movement that takes us to the point where we can repress as "idea" what we earlier repressed in more primordial ways. Rationalistic theorizing is the mirror image of the neurotic process, the obsessional working of the desire to reduce everything to ideas in order to avoid realities that resist such tidy resolution.

We move toward a better model of how psychic structure develops when we begin with the notion that there are certain experiences we hang onto and keep reworking, projecting them onto subsequent situations, because we continue to be haunted by the conflicts they established; thus, on analytic scrutiny, we find that our agency throughout our lives has been determined by the need to assert and project the desires first formed by these experiences. The origin of the psyche is not in "instinct," but in conflicted interpersonal relationship. To be more specific, its origin lies in the family, and a psychoanalytic understanding of that institution is the task we must now undertake.

THE FAMILIAL GENESIS OF THE PSYCHE

Because the psyche is inherently interpersonal and familial, psychoanalysis is essentially a theory of the family. The core conflicts that define the individual psyche are generated by one's insertion into the family complex. Each individual may be seen, in fact, as the effort to mediate the unresolved and suppressed conflicts of its family. Such an "origin" is not formed by the force of a single event or produced by a single period of time. Psychic structure never follows a simple chronological order but takes form through the growing awareness of one's insertion into a set of conflicts—among parents, siblings (real or fantasized), grandparents (present or not)—in which every event requires and undergoes constant reinterpretation. Chronology is constantly disrupted by delayed effects. Even the most basic things that supposedly had to happen for other things to happen never happened once and for all or without requiring subsequent events to establish their reality. In a world of simple linear time, the past would be utterly that; but a primary lesson of psychoanalysis is that the past is never past.[21]

One of the primary sources of confusion in psychoanalysis has been the tendency to separate into stages and time periods, and to distinguish in terms of gender roles and the distinct "contribution" of each parent, what is always the result of complex relationships that are present from the beginning. They are at the breast, as it were, but that experience is never a simple presence or dyadic symbiosis. While it is natural to speak of conflict in a dyadic language—especially when only two people (mother and child, say) are literally present—conflict is almost always a good deal more complex. This is especially so when the subject is the family. Psychoanalysis could have avoided a number of false issues, especially regarding gender, had it realized that it is not a question of what the mother or the father does—or of distinct pre-oedipal and oedipal periods where each has their distinct part to play—but of the parental relationship, which is present even when one member is absent.[22] Alone with the mother, one is actually with the wife of a particular husband/ father, inserted into a complex relationship which usually reveals its terms only when one recognizes the role of grandparents, siblings, and other relatives. One is the child never simply of this mother, but of this wife, the son/daughter never of this father, but of this husband. If the mother as wife transmits to the child her conflicts with her husband,[23] they derive in turn from the conflicts both partners have with their parents (and siblings etc.). As Hamlet said, in addressing Claudius, "Father and mother are man and wife / man and wife are one flesh, therefore my mother."

The family is a rats' nest of conflicts, and there are many ways in which the whole thing is present at the breast. When, for example, mothering revives regressive sexual fantasies that are threatening to the mother, activating resistances that are communicated to the child as a fundamental confusion about bodily pleasure, the place we may have to go to find the "source" of the child's difficulties is the parents' bed and the actions there of the father. Or, to be more exact, we may have to see how the sexual conflicts between the parents are an unsuccessful mediation of conflicts both parties have with their parents. Such conflicts are often revived and exacerbated by the arrival of a child who may represent the father's rival or the recognition one gets and the revenge one exacts while mothering under the ever-watchful eyes of one's own mother. If we want to define the first form of "psychic integrity" by exploring in a concrete and noninvidious way the conflicts that derive from the child's experience of mothering, we must foreground such connections.

The point of the example is that one never gets a simple origin that exists outside a network of relationships. Nor is what gets "imprinted" on the infant psyche at different "stages" of psychological formation (mirroring, symbiotic, narcissistic, pre-oedipal, oral, anal, urethral, oedipal, phallic) ever set down once and for all. Numerous confusions could have been avoided had psychoanalysis realized that it is impossible to fix the mother's part or the father's part—let alone "assess the blame," this being the hidden agenda of many theories—as if the parents ever were discrete realities. Many of the distinctions Freud made, partly as a result of his reluctance to confront his relationship with his mother, generate oppositions that come a cropper in Lacan's structuralist separation of pre-oedipal and oedipal experience into the reified realms of the imaginary and the symbolic. A more phenomenological view shows that it is not possible to make neat separations between pre-oedipal and oedipal stages, nor to give the particular oedipal drama Freud favored, no matter how dominant in our culture, the binding power Lacan confers upon it when hypostatizing it as the symbolic. No matter how much it may help to map the drama of the family by referring it to that model, the greater truth psychoanalysis must fathom is the one Tolstoy knew, that "each unhappy family has a story of its own." It would be nice if we could chart such complexities in terms of a single drama, order its acts as a series of discrete stages, and define the part/role and distinct contribution of each participant, thereby assessing blame and establishing both health and sexual identity at a single stroke, but the main lesson of clinical study is that such models blind us to the complexity of the phenomena.

I have no wish to deny the sociocultural dominance of the patriarchal model of the oedipal drama or the political desirability of crushing it. It is one of the contexts that intervenes in any family since the cultural roles it sets down exacerbate the conflicts already present within the family and frequently superimpose themselves on richer dramatic possibilities, as when all drama is arrested in the blind assertion of one's proprietary rights or the complacent assumption of one's proper female role. But, if our task is to uncover the complexities of psychological conflict in the family, the intellectual symmetry of a single oedipal pattern can serve as no more than the grid for measuring difference.[24] The potential of psychoanalysis is to understand the family not as a simple social institution reflecting the dominant structure but as a conflicted institution where the plumbing gets clogged.

The birth of the psyche lies in one's insertion into the nest of conflicts that make up "the family system." Each individual can be understood only when all the parts of all the parties in that drama are coordinated and the system is known as a whole. This is the object of psychoanalytic search when the analyst asks the patient to reconstruct the family story. The complexity and conflicted nature of that story should not be underestimated. For example, the different ways either or both parents relate to a child's siblings of either sex, vis-à-vis the way they relate to the child, coalesce in personal attributions[25] and gender confusions which are resisted far more often than they are accepted because they are perceived, by the one who must also deny the perception, as manipulations rather than choices, rejections rather than bestowals of worth or love.

The struggle for individual autonomy might be conceived of as the attempt to establish one's own desire and reality as a term over and against the attributions that have inserted one in a slot in the system of others' conflicts and desires.[26] Once we adopt this perspective we bid farewell to two myths of origin.

The psyche originates not with a single event or through the activity of a single privileged other, but in the midst of a familial confusion that only slowly reveals its terms, if at all. To understand oneself one must undertake the quest to know one's parents: to comprehend as conflict what they try to present as natural, eternal, essential, good. To pose the problem in terms of a striking implication, the child's emotional turmoil isn't confused perception; it's the engagement that makes knowledge of the family possible. The child's emotional reaction to the parents is an attempt to act out and give them the knowledge they deny. Children are, in effect, the last chance most parents have to understand themselves and the truth of their marriage because kids see what's really going on.

Knowing the truth, they pay the price, the "neurosis" being, in its initial formation, an attempt to intervene in the family and activate its arrested drama. Neurosis is always, initially, a legitimate act of protest.

In stressing the "parents' part" I have no desire to get the kid off the hook. The exclusivity and stubbornness of desire run from childhood straight through Lear's effort, even at the end, to "have his daughter all." Everything we established about the impossibility of desire in Chapter 1 will find a place in psychoanalytic theory. All I want to establish here is that if "his majesty the child" is a tyrant, he has a lot of help in mapping the ways to prosecute his tyranny. His choice in the whole matter remains the deciding factor, as we'll see, and what he actively does in living out that choice is the key recognition to which he must be brought if analysis is to produce the truthful reconstruction of a life history. But choice is never absolute, and no desire is free of the situation that establishes it as one possibility among others. When we formulate our desire and enact a definite relationship toward our core conflicts, thereby making them truly ours, we necessarily take up what has already been chosen for us by our parents. Once again, exclusive conceptual dichotomies blind us to the complexity of the phenomena. One can sublate only situations into which one is thrown; action requires adversity for its possibility. We always enter in the middle of the movie that is our life. We walk through our grandparents, and, if we succeed, we put them to rest. Aside from being a defense, the question of who's to blame always misses the mark.

A recurrent difficulty in the path of psychoanalysis has been to avoid the genetic fallacy without losing an understanding of the connection between developed neurotic conditions and their roots in early experience. The problem is threefold, for the task of interpretation is to understand (1) where "conflicts" start and what "form" they take in their genesis; (2) how they develop; and (3) the precise connections between the two, since it is on the establishing of connections that the reconstruction of a life history depends. The key to resisting reductionism is contained in Freud's concept of *Nachträglichkeit*, or delayed effect, if, that is, we reinterpret this notion along dramatistic and developmental lines.

One model of how psychic conflict "matures" may be outlined, in deliberately abbreviated terms, as follows. The psyche is born in the "desire" for the restoration of a particular kind of sensual closeness to the mother. That closeness never was biological bliss but existed as a tension-filled response to the imprinting of her "unconscious" interfamilial conflicts onto the child. That origin becomes, in turn, sexual fantasy and sexual desire once the relationship has developed a pattern of need, fear, and inhibition that both expresses and denies the degree to which one or both parties hang onto its exclusive and intimate (libidinal) character. The core conflict thereby established forms the ground plan one carries into the inescapable problem of establishing one's psychosexual identity. When that effort faces its own endemic crisis, the oedipal drama,[27] all of the stored-up, unresolved, and developing conflicts over one's relationship to both parents come together in what can for the first time be properly described as the *action* of an *agent*. By the same token, however, the pre-oedipal relations, which serve as the first "organizers" of the psyche, set the specific terms which give each individual's oedipal crisis its unique form as a drama.[28] Everything then takes on further determination by the way one "resolves" one's first "love story." There are two supposedly dominant responses: (1) one hangs onto the object of one's desire in the face of the hated rival, or (2) one rejects one's original object and makes that rival the new object of one's desire. But there are other equally note-worthy possibilities. Some agents welcome the Oedipus as release from a smothering, claustrophobic relationship; while others embrace it as a chance to take revenge on the rejecting object of their disappointed love. Some deny the fact of being the chosen one (son) who has already won the oedipal battle and must now seek some way to make reparation to a defeated father; others play both jealous parental lovers off against each other, making themselves the prize that can never be claimed. We are wrong to reduce the variegated forms the "oedipal" crisis takes to a single symbolic pattern so that we might argue that one must accept this culturally enforced solution or remain forever trapped in "imaginary" dyadic binds.[29] Triangular desire is present long before the oedipal moment, and the conflicts oedipalization engenders are a good deal too complex to admit of a single structural resolution. The real moral of the oedipal story is that everyone loses, especially those who appear victorious. For the cost of "victory" isn't simply the need to deny the fact or to develop a punishing superego. That would be enough to lay sufficient seeds of future conflict and defeats, and I have no desire to minimize these reactions. But the greater cost may be paid by those victors who need to reenact the drama, while denying that it ever took place. To invert Sartre, the moral of the oedipal story is that "winner loses." Those who successfully commit the oedipal crime have gained a prize that necessarily turns to ashes in their mouth. (We will see later, however, that the oedipal may also be the transgression required for any liberation of the psyche and of the desire held onto by even the most passive, compliant beings.)

One rarely achieves significant dramatic agency at the first try, and that is why the Oedipus, though a turning point, is usually resolved by compromise formations and followed by that period of exhaustion known as latency. But compromise only lays down the terms of future conflict, and although the Oedipus is usually resolved by repression, renunciation, and the development of the superego, this holy trinity will enact a heavy price at adolescence and often ever afterward. Adolescence, the search to find the terms of intimacy, revives everything one struggled with in the oedipal but with those conflicts now projected primarily into one's relationships with members of the opposite sex. Those conflicts reawaken in all members of the family, incidentally, and often with far more disturbing consequences than before as a result of actions now taken by the father or mother who resists losing what he or she dare not admit is far more than just daughter or son.

In a sense, the development of the psyche might be seen as an attempt to break out of the family and enter the world of concrete relations with others.[30] But leaving home may also be the drama that never really ends. For the oedipal drama, revived at puberty, guarantees that interpersonal relationships will be full of conflicts that it may take the rest of one's life to understand, let alone solve.

At each "phase" of development, the psyche simultaneously moves in two directions. Whenever an effort is made to mediate them, earlier experiences are both understood anew and activated as conflicts of a certain kind for the first time. Sexual desire for the mother, for example, often reveals itself as such only when one finds one must, in effect, betray her by choosing another or when one finds one can't do so without feeling guilt and the need to seek restoration by undoing each new relationship. Similarly, one often learns what was going on with "daddy" only when one takes delight in toying with men or finds kindness feminine or when one discovers that one needs to play the part of the other woman in a repeated pattern of triangular transgression and subsequent rejection.

Any attempt to mediate conflicts both establishes their power and gives birth to them in more involved forms. This process constitutes the uncertain path of psychic development.[31] Nothing ever happens once and for all in the formation of the psyche because everything is what it becomes. And that process has the ability to reach back and transform the beginning. This recognition provided the solution to Freud's long vacillation on the subject of infantile seduction fantasies: the truth of the matter is that father and daughter, mother and son did and didn't do it together numerous times in ways that we will never know until subsequent experience lights up the past with the shock of a recognition that is creation as much as discovery. Conflict is not something we can escape, because it forms the very way we act and interact. The self is its conflicts, and whatever "identity" we achieve derives from how we live them out. Conflict does not disappear—it issues. A conflict is what it becomes, and that becoming is always greater than and irreducible to its origins.

Such connections hold the key to seeing why adulthood is so often marked by conflicts which have the character of a "return of the repressed." As adult relations (especially marital) develop, the "unconscious" motives that informed what Freud termed one's conditions for loving, and the conflicts one hoped to escape, surface. Trauma presents the bill —the task of confronting all the avoidances that have shaped one's life —but now in a situation a good deal more complex and confused, with responsibility all the more exacting for being so long deferred. As we shall see, psychoanalysis is essentially a theory of (unhappy) love, and this must be kept in mind if we are to achieve a nonreductive understanding of the centrality it assigns to sexuality in the genesis of "neurosis."

Freud was fond of the adage that in love relations there are always four people present: the man and his mother, the woman and her father. The mathematics are actually a good deal more complex, but Freud provides a good starting point. Finding one's other—and not just refinding the original object—is a rare act, perhaps the rarest. And making a family of our own is necessarily among our most complicated attempts to mediate the entire complex of conflicts that defines us. It is also the scene of our most persistent failures not only because, as Freud notes, we often choose someone unlike the parent of the opposite sex and then turn him or her into someone similar, but because we just as often find that we've done no such thing but were simply kidding ourselves all along with the illusion of difference. There are no safe or innocent choices, and those that appear so frequently hold the biggest surprises and the most shocking connections.

Love is also our most significant project because, in bringing the entirety of the psyche into action, it contains the possibility of a new issue. Once again, psychoanalysis asks us to conceive opposed alternatives of a single dramatistic concept. Love always activates a dialectic between the repressed and the emergent because the other holds out—or inflicts— the possibility of self-knowledge. Projecting onto another woman what one hasn't faced about the relationship to one's mother, for example, puts one in a position to understand one's activity for the first time. Projection breaks down because it runs up against an otherness that exceeds it, an other who is different and confronts one with a world of difference. Such is the fortunate result that may befall us—unless, that is, we love successfully and find the perfect "other," the mirror image of an arrested "self."

The beauty of relationships is that the conflicts we project come back at us from the outside. Two people, each with conflicts, meet and either disguise or welcome the struggle in store for them. If this image suggests a fundamental disorder that accounts for the frustration that so often characterizes our experience in loving, it also posits that love always activates the chance for a drama of emergent possibilities. Love need not be simply the clash by night of frozen projections or the ceaseless, Proustian pursuit of the lost object, which is itself, ironically, the self-defeating attempt to reinstitute an old conflict. Love can also be the process of interaction through which the clash of conflicting projections submits to drama. Failure may be the usual issue, but the permanent possibility of love is that it need not fail—if, that is, we learn to conduct this affair in a way that welcomes its inherent and necessary conflicts rather than avoids them.

Love is also the experience that most often brings one to the experience of trauma because it collects and brings to a head everything that has been held in suspension or deferred in the psyche. The psyche in trauma circles back to its beginnings and picks up the thread of all the significant efforts it has made to mediate its conflicts. Methodologically, the overview we have presented in this section points to a determinate, dialectical connection between "repetition" and the emergence of the new, a connection that should put an end to reductionism. Conflict begets a drama that is irreducible to its origins. Desire isn't a fixed point: desires are canceled, preserved, and uplifted as they are lived out in the new and progressively more complex interpersonal relationships that make up the course of significant experience.[32] Development is neither the dissembled howl of endless repetition nor the fitting of oneself into a prearranged structure. The only development given to the psyche is the "projection" of its conflicts into a world that always bites back.

REPRESSION AND THE UNCONSCIOUS: "YOU CAN PAY ME NOW
AND YOU CAN PAY ME LATER"

We are now in a position to reinterpret repression and the unconscious in dramatistic terms. Freud's great discovery was not the existence of the repressed, but the activity of the repressed. His true insight was into the psyche as a dramatic structure that constantly expresses its conflicted positions in each of its modes and activities. Dream as disguised fulfillment of repressed wish, symptom as sexual desire and denial are merely the clearest examples. For this insight is also the key to understanding the foundation of the whole edifice—repression.

Standing in the way of a correct understanding of repression, ironically, are psychoanalysis' two main notions of what we repress: instincts and/or ideas. Both positions derive from opposite sides of the naturalistic-rationialistic dichotomy according to which consciousness is either thinking machine or mind connected to body. The psychological subject is the lived transcendence of these alternatives. Its birth is in conflicted desire, which is a reality that surpasses both frameworks because it defines the subject not in terms of behavioral or cognitive processes but in terms of a certain kind of agency. It is the nature of that agency that we must conceive in order to understand repression.

The recurrent and most significant discovery in analysis is that beneath all the distortions and defenses, resistances and denials, beneath all the fears and inhibitions, and beneath all the tales of victimage and passivity, an affirmative voice can be heard. Desire is the true author of the neurotic process. One powerfully desires something one was not given or has lost; and one has refused to renounce that affirmation, let alone admit it. The pivotal analytic discovery that provides the basis for reconstructing a life history is the discovery of hidden, disclaimed desire. Repression is first and foremost the repression of desire. And, as such, repression is also the great sustainer of desire because it gives birth to a series of denials and disclaimers which keep desire alive by keeping it disguised. The key to "health," as we'll see, is not to tame or eradicate desire but to "free" it.

Affirmation is what generates and sustains the unconscious—and that is *why* the unconscious remains constantly active. Struck by the many ways in which it finds expression—dreams, jokes, paraphraxes, fantasies, symptoms, etc.—we may lose sight of the connections and order of importance among these phenomena. This is what happens when one gives in to the temptation to conceive of the unconscious as an independent agency and to picture it as a "cauldron" seeking discharge at any cost and at any available exit. In gaining an encyclopedic perspective on a wealth of phenomena, such a conception loses sight of the central fact. The unconscious is one term in a dramatic process where desire is the foundation of human agency and the repression of desire our primary mode of operation.

Repression is a two-edged sword. It affirms both the importance of a conflict and our inability to deal with it. It reveals the centrality of a desire at the very core of subject and yet how strenuously the subject, in suppressing that desire, has had literally to take flight from itself. Repression splits the psyche, and once one has resorted to repression, the psyche *is* this split.[33] Subject is not outside the split but is the way one lives it. Once "born" through repression, one has become an agent acting a conflict. As Freud came to see, splitting is the initial and most primitive defense mechanism.[34] It is also the starkest way of establishing the conditions for drama. It will be succeeded by much subtler defenses, which may be most noteworthy finally for the indirectness whereby they delay and detour a clean dramatic expression of the conflicts they harbor. Every repression requires and creates a *defense* both in order to keep something out of awareness and as a way of dramatizing that fact. Defenses thus share a characteristic that makes them prime sources of drama: they establish the importance of a conflict they refuse to face. As such, they give birth to a history made up of the successive crises in which one defense collapses or outlives its efficacy only to be replaced by another. One of the most revealing ways to decipher an agent's narrative, in fact, is by retracing his defenses. As the drama of life proceeds, each product of conflict deferred and denied requires a new and more sophisticated defense to sustain the process. When all this functions smoothly, one eventually attains the sophisticated intellectualizing defenses that constitute the characteristic baggage of what we term the mature, adult, reality-testing ego.

Since repression is the distinguishing human act, from the perspective of psychoanalysis to be human is to live a relationship to oneself defined by a core conflict—to be internally conflicted in one's very desire. This formulation offers a new understanding of desire.

Desire is active not because it craves release, but because it seeks to achieve a certain kind of relationship. It is frequently noted that this quest, and with it the very pulsion and peremptory force of desire, derives much of its power and poignancy from the loss of the original object of desire. The less recognized fact is that these characteristics indicate that the initial relationship was not the tranquil paradise pictured by nostalgia —as when Freud speaks of the child at the mother's breast as the central symbol of reverence in our culture—but was itself internally disrupted. Perhaps the deepest secret desire keeps from itself is that the ideal it keeps harking back to was not ideal at all. The violence of desire would never have arisen as the response to the loss of paradise. Desire needs betrayal as much as succor and finds disruption in every presence because the initial presence it harks back to was fraught with it. Desire has its springs not simply in loss, but in a loss that can't be accepted because it brings into the open conflicts that were already present in our original relationship and that constitute its suppressed truth. This understanding of the matter is crucial to understanding the repressive process. Its confirmation is usually found, however, only at the end of the line when, like Gatsby, we attain our desire only to discover that it is empty, or that the real payoff lies in losing or destroying it. Just as the outcome of the story of desire is often full of surprises that are rarely romantic, so its original position is a good deal more conflicted than any sentimental thematic of "paradise lost" can conceptualize. The true story of our first story is the one we don't tell— or tell incessantly in reenacting its conflicts.

We thus arrive at the central irony, the basic fact: repression is not a way of getting rid of a conflict; on the contrary, it is the act that gives a conflict greater force and extended sway over one's activity. Eternal vigilance is the price of the repressive process because whenever experience presents situations in which the repressed conflict is brought into the open, renewed repression is required. And that is merely the surface, the way things get pictured when it seems our misfortune is to keep running into things we want to avoid. The truth of the matter is that we actually seek out such situations or take situations capable of going in another direction and turn them down this predetermined path.

Because repression insists on the importance of a conflict we try to deny, and affirms desires we project while disclaiming that we are doing so, it creates what George Klein terms "unconscious cognitive, affective, and motivational schemata" that have a controlling force in the way we organize "experience."[35] In Kantian terms, repression creates the a prioris of our interpersonal experience.

The repression of a conflict is never the solution of a conflict, but the beginning of its drama. Through repression we "store" conflict in such a way that, as Klein shows, we simultaneously try to avoid situations where that conflict will be primed and actively seek them out. The subject continually strives both to realize its founding desire and to run from it. Repression thus reproduces conflict in that double form that constitutes both the precondition and the inevitability of drama. Defense is man-dated, but self-alienation paradoxically becomes the movement toward self-discovery—or "falling ill"—for the act of repression establishes the psychological conditions for what Aristotle termed *reversal,* an event he saw as the precondition for recognition and genuine change of character. Repression is the act that first makes drama possible. For it establishes the primacy of a core conflict on which we continue to act while at the same time denying our activity. Initially, to be a dramatic agent is to find oneself caught up in conflicts that one produces out of one's deepest needs without recognizing *that* or *why* one is doing so.

To forestall a false issue let me reintroduce an important qualifi-cation. Psychoanalysis is a study of how the subject acts in the face of situations that involve its "ultimate" and most basic concerns. It is only in such situations that the processes we are talking about operate to produce the irreversible developments that constitute the history of the psyche. There are many things both in the daily operations of consciousness and in the sum total of "events" that make up the empirical story of the years that have nothing to do with psychoanalysis. There are also, as Freud and Joyce show, many times in the midst of our quotidian affairs that the deeper concerns of the psyche announce themselves. But this fact can easily lead in the wrong direction. Contra Heinz Hartman, psychoanalysis is not a general psychology, nor should it aspire to become one. As with literature, its value is as a study of the engaged psyche. That is where our true history lies and where we take those actions that "determine" the content of our character. Much in our daily existence and (sadly) in the accumulated story of the years has little to do with that drama. But empirical psychology grasps the unessential relationship. The significance of its subject lies in its insignificance, its revelation of the wasted time stretching before and after those experiences that really matter.

THE UNCONSCIOUS DRAMATISTICALLY CONCEIVED

Experience structured as drama consists of those actions through which primary repression gives birth to situations that require further repressions, thereby making life one long, continuous, subterranean move-ment toward and away from those key events and episodes when every-thing comes together in a way that makes trauma and recognition pos-sible. As the force regulating the series of complications through which a core conflict develops, repression constitutes the hidden "logic" of our experience. That logic basically works as follows. Whenever experience presents situations where the repressed is brought into play—i.e., either threatened with detection or cunningly engaged in projecting itself—a new repression is required in order to maintain the self-deception. Another event or area of experience has thereby been incorporated under the sway of the repressed. We have increased both the number of situations in which we are likely to become anxious and the likelihood of finding ourselves in precisely those situations.

A similar logic shapes the development of defenses, with each new defense building on previous ones in a process that is progressively more limiting and desperate. This is especially true when that limit is the "academically" hallowed defense, intellectualization, which is the foolproof means of achieving a state in which one has escaped the possibility of understanding one's psychological processes. This logic of dramatistic doubling also offers the proper conceptualization for a number of distinctively psychoanalytic discoveries, such as selective inattention (ironically one of the keenest acts of attention), reaction formation, and the multitude of other ways in which we systematically maintain in the face of anxiety a particular kind of gap or blind spot in our awareness. Specifically, these are ways in which we deny desires (or their derivatives—wishes, fantasies, forbidden thoughts) in the very act of affirming them, ways we refuse to recognize the importance of conflicts we author, at the very moment in which we express them.

The irony of all such processes is that while they may produce *gaps* in our awareness, there are no gaps in our actions. The unconscious as an evolving system and the real world as neurotically lived are structured simultaneously through the process in which primary repression gives birth to derivative repressions. The unconscious is not a substance or script set down once and for all through a primordial act that occurred at some hypothetical time in childhood and that has since remained dormant waiting to be unlocked by psychoanalysis and resolved through the recovery of early memories. It is an evolving system of disclaimed acts, motives, desires, and conflicts—and its structure corresponds to the life history of which it is the underside. There is nothing substantialistic or reified about the unconscious. Its structure is that of a continued structuring. It has a birth and a development and it always remains open to further modification, for it is the growing, still-active "product" of what we have not mastered in the experiences that have mattered most to us because they were the ones in which our core conflicts were most in force yet dealt with least.[36] This is why analysis so often resembles peeling the layers of an onion. As one goes back through one's psyche, uncovering defenses and denials, the most shocking discovery is that they form a highly structured order. That order provides explanations that fill in the gaps in our narrative by revealing our experience as a continuous drama of "repressed" desire. The unconscious isn't a fixed desire that remains static throughout time, but a system and history of what desire goes through in its convoluted passage. Rather than a substance, the unconscious is an activity; and the primary way in which it acts is not in dreams or para-phraxes but by organizing experience so that we seek out situations where we can express our conflicts but always, and with increased insistence, at a further remove from awareness. That process constitutes the development of the unconscious, and reveals it, not as a collection of discrete repressions, but as an ordered structure of interconnected ones.

As a dramatistic system, the unconscious evolves as new repressions are called on to sustain earlier repressions. The conflicts that structure the unconscious are thus lived out in experience in a way that puts the psyche on a collision course with itself. The unconscious and experience coincide because the "developmental" process brings repressed conflicts to a head. This happens for one simple reason: it is well-nigh impossible to live without relating to other people. Thus the situations that called for repression in the first place have a way of turning up with persistent regularity and greater urgency in the course of "adult" life. The beauty of experience is that it always runs to meet us halfway. Those supercharged experiences in the realm of human interaction involving conflicted feelings of love and hate, dependency and aggression, erotic longing and the fear of punishment that shaped the psyche's core conflicts simply won't go away. It is impossible to live among other human beings without facing many situations where repressed conflicts will come into play. Hell may be other people, but if so it is because the other is always both the occasion for projection and the power urging self-discovery.

To such commonsense observations, psychoanalysis adds the deeper connection. It is unlikely that our conflicts will become less intense as we "mature," for failure to deal with a problem only exacerbates it. As the contexts of human interaction become more demanding, in terms of both what we ask of others and what they ask of us, the chances of "running into oneself" multiply. The fact that most people settle into their ruts, maintaining their "mental health," through whatever deadening of mind and feeling, managing to forestall the day of reckoning beyond the successful end of their successful lives is not really an argument against this proposition. It is one of its finest confirmations. Trauma is probably never more apt a designation then when applied to those devastated beings who spend their whole lives denying trauma has occurred or who think the avoidance of drama is anything but the marionette show in which, under the sign of normalcy, they enact their desire in parody form. But to see this as the most consoling truth of psychoanalysis, we must describe the basic choices we face insofar as we are beings who live condemned to drama.

THE DRAMA OF THE PSYCHE: BASIC MODES AND DEVELOPMENTAL LINES

Many outcomes are, of course, possible. Such is the nature of drama. In its most virulent form, repression becomes so massive, with the unconscious growing to such a degree, that experiential possibilities are eliminated. One lives in the constant presence of a danger one can neither avoid nor face. The repressed becomes omnipresent, voracious, and desperate. Wherever one goes one meets only oneself—and flees in horror from the encounter. As Fairbairn shows, the paranoid displacement necessarily moves toward psychosis. Attaining that certitude, it achieves the dissolution of drama.[37] It thus provides a point of contrast enabling us to define the principles that make more complex dramatic outcomes possible.

To be an agent is to live a relationship to one's core conflicts and to organize experience in terms of the conflicting motives and desires they establish. Interpersonal relations are, at base, attempts to mediate one's core conflicts; action is the attempt to resolve incompatible demands. Given the activity of the repressed—the continued denial of an affirmed desire—our acts as agents always have a doubleness: they are efforts to escape our conflicts, but they are also efforts to resolve them by fulfilling the "desire" at their roots. This fact suggests why our efforts so rarely meet with success.

Experience is essentially a process in which one generates new conflicts out of core conflicts. This is what informs the unity and recurrent instability of its dramatic structure. Experience as dramatic process is thus a dialectic defined by poles which George S. Klein has termed *fractionation* and *active reversal*.[38] In what follows, I reinterpret dramatistically what Klein formulates in terms of a cognitive ego psychology that is tied to a quasi-Eriksonian theory of the maturational process as proceeding along fixed developmental lines, with each phase contributing a solid "content" to a relatively stable identity. My implied argument is that this framework, however inadvertently, deprives these principles of their dramatic character. When everything becomes a matter of Piaget's cognitive sets and Erikson's abstract needs for basic trust, identity maintenance, etc., active reversal becomes an adaptational category rather than a dramatic one, with the reality principle of American society covertly controlling the entire process. A dramatic development of these categories will liberate far more disruptive possibilities.

Although experience looks like a random and discontinuous process, full of twists and turns, apparent progress, and abrupt regressions that rarely assume the clarity and order given by retrospective schematization, fractionation and active reversal define the general lines of psychological development because they define the two ways in which one lives the drama of the repressed.

Fractionation

In *fractionation* the psyche contracts, becoming progressively more defensive as it repeats the refusal to recognize or renounce the repressed desires on which it continues to act with increasing insistence. The existential consequence is a progressive shrinkage of experiential possibilities. Action becomes progressively more blind, more automatic, more a thing of insatiable and peremptory urges and fears. As the repressed in this malignant form extends its sway, all of experience becomes charged with the presence of a danger, a confusion (Emma Bovary's "fog in the head"), and a frenzy that drives one along in that rattle-trap streetcar of desire toward inevitable confrontation with the very thing one fears: the desire that has structured one's experience finally brought home in its most frightening and appropriate form. Such is the basic logic characters such as Emma Bovary, Charles Swann, Bob Slocum, and Blanche du Bois live. As fractionation progresses, one is constantly on the lookout for occasions both to flirt with the repressed and to renew one's flight from it. One gravitates toward those defenses that are automatic and frenetic (undoing, isolation, regression). Anxiety becomes omnipresent, and panic becomes the only possible response to "truths" which become unmistakable. Eventually one attains psychic agoraphobia. As a consequence, one runs into the repressed everywhere. There are no longer any obstacles to one's "will." Reality can no longer interfere with the pure fulfillment of one's dreams. The psyche has now become the unity of two moments: projection and distortion. One's activity takes on, in reified form, the characteristics Lawrence

Kubie uses to describe neurotic behavior: repetitive, obligatory, insatiable, and stereotyped.[39] In terms of Klein's cognitive psychology, we can say that in such a condition no "accommodation" to "reality" is any longer possible; instead, one blindly "assimilates" all experiences to a repressed schema that is frozen in its abstractness.[40] One lives a repetition compulsion in the worst sense of the term: utterly estranged from oneself, one's life becomes the big lie. As Emma Bovary learns in enacting this movement with exhaustive naturalistic regularity, it takes a long time for experience to come to this, but this point is the telos of one way in which conflicts can be lived. The price of blindness to oneself is the repetition of one's conflicts in progressively degenerate forms so that one's life becomes not the fulfillment but the parody enactment of one's desire. In such cases, conflict hasn't been banished; it has merely assumed its most reductive form. Everything is made to look like an impersonal process in which one is victimized by the external world, the irony being that such a world no longer exists.

Active Reversal

Fortunately, there is another, though far more exacting, possibility. It is also harder to conceptualize because it finds its beginnings in the experience of trauma. While fractionation shows a life sliding to its "happy" end on the grids of a continuity that is really that of breakdowns deferred, denied, and displaced in ceaseless repetitions, active reversal becomes possible only when such processes are shattered. Everything grinds to a halt, past and present converge, and one is flooded with "connections" that are initially experienced as a vague, free-floating, yet omnipresent anxiety. If successfully sublated this experience leads to a genuine depression in which, like Hamlet, one takes action within oneself. This process is the foundation and beginning of active reversal: the internal change through authentic reflection that makes external change possible.

A description of how an analysis moves toward active reversal will put us in the best position to understand how active reversal must operate on the larger stage for which analysis is merely dress rehearsal. The following description refers simultaneously to both performances, however, in order to illuminate the connections between what happens on "the couch" and in the world.

The movement toward active reversal is essentially one in which, through the breaking down of defenses and the opening of oneself to anxiety, one "repeats" one's core conflicts in a new way. Intellectual assimilation of the repressed into one's consciousness is only a beginning; and as long as working through is confined to one's transference relationship with the analyst, it will never effect genuine change. To get that, one must plunge into one's experiential conflicts in an effort to transform the nature of one's activity. Analysis can be most meaningfully defined as the controlled production of and working with anxiety. That is both its virtue and its limitation as preparation for living. Life is greater drama because its anxieties assault us unbidden, because we have no sure means of control when we find ourselves thrown into situations unanticipated yet in some way deeply chosen. If analysis rids us of anything, it's of our way of avoiding conflicts in order to prevent both the understanding of our experience and the fulfillment of our desire. Virtually everything that makes up this description of the goal of analysis constitutes a critique of the general drift of things in the American mental health professions, where a gross recidivism rate lies hidden, cloaked in its proudest product —the happy, adjusted psyche confirmed in its need to "feel good about itself."

Effecting the movement toward active reversal involves three distinct dramas that usually constitute three distinct phases in the course of an analysis.

1. *Uncovering Defenses.* The first step is to become aware of the ways in which one distorts one's experience. The analysis of resistance, of defenses, projections, and reaction formations in terms of the specific situations in which they are used, focuses on this activity. Its purpose is to recover the true scene of one's life. It does so by showing that the babble of displacement and hyperempiricism that characterizes the early stages of analysis—and of most relationships—is a systematic veering from the real issues. One would not go as far as Clara Thompson who said, "The analysis of the resistance is the cure,"[41] but uncovering defenses is the necessary first step. As Freud put it, "One must listen to the details of one's illness."[42] Defenses are employed not randomly but only in situations where there is something we do not want to know. The irony is that we defend against knowledge only when the matter is one of deep personal concern. The situations that call forth defense thus contain the clue to discovering our true conflicts.

How one defends is an even more important discovery because it gives us an insight into our dramatic method, or the nature of our dramatic agency. Projection, for example, is the mechanism whereby I have my action come back at me from the outside as an assault by the other, thereby securing my protected place as spectator-victim at the staging of my own drama. Discovering *what* we need to distort about our experience and *how* we do so are crucial acts; but they are also mere prologues to the question *why*.

The reason *why* one distorts and defends is the ultimate object of inquiry because it reveals the desire at the foundation of defensive processes. It also brings home the recognition that we have been the active agents all along in sustaining the neurotic process and that we have done so because of desires we continually project onto experience while refusing to face the fact. Once one achieves this standpoint, one's life history begins to reveal its fundamental dramatic pattern. (It even becomes possible to start dividing it up into its acts—pre-oedipal, oedipal, adolescent, young adult, midlife, etc.—in a way that makes sense of those periods not as preformed structures but as parts of a continuous personal history.)

2. *Moving to the Active Voice.* Roy Schafer has argued that a successful analysis can be described as a movement from the passive to the active voice, with its stages and the kind of personal narrative told in each illuminated by Northrop Frye's theory of the four great literary modes.[43] Beginning in a comic paradigm, one pictures oneself as the passive victim of circumstances. Without knowing it, one begins to reveal the active side of one's agency when, in the romance or transference phase of the analysis, one goes in quest of the analyst's love. If successfully interpreted, that act—the significance of which lies in reviving the emotional force of one's original desire—brings one to the tragic recognition that one has been the primary author of one's unhappiness. Tragic recognition is thus the point at which reliable narration becomes possible, such telling being a pitiless attempt to track down the basic fault that has shaped the pattern of our experience. Schafer goes on to describe an ironic phase (which he admits overlaps the tragic) in which, through a detached contemplation and intellectual acceptance of the truth about one's life, one gains release from bondage. Schafer's tie to ego psychology and its view of therapy as "reality testing" here exacts its revenge. For reasons that will become apparent, we must reverse the order of the last two phases, seeing the ironic as either the attempt to arrest the tragic (as in Joyce and Spinoza) or as the process of readying oneself for it (as in Hamlet and Nietzsche). It is also worth noting that the ironic phase will circle back to the beginning, à la Fryean desire, only if one's entire analysis has been a sham. The circle is an endless source of fascination because it cleanses us of the sin of existence. But analysis is necessarily concerned with the *irreversible* in

human experience. Its greatest cultural contribution may, in fact, lie in restoring respect for tragedy as the truth of the human spirit.

As Schafer shows, the key to progress in analysis is the recognition that the neurotic process is constituted not by what has been done to us but by what we have done. An analysis can go on forever,[44] but its secrets are given only to those who recognize their complicity in the neurosis from its inception. This is also the reason why analysis actually reaches back and transforms the past. It does so because it has to. Tragedy isn't the only version of one's experience; it's the most honest and useful version. It is self-defeating to blame those no longer around. The only one whose activity matters is the one who is still performing the actions that bring about a suffering they alone are capable of reversing. One's complicity in the neurosis is the essential discovery because in revealing one's agency, it restores one to that agency. With the hard-won recognition that one has been the author of one's suffering and the active agent all along, sustaining the neurotic process out of a desire one has persistently refused either to relinquish or to admit, one begins to reclaim oneself as an agent.

3. *Reclaiming Desire—The Act of Reversing Oneself.* What does one do with all the painful facts analysis dredges up? This question, which is most often raised dismissively, is in fact the question most worth asking. Even those who chase the myth of an exhaustive analytic self-knowledge still remain agents. That is the one thing from which psychoanalysis can never deliver us. Every time it thinks it can, it gives in to the error of substantialization and suppresses its true discovery: that the subject it studies is action through and through and has no point of substantiality where reifications, however well intended or socially dominant, can take root. Analysis may prepare us to know ourselves, but even in the best of possible worlds to do so one must go forth and act.

The crucial third step in any process aimed at self-knowledge, and the step required for genuine change in the structure of one's personality, is active reversal. Insight and working through are prologues. Action got us into our situation and only action will get us out. The real change psychoanalysis makes imperative is a change in the modality of our activity. That is why change requires plunging into our conflicts in an attempt to find some new way to live out the life of our desire. One moves toward that possibility by attending to situations with an eye to detecting both the continued activity and the self-frustrating pattern of one's desire. Making that connection puts one in a position to cancel repetition and reclaim desire. In many ways, active reversal requires working up the courage to go after what one has been after all along. The desire that forms the "core" of the psyche is ineradicable—as long, that is, as one remains an agent. The suggestion that we act upon it is not as "scandalous" as it may initially sound. For it isn't as if we haven't been acting on it all along. On the contrary, our whole life has been that action and its indefinite deferral: the projection of a desire and the self-frustrating denial of that very desire. Active reversal is not an *Umkehre* or an unraveling of the psyche, but the process of trying to liberate something that has been consistently at work throughout our life. While the "developed" forms desire takes assume from one perspective the monstrous proportions of a repetition compulsion, from another angle they reveal a flawed history of attempted mediations that contain, even if under the sign of defeat, the scars of possibilities well worth recovering. Each episode in which the psyche suffered genuine defeat was necessarily one in which it was also engaged in some significant effort to emerge from its prison. The true task of analysis, accordingly, is to recapture failed projects and restore the continuous thread or through-line of our defeats in order to point us toward the actions we must take to renew the drama of our possibilities.

One of Freud's most challenging and far-reaching ideas is contained in the statement "In our unconscious we never renounce a desire we've once had." The problem is not to get rid of desire, but to find a way of unlocking and realizing it. The basic contradiction in those psychoanalytic theories that preach adaptation and renunciation, or picture health as a condition in which the ego as "function" maintains control over drives under the sovereign dictates of socio-economic normalcy or "the reality principle," is that in dissolving the dramatic agent they deny the reality of the psyche. In opposition, we derive our most controversial hypothesis from an attempt to sustain this dimension of the subject: the purpose of analysis is to reclaim and free desire.

Freud's papers on therapy and technique are often far ahead of his theoretical articulations and contain some of his most provocative insights into the nature of drama. One of the most suggestive remarks is this: "He [the patient] must find the courage to pay attention to the details of his illness. His illness itself must no longer seem to him contemptible, but must become an enemy worthy of his mettle, a part of his personality, kept up by good motives, *out of which* things of value for his future life have to be derived" (italics mine).[45] Much of what we've said above provides one gloss on this remark. Its richest implication we will now develop.

Let me introduce it through a relatively safe example. Consider the fairly typical case of a person who is inhibited from having a satisfying sexual *and* interpersonal relationship with his or her spouse because of an unresolved oedipal tie to the parent of the opposite sex. The key to the dilemma: one can't live fully as long as one has divided one's desire and left the bulk of it trapped in a conflict one refuses to face. Through analysis the erotic energies bound to the parent are not done away with. Were that the case, the person would remain where he is, acquiescing in his "inherent" limitations. Active reversal entails a more exacting and enriching possibility. The erotic desires bound to an internalized object and an "infantile," self-punishing relationship are transferred to the present and set free in such a way that they can be invested in the real world in a fully liberated erotic and interpersonal relationship, which we may term, with a bow in the direction of romanticism, the resurrection of the body.[46]

In *fractionation* one "repeats" one's conflicts *passively*. That is why fractionation progressively shrinks existential possibilities. In *active reversal* one "repeats" conflicts not in an effort to defer, escape, or resolve them, but in order to transfer, transform, and realize reclaimed desire. Understanding its terms, one plunges into one's conflicts vitally engaged in the effort to bring the whole thing to an issue. Successful outcomes are not guaranteed, and we may leave their proclamation to the mental health professionals. The key to the concept of active reversal is to see it as the turning point in the nature and power of one's agency which produces a change in the kind of drama of which one will be capable. The effort of active reversal is to see *if* desire can be set free of its infantile moorings and its self-defeating identification with a frustrating or forbidden relationship so that experience may become the existential drama of desire canceled, preserved, and uplifted. "Repetition" of this sort might be described as a process of self-overcoming in which one's basic task, following Nietzsche, is to "become who you are." The task of psychoanalysis is not to undo things, but to recover them, not to cleanse the psyche but to restore its power of activity by showing it that it has always been active and must remain so. The goal is not static acceptance or acquiescence in necessity,[47] but the need to *become* who we are by assuming responsibility for the actions we have already performed and must now undertake in order to live out our drama.

This view of the goal of analysis may be too challenging, but it alone preserves the essential contribution psychoanalysis makes to a theory of subject. The late resistances on which many an analysis flounders are not so much resistances to knowing things about oneself as refusals to give up a desire one has not yet found a way of realizing. As psychoanalysis shows, one would rather have a frustrating object than no object at all. Until one finds a way to get one's desire into the world, one hangs onto it in disguised, distorted, and self-defeating ways. As Freud learned, all psychoanalyses are the reconstruction of love stories. The deepest attachment of the psyche, the act which in many ways constitutes its self-definition, is not something that can be renounced. For this attachment isn't an attachment to an object, but constitutes the very inwardness of the subject.[48]

From the beginning, desire isn't wish but dramatic conflict. It is that erotic tie one cannot but choose to act on in some way. Transference is the essence of psychoanalysis, but the main transference it tries to affect is the transference and transformation of desire. It is only when desire is being transferred from an internal object to the real world that new possibilities emerge. That, in a nutshell, is the slow and agonizing task of active reversal: not willed necessity (Freud), or expanding the conflict-free sphere of the ego (Hartman), or changing one's cognitive schemata (Klein), or altering the attitude one takes toward one's actions (Schafer), but summoning the courage to put one's all into the irreversible deed. Active reversal goes even further than the powerful idea that analysis tries to bring about a change in the structure of one's personality; for it reveals that intrapsychic change comes only through changing the way one acts in those situations which one has, from the beginning, hallowed out for oneself. Change derives not from dissolving or minimizing one's conflicts, but from acting them in a new and necessarily more engaged way.

There are, of course, no magical acts or final victories. Almost every progression entails regressions. A conflict is never solved by a single "privileged situation" or "gratuitous act." One can always regress, but there comes a point when if one does so it is because one has deliberately chosen to lapse in one's being, unable to sustain not only all that one has learned about oneself but all that one must do to prove worthy of that knowledge. There is no closure short of the grave. The reconquest of one's humanity is, as Nietzsche said, one's daily task.

For most of us, the possibility of active reversal comes only when we have brought ourselves to the point of crisis or trauma, which is why trauma is the dramatic category par excellence. Trauma leaves us with two choices—the long march to recovering the truth of our actions and the courage to act them in a new way, or the search for the quick fix and some new means of denial to ease us down the slow and tedious road of zombification. Most of us, of course, contrive to live our lives somewhere between the poles of fractionation and active reversal. We make our meek pragmatic adjustments, settle for our partial fulfillments, function with our defenses carefully in place, and conspire, with conspicuous success, to forestall the day of reckoning. But what is such living, for all its health and normalcy, but holding things at bay—even perhaps a manifestation of thanatos? Only when confronted with crisis do we have any way of knowing our character, in any case, for as Aristotle observed long ago, "It is by virtue of one's actions, and not in terms of a quality, that one is happy or the reverse."[49] What he might have added is that in the course of our life we all perform but a single action.

Experience may be defined psychoanalytically as a dialectic of the disclaimed and the emergent because the repressed always organizes experience in a double way. Action is both a process of alienating oneself from oneself and a process of coming toward oneself. Experience is both flight from and flight toward. We are always in some way moving toward either fractionation or active reversal. Though its forms vary, the one thing we can bank on is trauma.

BASIC PSYCHOANALYTIC CONCEPTS DRAMATISTICALLY REINTERPRETED

The Drama of Defense and Anxiety

The analysis of defenses, which has today become a major focus of analysis, bears out this line of thought. One of the subtler and more exciting discoveries of recent clinical psychoanalysis is that defenses and their corresponding affects present a layered structure.[50] Uncovering the connections leads to some of the most valuable inferences in reconstructing a life history. As a "mature" defense gives way to analytic probing, a new defense and a new affect come to the fore. This order reveals in reverse the process whereby the defenses initially came into operation. Each new repression requires a new defense in order to ward off the affect and the attendant conflict that pours forth once that defense breaks down. Freud argued that each new stage of psychic development demands a new censorship. Analogously, each emotion or experience we can't deal with requires that we either find a new defense or force an old one to strain under a new burden. In Sartrean terms, what is uncovered regressively through the analysis of defenses provides, when reinterpreted progressively, a fairly reliable picture of a person's life history *condensed* into its purest dramatic terms. The countless "naturalistic" experiences that went into a given way of *not* dealing with experience are, in a defense, represented as the act of one agent versus another. Schizoid withdrawal, for example, struggles to freeze an overbearing anger. The outcome of that drama forms the arrested unity of such a subject: the charming set of resultant behaviors is termed the passive aggressive personality. The popular view that the early Freud concentrated on finding the id and the later on showing the ego's success in defending against it misses the dialectical connection between the two "agencies." In looking at either, we are looking at the other; their dramatic relationship is the sole reality.

The layering of defenses and affects conceals and reveals the "stages" through which secondary repressions have built up a structure of disclaimers that simultaneously sustain and displace the desire at the basis of the neurosis. The layered relationship of defenses and affects thus represents the strategies the subject has devised in the face of its drama so as *not* to enact it. Because we all employ an array of defenses—with superfluity perhaps a necessity—it is naturally hard to sort things out. But, with enough patience, specific defenses can be correlated with specific situations. Both can then be traced back to specific episodes and relationships in our life in which our core conflicts had to be handled or avoided with some urgency. The defense came into being and derived its appeal from how well it did the job. Having done so, it found steady employment. The thing we've lost sight of in the effort to gain an encyclopedic catalogue of defenses[51] is that defenses are derivative phenomena that make sense only when dialectically connected to the *situations of anxiety* from which they endeavor to deliver us. The hidden story of defenses is a story of underlying motives. The main implication of this line of thought, of course, is the critique of the defense ego and of those psychoanalytic theories that define the subject in terms of the ego's need to maintain control over drive.

Anxiety and defense are the central concerns of psychoanalysis and they are correlative concepts. Defenses are the measures we take to avoid knowing what we are doing. Anxiety is the momentary breakdown of those shields.[52] Anxiety is in many ways the most important experience we can have, if we can learn to stick with it and listen to what it announces. For although anxiety is still viewed as a vague and transitory, almost somatic experience, which simply assaults us from time to time and bears no connection to our normal everyday life, anxiety is actually radically concrete and always situational.

Freud's vacillations on the problem of anxiety are worth careful consideration since they provide a perfect recapitulation of the problems and changes in his thought. In his most mature thought on the matter, Freud defines anxiety as the unconscious response of the defense ego to *danger situations*.[53] By definition, these are situations in which the repressed is in some way impinging on awareness. Although we like to picture anxiety as a momentary, quasi-physiological experience that intrudes on our consciousness from nowhere only to pass away just as quickly leaving no residue but the "It was nothing" response Heidegger analyzes so brilliantly, the mature Freud reveals that the ordinary understanding of anxiety is itself a primary defense against it. Our anxiety over anxiety—our need, as Sullivan shows, to get rid of this feeling quickly and at any cost[54]—rules our conceptualization of it. Psychoanalytic theory is hardly immune from complicity. Wanting to be delivered from anxiety, we like to think of it as a passivity of the subject, when it is really an act we perform in response to a situation. It can, in fact, be regarded as the first act we perform— though unfortunately for most people it is also the last.

Initially, anxiety is the act both of alerting oneself to danger and of trying to make that danger appear vague enough that one will have no choice but to flee. The personal and situational is thereby made impersonal. That irony defines the characteristic doubleness of anxiety as both an act and an emotion. It is as if the psyche were bent on taking flight from the world precisely at the moment when the world deeply engages it. We seem to live determined to run from desire the moment desire has been quickened.

What is true of anxiety is true of all emotions: they are ways in which we enact a drama in situations of conflict. Anger, for example, isn't a fixed quantity of stored-up energy seeking discharge, irrespective of the occasions to which it arbitrarily attaches itself. Nor is it a hidden substance that explains everything in one's life when, on that wonderful day, one finally gets in touch with it. There is no such thing as an "angry person." One's anger relates to certain definite situations, and one doesn't begin to understand or deal with it—let alone consider, contra mental health jargon, whether it may be healthy or appropriate—until one looks at the situation. No emotion is abnormal or bad per se, though the desire so to classify certain emotions is. The key to understanding emotion is to specify the situation, the conflict that calls the particular emotion forth, in order to probe what that emotion, as incipient action, reveals about the nature of one's engagement with the situation.

This general point about the nature of emotions, to which I will return, has special significance for the understanding of anxiety because anxiety is in many ways the prototypical affect from which others derive —as defenses, displacements, reaction formations, etc. Harry Stack Sullivan argues that the primary act that forms and regulates the psyche is the attempt to ward off anxiety. That effort is, in fact, the origin of what Sullivan terms the self or "self-system," which for him is no more and no less than "a system constructed to avoid anxiety."[55] Therefore, this system might with greater justice be termed the false self, for the truth of the construct Sullivan describes is that it doesn't work, or works at the cost of too great an impoverishment of the subject. Consensual validation aside, the false self will continue to impoverish the subject until anxiety is seen not as an uncanny and terrifying feeling to be avoided at all costs, but as an annunciatory experience to be probed in depth.

To so understand anxiety, one must get it out of the category of the impersonal and into the category of the situational. For "danger situations" don't just happen. They are personal. As Schafer has shown, Freud's mature understanding is that all danger situations are one's own danger situations, because of the "meanings" (usually unconscious) one has invested in certain experiences. The fact that the meanings are "unconscious" yet peremptory is the tip-off. Danger situations are chosen— indeed, they are often actively sought out—because they are the situations that are of most importance to the subject, those where it confronts, if only momentarily, its buried history. Even if anxiety assaults me when I'm in a room alone, doing nothing, it remains situational, for it refers to some conflict that is impinging on my consciousness. We are always in danger because the one vacation one can never take is a vacation from oneself.

The analytic process, accordingly, is only as good as the danger it is willing to run in the production of anxiety. Whenever the patient is coasting along free of anxiety, the analyst had better see that he or she regains contact with it. The absence of anxiety is not a sign of progress, but a reliable index that the analysis is off target. As an analysis proceeds, it is not so much the case that anxiety lessens or disappears as that it becomes specific and articulate. As one comes to understand one's core conflicts, it is no longer necessary to have anxiety over everything, to displace it frenetically into innumerable inhibitions and symptoms, or to project it randomly onto every available occasion. Having unmasked the unconscious meanings and symbolizations that allowed one to extend and displace anxiety onto relatively "innocent" situations (i.e., agoraphobia, writer's block, hypochondria), one now has one's anxiety concretely and in face of the actual situations from which it derives. Once we know what our anxiety is about, we can begin to interrogate it. What was originally a curse has become a blessing: the true inner voice that comes unbidden to level our complacency by putting us in touch with "unfinished business." Thus the existential consideration of anxiety initiated by Kierkegaard complements the psychoanalytic understanding, which in turn concretizes it. All anxiety is ultimately anxiety before oneself and over oneself; it is anxiety over the core conflicts that make a given situation one's own situation. "Anxiety tolerance," or its lack, is not a given of one's natural or biological constitution, though such a view is a good example of psychoanalytic conceptualization as a defense against anxiety and an expression of a certain passivity and ill will toward the task of being human. Being overwhelmed by anxiety, displacing it, being unable to interrogate it, actually means being estranged from oneself and passive toward oneself in that estrangement, just as readiness to project oneself into anxiety is the beginning of insight and the sine qua non for active reversal.

Defenses also deserve closer dramatistic scrutiny than they have generally been given. It was impossible to explore this connection until the more dynamic orientation of recent ego psychology established the ego "as a system of motives, rather than of functions,"[56] endowed with drives and desires of its own, most of which are "unconscious." With the shift to study of the conflict between ego wishes and id wishes—rather than between ego functions and id wishes—defenses began to be seen as "dynamic tendencies having mental content."[57] The task of their interpretation, accordingly, was no longer one of identifying or reinforcing them, but of scrutinizing them in an attempt to discover the wish that they express—albeit in disguise.

Though few ego psychologists picked up the implication, their view of the ego and of ego development had begun to totter. Most of the ego is unconscious and dark to itself. Our self-knowledge here is as fleeting as it is in the case of our desires. We have, at best, intermittent insight into what is going on in any of the rooms of our divided house, and we strenuously resist the little insight that comes our way. But while we are quick to concede blindness when it comes to the id, we resist any attempt to undercut the identification of the ego with conscious intentions and transparent rationality. The possibility that the ego may be the darkest continent has not yet been plumbed because that possibility destabilizes every conceptual and social scheme on which psychoanalysis has rested. Perhaps we have struggled for so long to see the ego as a rational or reality-testing function in order to avoid seeing it as yet another manifestation of conflicted desire. In spite of itself, the great achievement of ego psychology is to have removed the ego's last and most cunning hiding place, the citadel of reason, even though it has just as persistently tried to reestablish reason's reign under the guise of the ultimate mystification, "the conflict-free ego sphere."[58] Psychoanalysis implies leads to a single overwhelming question, which bears on all the practices we identify with the disinterested exercise of mind: What isn't a defense—and what defense can withstand scrutiny?

Freud was fond of reminding us that what we strongly fear we often strongly desire. Defenses are clever and compromised agents sustained by complex motives. Maintaining a defense may have as its primary significance a continued insistence on the very thing the defense is supposedly warding off. Defenses often bear an uncanny similarity to the specific anxieties and conflicts that call them forth. Analytic scrutiny shows, with great regularity, that the precise defense used in a given situation *mirrors* and in some way *satisfies* the repressed desire it is supposedly combating. Schafer has argued, in fact, that defenses are double agents which always in some way fulfill the very desire they supposedly deny.[59] One factor supporting this view is the pleasure, and not just relief, that results from the successful employment of a defense. Adaptation, the reality principle, and the need to assert the ego's control over drives have little to do with the glee we feel when a defense works: something closer to a pure expression of the pleasure principle gleams forth on such occasions. It is as if one has successfully escaped detection and can now serenely persist, secure in the hidden life of one's desire.

The erotics of that life come into view when one probes the close connection, often amounting to a covert identification, between a defense and the desire it wards off. Defenses are selected, and one of the most significant questions one can ask is why, from the innumerable ones available, does a person "choose" this defense or set of defenses, rather than others? In pursuing this question, one finds that often a particular defense is appropriate because it fulfills the desire it is a defense against, but in reverse, or, as it were, in drag. Robert Waelder found an intricate, if somewhat forced, connection between projection, paranoia, and unconscious homosexual urges: fear of being assaulted from the outside was a disguised way of affirming homosexual desires.[60] Less ornately, we may note how hysterical symptoms attribute hysterical desire to everyone, while daring them to detect the hysteric's insistent projection of a randy atmosphere charged with constant innuendo. Analogously, schizoid withdrawal provides the perfect defense for a passive aggressive personality, since it is the posture best suited for denying the actions one takes in an effort to drive the other into a rage.

The dialectical relationship between desire and defense points to a larger concept that bears on all psychological processes. Like Leibniz's monads, every act of the psyche mirrors the psyche as a whole in its conflicted position. If we begin to look at defenses from a perspective alive to their dramatistic doubleness, the following considerations point to a single conclusion. Defenses are far more than "mechanisms," and their employment is far from automatic. As enactments of the "unconscious" part of the ego, they are much closer to the "id" than has been generally recognized. This closeness becomes particularly suggestive, according to Schafer, when one notes their archaic nature, and their source in primary process ideation.[61] Add to this the irrationality with which even the most "rational" of them are maintained when threatened—the "academic" defenses (i.e., intellectualization, idealization, isolation of affect from content) being, all things considered, the hardest to dislodge—and combine that insight with the pleasure resulting from their successful employment and one begins to appreciate the "erotics" of pure mind and related phenomena. Defense is the most fun many of us have because it's the only fun we have. But, like the murderer who gets no pleasure from his crime, it's a kick we can't admit because that would bring the submerged story of the defense into the open. That story can now be told, unfolded and conceptualized in its basic terms.

Defenses are always attempts to flee from a desire one has already in some way acted upon. By and large, they have the character of reaction formations: they sustain a desire by disguising and displacing it. The logic of their development is a good deal closer to Derrida's logic of the supplement than to any logic based on the principles of identity and contradiction.[62] Defenses are substitutes: they supplant desire in a way that resembles an inversion of the logic of *Aufhebung*.

What is true of a single defense is most revealing, in fact, when applied to the layering of defenses and their corresponding affects. In the course of analytic struggle, as one defense gives way, another defense of a more archaic (and often quite different) nature comes to the fore. This order constitutes "a continuum of conflicted positions,"[63] which, as a sequence, holds *in suspended animation* an incisive "picture" of the subject's life history. It does so because the unconscious defense ego is finally no more than a mirror image of the id: not so much its antagonist as its double. Once one sees disclaimed activity and substitute gratification as the key to defenses, it is possible to see their history as the parody enactment of one's desire. A defense is like a symptom: it cries out for a deciphering of the desire it stages. It is also analogous to Freud's definition of the dream: "the *disguised* fulfillment of a *repressed* wish." That is why even while resistance is uppermost, close attention to the phenomenological character of defenses gives analysts considerable insight into the frozen conflicts and desires for which they must reconstruct a history. It also gives them considerable insight into the difficulty of the case: for our defenses reveal both the kind of drama we've engaged in and the kind of dramatic activity of which we are currently capable. Consider, for example, the difference between schizoid passivity and projection; even at its most histrionic, the latter at least puts us in motion and drives us, however desperately, into the world.

One key to analytic progress lies in depriving defenses of their semi-automatic and mutually reinforcing character in order to restore their dramatic significance as stages in a conflicted history. This is the kind of development Clara Thompson had in mind when she said, "The analysis of the resistance *is* the cure." Resistance isn't an abstract static thing but an ongoing drama which we term, somewhat misleadingly, the transference. The defenses and affects uppermost at one stage of this process are seldom what one encounters at another. Moreover, since transference sustains drama, it recaptures, in series, the acts through which the subject has dissembled and displaced its core conflicts. Exposing the contradictory nature of the defenses a subject has used restores the contact of defense with the desire underlying it.

But before we can liberate this connection we need to complicate its context by showing how emotion, which is frequently taken as the opposite of defense, is really its double, caught up in a similar dramatic struggle, and equally in need of analytic scrutiny.

THE DRAMA OF EMOTIONS

What isn't a defense? This is the question to which psychoanalysis is led, often in spite of itself. Some of its most cherished and least analyzed concepts—normalcy, health, reality testing, adaptation, the conflict-free ego sphere—are implicated in the crisis signaled by this question. The emotional life doesn't escape that interrogation; it, too, is called upon to give an account of itself. In our romanticism we like to think that our feelings are above suspicion, antithetical to our lies, or, in more sophisticated terms, that emotion is that self-presence that provides incontrovertible evidence. We keep telling ourselves, "If we can just get in touch with our feelings." Feelings are safe preserves, in any case, since they can't be critically analyzed. Feeling, like belief, is a performative; it isn't something we analyze but something we do. In my emotions I am self-evidently present to myself and I am free. Those who hold such beliefs may find that psychoanalysis offers yet another surprise.

The great contribution psychoanalysis makes to the understanding of emotion has been repeatedly arrested and lost in metapsychological speculations.[64] And there are so many things both within and outside psychoanalysis that one has to cut through in order to get to the emotions that one could easily spend a volume simply clearing the ground, only to arrive by that laborious route to a single conclusion: emotions are that which we understand least—and want to understand least. Theories are not innocent, value-free constructs, but are often themselves defenses against, or attempts to get rid of, the very phenomenon that is their subject matter. Little wonder that the dominant theory in psychoanalysis holds that emotions are "discharge phenomena," thereby illustrating through theory the archaic defense of undoing. We take the emotions and "blow them away." Emotion is what we deal with after we've dealt with more important things, or what we want to know quickly along the line of least resistance to gratification *sans* understanding. Whether we cherish the emotions or distrust them, when we get to them most of us simply want to express ourselves and be done with it. The interrogation of emotion always occasions strong resistance because it implies the "scandalous" notion that we may be "wrong" in our "subjectivity," that perhaps emotions are the place of the greatest deceits, where the real battle for change and self-criticism must be waged.

One of the most curious things in Freud is that, while he continues throughout his work to theorize about emotions in a severely abstract natural science framework—defining affects as discharge phenomena in a reflex arc physiology dominated by the economic point of view—his clinical practice pivots on emotional struggle and the discovery of complex emotional connections. Franz Alexander argues, in fact, that therapy is essentially a process of finding and unlocking those "*archaic emotional syl-*

logisms which rule the unconscious processes."[65] Metapsychology and clinical practice are consistently at odds, and, with respect to emotion, psychoanalysis stands more in need of dramatistic and dialectical reformulation than anywhere else.

Like all psychological events, emotions enact the total psyche in its conflicted positions. As such, their "immediacy," regardless of its force or certitude, is never a simple phenomenon. Like defenses, emotions are often double agents. We feel one way so as not to feel other ways. Our strongest emotions often stand in stark opposition to the motive that sustains them: moral outrage often denies and defends against desire; exalted servitude provides a perfect cover for hate.

Like the dream, the fantasy, and the symptom, an emotion is a complex and conflicted text. Among such phenomena, it is also the one most worth learning how to decipher because it brings us closest to experience. This fact, which is often used to mitigate the importance of emotion, is the key to its uniquely revelatory power. While dream and fantasy have a certain freedom, emotion is always in some way pinned down to the world it wants to flee or magically transform. Emotion has its origin when in the course of experience I would like to enter the freedom of the dream, the fantasy, or the joke but cannot. That doubleness or double bind is what the emotion both conceals and reveals. Although we like to think of the emotions as expressions in which we are most free and direct, it makes more sense to see them as efforts at deception when it has become hard to fake yet imperative to do so.

Emotion derives its force from the fact that it is the last step in the effort to complete a distinct kind of psychological process. Emotions aren't by-products but end products. They make sense not as a release of leftover tensions, but as the *action* in which I try to finalize my stance toward a situation in a way that will put me in control and make me fully present to myself. This need, and not the need for discharge, is what gives emotion its peremptory character. Not surprisingly, it also informs theoretical attempts to protect emotions from scrutiny and give permission for their expression by identifying the emotional life with personal idiosyncrasy, subjective freedom, and the unanalyzable natural constitution of each individual. The irony is that the supposed passivity of emotions—and the dispassionate objectivity of theories of emotion— conceal the urgency of an intense activity.

Emotion is the heart of the psyche because it is the act in which the subject tries to finalize and master its experience. As Spinoza taught, "An emotion can be overcome only by an emotion."[66] We have to live out our emotion or get a new one because an emotion is required to complete our dealings with any situation that has troubled us. For the most part, we do so by finding the emotion that keeps us safe and secure. This is one source of the persistent attempt to explain emotion in terms of discharge, adaptation, and a steady-state interpretation of both the pleasure and the reality principles.

But even if self-protection is the characteristic human operation, this does not explain its doubleness. The secret of subjectivity is that permission is never given: if we weren't up against the world, if the world didn't impose itself on us, we'd never feel. Conflict provides the experiential source of the processes which issue in emotion. Once we study their situatedness, most emotions reveal themselves as attempts to resolve this origin by suppressing one of its terms. If I can feel a certain way, I *don't* have to deal with something that is troubling me. That is why, for most people, feeling puts an end to all debates. It is but a short step from such an attitude to theories that identify emotion with "personal identity" and autonomous subjectivity and that defend it as the one thing no one has any right to interrogate, the last place in the modern world where we are still free from the objectifying and impersonal laws of science and technology. The circle of this line of thought is complete when one embraces oneself in the knowledge that, thanks to it, one's emotional life forever escapes scrutiny. One is entitled to feel whatever way one wants to. Emotion thus becomes the final defense that completes psychological processes in a way that reifies the psyche. The appeal of this healthy, quasi-adaptational view lies in what it conceals: when the motive for emotion is to suppress conflict, the emotion is a liar.

Ironically, our need for the lie establishes the inestimable analytic significance of emotion. Emotion is the attempted resolution of a complex drama. As such, it contains the entire conflict encapsulized and ready to reveal itself, to the right kind of scrutiny, in a way that makes concealed "truths" no longer deniable. The most important exercise of suspicion is suspicion toward one's emotions. It is here, if at all, that we will track our selves down. But this is the hardest task and the one in which resistance is uppermost because emotion is the most carefully constructed hiding place. Emotion tells the longest story; but because it condenses that story into the terms of immediacy, it is also the most elusive narrative. Like the dream, an emotion is a complex text represented in the mode of the instantaneous. Like the dream, it condenses volumes into a single stance or image. And, like the dream, it demands expression and seems to consume itself in that act, leaving no trace. We're glad when we've gotten it off our chest and can say of our emotion, as Heidegger's inauthentic being says of anxiety, "It was nothing." Even when we prolong their pleasure, we seldom allow the understanding of our emotions to progress beyond the stage of the Hallmark card.

Psychoanalysis will have achieved much if it gets us in the position to consider the heretical proposition that we can be "wrong" in our emotions, wrong not just in our response to *King Lear* or the latest film, but wrong in our response to our own life. The critique of one's emotions —and through that act perhaps the discovery of one's "true" emotions —should become "the basic rule" for psychoanalysis because emotion is what free association gets to when it's working. The fact that we have to labor to get at how we feel, and the fact that the emotions that present themselves first usually prove the biggest liars, derive from the same condition. Emotions are actors—some bad, some cunningly defensive, some genuine—whose roles are determined by their place in a historical drama, that of our relationship to our core conflicts.

Reconstructing the history of our feelings requires discovering that structure and subjecting it to critical scrutiny. But, to reconstruct, one must know how to begin at the end, that is, with the present and the interpretation of emotions as they present themselves in everyday life. For here, above all, our real emotion is usually the one we don't feel.[67]

To understand an emotion one must begin with its situational specification. An emotion is always an attempt to maintain some conception or "sense" of oneself in the face of some situation that is important or threatening because it relates to actions we want or do not want to take. Careful phenomenological attention to every component of this "definition" is essential. To understand an emotion, one must see what triggers it and what the emotion does to handle the provoking situation. One of the reasons why there can be no univocal definition of any emotion (anger, say) nor any single standard of normalcy or "morality" for judging emotions is that every emotion is defined by the situation to which it refers. Anger when warranted is admirable and articulate just as anger expressed without provocation is symptomatic.

The psychoanalytic notion of "unconscious affects" is a convoluted attempt to make an important point. Emotional life is a layered structure. That structure holds in "solution" the series of positions we have taken up toward our conflicts. It thus reveals the immediacy and self-evidence of feeling as an impossible myth. The function of our first and most cherished emotions is not self-expression but defense against those emotions we fear and are unable to handle even though they express our actual feelings far more accurately than the emotions we have carefully contrived to put in their place. This function, to use a safe example, is the deferred source of Hamlet's melancholy: his ambivalence toward his father comes through only when the language of exalted respect cracks under its own strain. Hamlet doth protest too much, because other feelings he can't handle keep rushing forth.

When analysis tries to get back to our "true" feelings, it's really after our buried conflicts. And the purpose of discovery is not to get us off the hook, but on it. For when we "get in touch" with such feelings, we don't find a fixed substance craving discharge, or a comforting romantic self-presence promising renewal. We find, instead, emotional complexes or knots that remain tied to specific conflicts. Our "real feelings" are the ones we've put off dealing with because doing so would force us to actively engage the core conflicts from which they derive.

If one wants to interrogate the emotional life with a view to "painful" discoveries, several ground rules prove invaluable. The emotions that matter are of two kinds: (1) those we need to have in order "to feel good about ourselves," and (2) those that burden us with ourselves, forcing us to work. The former derive from the defenses and avoidances that sustain our "self-system." Their peremptory character is not that of desire but that of need: the need to be rid of certain conflicts, by emotional fiat if necessary. Conflict, not bodily tension, is what such emotions "discharge." The latter emotions are significant, in contrast, because they bring us before a less automatic and self-serving process. Here *reality* functions as a term of genuine opposition to desire. What we do with these emotions provides a gauge of what it costs us to get back to the emotions we need or of the degree to which, in holding onto anxious feelings, we are embarked on the struggle toward active reversal.

Emotions are masks, poses, character armor. They are also imperfect actors who can be driven to self-revelation. When emotion functions as a defense, interrogation brings out its hysterical character. Insistence, blindness, and the need for emotional discharge indicate not the force or the authenticity of an emotion, but its desperateness. Such responses betray the infantile, primary-process character of many of our emotions, especially those that mask as the contrary. It is only when the serene, intellectually dispassionate personality strains to maintain that stance that we begin to know the stance for what it is. When we catch an emotion struggling to reassert itself, we uncover both its defensive function and its inadequacy to what one is being forced, however momentarily, to confront.

Analysis is an attempt to reactivate this drama by recovering and then exacerbating the conflicts emotions strive to resolve. As an emotion unravels—or blindly reasserts itself—the conflict it was designed to cover is recaptured, and other emotions come to the fore. The emotions that make up our lines of defense are the emotions "most worth having" if we are prepared to undertake their critique. For their value lies in their destruction—and in what emerges in their wake. Before emotions submit to destruction, however, they trot forth in the full pride of their assertion. Only a poor analyst would fail to pay careful attention to them in this guise, since the basic emotional profile one presents at the beginning of analysis indicates the basic stance one has taken toward one's life. Sartre holds that we choose our emotions and that a basic emotional choice constitutes the "core" of each subject. Our basic emotional disposition thus provides the key to our self-reference, our attitude toward reflection, and the stance we have adopted toward our existence. The popular notion that "we can't lie in our emotions" might be most profitably pursued along such lines. Emotion is able to express the truth of subject, not because immediate self-presence coincides with the expression of emotion, but because emotion is a complex disguised text awaiting decipherment.

Emotions, like defenses, can be distinguished in terms of whether they move toward fractionation or toward active reversal, in terms of whether they serve passivity or sustain anguish and the possibility of awareness. For all emotions refer to the subject's relationship to itself. Sustaining some mode of that relationship is their primary function. Emotion as defense restores normalcy, discharges trouble, and feeds on consensual validation. Its function is to deliver us from ourselves. The direction is always passivity and abstraction from the situation. In contrast, those emotions that burden us deliver us over to the world. Their function is to sustain experience as a problem. Keats calls melancholy "the wakeful anguish of the soul." The vitality of depression lies in its ability to sustain a drama of the mind in which everything lacerating that we know about ourselves and being-in-the-world is held in suspension before the question "What shall I do?" Depression doesn't remove us from action but prepares us to engage in actions that will be more than semi-automatic, conventionalized responses. Such capacity is the difference between Hamlet and Laertes.

Emotions that burden us offer the richest insight into emotion in general because they show that emotions are not passivities of the subject or discharge phenomena, but incipient actions. As such, they inaugurate existent reflection, grounding that possibility by presenting its burden. Sustaining painful emotion is the way in which we first summon ourselves to the possibility of self-knowledge and active reversal. Unfortunately, when reflection equals reestablishing security of "self," the revelatory power of emotion is undone. Then, of course, the emotions one prizes are those that restore harmony with social consensus or show our ability to adapt, defer pleasure, and conform to "reality." Given such an attitude toward reflection, the purpose of the emotional life is to get rid of disturbing phenomena. This is the hidden Kantian or rationalist legacy in psychoanalysis.

Analysis depends on the demystification of immediacy. Since most emotions are defenses, the proper question to ask is "What are they covering up?" Analysis answers this question with a recurrent discovery. When one finally gets down to the "real emotions," what one gets at is core conflicts. Bedrock emotions are capsulized summaries or figures of desire; they represent the ambivalence that attends the inevitable connection of desire with prohibition and transgression. Our deepest emotions are, in a sense, impossible projects. They invariably have more to do with what Lacan terms the register of demand, the absolute requirement to be loved without qualification, than with the compromises that make up the unstable mediations of interpersonal desire. That is why when one gets down to bedrock one uncovers never "the one true feeling" but an ambivalent conflict of feelings, and why demystifying the "law of the heart" and the romantic myth of an original emotional self-presence is an essential step on the road to self-knowledge.

There is something truly liberating in this discovery. For it suggests that our "true feelings" are a matter that has not yet been determined. The way we supposedly feel in depth is merely one side, and most often the frozen one, of an arrested drama. Our task isn't to get back to our feelings, but to bring their conflicts into the open in order to reactivate the drama they conceal. Psychoanalysis joins hands with the fundamental condition of true humanism: self-criticism is our primary duty. If we want to live out the romantic ideal of discovering ourselves by discovering the truth of our emotions, then feeling must be the first moment in a reflective process where self-criticism holds sway. Our true feelings are "feeling-complexes," defined by their relationship to unsolved problems. That is why Freud is wrong in his interpretation of Dora, for example, when he engages in a search for the single ultimate cause or affection (supposedly her love for Frau K) that will explain everything, and right when he describes the tangle of feelings and motives that implicate the entire cast of characters in that convoluted drama in one grand disorder.

What is true of developed emotional situations is also true of the original conflicts that impelled us on the tangled journey toward our "mature" emotional postures. This connection, in fact, illuminates both ends of the process. Whenever we trace desire to its roots, we invariably find an interpersonal relationship full of conflicted feelings, and with a wealth of "warring" characters contributing their voices to the drama's inception even when only two people are physically present. The interpersonal dimension maintains throughout our emotional life. Even when alone—or at the end of the road—we always feel emotion "up against" and in the presence of the other. There are no private emotions: emotions are appeals, gestures, and even when they apparently refer only to oneself they do so in terms of an image one needs to sustain—an image of oneself as lovable, hateful, misunderstood, worthy of redemption, or whatever. It is impossible to feel anything long without personifying and then staging some miniature drama in our heads because emotions are coalesced patterns of interpersonal interaction that make sense only in terms of the others to whom they refer. Thus, for all its intensity, emotion is a bare stage and a shorthand script. In emotion we stage interpersonal conflict purely in terms of self-feeling and dramatize our attitude toward the other purely in terms of our magical power to compel his love or undo the effects of his hate. This is one of the reasons why the interrogation of emotions is so important: magic undone restores our contact with those feelings and situations we don't want to face.

Something similar explains the power of emotional pain and its intimate connection with active reversal. The primary motive for having emotions in the first place is our need to rework experience. This is especially true of our need to hold onto painful relations and memories. Hurt alone does not compel us; the goal, which can also be the source of endless frustration, is to work out a new solution—to find, in effect, a whole new way we could have lived the relationship from the beginning. The refusal to let go, to be done with something, often breeds resentment, stored vindictiveness, and the masochistic need endlessly to reopen one's wounds. But not letting go can also be an insistence on facing something, on not being done with an experience until one has plumbed its depths, its quotient of necessary suffering. When carried through properly, emotional convalescence is not that failure to "grow up" that eventually produces a hardening of the heart, but an essential step toward active reversal. When we mourn properly, our goal is not to get even but to preserve that vital desire that has been misplaced and misspent. Reclaiming it bars the easy route of forgetting with a yield of painful truths, especially about oneself. Not letting go is the condition for saving desire, which is, in turn, the ultimate motive behind active reversal. Otherwise, there would be no reason to welcome suffering and use it as the test to find if we prove worthy of our experience. Our task as subjects is not to attain renunciation, tame desire, or refuse to internalize experience whenever doing so entails shame or depression, but to recapture the vitality of our desire by discovering the ways in which we have been the author of its frustrations.

As Robert De Niro observed, "The actor doesn't express emotion, he conceals emotion, for it is in the process of concealing emotion that the real emotions come out." This is more true off the stage than on, because on the stage of life, the audience each actor is most intent on convincing is himself. We are always in some way reflecting and taking action in ourselves; in fact, inwardness is where the most important actions take place. Emotion is trial action and incipient action. Keeping up an active conversation with ourselves is a deliberate and deliberative effort to affect processes that reach far beyond what passes simply inside our heads. Eventually everything we feel reaches directly into our experience—in one way or another. Since we are condemned to living out what we "really feel," it behooves us to exercise the greatest critical violence in this area. Our duty is not to save or indulge or trust our emotions, but to develop the right ones. The alternative to emotional self-indulgence is not rationality or lack of feeling, but the recovery and dramatic projection of one's abiding passions.

THE DRAMA OF PSYCHIC STRUCTURING: REINTERPRETING THE STRUCTURAL THEORY

THE DILEMMA CALLED THE EGO

The dramatistic perspective we have developed provides a new way to conceptualize Freud's final formulation of his discoveries, the structural theory of id, ego, superego. Properly understood, this theory is one not of separate agencies or blind impersonal forces but of the conflicted motives that are present in an agent's activity and that reveal the relationship that agent is now living to his or her core conflicts. Its schematism thus provides the most complete description we can give, in interpreting any particular event and its aftermath, of how an agent's core conflict is currently structuring experience. The key to understanding is to see the three "agencies" as dialectically or dramatically related to one another, with the changing character of each "agency" determined by the actions —or inactions—the subject performs. The structural theory is not one of fixed quasi-substantial "entities" but a theory of drama and of how to map change in intrapsychic terms. The only time the three agencies take on fixity is when one has successfully reified oneself, which is why they frequently so appear at the beginning of analysis. The task of analysis, however, is to enter this frozen world and introduce new possibilities; i.e., its task is to effect the drama of what one initially encounters as three hypostatized "forces," two of which are impersonal and overpowering and use the third as their sport and plaything. Their dramatistic reality is also the reason why all three terms, especially the ego, have resisted univocal definition. As we'll see, this resistance isn't a theoretical defect but a positive phenomenon and holds the key to a correct reinterpretation of Freud's thought.

Id

Characterizations of the id range from picturing it as a thinglike, seething cauldron that knows no limits in the rapaciousness of its erotic (polymorphous perverse) and destructive drives, to seeing it as a highly personal system composed of specific desires that are finally not all that frightening. Though it may come as a blow to romantic readings of psychoanalysis, the first characterization pictures the way the id looks when it is deeply repressed and strongly defended against. It has to appear impersonal and overpowering because one wants no part of it: one needs to disown it and to regard its eruption as tantamount to psychic dissolution. In one's passivity, one sees oneself as the victim of forces outside one's control. One runs from the id in horror, not knowing one is running from oneself. Or one embraces it in rapture to sustain the same blindness.

The theoretically significant point is that this picture derives from the way the id appears at the beginning of analysis. When this view is sustained, on either side of the couch, the purpose of analysis becomes taming the id and building defenses against it. Psychoanalytic theory is always implicated in its subject matter. Unfortunately, the main line of ego psychology—adaptation and defense's control over drive—is a movement of flight from the id. The disadvantage of that process, as we'll see, is the concept of the ego it develops. The opposite side of the coin, romantic glorification of the id, is also a defense but of a different kind. Romanticizing the id secures one from having to deal with its personal nature.

As one listens to and interprets the id, it becomes "domesticated" yet in no way tamed. As one confronts one's desires, the character of one's id gradually changes; it becomes attached to specific situations and conflicts. When desire is seen as the force shaping a whole pattern of actions for which we now claim authorship and responsibility, the id becomes once again our own. Those who see this development as a loss of the utopian and disruptive energies of psychoanalysis betray in their conception of the id their resistance to the painfully personal character of analysis. Freud's famous statement "Where id was, ego shall be" is capable of two quite different interpretations. It invites the reductive reading that has unfortunately prevailed. But it is also open to a much more dramatistic reading. As we move from passivity to active reversal, the id becomes the voice of those vital desires we must reclaim. And reclamation is not a function of the ego's control over drive but a transformation of its being. The purpose of analysis is not to tame the id, but to make it fully one's own, thereby setting it free.

Superego

Id and *superego* are dialectically related terms, and that connection, though often strenuously denied, is crucial for conceptualizing the latter. Characterizations of the superego usually begin with picturing it as a harsh, unremitting force of self-punishment that masochistically tears down each attempt we make to free ourselves from overpowering parental injunctions that have been planted in the defenseless infant self and now operate beyond modification or control. Bribing the superego is one of our favorite occupations, but the superego can't be bribed. It is insatiable, and its power is attested by the fact that it attaches itself to the body (impotence, frigidity, etc.) in involuntary and uncontrollable expressions that quite literally have their way with us. The neglected side of this description, however, is that this too is a picture of the way things look at the beginning of analysis. At this point, the superego is a perfect match for the unregenerate id.

Those who see in this distorted form of ethical self-regulation a voice worthy of salvation claim that the education of the superego changes its character into that of a "loving and beloved" source of inner comfort, close to an ego ideal, which functions as an inner tribunal regulating how to fulfill our desires without violating the inherently ethical dimension that makes them human.[68] I have reservations about the ways this view has been developed in ego psychology. A more dynamic orientation might describe the evolving superego along Nietzschean lines as that standard of noble valuation one establishes in order to test oneself by making self-overcoming one's innermost imperative. The point of agreement between the two views is the necessity of intrapsychic struggle with rigid and dogmatic ethical injunctions. The value of a phenomenology of the superego lies in revealing ethics as a psychological phenomenon. Such a description concretizes ethics by exposing how many of our "moral values" we have incorporated out of disappointed love or produced out of righteous fear. Thus a self-critical awareness of the psychological bases of our values becomes the starting point for any ethical theory.

Like the id, the superego is one's own—and making it so is the task of analysis. The superego has to appear impersonal and overpowering as long as one fears to take any actions that would bring one into conflict with it, or, more to the point, as long as one refuses to confront the desires (erotic motives, not energies) that sustain it. This is the connection Freud was after when he called the superego the mirror image of the id. It is also the connection that occasions the strongest resistance, and we will have accomplished much on the way to active reversal when the impersonal superego is repersonified and assumes the character of parental voices. However distorted, such voices point to definite conflicts and desires. As long as the superego is the voice of God we have little chance of addressing it or of finding out what God is really saying.

Freud shows that as the "heir of the Oedipus complex," the superego is not a resolution of the complex but a displacement, inversion, and prolongation of it. It springs from "identifications" with the parents that one refuses to give up because they sustain the desires for which they provide a substitute. The extremity of the superego is the first tip-off. This voice, though derived from the parents, usually exceeds them in both the rigidity of its prohibitions and the virulence of punishment for transgression. If this is "the Law of the Father," it is that of the father avenger.

Even violations in thought or fantasy are often punishable by death—or its equivalent, psychic dissolution. It is only when the quest for failure exhausts all available occasions, or the delight in self-punishment rises to take a bow after some particularly brilliant performance, that the reaction formation character of the malign superego emerges. It then invariably reveals the lineaments of desire in the visage of hate. Its statement: "You refused me; now I'll become that refusing voice." Do unto others. The turning point in reversing superego pathology is a recovery of the desires that hide within moral injunctions.

A "benign" and ethically courageous superego requires freeing parental introjects of their allegorical character as those unremittingly judgmental personages bearing apodictic imperatives before which we shrink to insignificance, even when obeying their commands. Change lies in discovering the roots of such exaggerated feelings in twisted love. The superego is that product of ambivalence most intent on concealing its ambivalence. Once we face our true feelings toward our parents and theirs toward us, the lies sustaining the harshness of this structure are undermined. That act is also the beginning of genuine ethical agency; for through it one begins to evolve a context in which ethics is not opposed to psychological insight but takes its origin in a recognition of the complexity of motives and experiences (including ones of moral failure) that must enter into the construction of an ethical theory that, in truth to the human complexity, will transcend what moralistic and categorical imperatives allow. In fact, the malign superego might be best defined as the hostility of abstract ethics to probing the psychological desires that sustain it.

The goal of superego analysis is not its dissolution, but the freeing of its ethical potential. Lest this sound too friendly to ego psychology, let me underscore the challenge it entails. Defining the healthy ego in terms of adaptation to the ruling order is little more than a sterling example of our collective neurosis. Ready acceptance of social norms and "values" is superego pathology cleverly disguised. The triumphant secularism of such formulations hides their complicity with the malign superego and their attempt to soften the bow before its dictates by having big brother, in executive dress, replace big daddy, with both suitably disguised as "the reality principle." A series of simple substitutions takes us from the God of Abraham and Isaac to the deification of American society; and, as usual, Reason (pragmatic, operational, cybernetic, or otherwise) is the humble servant, diligently at work, laying the foundations of the temple.

The reversal of self-punishment and the recovery of desire depend, in contrast, not on seeking peace with the superego at any cost but on struggling to uncover the story it conceals. That story is largely one of rejected love sustaining itself as desire by taking on the voice of the rejector. Our love is often so deep and so desperate that we will inflict any punishment on ourselves in order to sustain the connection. The answer to our dilemma is not to dissolve the bond but to unlock its knotted nature. As always, we would rather will nothing than not will; we would rather love the one who prevents our loving than give up the "dream" of love. An "internal object" that punishes is better than no object at all. In the loneliest night of our masochism we thus embrace a beloved who comes to observe and sanctify our pain with a fixed and icy stare. The one marriage that can't be dissolved is that between the id and the superego. This is the truth to which its child, the ego, must come.

Ego

Characterizations of the ego range from regarding it as little more than a passive by-product of the struggle between the other two "forces," with reality, a third stern master, thrown in for good measure, to seeing it in the role of that truly executive function that synthesizes all the forces, motives, and contexts of human interaction making up the total life of the psyche. But what can such a synthesis be? We have little chance of knowing as long as we stay within the conceptual framework of ego psychology. The best it can offer is a hodgepodge of discrete functions in search of an organizing principle. In their survey of its development, Arlow and Brenner list the following as the main ego functions: (1) consciousness; (2) sense perception; (3) the perception and expression of affect; (4) thought; (5) control of motor action; (6) memory; (7) language; (8) defense mechanisms and defensive activity in general; (9) control, regulation, and binding of instinctual energy; (10) the integrative and harmonizing function; (11) reality testing; (12) the capacity to inhibit or suspend the operation of any of these functions and to regress to a primitive level of functioning.[69] The alternative to this conglomerate is to use the ego in a way that makes it virtually indistinguishable from the terms "self" and "identity." At this point, the need for someone like Erikson, who uses such terms with a certain calculating naiveté, trusting his examples to substitute for concepts, becomes apparent.[70] At a later point Kohut will attempt metapsychology by adding a distinct "psychology of the self."[71]

Conceptualizing the ego has been the bugaboo of psychoanalytic theory, and the inconsistencies that abound will not be resolved as long as we use the ego as the umbrella term for everything we regard as positive, fashionable, or would prefer not to interrogate. After surveying its history, one of its foremost practitioners, George S. Klein, concluded, "There is little reason for satisfaction with ego psychology."[72] We have little hope of altering that judgment as long as we stay trapped in the positions summarized above.

A DRAMATISTIC SOLUTION

The looseness of definition that has characterized discussion of id, ego, and superego contains a positive possibility: a dramatistic development of the issue, offering a different kind of conceptualization. The range of meanings that is necessarily included in each term recapitulates the stages that make up the analytic process and describes the nature of the change effected by it. The way an agent views and relates to any one of the "agencies" is strictly correlated to the way that agent experiences the others. By the same token, any change in one entails corresponding changes in the others. One always experiences and articulates all three as a whole—even when speaking only of one. Their dramatic relationship defines our intrapsychic integrity. And that relationship is determined by the way the subject is currently living its conflicted positions. Freud's notion that one addresses the "id" at one stage of analysis and the superego and ego at others misses the fact that one always speaks to all three: the "agencies" are inseparable mirror images of one another. Drama is both the source of psychological change and the permanent reality of our intrapsychic constitution.

This view of the structural theory clears up many of the difficulties in conceptualizing the ego. The confusions of psychoanalytic theorizing with respect to the ego expose the main contradictions within psychoanalysis: the desire to become a general psychology, along positivist and quasi-behaviorist lines; the complicity of its concepts of normalcy, health, and the conflict-free sphere of ego development with the dominant social orders; the failure to develop a nonsubstantialistic understanding of self and identity and the inability to fill this lacuna within the terms of metapsychology.[73]

Psychoanalysis has persistently used reifying such concepts to limit the impact of its discoveries and to assert control over the analytic process. Analysts do not want to be too deeply implicated in their discoveries.

Even when they exalt empathy and claim that psychoanalysis is essentially a process in which, as Kohut says, "the unconscious of the analyst listens to the unconscious of the patient," they are loath to let their hermeneutic impinge on their method of conceptualization.[74] Analysts want in some way to stand outside the process in order to limit its impact on both their theory and their lives. The "healthy" ego remains the primary hiding place for such tendencies as well as the angelic mask hiding the function of analysis in sustaining the dominant social order.

Reinterpreted dramatistically, the vague and shifting meanings the ego assumes highlight, better than anything else, the movement of analysis from passivity to active reversal. Through a dialectical reinterpretation of the range of meanings Arlow and Brenner summarize—showing how different conceptions of the ego have their place at determinate stages of the analytic process—we can show how reified, substantialistic theories of the ego, such as those that identify it with the successful assertion of defense over drive, function as way stations rather than permanent havens on the journey toward a psychic integrity that transcends them.

In the beginning, the patient usually presents him or herself as the passive victim of impersonal forces outside his or her control. The ego is timid and weak: both id and superego in their irrational, massive, and uncontrollable force appear very much what Lacan calls "the discourse of the Other." Starting here, much of the work of analysis is an effort to bring the "victim" to agency through a recognition that both id and superego are one's own. They have assumed an impersonal and terrifying form precisely because their personal nature has been so persistently and vehemently denied. But as defenses break down, one discovers the desires out of which id and superego take their common origin. With that discovery, their "character" changes. They become more concrete, less awesome, and far more intimately connected to the precise fears, frustrations, and desires defining specific conflicts and situations.

This process is both the activity and the self-transformation of the ego. The notion that the ego both directs the analytic process and is its result poses a conceptual paradox or aporia only to those caught up in a substantialistic version of identity and a myth of absolute beginnings. In terms of emergence and *Aufhebung*, however, this notion concretizes the question of *synthesis* by showing that the "synthesizing power of the ego" develops only as subject mediates its drama. The ego is, in effect, the architect of its own becoming—a fully existentialized principle of negation and self-overcoming. Not surprisingly, such a change in the ego's self-understanding inevitably activates the greatest resistances of the defense ego. The need to make id and superego more terrifying than ever before is never stronger than when their personal character is coming out. Though many an analysis ends here, exacerbating this conflict is the necessary analytic gambit.

The reason why a successful analysis can be described, following Schafer, as a movement from the passive to the active voice is that a successful analysis is both the product and the coming into being of an autonomous ego. Such a psychological reality becomes possible only as the ego reclaims those "parts" of itself it has split off and disclaimed. The "growth" of the ego is neither a quasi-biological nor an adaptational process. Nor is it one in which identity is achieved and maintained in a quasi-substantialistic manner as one gets inserted into a series of prearranged grids that constitute "the maturational process" and, conveniently, the going concerns of the dominant social order.

Genuine ego development operates in a way comparable to the principles that shape the dialectical development of subject in Hegel. The ego has been the shifting term, defined in so many different and contradictory ways in psychoanalytic theory, because it is the shifting reality upon which psychoanalysis operates. Its meaning changes because it is the process of change itself. *The dialectic of its self-reference constitutes the psychoanalytic process.* As ego becomes strong enough to admit its disowned and disclaimed motives, they change because it has changed. While it remains passive and weak, these motives remain virulent and impersonal. As ego becomes active, it integrates them into its activity, recognizing them as most worthy and most in need of reclamation because the "cathexis" of "energy" they contain is "always already" interpersonal. Only the tangled name of love can serve to define them.

In describing the therapeutic process Freud said, "Where id was, ego shall be." He could just as easily have said, "Where superego was, ego shall be." But both ideas refer neither to the taming of disruptive forces nor to Lacan's odd inversion of Freud's statement: "There in the place where I was, It will be for me."[75] In a successful analysis, repressed desires and motives aren't eliminated, but integrated into the "self" and assimilated into the self's activity. Just as the interpersonal conflicts sustaining the id and the superego aren't banished but made ripe for dramatic engagement, the achievement of the "self-identity" capable of undertaking that effort has nothing to do with adaptation and transcends both the reality and the pleasure principles.

Of necessity, the battle of interpretation in psychoanalysis is simultaneously waged on three fronts: the ego becomes acquainted with the id and superego as its own defenses against knowing these "parts" of itself are explored. But while that act of interpretation progresses, something far more important must take place: the struggle for change, a battle that is waged in the "ego" alone and that takes place not on the couch but in the world. Otherwise analysis will eventually amount to little more than an intellectual game.

In contrast to the old view that one shouldn't make any major decisions until one's analysis is finished, it is now generally recognized that the things one does and doesn't do during analysis are perhaps the most important part of it. It is impossible to bring our mental life into some sort of order prior to taking actions in which we will both risk and discover ourselves. We are always acting—even when trying not to. Finding the courage to act in new ways in one's specific anxiety situations is the primary sign of analytic "progress," for it is through action alone that one's conflicts are worked out. Our being resides in action. Drama is the destiny of the psyche. And that is why when an analysis is working things outside the analytic hour come to a head. Once defenses and denials are no longer possible, experience becomes an intensification of one's basic drama. The task of analysis is to encourage this process rather than retard it.

One necessarily lives an authentic analysis and doesn't just think about it. What one does outside "the analytic hour" is, in fact, the most complete enactment of the transference: for experience is where one goes about recapitulating the significant past and risking the actions one must take in order to mediate one's core conflicts. Obviously, none of this happens with perfect chronological symmetry. False starts, regressions, and downright confusion play a part in any process of change. But if one watches what happens over a period of years, the events since the analysis began form a pattern shaped by attempts to relive and reverse the sequence of conflicts that structured one's life prior to analysis. Current experience is always the finest teacher—and the primary text for analytic scrutiny.

Analysts could worry less than they do whether they are providing all the transferences their patients need. The one thing we can bank on is that someone out in the world is being cast in the required role. And it is to that relationship one must look to see what may be struggling to be born in the patient's psyche. That said, it's worth noting that one of the arguments for the value of group psychotherapy is its ability to facilitate multiple transferences among the members of its "family." Group is a hall of mirrors in which all project their conflicts and confusions upon one another. Dramas and desires constantly intersect and oppose themselves to one another. The inadequacy of interpretations—and the motives behind them—comes to the fore. The chance of meeting oneself in the distorted image one projects upon others engaged in similar pursuit multiplies. Striving together as a group to put the shoe on the other foot, we enact the possibility of moving toward a more complex self-reference. If the group is analytic—and not supportive—its psychology embodies the effort of the members to effect psychological change in one another. Together we tell one another the thing we least want to hear—no holds barred. This "basic rule" is seldom followed, but that does not alter its conceptual status.[76]

HOW TO CRITICIZE ONESELF

Reformulated, the principle of overdetermination or multiple function provides the best conceptual completion for this line of thought. As first formulated by Robert Waelder, this principle was meant to correlate the kind of clinical findings that resulted in Freud's structural theory. Any action serves a multitude of purposes or motives—and these motives are often not only in conflict but downright contradictory. The psyche is a storehouse of intersystemic and intrasystemic conflict. The first step toward analytic competence is to become aware of all the different motives that may be at work in any one of our feelings, attitudes, defenses, or actions. Motive hunting can, of course, be an endless process. The key to sorting through "God's plenty" is to focus on the motives one tends to discount, ignore, or deny—especially when those motives are less than self-enhancing. The question of why we feel or act a certain way can appear full of almost limitless possibilities, and it is easy to lose the "obvious" in a wealth of narcissistic or Hamlet-like detail. This is especially true when motive hunting assumes a masochistic cast or becomes itself a defense, i.e., the sheer complexity of my case delays any point of definiteness or decision.

Psychoanalysis hardly invented such behaviors, but it has unfortunately encouraged them because the exercise of suspicion depends on an initial effort to make us acutely aware of multiple motivational possibilities. The intricacy of an explanation is not necessarily an argument in its favor, however. Once one has become adept at tracking down the competing motives that may be served by a single course of action, the task is not to put one's reductive money on one motive but to establish a determinate relationship among all. There is no single ultimate cause for our actions. Nor is the "deepest" or most intricate motive necessarily the most important one; though those motives which give anxiety or are most strenuously denied deserve serious consideration by reason of that fact, just as the motive one favors deserves, for that very reason, to be held suspect. A commitment to self-criticism demands no less. But when motive hunting has exhausted itself, one is usually left with a number of motives, many of which stand in marked conflict. Altruism can serve sadism and still be altruism; one can at one and the same time wish a person well and ill; that which serves love can also increase dependency and sow seeds of future aggression.

Motivation is one of the places where psychoanalysis, like all implicitly dialectical philosophies, is forced to go beyond the principle of contradiction and beyond both a structuralist logic of binary oppositions and a naturalist logic of a single underlying cause. Contrary to popular opinion and practice, psychoanalysis goes wrong whenever it becomes a reductive search for the one motive into which all others can be resolved. To describe an action with any degree of adequacy, one must assess all motives and establish a determinate relationship among them. But since motives are themselves often conflicting and contradictory, such a description will not be able to resolve things into a simple picture or single alignment. The establishment of a more dialectical relationship is the true task of analytic interpretation.

Waelder's explanation of the principle of multiple function both enlightens and straddles this issue. As he explains it, any action will express the "drives" of id, ego, superego, and the "repetition compulsion" in the two ways in which we always relate to their demands—both passively and actively. As long as maximum complexity is what one is after, Waelder's formulation provides a methodological assurance of descriptive adequacy. But unless we go further, it leaves us with the kind of classically complete yet somewhat static descriptions that are the hallmark of the essays one finds so often in psychoanalytic journals where the effort apparently is to show just how encyclopedically rich and intricate a psychoanalytic explanation can be.[77]

To achieve a more determinate principle of explanation, we must return to the analytic process. For the concern there is not simply the uncovery of multiple motives, but the study of how motives change in experience and through the therapeutic action of psychoanalysis. All of the motives which "make up" the psyche have a way of hanging around, and it is always possible—even at the advanced stages of an analysis—to find the same "bundle" of "forces" at work in one's actions. But the return of the revenant motive, lurking beneath what looked like progress, does not mean that one is back at square one. A motive that may have once been dominant, because strenuously denied, may now be significantly modified by other motives that were previously far less powerful or hardly present at all. The importance of this distinction becomes especially clear when studying what happens when one is in the throes of one of those "creative" regressions that often mark turning points in an analysis, but that are characterized by the return, often with accumulated force, of motives, anxieties, and conflicts one would have thought by this time to have overcome for good.[78] Should we welcome this experience as a sign we have summoned ourselves to further necessary work, or decry it as proof that eventually all efforts collapse and we end up back where we began?

Before analysis, it is generally the case that strongly repressed motives have a peremptory force enabling them to take over any situation of anxiety, blocking out all other motives and considerations. As Loewald notes, like the dead in the *Odyssey* they crave blood and will not speak until they've been sated.[79] By that time, unfortunately, other possibilities will have long since vanished. In such cases, reductive explanation is appropriate, because reification is the self-reference such an agent is living.

As an analysis progresses, however, even the most violent motives become articulate and address, even during the very act of regression, a larger picture. That picture is not of the ego defending itself or asserting control over drives, but of the ego expanding itself through the recovery and projection of desire into the world. The "return of the repressed" means one has further work to do, but the larger context to which repressed motives are now referred is the truly significant fact because it reveals what one wants to do with desires one now has the courage to face. If we prove worthy of it, regression is never repetition. We regress deliberately in order to test ourselves and, more important, to recover motives we don't want to lose. Artists are not the only ones for whom "regression in the service of the ego" is an essential activity. Perhaps it is the deepest need of all who would live a creative rather than defensive relationship to their desire. Regression is often the clearest sign that one is engaged in active reversal, in fact, since, to paraphrase Freud, it is impossible to "cure" a patient who is not present. This is also why regression should not be confused with resistance. For in regression one hangs onto a desire, not a defense. Rather than sustain a lie, one recovers a conflict. A person engaged in active reversal needs to open up to anxiety, renew conflicts, and even initiate actions leading to situations of "danger." It is when none of this happens that we should become suspicious; for in such cases the psyche's "health" depends on minimizing—and re-repressing—some of the most significant "parts" of itself. When one does so, of course, the repressed eventually returns later in life in all its original virulence and with a new authorship and hidden story to its credit.

The key to the psyche is the way in which its drama sustains as it realigns everything that entered into subject's original constitution. As Freud knew, "We never give up a desire we've had." The question, rather, is what we do with it. In reconceptualizing the structural theory, we preserve this question by offering the following as a final definition of the ego: the goal of analysis is to achieve a condition of psychic integration in which id, ego, and superego motives have become one; in which all are actively engaged in structuring one's experience so that when tensions reemerge, none takes over to the exclusion of the others; in which all are continually modified by one's developing situation; and in which, when this is not the case, one knows that one needs to undertake anew an in-depth probing of oneself.

This line of thought enables us to conclude with a dramatistic explanation of the claim that the goal of psychoanalysis is to effect a basic change in the structure of the personality. Psychoanalysis neither promises nor gives a fresh start. Analysis doesn't make one a new person. In fact, in many ways one remains as one was. The desire to be delivered from oneself—to re-repress (through hypnosis, say) all memory of the events that precipitated trauma—is a common desire that is voiced with regularity at the beginning of analysis. It is also a perfect example of magical thinking, which is a primary mode of passivity. But the lesson of analysis is that nothing is ever lost. At best what happens instead is something like this: a basic change of personality is activated as one comes to live one's core conflicts in a new way. One *is* and acts in a new way because, through a painful process of reflective action, one has grasped one's conflicts not in order to be rid of them or bring them to a successful "resolution," but in order to ready oneself for their ripest issue. When, through analysis, the personality has undergone a fundamental change, the primary evidence is that one structures experiences not in order to avoid conflict but in

an effort to seek out occasions for the fullest realization of what one is
and must remain: an ongoing projection of the drama one must live out
in relation to the core conflicts that define one's being. This is perhaps
the most significant challenge we can derive from Freud's insight that we
never renounce a desire we've once had.

Subject and "The Large Glass"

IDENTITY AND SEXUALITY

Love is a noble selectiveness of sensuality.   —NIETZSCHE

I have kept sexuality in the background thus far, but actually I've
been talking about it all along. We can now address it explicitly because
the previous discussion establishes the context enabling us to define it in
a way that circumvents the characteristic objections that have attended
psychoanalysis' contribution to its understanding. Sexuality is at the center of analysis, but irremediable confusion results unless sex is conceived
of from the start as a psychological and not a natural or biological phenomenon. Sexual conflict is central to every "neurosis" not for naturalistic
reasons but because sex is the primary and most revealing enactment of
our "identity." Identity is not a fixed principle to which sexuality later
attaches; it derives, rather, from the way we live out the conscious and unconscious conflicts connected with the discovery of our sexual being and
the need to fashion a response to this inescapable "fact of life." More than
death and taxes, sex is an issue to which indifference is impossible. Even
those who would "prefer not" must practice that refusal in their pores.
The body is revelatory because it always gives out a more complex text
than consciousness anticipates or can comprehend. The commonplace has
it that there are no lies in bed, but the truth of the proposition remains
unexplored because we have forgotten how to read the signs. As interpersonal beings, we are condemned to live out a relationship to self through
our relationship with others. In sex, the truth of both is made manifest
in immediate terms. The sexual body enacts the truth of our character;
the nature of our engagement with life and our basic attitude toward the
duties we face as interpersonal beings here incarnate themselves in their
most basic terms. This is the reason why there are no lies in bed—and
why we need to work so hard to disguise or escape what is staged there.

The clinical understanding of sexuality—and a correct phenomenological description of any sexual behavior—derives from this line of
thought. Its yield can be set forth in a series of propositions that extend,

reinterpret, and complicate everything argued in this chapter. But first, an introductory observation. Why, when one sets up the project of grasping the connection (or identity) between identity and sexuality, does one usually confront this situation: men ask for a definition of terms while women already know what the statement means or assume they must possess such knowledge. There is no way one can discuss sex without activating defenses; the hermeneutic engagement here is such that both the discourse and its reception reveal a great deal about both parties.

1. In sex, body and psyche are joined in a relationship that is misunderstood as long as we remain good Cartesians, invoke natural law, posit biological drive discharge mechanisms, or assume that to understand sex we must reduce everything that goes on in people's heads to the status of an epiphenomenon. Those who so think forget that the mind is the primary erogenous zone, the place where the orgasm dances or where its occurrence is arrested, barred, or requested to provide some strange ticket of admission. Sex is philosophically significant because it holds out the possibility of putting an end to dualism by exposing the inadequacy of both rationalist and naturalistic theories of the subject. In establishing the reality of incarnate mind, sex provides a model for conceiving situatedness in general.

Several striking "facts" suggested such a line of thought to Freud.[80] (1) The endless variety of substitutions in the object, aim, manner, and "organ" of satisfaction not only gives sexuality the ability to assume many symbolic meanings, but makes it impossible to disconnect the act from its meanings. (2) There is no single norm or purpose that can be used to legislate the diversity of sexual behaviors. Sexual identity and "normal," "healthy" sexual behavior aren't natural or fixed realities. The proper "posture" is assumed only reluctantly and throughout life occasions strenuous resistance. The cultural, moral, and gender-determined contexts that try to fix sexuality always prove a poor fit. Sexuality is disruptive to any and every logic of the proper, to all attempts to establish what is natural, rational, essential, and lawful in order to measure the marginal and deviant.[81] One of the most significant aspects of sex is its ability to call dominant modes of conceptualization into question while exposing their complicity in sustaining sociocultural and ideological realities that wish to give themselves the stamp of the natural and the "eternal." (3) We discharge other "instincts" and are done with them; sexuality seems to begin at the other end of the line. It has its origin in an experience—sensual sucking—that arises only after physical need has been satisfied; it is prolonged for a distinctive pleasure, a near oceanic sense of well-being that transcends *bios;* and it is pursued, throughout life, for ends that involve far more than physical need. Unfortunately, Freud's natural science framework, especially the economic point of view of metapsychology, forced him to nip all of the above discoveries in the bud.

2. In analyzing any sexual phenomenon the proper analytic question is: What are the conscious and unconscious conflicts and meanings that are here being enacted? Psychoanalysis has consistently resisted its own discoveries. As George Klein has shown, Freud conflates two distinct and incompatible theories of sexuality, one psychological, the other biological.[82] The latter, the drive discharge model, is a reductive attempt to contain the disruptive significance of sex; it is mirrored in experience by those who contrive to live toward their sexuality the kind of relationship it describes.

3. The identity of sexuality and identity—or, to put the thesis in somewhat weaker terms, their intimate connection—derives from the following condition. Our sexuality has its origin in the precise and usually disruptive way in which our being is affirmed in that prolonged sensual symbiosis that constitutes our first love relationship. This is the original experience that establishes the possibility of experience and its inherently conflicted terms. Mothering is "origin," but no simple beginning. The mother imprints her unresolved sexual conflicts—and those of her current relationship—onto the child. The psychic coalescence or "identity" thereby formed has as its task the mediation of the conflicts that define it. Lichtenstein terms this mediation the primary affirmation of one's "I am," arguing that the *adaptional* function of sex throughout life is to reestablish and maintain the identity, or identity theme, thereby established. Less reified and more dramatistic terms suggest viewing this experience as the source of the core conflicts that surface in one's subsequent response to sexuality and the problems inherent to intimacy. In founding the possibility of this history, our first love relationship shapes in profound ways the nature and power of our dramatic agency. Those engulfed in destructive mothering begin "already weary of ardent ways," bent on passivity and avoidance; those chosen ones like Freud, affirmed in their being, strike forth boldly to confront life. Sexuality is an identity attained only by living out a relationship to certain conflicts. It is not a natural or biological given but the product of a history.

4. That history is marked in its origin and development by the inevitability of conflicts that derive both from the complexes of one's

family and from the larger sociocultural order. The two, however, are not identical, and reductionism here, while "politically" inviting, levels off the complexity of the phenomena. To avoid hypostatization, the cultural understanding of sexuality in terms of gender and its discontents needs to be dialectically integrated with a clinical focus on specific individual conflicts, because the family is never a simple reflection of society but a conflicted representative where suppressed social conflicts come out—or come home to roost.

In this regard, a word about the French connection. The appeal of Lacan's hypostatization of the Oedipus as symbolic law is akin to the magical thinking of its abstract feminist inversion: by establishing a number of abstract connections—patriarchy, gender, capitalism, and logocentric metaphysics—one confines the disruptiveness of the sexual to the abstract symmetry of the ideological. Thus the utopian potential of such arguments for those who think they can constitute a content for themselves, and liberate a new "identity," by simply inverting the dominant scheme. But in so doing one sacrifices the concrete on the altar of one's need to worship a purified image of oneself.

We abridge the range of dramas open to us whenever we posit a monodrama. The Lacanian hypostatization gives credence to the curious notion that male sexual identity is fixed and stable while the disorders of desire devolve upon the female. But the only thing such a "representation" fixes is the need of males dominated by it to deny their sexual anxieties by propagating such an image. The same can be said for the abstract and equally magical notion that its simple cancellation—through *écriture féminine* or Gyn/Ecology—will recapture a pristine identity freed of all phallogocentric contaminations, when all such cancellation does is to arrest its adherents at the first moment of dialectics in a sort of anti-*Aufhebung* in which abstract negation of the given is coupled with its necessary double, flight into worldless abstractions.

The supposedly "natural" language of activity and passivity Freud uses, as well as the sociocultural gender designations to which he ties that language, are both implicated in a larger dialectic in which sex expresses discontents that come out regardless of one's position. Gender provides a perfect stand-in for mutual cruelty. That is the reason for its reductive appeal as an explanatory hypothesis. But the secret of sex is that it always incarnates a complex drama in which there are no secure positions, in which "passive aggressive" behavior, for example, has its finest hour, and in which the one thing certain is that we all know how to get the par-

ticular pleasure we crave and communicate the festering message we want
to leave behind. One source of sexual inventiveness lies in our cunning
ability to devise a way to express our true feelings, whatever our station.
The problem of sexual identity cannot be resolved by either an abstract
alignment or an abstract inversion of gender designations because it has
its basis in a prior order of conflict.

 5. The task of analytic inquiry is to discover the specific values,
meanings, and conflicts that sexual experience has had in the motivational
history of the individual person. The motives behind the act define it
and make sense only when seen as part of a unified history that has a
complex and rigorous dramatic structure. This, our most hidden story,
is also our most coherent and unified one: that of the relationship we've
lived to our sexual conflicts. The analyst's task is to order data so that
they tell this story. The same consideration holds for the effort any of us
must make to fathom our sexual identity. For that "identity" is one we've
achieved by projecting a relationship to conflicts we can't avoid because
they define us. The "epigenetic" development of sexuality is structured
not by our maturation into prearranged slots, but by our response to the
crisis situations in which sexual identity is gained, lost, or put into question. Conflict and crisis are the key experiences because they bring out all
that may lurk beneath the surface of triumphant sexual adjustments and
roles. Experience is definitive, moreover, because we can know our sexual
being only as it comes to be for, through, in, and with the sexual being of
another.

 6. In getting to this drama, there are three distinct ways in which
we can experience our sexuality: unconsciously, traumatically, and toward
active reversal. In the first, conflict deferred and unmediated accumu-
lates the steadily growing pressure of that avoidance we term normalcy.
Through trauma the sexual conflicts we've struggled to avoid—by covertly enacting—become unmistakable. Trauma also brings home the
recognition that our very identity is implicated in our sexuality. This is the
crucial experience because in it everything significant in one's life comes
together. If we take up the burden of trauma, we attain the possibility
of an active reversal that is itself dependent upon two things necessarily
experienced together: a painful recovery of one's buried sexual history,
and the struggle to act toward a new sexual identity.

 These three ways in which we can experience our sexuality apply
both to the stages (or crises) that make up childhood psychosexual development and to the later dramas in which unresolved conflicts from

those earlier experiences are revived and submitted to the possibility of a new issue (puberty, adolescence, adulthood, etc.). In both cases, sexual development isn't a natural and irreversible fruition based on our insertion into prearranged structures that guarantee a secure and substantial identity. On the contrary, sexual development is largely a process of deferred conflicts that refuse to disappear, living on with increased urgency beneath the surface of their apparent resolutions. One of the best examples is latency, that long period of exhaustion before, in puberty, sexual conflicts spring forth with redoubled force. A similar story is the still largely untold one of marital sexuality prior to its endemic crisis. Contra reductive psychoanalysis, the beauty of sexuality is that it is never fixed and its development never guaranteed because its transformation depends on the kind of change which is possible only when one projects a new relationship to one's conflicts. Repetition has its truth because conflicts are never resolved by irreversible ego developments that place us beyond the pale of regression. But repetition is also the defeated, passive relationship to one's conflicts, the dominant human story but not the theoretically significant one.

7. To understand any sexual experience and expression, we need to coordinate current conflict with all that it revives, collects, and brings to a head. Our sexual history is a complex web of interconnections that make sense only when seen in dramatistic terms. Otherwise we lop off the past in the fallacious belief that we finished something once and for all or can begin anew, now that we've gotten something out of our system. However, sexual identity is never secure. This is the key to the anxiety that permanently attends it and its discussion. Fixations and regressions are always possible, as are striking reversals. We are permanently, existentially at issue in our sexuality because we can never be sure experience won't bring our suppressed text into the open, giving the lie to all we think we've achieved. Such is the kind of history to which sexuality condemns and frees us.

The diverse phenomena characterizing human sexuality make sense only when placed in such a context. Inhibitions, symptoms, "dysfunctions," and phobias, for example, refer to unresolved and "unconscious" conflicts over sexuality. They are the ways we express contradictory motives and enact the frustration attendant upon our inability to deal with some specific conflict. As Schafer argues, we don't have inhibitions; *inhibitions* are actions we perform.[83] Their sexual flavor derives from the fact that, despite apparent avoidance, they mark off an area of deep concern;

like defenses, they present desire in disguise. *Symptoms* elaborate such operations into symbolic actions that, like the dream, represent contradictory desires as unresolved and unresolvable. Just as sexual fantasy stages a garden of sexual conflicts we rarely face, symptoms and inhibitions are statements that epiphanize and hold in lyric suspension the complex drama they arrest. *Dysfunctions* enact it. Their significance is neither biological nor technological. Premature ejaculation, for example, stages anger, fear, and the need to withdraw quickly from the threat of maternal engulfment in the avenging, castrating female. Its perfect double, frigidity, feeds resentment while inviting the other to take responsibility for one's refusals and failures. The male who lives his sexuality true to the slogan "Wham-bam, thank you ma'm" lacks more than technique; what he persistently enacts is an inability to connect the sexual and the psychological. The female who sees herself as an object, the receptacle of another's pleasure, has taken an equally easy exit from danger and discovery. Such examples—here presented in deliberately abbreviated narratives—reveal sex as an act expressive of comlex meanings incarnated, of necessity, in the terms of immediacy. Sex is psychosexual identity made fully present and, in quasi-Hegelian terms, momentarily aware of itself as such.

The beauty of the situation, of course, is that we're in it together. Sex is inherently interpersonal in origin and in each and every expression. The way one conceives of and expresses one's sexuality is always a result of the way one conceives of the sexuality of the other. Those who think/make men brutes or women objects might begin to reverse their paralysis by seeing what that conception makes them and what motives that self-image serves. By the same token, the strength or weakness of one's sexual appetite—and the importance sex or the lack of same has for different persons—derives not primarily from an innate biological constitution, but from the meanings and conflicts that sex has assumed in that person's history. The biggest ruse we've played on ourselves is to impersonalize sex in order to make it, as in Masters and Johnson, a matter of technological manipulation and training. The drive discharge model is the prototype of such a reification, which is not to say it isn't one of the most convenient ways to conceive of and live one's sexuality, since it absolves one of responsibility and self-knowledge in this area. That is why its negation may be the first step toward active reversal. Deprived of the reductive defense, sexual phenomena become again what they've always been, self-revelations of our efforts to mediate the conflicts central to our identity, because those conflicts necessarily announce themselves whenever we engage in that act in which we most deeply express or are most deeply burdened with ourselves. That is the proper analytic focus, and with its attainment all sexual phenomena reveal their secrets as parts of a larger history, that of our struggle to achieve identity or escape the issue.

8. The different character types psychoanalysis distinguishes might be most meaningfully defined in terms of the distinct sexual conflicts they enact. Thus we have the hysteric, for whom sex is overpowering, destructive, omnipresent, and utterly familial; the obsessional, trying to maintain control over that which forever slips through one's hands; the narcissist, forever seeking identity in the image of a self-sufficiency projected as the lure to blind others to one's emptiness; the compulsive, bent through ceaseless repetition upon the project of reducing psyche to soma, sexuality to an insatiable yet impersonal mechanism; the passive aggressive, adept at all the nonstatements that force the other to take on the rage underlying them; the manic-depressive, for whom sex is euphoric release from the endless mourning that sits shiva in one's soul. Perhaps the primary motive for sex is that it's the clearest method we have yet devised for making a statement.

9. Unless one defines sexuality in terms of identity, all the old reductions eventually creep back in. But once we look at it along such lines, certain characteristics that have been persistently overlooked or marginalized come to the fore. Three are worthy of particular emphasis.

First, sex is dangerous. We can lose ourselves sexually because sex touches our intersubjective identity to the quick. The myth of isolated individuality dissolves. The precariousness of "the rational self" is revealed as it succumbs to a more basic drama. Defenses pass from their habitual and unconscious status to impinge painfully on awareness. Identity is always at stake in sex because the other has the power to reveal things we don't want to face or to inflict a wound that will shatter our very relationship to ourself. The sexual wound may, in fact, be the most revealing phenomenon for the attempt to conceptualize sexuality. To put the possibility in quasi-Kantian terms, "What must human sexuality be like for us to be capable of being wounded sexually in a way that may even destroy the very integrity and value of our identity as persons?" As clinicians observe, sex frequently becomes insistent only after a traumatic sexual or interpersonal experience. We seek through sex to restore our self-esteem or to find the identity we just discovered we never had. The erotic upsurge is not that of a drive, but that of motives and conflicts the wound brings into the open. Sexual conflicts that were already present, in deferred or disguised form, must now be faced explicitly. The temporality of this formulation calls attention to the dialectical connection. In sex, we can suffer a psychological wound only because there are unmet conflicts and suppressed meanings already at work in our sexuality. Trauma merely brings out the truth of what is already there. That is why sex is always dangerous: the danger lies in the fact that it threatens to expose conflicts that fester at the core of the personality and that are terrifying precisely because there is no easy way to vanquish them once they've announced their presence.

Second, sex can become peremptory. The peremptory character sex often assumes after a traumatic experience requires the dramatistic connection to render its secrets. The craving for physical contact is not the pulsion of a drive, but the urgency of conflicts that must be expressed, however chaotically, because their centrality to our very identity has announced itself. Sex is sought not for release of tension but as part of a quest to attain a new relationship to oneself which can come only through our relationship to another. Lichtenstein talks about the "adaptational" role of sexuality in maintaining one's "I am." Such reassurance is the sexual quester's primary need. But to work, the affirmation must be of a particular kind. A repetitive urge and a hunger that is often most acute immediately after sexual fulfillment so often characterize the struggle for sexual liberation because the need isn't to compose one's own catalogue aria or find Mailer's perfect orgasm, but to go through a particular order of intimacies in order to mediate one's sexual conflicts in a way that will bring about a completely new intrapsychic integrity. Sexual experience is not a matter of quantity, but the search for a certain kind of quality. Repetitive coupling until one loses count, or gets the notches that assure magical thinking, won't do the job because mere sex is never what one is after. If there were such a thing we could do it and be done with it. But, as with Hegelian desire, the anguish of sex is that hunger arises in the midst of plenty; and repeated frustration merely weds us to the impossible project of reducing our sexuality to a thing. Repetition doesn't work because it is finally the supreme avoidance: one tries to substitute the act of intercourse for the act of taking psychological action within oneself. Only when the latter is in progress does the sexual act assume the significance proper to it. And only then is sexual experience a possible means of self-transformation. If we try to gain a new identity through sex

—and these pages suggest we may have no other way to do so—then our effort must be to express and confront the conflicts inherent in the act.

Third, sex always entails the possibility of self-discovery. The other side of danger is always blessing. Sex is sought and prolonged above and beyond any discharge of instinct because it is a way of communing with the deepest springs of our subjectivity. Unfortunately, sex is often avoided —or abridged—for the same reason it is sought. It must be constrained when conflicts we don't want to face arise in the midst of our attempt to enter a safe haven where we can reduce the problem of subjectivity to the conditions of a drive. Naturally we sometimes use sex just for the release of tension, but we also know when doing so that we are minimizing it. Here too, then, the meaning of the act is what defines it from inception to consummation. That is why touch is of inexhaustible variety.

10. The most important characteristic of sex is its self-revelatory character. We can maintain all sorts of "myths" about our rational identity and our moral character, but in sex we give ourselves away. As with the other forms of great acting, however, De Niro's point holds: it is in the process of disguising our emotions that our true emotions come out. There are no lies in bed, but deciphering the truth of what is staged there is an intensely subtle act of interpretation in which objective observation is impossible. In bed we confront one of the primary situations where knowledge demands that we transcend objectivity. We can know our own body only by incarnating the body of another.

The way we conceive of and, of greater importance, the way we relate to the sexuality of the other are the clearest index of our own sexuality.[84] The most significant implication of Sullivan's great insight that "the attitude we express toward others must express the true attitude we have toward ourselves"[85] lies in this unexplored area. The beauty of sex is that it brings into the open everything we'd like to deny. If we regard the other as a medium and ourselves as an instrument, or see ourselves as the object taken for another's pleasure, we may find many ways to disguise the truth from ourselves, but what everyday life conceals sex represents in unmistakable and immediate terms. Thus, those who become the perfect object embody both their refusal of the other as subject and their self-contempt for failing to be anything but an object. Frigidity is the perfect realization of such a subjectivity. Those, in turn, who attempt to assert dominance by compelling all relationships to conform to the basest model exorcise anger and fear at a stroke by reducing the other to an

object. Premature ejaculation embodies the fear defining such a subjectivity, priapic rigidity its Bergsonian comedy. In either case, the truth of
the subject is assured and revealed: thinghood and the use of relations to
deny relatedness.

Sex is most revealing when the primary condition for the arousal
of desire is the experience of feeling desired. The other's attempt to
incarnate my body as pleasure creates my desire. This is the real turn-
on or the thing we wait for that never comes. This affirmation or its
absence is thus perhaps the most revealing moment for all concerned. The
particular way in which I am made to feel desired—and especially what
I am desired as—tells me what I am as a subject "objectified" for another
subject "objectifying" him or herself through that act.[86] The manner of
this "interchange of state" is the secret of communication as attribution.

11. If we can read the signs, our sexuality gives us the clearest insight
into the conflicts that are currently structuring our life. The significance
of disruptions and changes in our sexual behavior lies in their power to
cut through our mutual deceits in order to present the actual terms of
our relationship. The truth of our tangled and conflicted history lives
on in whatever solution we have imposed to arrest its drama, unless or
until trauma brings back, as a continuous whole, the history of all we
have failed to face about our sexual being. Analytic scrutiny is an attempt
to discover the truth of the phenomenon—and what that truth reveals
about the structure of our lives and the nature of our relationships. We
can know ourselves in and through our sexuality if, and only if, we are
prepared to see it as the place where we are laid bare rather than as
another rat's nest where we can hide.

To do that, however, all sexual behaviors must be interpreted historically by making unmistakable the contradictions of the core conflict
that they represent. In the sexual, incompatible desires cohabit. It is nice
to regard sex, like the dream of full speech, as the act in which we become fully present to ourselves. But the truth of this presence negates
the romantic, utopian, and anti-oedipal glorifications that have obscured
its meaning. Sex shows that the dream of presence is best when it gives
us over to ourselves not by releasing us from conflicts but by uncovering
them. Sex is always disruptive because it touches, however momentarily, on the possibility of a relatedness that transcends mutual cruelty and
Sartrean struggle. No doubt that is why the experience has to be trun-
cated or routed into more serviceable channels. We are preoccupied with
sex because it is the truth about ourselves we don't want to know. That is

why it is so important to develop a new sensitivity to its nuances; as with all phenomena of analytic significance, the truth announces itself only in the breaks, the gaps, the unexpected, the neglected.

LOVE STORIES

The justice of living is that we do unto one another. Relationship is the sole reality. Progress in psychoanalytic theory depends on the conceptualization of relational complexes. Individual personality disorders are always parts of a larger story which is the one we must learn to tell, especially if our concern is "to trace the visionary company of love." The unfinished business of psychoanalysis is thus the development of an erotics of the self. Such a theory of the ego and of ego development would be well worth having as well as one that would give the quietus to much of what goes on under that name. The analytic interaction turns on the telling and deciphering of love stories. No matter how far afield they may range, it is the story of their love that patients insist on telling. And no matter how hard they may try to put the analyst off the track, this is the story that must be reconstructed. Love is not only the key to the transference; it is also the key to the historical reordering and interpretation of everything that happens in the course of an analysis. Learning to tell the story of one's loves correctly may be our primary duty—both in and out of analysis.

Because interpersonal conflict is the bedrock of the psyche, the issue of "personality types" might best be approached, in fact, not in individualistic terms but through a classification of the dominant types of love conflicts. What Freud termed the "conditions of loving" or of object choice—i.e., the whole issue of whom one falls in love with and why[87]—can be understood only if we take them out of the realm of the "solipsistic" and "romantic" and put them into the realm of interpersonal conflict. In a sense, the individual never chooses: we choose one another. The match is the truly concrete phenomenon and holds the key to understanding both psyches. Our surest "instinct" seems to be for finding the one who is worst for us—or best in terms of the conflicts we must project in order to love.

Like happy families, most happy lovers have the same story. One also suspects that they have no unconscious. "Falling in love" may appear mysterious; but the mystery lies in the perfect adequacy of our choice to our deepest needs. We fall when we find that other best suited to whatever relationship we are currently living toward our conflicts. The "course of true love" then brings to fruition what was present in that beginning, for those who have eyes to see. The condition of object choice is that, even when our goal is avoidance, we choose the one who will eventually force our conflicts into the open, even if that openness lies in the vapidity of the successful American couple. Whenever we find the "one who is right for us," what we really find is some hope of mediating our conflicts. Lover's euphoria derives some of its force from the contradictory sparks that go off at the lower registers of the psyche.

Thus far, sadomasochism has been about the only disorder illuminated by the analysis of a relational complex. Seeing the dialectical connection here proved unavoidable given the perfect symmetry of the match. The two projects require and feed off each other. The roles are doubles, and the only thing barring "perfection" is the scope of each party's inventiveness. How can I devise a new humiliation? How can I find a new way to savor my victimage? The primary reason for the hypertheatricality of the sadomasochistic drama is the need to substitute spectacle for action. What Aristotle regarded as the least important component of drama here becomes the whole story. Repetition, accordingly, is the only dramatic possibility. The payoff lies in the dissolution of drama and the reduction of the body to the condition of a thing.

But there are many other ways to make a perfect match. Narcissistic lovers exhaust one another propping up identical absences. The bottomless need for an impossible reassurance defines their coupling. Female hysterics and their male equivalents (Don Giovannis) are made for each other because the protest of one against her sexuality is a perfect match for the insatiable need of the other to reestablish the existence of his organ.[88] For both, sex is a weapon, the punishment one inflicts on the other in order to torture oneself. The ironic adequation lies in the fact that the hypersexuality of both is dominated by a body that withholds and denies pleasure. For schizoid personalities, the best relationship, in contrast, is one where emotion is minimized. Feeling always threatens to dissolve a precarious psyche incapable of dealing with conflict. The schizoid project is to turn the other into a model of tranquillity or, failing that, to prove that all ills reside in the angry reactions of those who resist their zombification. In either outcome, success is assured because all psychological disorders are projected, externalized, and located in the other, who can either purge the schizoid's being of anything troubling or bear the stigma of angrily acting out the mutual frustration that defines the relationship. All the above relations are success stories. That's their secret pride. Success lies, however, in embracing a corpse and displacing anger over one's emptiness into a pattern of mutual frustration and mutual cruelty. Finding each other, such lovers lay down as the term of their relationship the refusal to undertake drama and the struggle toward a meaningful identity.

A richer order of conflicted loving derives from the intricate psychological connection between idealization and devaluation. Idealizing lovers invite and feed on rejection. The secret spring of idealization is the need to deny the threat posed by the other. Idealization goes hand in hand with devaluation because splitting is the primary defense mechanism romantic lovers use to avoid facing the conflicts behind their infatuations. Whenever hopes are dashed—or the other fails to conform to the ideal—flight into a new romantic illusion is the only way to displace the aggression that underlies the entire project. As in Hitchcock's *Vertigo* the attempt to fix the other in the image we project is an attempt to contain our rage over all that we can't control and that would necessarily come out if we had to interact with a real person. Devaluation is the true mother of idealization; for idealization is an attempt to set to rest our beliefs regarding the other's true nature. Need we add that the ever-recurring suspicions and doubts invariably derive from an arrested oedipal drama? The incessant fear of the idealizing lover—Swann, Othello—is that when the beloved is alone, even in her thoughts she's with another man. For convenience, I've used examples featuring male lovers. The same principles hold for women, though usually their perfect object is a narcissistic rake, the payoff being his seduction and betrayal of them or their sacrifice of self-respect as the ritual through which they prove their love. Their jealousy tends to focus its aggression on the other woman, however, in keeping with the oedipal triangle from which it derives.

Idealization necessarily pictures the other in terms of external signs —money, beauty, virginity, etc.—because the other can have no qualities suggesting interiority or otherness. The perfect object has achieved successful externalization and is one with his or her image. But this is also where the whole project begins to unravel. For such a one is open to endless appropriation by others and by the power (itself ultimately monetary) of the images they project upon that eternally blank screen. The condition of availability is the desire of the perfect object to coincide with the image others project to cover over a desperate need to get constant reassurance from others that one is not bad, hollow, or unlovable. Of necessity, anyone who gives love to a perfect object introduces doubt and must be rejected as having been duped by an image, blind to the emptiness beneath. A great play was not written on this subject—its substitute is called *After the Fall*.

For idealistic love to work, nothing must be said. Everything must remain perpetually suspended. The perfect object must remain "forever young and still to be enjoyed" so that the perfect lover can forever be warmed at the fires of fantasy, like Benjamin's reader warming himself over another's death. Lacking success in the project of mutual reification, the idealizing couple must face the mutual aggression that underlies the attempt to keep each other in a state of perpetual illusion.

The beauty of more complex psyches is that they engender more complicated dramas. With inwardness comes the recognition of ambivalence, guilt, and the need to assume responsibility for experience by internalizing its results. The ghostly peace of repetition is disrupted by the imperative of change. What one did in a situation of conflict now becomes the basis of one's struggle toward active reversal. Such are the achievements of what is termed "the oedipal stage" of experience. Before we celebrate this "development" along the substantialistic and adaptational lines of ego psychology, however, it might be wise to consider quite different directions for the project of loving. Once desire turns on transgression and triangular situations, we have achieved the perfect conditions for perpetual failure. Victory is necessarily defeat since it puts us in the position of the one we earlier violated. When the condition of object choice is that the object belong to another, desire reenacts transgression only to load itself with guilt. Losing the oedipal battle and submitting, under the threat of castration, to the "Law of the Father" may be a harsh fate, but victory may be a harsher one. Victory is, of course, a psychological category: actual incest is not the issue. There are many ways to defeat the older rival or, as parent, to bestow the prize on a favored child. But the price of winning is always the same. The only way to make reparation to the one we've vanquished is by identifying with his defeat and bringing a similar fate upon ourselves. We do so best when we internalize his pain as the very condition that must accompany the experience of our body. If a man wins victory over his father he must become his father's pain, through some self-castrating denial of his own sexuality. The part of the uxorious male is perfectly designed to fulfill this imperative. Or if a woman replaces her mother as the object of her father's desire, she does so at the cost of freezing her pleasure by self-punishment (nymphic promiscuity) or denial (frigidity). In all these outcomes pleasure is impossible because its onset coincides with a feeling of psychic dissolution in which we are flooded with guilt.

The resources of bodily denial are truly remarkable, but a deeper lust compels "oedipal" victors to reenact the crime by structuring their life around situations in which they will find themselves in the role they forced on their initial victim. Adultery derives much of its appeal from motives that have little to do with sex. Driving one's beloved into the arms of another male who, in terms of stereotypes, seduces as a result of greater sexual attractiveness and power, conveniently casts the offended party in the position of the castrated father and also gives him the opportunity to punish the offenders as that father should have. Cuckoldry is an inviting position, serving motives that have little to do with the anxieties regulating male humor. The charm of being cast in the position of "the other woman" draws its appeal from equally complex and convoluted motives. One can renew the attempt to break up the family while assuring that one will get the rejection one deserves. Finding oneself alone again, abandoned by the male, one rejoins one's mother in her pain. The stereotype of gullible women victimized by calculating males conveniently covers motives we'd prefer not to confront.

Sartre loves to demonstrate the proposition "Loser wins," but the truth of the psyche is a good deal closer to the notion "Winner loses." Triangular, "oedipal" desire is not a situation in which one can't win, but a situation in which one had better not win. For the triangle completes its history only when we put ourselves in the slot of the loser. That is why one of the dominant patterns in such loving is the search for the destructive other. The streetcar always stops there. Blanche Du Bois, haunted by a guilt she needs to deny, flees and pursues the destructive other in order to bring the required punishment on herself. Meeting Stanley she knows immediately that "that man will be my destruction" because she has finally found the perfect embodiment of what she's always sought and provoked in men. She can't help making fun of Mitch, whose love appears foolish even as she clutches for it. Her search is for the one who will unravel the psyche. Any other kind of man is necessarily weak and contemptible, an object to play with. Loving her is the proof of one's disposability. Only the destructive other fascinates. That is the person one keeps meeting up with because, going forth, one always meets only oneself. In bringing upon herself the precise disaster she requires, Blanche Du Bois is far from alone.

Perhaps our abiding desire is the desire to open ourselves fully to the other and be rejected.[89] Our very being has then been found wanting, valueless. We justify numerous behaviors by calling rejection our greatest fear; but perhaps Freud's notion that what we deeply fear we also deeply desire finds in unhappy love one of its most important implications. Through rejection, the project of loving receives the rebuke that puts us for the first time in a position to discover what it is really about.

Here is one version of our malaise: what Aristophanes didn't know. Maybe what joins us is the desire to be the object of desire for one who has never found a satisfactory love and therefore represents an ideal subjectivity, recognition from which would complete our being. To be that, however, the other must be lacking, in need of an affirmation he has never found and which our love will bestow. Loving will complete both of us. It is the proof of the other's worth, the declaration and perpetual act that will heal the wound that lies at the origin and center of subjectivity. Unfortunately, rather than healing the wound, love reopens it. When we are made for each other we meet under the sign of the unvoiced question that hangs in the air, structuring the relationship: how could I love anyone who loves me? That is why we all find our perfect match in those who betray a fundamental indifference and need to devalue those who love them. Giving ourselves to them proves our lack of worth, confirming a "truth universally acknowledged" since adolescence; the courting of rejection finds its perfect object in the pseudotranscendence of narcissistic personalities.

It also brings us to the more significant fact we must internalize if the pain of love lost is to do its work. Whenever we love we necessarily dramatize our fundamental frustration as subjects. This frustration is the common spring in all our examples and the condition for their dialectical ordering. The beauty of rejection is that it brings the impossible desire at the heart of loving into the open. We need not fear rejection because it is inevitable; we should not because it is the condition for self-knowledge and active reversal. The dignity of tragedy—and of "ordinary human misery"—lies in the act of finally locating the flaw in oneself.

When we love we necessarily reawaken the psyche's core conflicts. Unfortunately, most of us spend the rest of our time together denying or displacing that fact. Loving reactivates our entire history. Unfortunately, for most it does so only by producing an anxiety we flee by trying to avoid the problems that made us unhappy before, which is why they so patiently ready themselves in the wings, anticipating the day when they can spring forth with increased venom. Just as mutual duplicity in the need to perpetuate our deferred conflicts is the thing that brings us together, the coming to light of that fact is the slow march of a relationship toward its point of crisis. Only at that point does the true drama of love begin—but that is a story that is seldom told.

Freud noted a common pattern in which one chooses a partner unlike the parent of the opposite sex only to turn him or her into someone like that parent. One chooses in order to avoid a conflict and ends up creating it. This pattern is but one variation on a larger theme: the intricate connections between one's initial love and the history of one's loving. Many attempts have been made to schematize these connections and to suggest, despite massive evidence to the contrary, irreversible developments. The connections are a good deal more complex than we have yet imagined, however, because there is no secure place from which to begin, either in the mature present or in the archaic past. Nor is there a single model, either of post-oedipal ego development or of cultural law, that can be used to regulate all the conflicts that love activates. The best we can do is stay open to the discovery of unexpected connections in the recognition that nothing is ever lost or definitively sublated in the life of the psyche because conflict does not develop or resolve itself in substantialistic ways. In a sense, we are all like Lear and must be ready at any time to be shocked by all we have still to learn about ourselves. The only thing we can know for sure about conflict is that it matures—as conflict. If we are lucky, when it surfaces it will find us ripe for the struggle with all that it brings to fruition. Let us then attempt the epiphany, the sonnet, the "lines composed in lieu of many moniments," celebrating what love enables us to know. If we strive through erotic love to renew contact with the original sensual affirmation that is the spring of our psychic integrity, we need look no further to see why anxiety, loss, mourning, and grief so often attend us before, during, and after the act. Love brings us into contact not with how far we've diverged from the pristine presence of our origin, but with how deeply we've failed to live out a mature realization of the possibilities and conflicts that it founded. Contra Freud, human sadness is not over the loss of the mother, but over the loss of oneself.

5 *Methodology Is Ontology: Dialectic and Its Counterfeits*

The end of all our exploring
Will be to arrive where we started
And know the place for the first time.   —T. S. ELIOT

The most valuable insights are arrived at last; but the most valuable insights
are *methods*.   —NIETZSCHE

Paranoia is the ability to make connections.   —THOMAS PYNCHON

DIALECTIC AS DISCOURSE

PRELIMINARY DEFINITIONS

My effort in this chapter is to construct a dialectic of theories of dialectic and a capsulized history of dialectic's internal development which
will demonstrate that subject is the only principle adequate to the dialectical task. I thus here take up in methodological and ontological terms
what the prior chapters established experientially.[1]

To focus the discussion, I will use Plato and Hegel as my primary
examples. I choose them because they represent the nodal figures in the
history of dialectic. In one sense, this chapter attempts to complete in-
terrupted conversations with R. S. Crane, Robert Marsh, and Richard
McKeon.[2] Crane and Marsh saw dialectic as the root error in modern
criticism, while I argued that the problem was not dialectic but the inadequate understanding its contemporary practitioners had of the methodology. My quarrel with McKeon was subtler, my argument being that
Hegel transforms dialectic by overcoming the "defects" in Plato's under-

standing of the method. Hegel brings dialectic to one kind of end and a new beginning. After Hegel the only possibility is a dialectic of subject which explicitly cancels any movement of transcendence. The *Phenomenology of Mind* is the struggle with and toward this realization. By identifying Hegel's methodological contradictions I will here attempt to complete the revolution he initiates, to do for dialectic what it has always done to itself: enact, through the act of reflection on itself, a complete and irreversible transformation. Eradicating Hegel's speculative intrusions and transcendental guarantees (*Geist,* Absolute Knowledge, Historicism) completes our argument for a dialectic of situated subjectivity.

To do so, I will demonstrate the necessary logical progression of the following definitions of dialectic. Since in dialectic the only context is "the whole of things," each formulation depends on those that follow and achieves its proper meaning only at the end of the inquiry.

1. Dialectic, following McKeon, is a universal and interdisciplinary method which uses comprehensive principles in order to relate apparently separate entities and activities, thereby discovering the "englobing truths" in which all things participate.[3] The founding assumption is that "the whole is all there is." The search for connections defines the act of mind because nothing can be understood apart from its place in that totality. Procedurally, dialectic accordingly rejects isolated phenomena, univocal definitions, and clear and distinct ideas.[4]

2. Conceived of in terms of the process through which it develops, dialectic is the movement of conflicts, oppositions, and contradictions toward the ever larger complexes of meaning and relationship in which all things participate. The dialectician's task is to discover the primary oppositions that characterize experience and then to trace, in a necessary progression, the range of phenomena that can be comprehended as the outgrowth of their clash.

3. In terms of content or doctrines, a dialectical system evolves comprehensive categories in order to articulate those internal relations among diverse phenomena which lead to the insight that all of experience is unified by the activity of a single, unconditioned principle. As the ground and telos of dialectic, this principle must be the sole source which generates and accounts for the contradictions through which the dialectic proceeds.

Consequently:

4. "The whole of things" is no more and no less than a working out of the dynamic inherent in its first principle.

5. In its internal constitution this principle must, accordingly, be (1) self-grounding since it can depend on nothing outside itself; (2) inherently dynamic since it alone produces the oppositions and contradictions through which the dialectic proceeds; and (3) necessarily related, for its actualization, to the many separate phenomena which it binds together into the whole.

The trouble with most accounts of dialectic lies in a fallacy of premature concreteness. Concentrating exclusively on one of the above characteristics, they substitute a part for the whole. The result is always the same: dialectic becomes formalistic and loses its rootedness in human experience. This is especially true of the ever popular "thesis-antithesis-synthesis" account in which the concrete drama of dialectical progression is reduced to a mechanical formula so abstract that it is indifferently applicable to anything. An analogous fault characterizes romantic fascination with conflict and opposition as ends in themselves; dialectic becomes no more than the undifferentiated collecting of all the creative oppositions that can be found in nature, society, art, and culture. The limitations of such an account are obvious: an indiscriminate collection of oppositions gives us no more than a conglomerate in search of an organizing principle. Recent dialectical efforts are characterized by a more troubling exercise of abstraction: the positing of huge dichotomies into which all of experience can be subsumed—Poetry and Science, Nature and Culture, Eros and Thanatos, Male Patriarchy and Feminine Liberation. Such constructs totalize by hypostatization and depend for their development on constant analogization and a thoroughgoing neglect of experiential particularity.

To correct such counterfeits we must begin at a point that initially appears "abstract," but which the greatest dialecticians (and their severest critics) agree is the key to the method—the assertion that "the whole is all there is."

The Primacy of the Whole

Numerous misunderstandings can be avoided by a preliminary clarification of what the dialectician means by the whole. The whole is not an ensemble of physical things or an encyclopedic collection of information about a multitude of topics, but a unity of experience. Human life and not the physical universe is the primary object of dialectical thought. Dialectic is not cosmology but philosophic anthropology. Its effort is to formulate the "laws" of human development, and the concept of the whole it advances makes sense only in that context.

But there are many reasons why this goal is a stumbling block to common sense and traditional ways of reasoning. If nothing is intelligible apart from its place in the whole, one can't proceed to such an understanding through a series of discrete perceptions but must somehow begin with it. If we can know any single thing only by knowing the whole of things, then our immediate knowledge of any single thing must be false or, as Socrates claims, possibly true but partial, unaccounted for, and therefore false. The whole, which is all there is, initially is not. To attain it one must begin with those experiences in which common sense and scientific understanding prove inadequate. Empirically minded thinkers may accuse dialectic of willful abstraction, but intending the whole of things actually implies a procedure of the utmost concreteness. The first thing Diotima teaches Socrates is that he must study love if he wants to learn how to think dialectically. A similar rationale makes Hegel take desire, not knowing, as the starting point for a study of subject. *Dasein,* in Heidegger, is the self-reference that emerges when all tidy compartmentalizations of experience have broken down; Heidegger begins with *Angst* because that mood reveals the world as a totality in a way that is "prior to cognition and volition and beyond their range of disclosure."[5]

Notwithstanding their power, such experiences provoke major objections to dialectic because their understanding requires that we bracket much of what we regard as discursively axiomatic, including the ingrained assumptions of Aristotelian logic. For the dialectician the only way to get to the whole is by evolving concepts that will progressively expand their meaning as one discerns connections among seemingly separate phenomena and disciplines. This is the requirement underlying the distinctly non-Aristotelian procedures that characterize the logic of dialectical discourse.

THE CHARACTERISTIC PROCEDURES OF DIALECTICAL DISCOURSE

ON DIALECTICAL TERMS

Dialectical discourse depends on a rejection of univocal definitions. The seemingly inconsistent and often equivocal use of central terms (Eros and Imitation in Plato, subject and object in Hegel, *Dasein* in Heidegger) is necessary to a philosophy which is circular, organic, and totalizing. As Hegel argues, dialectical method requires an "absolute skepticism" in which all assumptions are challenged by a self-critical thought that is self-grounding since it coincides with the very process in which it comes into being. Form and content are radically one; the content of philosophy arises out of the act of philosophizing, and nothing achieves determination until the end of that process. Ontologically, if the whole is all there is, each thing requires every other thing for its determination; nothing can be understood apart from its place in the totality. The only way to define any thing is by tracing the circuit of its interdependencies.

As a consequence, the central terms in a dialectic must wind through curious reversals, doublings, and extensions of their basic meaning as they gather together dispersed realities. Dialectical definitions are necessarily ambiguous, provisional, and subject to progressive reformulation because radical reflection requires that the terms and concepts of discussion be constantly called into question.

Perhaps the most striking example of this requirement is the concept of the whole. The whole and the search for "the essential connections among all things"[6] are concepts that achieve determination only in and through the dialectical process. Their meaning cannot be fixed prior to that process, but must be established by it. They thus take on a meaning quite different from what one assumes when one adopts the stance of common sense or scientific understanding. For common sense the primary meaning of "thing" is physical entity; "connection" signifies physical reciprocity; "essence" remains for the most part a mystery (the "I know not what supposed support of sensible species"); and "the whole" is no more than the ensemble of entities standing in physical proximity and resolvable into their component parts. Such conceptions are fine, but they preclude understanding a philosophy such as Hegel's, in which the physical world is neither the primary reality nor a constant, but is ontologically transformed through subject's development, and "the whole of things" is not a subsistent but a historical reality.

Those who attack dialectic for loose terminology forget that fixed, univocal definitions are appropriate only when it is important for distinct disciplines to isolate the objects under investigation from other things; and such definitions can be maintained only when those objects remain fairly stable.[7] For the dialectician there are no such entities. A network of interrelationships defines all objects and activities. Terms must accordingly be capable of undergoing a continuous expansion of meaning. Plato must use imitation "inconsistently" and within the same discourse apply it at one point to poetics—to which Aristotle would restrict the term—and at another to much larger epistemological and ontological issues because everything in the phenomenal world is an imitation for Plato and must be approximated to the transcendent objects of thought.[8] Eros cannot be confined to biology or psychology since its function is to comprehend the place that all the modes of our affective interaction with the world have in a single hierarchical order. A similar rationale underlies the transformation of the meaning of both subject and object at each stage of Hegel's *Phenomenology*. Refusal to fix those terms is essential to demonstrating how "consciousness" progressively overcomes its own limitations.

Dialectical concepts don't signify entities with fixed properties. They signify forces that pervade all of our thoughts, desires, and actions. That is why their meaning coincides with their development. A dialectical logic is not a system of classifying genera and differentiae or an organon for establishing the rules of demonstration and probability for distinct disciplines. It begins precisely where scientific and disciplinary systems of logic leave off: with the problem of establishing comprehensive categories of thought which are applicable not to genera but to being or reality-in-general. As Herman Sinaiko shows in an excellent book on Plato, eros can't be treated as a generic concept, for it is not the object of any one of the sciences or of their combination, but a force moving through all things.[9] It can't be defined by anything else because everything is defined by it. Such categories are not abstract nor are they empty of content. Understood properly, they reveal the immanent principles of dynamic movement which pervade experience. Universal in extension, they point to a comprehensive order of being. While previous dialectical thinkers hypostatized such principles, with Hegel they come to depend on subject's development. But even with this rationale restored, dialectical terms remain a conceptual puzzle to those whose awareness is focused on particulars. For the quarrel over terms and their definition is really a battle over the nature and limits of thought.

DIALECTICAL THINKING VS. ANALYTICAL THOUGHT

In asserting the primacy of the whole, dialectic implies, as McKeon notes, "the impossibility of independent finite substances" and "of clear and distinct ideas."[10] It thus stands in conflict with the rationalist and scientistic logos that has dominated Western thought since Aristotle. Clear and distinct ideas are formed to give thought the analytic precision needed to separate questions and resolve complexes into their fewest parts. Dialectical thinking, in contrast, requires what Coleridge terms a synergic or esemplastic power of mind capable of discovering essential yet hidden connections. As a token of this difference, dialectical philosophies are always marked by a sharp contrast between dialectic and other ways of thinking. Such is the function of Plato's divided line, of Coleridge's distinction between fancy and imagination, of Hegel's critique of Kantian understanding, and of Heidegger's effort to liberate poetry and authentic thinking from science and technology.

The numerous issues that converge over the question of mind's powers and limits can be illustrated most economically by the conflict that has developed between continental thought and the Anglo-American analytic traditions. The two movements operate from totally different logics. Analytic thought seeks to resolve things into their components, whereas dialectic strives to establish overarching contexts and connections. For the dialectician there are no least parts, whereas for the analytic thinker any whole is no more than the sum of its parts. Analytically, to give an account of any single thing is to discover its elements and the laws of their combination, whereas dialectical explanation sublates the particular by establishing its place in an evolving and irreducible totality.[11] The lines of thought drawn at this fairly abstract level of logical assumptions are maintained with remarkable consistency.

As an epistemology, the analytic tradition is dominated by the question of how an essentially passive mind, a tabula rasa or behavioral mechanism, comes to know "objects" and is shaped by them. By reducing ideas to copies of impressions and reflection to trained response and social consensus, analytic precision produces the naturalization of consciousness. Subject is no more than a thing among things; the determining factors are external givens. In its broader reaches, analytic thinking is characterized by an antimetaphysical bias. Philosophy becomes suspect; its linguistic imprecision is exorcised. Clarity is everything, even if purifying discourse leaves us with nothing to say. In an early phase, the movement demanded that all statements satisfy the requirements of factual propositions about states of affairs verifiable by precise scientific and mathematical criteria. More recently, a "commonsense" concern with ordinary uses of language frequently eliminates philosophic problems by convicting them of ambiguity, category mistakes, or lack of consensual validation by the shared yet wholly arbitrary agreements of an authorized linguistic community.

Ontologically, the analytic movement abides in what Hegel termed the standpoint of observational reason. Reality is the undifferentiated totality of "objects" (including subject) that are amenable to scientific investigation. Philosophy has no original mode of access to reality. Explaining and justifying science has become its primary task. Since scientific method supplies the only rigorous model of knowledge, all phenomena become intelligible only when so conceptualized. Thus, in psychology and ethics analytic thought gravitates toward behaviorism. The subject follows the same laws that determine all natural organisms. Adaptation is the ultimate "reality principle." Freedom consists solely in the ability to perform calculations of greater and less among pleasures and pains. Social convention contains the solution to all questions of value; politics acquiesces in the status quo and the impersonal laws of an impersonal system.

Dialectic contrasts sharply with each plank in the analytic platform. As an epistemology, dialectic emphasizes the speculative and a priori dimension in knowing. It begins with those vital precognitive experiences which reveal a *Lebenswelt* more primary than the world of science. The problem of knowledge is posed in terms of the primacy of those engaged experiences in which intellect, will, and feeling are one and in which we know things to the extent to which we project possibilities upon them. Dialectical discourse strives, in Heidegger's words, "to liberate language from the tyranny of logic" in order to articulate the cognitive and ontological significance of those existential experiences that have been consistently marginalized during the long reign of Cartesian and Aristotelian assumptions. Science and the problem of knowing the physical world are referred to a more fundamental problematic. Reality is a result of human mediation. All conceptions of reality, science included, must be ordered in a single hierarchy that interrogates the attitudes and motives upon which distinct theories are based. Because that order is ontologically binding, philosophic anthropology becomes fundamental ontology. Philosophy's task is to reverse the positivistic flight from life by rethinking the question of being from the perspective of human activity. To reverse the analytic reduction of subject to no more than a what, a thing among things, dialectic begins with the act of existence itself. Its effort is to grasp the "who" of subject in terms of the radical self-questioning that defines us. Because subject is "that being whose very being is at issue," a dialectical psychology emphasizes the integrity of the psyche, against all attempts to separate faculties and functions, in order to show that authenticity and freedom, while only possibilities, define and measure whatever derivative behavior arises as we flee them. Ethics shifts, accordingly, from a formalism of categorical imperatives—where a conflict of duties is a priori impossible—to a study of those situations in which values emerge out of the irreducible conflicts that define their possibility. Values exist only when they are projected in situations in which irretrievable loss is a definite prospect. Politics accordingly becomes the search for a nonutopian praxis that does not underestimate the dehumanizing conditions that any action today confronts as its coefficient of adversity.

In centering thought on those concrete experiences, such as anguish, in which subject intends both the integrity of its existence and "the whole of things," modern dialectic revolutionizes the understanding of its own central concept. The whole is the world, an existential and historical rather than a cosmological totality. It refers to the totality that emerges out of the projects we undertake in an effort to create a human order adequate to our fundamental needs. So understood, dialectic and analytic thinking are not in conflict, but simply address totally different realities.

DIALECTIC VS. THE SEPARATION OF DISCIPLINES

But this distinction leaves us with another difficulty in the path of dialectic. Dialectic rejects isolated problems and distinct disciplines. It thus clashes with the main canon of inquiry since Aristotle—the belief in separate, self-contained disciplines with distinct questions and different kinds of reasoning appropriate to them.[12] (Such a concept of pluralism underlies the critical practice of the Chicago neo-Aristotelians.) This conflict cuts both ways. A plurality of distinct disciplines each treating a particular subject matter, as in Aristotle, is possible only if there are separate objects and activities that can in fact be isolated from one another. But if "the whole is all there is," all things and activities, must be seen in terms of their interrelationships. All problems are, ultimately, related, and all activities are comparable responses to a single overarching question. As a universal method,[13] dialectic has as its task to unify knowledge and experience by discovering the essential connections that cut through disciplinary boundaries.

Much can be said for limiting oneself to a single subject and bracketing all the questions and fields one doesn't want to get into, but the practice of Chicago pluralism rests on a precarious foundation which makes it hard for it to examine itself. How, for example, can one exclude politics, ethics, and psychology from literary study or leave such questions to outside experts? Limitation may appear necessary, but the price paid sooner or later is formalism and the arbitrary exclusion of questions that are inseparable in the experience of a literary work. As Socrates showed, questions are related. The experience Socrates offers his interlocutors is that they can't make the most casual assertion without implicating themselves in a host of problems. Any statement—such as Thrasymachus' "Justice is power"—if properly pursued generates a succession of questions and an evolving awareness of complex interrelationships. As Plato demonstrates in the *Republic*, questions of poetic judgment and educational pedagogy are finally inseparable from ethical and political inquiries, with all four topics necessarily connected to complex ontological questions about the nature of knowledge and the good. Hegel's analogous procedure in the *Phenomenology* takes us from the restricted epistemological focus of traditional philosophy (section A) through a dialectic of desire (section B) that propels us into the study of cultural and historical being. The necessity of this expansion derives from the fact that each position Hegel considers, whatever its disciplinary focus, rests on a distinct self-reference of subject. The disciplinary thinker maintains his program by suppressing this self-knowledge. With its recovery, contradictory positions become moments in a movement toward an understanding of the interaction of all activities.

Dialectic challenges the disciplinary assumptions that have been axiomatic for many since Aristotle. Establishing a plurality of separate sciences each with its own particular subject matter, unanalyzed first principles, and particular rules of demonstration requires a logic that has an architectonic status only as an organon. It does not itself have an object, but formulates distinct rules of demonstration, probability, and evidence to be used in the treatment of distinct problems.[14] For the dialectician there is no way to maintain such a program. Discovering the single order of questions in which all activities are implicated demands that one unify all disciplines within a single context of thought. To achieve such an understanding, everything depends, as McKeon shows, on a logic of comprehensive categories capable of constructing a hierarchy that orders all of experience in an ascent which either culminates in a fundamental dichotomy, as in Plato's divided line, or enacts a continuous movement of *Aufhebung,* as in the progressive transformations of subject and object in the *Phenomenology*. The order of being thereby established simultaneously ranks the objects of knowledge, the ways of knowing, and the modes of meaningful discourse. According to McKeon, the logic through which such comprehensive categories arise and expand their meanings is "regulated, *as a whole and at each stage,* . . . by a principle which is not itself the object of direct consideration."[15] This unconditioned first principle is the ground and moving force of dialectical thought.

As long as this principle is not made an object of direct consideration, however, the logic of dialectic remains open to charges of abstraction and hypostatization. Three major problems remain unanswered. How do comprehensive principles arise *in* experience? Why do they develop as they do? And how must the unconditioned first principle be internally constituted if it is to inform this process? Without knowing how the first principle is internally constituted, we cannot grasp the logic of dialectical movement.

McKeon's description is unexcelled as far as it goes. But he leaves these questions unanswered because the thinker he takes as the paradigm of dialectic, Plato, is at best paradoxical on them. Given his skepticism about language,[16] Plato always resorts to myth to figure forth the highest reaches of his thought, especially when it is a question of the connection of transcendent ultimate being to the world of becoming. Though both the *Phaedrus* and the *Symposium* give an unforgettable picture of the development of eros and the hierarchy of experience that results from that development—the famous progression from a particular beautiful body, to an aesthetic appreciation of body in general, to the love of noble laws and institutions, to that love of ideas which culminates in the love of beauty itself—the logic informing that progress remains a mystery. The "ladder" of ascent accordingly strikes many readers as a noncontinuous series made possible by several broad leaps of sentiment. The connection of stages and the necessity of the total structure remain vague.

Plato offers even less about the unconditioned principle toward which the entire process moves. According to most commentators, about all we can say of the good is that it subsists in unchanging perfection, beyond human discourse. It can be intuited only in a moment of vision. Supposedly outside the realm of becoming—and thus curiously removed from the process that draws us to it—it subsists as a changeless model, an unmoved hypostatized end, mysteriously apart from a world it just as mysteriously draws toward itself. For all the striving that characterizes his thought, Plato's dialectic remains essentially one of transcendence in which motion exists for the sake of rest. His unconditioned first principle is not an indwelling but a transcendent cause. As a result, it is difficult to conceive its connection to the immersion of eros in concrete experience. As the climax of soul's self-movement, the good strikes many as an abrupt leap into another realm which violates the continuity of experience eros has established. As Nietzsche saw, the good feeds on a *contemptus mundi*. Once we attain it the phenomenal world drops away. The connection of dialectic with experience is rent asunder. Hence Platonism (despite Plato) and the long march of dualisms which will persist as long as the first principle of dialectic remains a religious or metaphysical pathos, rather than an indwelling cause.

Plato's ultimate good is exhilarating as an object of reverence, the clearest expression of that dialectical drive for the unconditioned which Kant recognized as a permanent desire of human reason. But it remains abstract, and once we attempt to bring it into meaningful contact with experience, the contradiction between its unconditioned transcendent status and the dynamics of the dialectical process becomes painfully apparent.

"Explanation means monism."[17] As Spinoza saw, to overcome the dualisms that have plagued its history dialectic must become a self-contained system: the unconditioned first principle of the system must inhere in and coincide with the whole of things and can have no existence apart from that totality.

But the ontological requirements such a principle must satisfy in order to establish its dialectical veracity are immense. In its immediate unity—and as a direct result of its internal constitution—subject must mediate the basic ontological oppositions that have characterized the history of thought: identity and difference, being and becoming, the finite and the infinite. Out of its own internal necessity, subject must generate a process that moves from immediacy to absolute knowledge in a necessary structure that is without leaps and that never transcends experience. Subject must bring "the whole of things" into being; and the comprehensive categories that structure our advance toward that totality must be directly generated from subject's activity. To assure the experiential concreteness of the dialectic, Hegel must apprehend subject at work, in the very process and necessity of its labor, and must trace its evolution from its initial to its most developed form.

It is a tall order, and to establish its possibility we need a new and more concrete beginning. A procedural account of dialectic, such as McKeon's, has taken us as far as it can. It resolves many misunderstandings, but it is unable to give an internal account of how dialectic arises in experience. To do that we must immerse ourselves in the dialectical process and articulate the principles that shape it from within. To preserve the totality of concrete experience the first principle of dialectical thought must be conceived of as itself inherently unstable and vitally in need of the dialectical process for its actualization. Hegel took that step by introducing lack and the need for development right within the "unconditioned" first principle of his thought. That is one of the primary meanings of the shift from substance to subject: the movement from a static principle, immune to change, to one that not only demands development but both preserves and realizes its identity through that process. That shift has two important ontological implications: "the whole of things" is not a preexistent state of affairs but the emergent result of a historical labor; the "unconditioned" status of subject is not a secure possession from the start, but a possibility requiring the entire dialectical process for its actualization.

Subject replaces substance because it alone supplies the principles required for a dialectic of experience. The noncoincidence which constitutes its "nature" impels it constantly to overcome its previous limits by plunging itself into experience. Only such a principle truly inheres in the dialectical process rather than abiding outside it.

DIALECTIC AS PROCESS

From Abstract Understanding to *Aufhebung*: Conceptualizing Dialectical Opposition

Contradiction, conflict, the clash of opposites, process, drama. No constituent of dialectic is more discussed than its emphasis on these characteristics of experience. Any partial understanding of these concepts obscures the internal logic of dialectical thought. The only way to understand them is by specifying their function in the structure of dialectical thought as a whole.

Observing the mere fact of opposition, many commentators make the valorization of conflict the essence of dialectic. Collecting dichotomies and arranging them in lifeless triads or equally mechanical binaries, such accounts reduce dialectic to a fixation on conflict as an end in itself. So defined, the dialectician is no more than a *bricoleur*. For in principle all such accounts offer is a conglomerate in search of an organizing principle. While observationally most concrete, it is conceptually far too abstract. As a result, it promotes a characteristic degeneration in which dialectic becomes the fetishizing of whatever opposition a given thinker favors: nature and culture, male and female, poetry and science, etc.

To achieve a more adequate concept of conflict, one has to articulate the logic that informs the clash of opposites and conceptualize the nature of the "realities" that emerge from their clash. One must study conflicts in their development and seemingly distinct pairs of opposites in their convergence. Conflict and opposition are dialectically significant because they reveal situations in which "things" are not frozen in their substantiality or isolated in their particularity, but stand in necessary connections and are implicated in an expanding context of relationships. So apprehended, conflict and opposition start one on the road to a knowledge of "the whole of things." For in a world characterized by the primacy of conflict there are no separate substances or isolated situations. "Things" are determined by their dynamic relationship to their opposites. Rather than breaking entities down into their components, one must view realities fluidly in the context of their developing relationships.

THE PRIORITY OF CONFLICT TO ITS TERMS

The starting point for such a conceptualization is the recognition that conflict is prior to its terms. In a world where conflict is primary, change rules. Nothing persists in its original state; everything is caught up in a developmental process. Apart from their relationship dialectical opposites have no being. Within their relationship both sacrifice forever their initial form. Dialectical opposites *are* the new and irreducible realities to which they give birth. Once the dialectical process commences— and it has "always already" begun—there can be no return to an "origin" outside the process. In an ontology of process, the emergent is the reality. Moreover, there is no way to halt the process. The realities that emerge from a genuine clash of opposites remain fraught with the tension that gave them birth, and thus with the need for further development. "Synthesis" is not a bland resolution in which conflict is overcome or dissolved, but a new and richer manifestation of the initial opposition. As in drama, where the opposed motives and desires of vitally connected characters produce a progressive development of conflict toward an irreversible outcome, in a genuine dialectic nothing is ever lost or simply canceled. At each stage of dialectical development the initial conflict incarnates itself anew in a more complex form. The Blakean adage "Without contraries is no progression" formulates two basic laws of the dialectical process. Apart from one another, contraries atrophy. Joined, they are infinitely productive—of further conflicts.

THE NECESSITY AND NATURE OF MEDIATION

Dialectical opposites stand in sharp contrast to the dualistic and binary categories with which they are frequently confused. Dualistic oppositions separate distinct orders of being, experience, and value, establishing the "purity" of one term while loading all ill onto the other, in such a way that conflicts are resolved.[18] Dialectical opposites, in contrast, are inseparable, mutually determining, and vitally in need of one another for their very being. Their *union* is grounded in the fact that the tension between them *defines* each. Such fusion is dynamic and necessarily generates mediations which give birth to irreversible developments. Mediation isn't after the fact; it is the primary fact. Dialectic overcomes reductionism and the genetic fallacy because origin is "always already" in process.

Hegel's concept of *Aufhebung* attempts to grasp the logic of that process in a single term. In *Aufhebung*, the situation that emerges from the clash of dialectical opposites *cancels* the initial form of the opposition yet *preserves* the essential terms of that conflict in a more complicated form which *extends* that conflict to a wider range of experience.

The ever popular thesis-antithesis-synthesis account of dialectic is the parody of this logic: dialectical progress is reduced to an abstract schematism in which every step constitutes an inexorable advance toward a single predetermined conclusion. Such is the way mechanical understanding arranges experience into abstract spatial patterns. "Synthesis" becomes a bland resolution in which opposites really do no more than cancel themselves in fixed, wholly positive results, risen above the conflicts that gave them birth and freed of the need for further development. Conflict is resolved only because it has never been met.[19]

In the concrete dialectics of *Aufhebung*, in contrast, conflicts are not dissolved but developed. Each successive "synthesis" coalesces what is dynamic in the clash of opposites by taking conflict to a more involved stage. The "essence" of a "synthesis" is the further development it demands. Rather than producing static outcomes freed of tension, a "synthesis" explodes with new developments. Thus the task, with any opposition, is to trace the stages of its *total* development or what Hegel terms "the self-movement of contradictions." Because no term, concept, or opposition can be stabilized outside the dialectical process, whatever perspective one takes on conflict and beginnings will lead to the whole of things. As we'll show, this proves true whether one *begins* with (1) a simple, primary opposition, (2) a random collection of opposites, or (3) a large, all-inclusive dichotomy.

THE PROBLEM OF BEGINNINGS: THREE APPROACHES

1. If one begins with a single, primary opposition—desire and the other, anxiety and inauthenticity, eros and thanatos—one is caught up from the start in the forms of experience that emerge from the clash. There is no way to retreat to a prior "origin" because such conflicts found the very possibility of experience and engender its basic forms. The primacy of conflict puts an end to both positivism and nostalgia. That

primacy also eliminates any simple resolution or predictable issue. Hegel's discussion of desire provides a paradigmatic example. The contradictions defining desire force subject beyond its initial hedonistic stance toward the world into a sufferance of the complex conflicts of self and other, master and slave, which give birth to history and culture. Such developments are not realities superimposed upon desire but an unfolding of the dynamic implicit in it. Desire is its issue. The contradictions defining it mandate the continuous overcoming of its previous forms.

Beginning with an initial primary opposition, dialectic thus evolves a hierarchy of subsequent oppositions. Incessant expansion of context is the primary law of dialectic. Expanding contexts of meaning and relationship generate progressively more inclusive totalities. A primary opposition is that process. Ontologically, its being is the elaborate structure in which it eventuates.

2. The same logic of expansion and convergence holds when one *begins* with a random collection of oppositions. Dialectical understanding discovers that there really is no such thing. In the ever larger, more comprehensive contexts which their development generates, distinct and seemingly circumscribed oppositions continually converge. One of Hegel's greatest contributions to this line of thought was his pioneering effort to show the ways in which distinct areas of thought and action come together as expressions of the single overarching contradiction characterizing a given historical situation. Setting aside unfortunate mystifications about *Weltanschauungen* and the *Zeitgeist*, the value of such a methodology is that it leads Hegel to the following insight into his own historical movement. The contemplative stance rationalist philosophy adopts toward reality, the otherworldly and self-alienating character of religion in which consciousness places its inherent powers in a suprapersonal agent, the flight of aesthetics from the existential import of art to a formalism of pure aesthetic qualities, and the belief of laissez-faire ideologists that economics obeys blind, impersonal laws are related phenomena deriving from the single root contradiction that defines the state of unhappy consciousness at the beginning of the nineteenth century: the contradiction between consciousness' recognition of the universal power of thought and its inability to root thought in the world. Adopting this method, Marx, Lukács, and the Frankfurt school will later show that the task of dialectical or ideological understanding is to correlate cultural and intellectual contradictions with the historical situation to which they correspond.

3. But to sustain such connections a further step is needed. The distinguishing mark of the dialectician lies in the search for what Thomas

Mann calls "the true or ultimate dichotomy": that single comprehensive opposition which generates and sustains the progressively more inclusive oppositions that make up the dialectical process. The essential dialectical task is to discover such an opposition and show how everything functions in the structure of its totalization. Lacking this principle, all connections remain subject to dissolution and fragmentation. The whole can be no more and no less than the total development required by a single comprehensive opposition for the movement from its initial manifestation to its most developed form.

The grandest attempt to fulfill this methodological and ontological ideal is Hegel's effort in the *Phenomenology* to trace the necessary structure of development implicit in the comprehensive opposition of inwardness and existence. The book resists any fragmentation of knowledge and experience because at each stage in its advance the contradictions of previous attitudes give birth to a new position which reinterprets the foregoing and broadens the context of the entire inquiry. The understanding of experience that emerges is necessarily one in which events are overdetermined. That is why history in Hegel is the product as much of economic forces as of ideas; why religion, which cannot be understood apart from the sociohistorical situations in which it develops, is a genuine force in history; and why the existential problematic of unhappy consciousness remains the permanently destabilizing center of the totalizing understanding to which Hegelian thought proceeds. The necessary plurality of attitudes, irreducible conflicts, and fundamental contexts of existence that are established in the course of the *Phenomenology* must all be maintained in the concrete way of thinking about the world to which the work proceeds. The richest concept we can form of the concrete is one which suffers that fact. There is no way "absolute knowledge" can transcend the human condition without contradicting itself. In resisting this recognition, Hegel reveals the contemplative drive of philosophy as the last and most alluring form of unhappy consciousness. A concrete dialectic renews itself in the teeth of this apparent end. The only end is an articulation of its present state that points to its future direction. The secret of sublation is that nothing is ever finally sublated. It is also the key to the next problem we must take up.

THE DIALECTICAL PROCESS AS A TOTALITY: CONCRETE VS. ABSTRACT DIALECTICS

While the search for a comprehensive opposition is the essential dialectical task, it also invites a characteristic degeneration of dialectic which has been prevalent in recent years. Nothing is quite as easy as inventing a comprehensive opposition: Reason and Revelation, Poetry and Science, Nature and Culture, Patriarchy and Feminism. Once one posits abstract dichotomies of this sort it is fairly easy to subsume all phenomena under one category or the other, thereby constructing a "universal" system, full of profound generalizations, but with little contact with the complexities of concrete experience.

Over a long career, R. S. Crane devoted considerable energies to criticizing such procedures in literary studies. Seeing hypostatization as the ground fallacy, Crane defined dialectic as a method of false reasoning which depends for its success on two rather arbitrary procedures: (1) the construction of a disjunctive major premise and (2) the subsequent analogization of all phenomena to one or the other side of that dichotomy.[20] Dialectic, for Crane, is a deductive method that moves from the general to the particular in flagrant neglect of both the canons of scientific inquiry and the historical nature of human artifacts.

Rather than an account of genuine dialectic, what Crane offers is an invaluable picture of what dialectic becomes when comprehensive oppositions are posited rather than generated. The striking thing about the practices Crane identifies is the abstract nature of the dichotomy and the consequent inability to ground it in a logic of immanent movement. The dichotomy between poetry and science, which the new critics popularized, and most of the ways in which the opposition between patriarchy and feminism is currently deployed, offer perfect examples. Once the opposed terms have been reified in their total opposition to one another, all dynamic connection between them is made impossible a priori. As a result, the dichotomy functions primarily as a means of separating phenomena in order to force a stark and essentially emotional or "ideological" choice between extreme alternatives. All sense of dialectic as a logos immanent in experience vanishes. The ruling desire is to prevent any complications from contaminating the purity of one's ideal. The popularity of this counterfeit of dialectic contains an invaluable lesson. The phenomenological route to dialectic is essential because only through it can one uncover the site of the real problems.

BEGINNING AT THE BEGINNING: THE LIFE OF INSTINCT

To earn a comprehensive opposition one must establish its rootedness in immediate experience. If it is to inhere in the dialectical process, the opposition must be present, inchoately, at the very origin of experience, and must contain in that initial and primitive form the dynamic required

for the entire development of experience. Two tests prove whether one
has found such an opposition. (1) If one begins with a developed stage
of the opposition it must be possible to trace that stage back to its initial
form. Otherwise the dialectic is posited rather than generated and floats
in precarious abstraction above all the phenomena it excludes. (2) But
unless this initial form also contains in itself the necessity of transcending
itself, developed stages of the dialectic face fragmentation and reduction.
Inherent self-mediation must constitute immediacy.

If Platonic Eros were not the child of both Poverty and Care there
would be no reason for love to immerse itself in sensual experience yet
demand an ascent beyond that form of experience. Unless Plato "begins" with a principle that unites both need and dissatisfaction there is
no way he can institute a process that will require a hierarchical movement through the whole of experience. If love were only dissatisfaction,
it would never enter experience, but would remain forever in an empty
narcissism. But if love were only need it would have no reason for dialectical advance, but would be naturalistically determined by its first object.
The myth of Love's origin and parentage shows Plato was well aware
of the need to root dialectic in immediacy, yet make the immediate inherently dynamic. What he expresses metaphorically Hegel formulates
in explicitly conceptual terms: as the union of poverty and care, need
and dissatisfaction, Platonic love is a metaphoric expression of desire as a
principle of determinate negation.

Large, abstract, and all-inclusive oppositions are wonderful things.
But to root itself in experience dialectic requires a theory of instinct.
Moreover, to escape reductionism, the primary instincts that form its base
must be implicated from the start in a drive toward self-overcoming. To
use an example that is not usually understood along these lines: *Trieb*
in Freud is not a reductive concept because instincts for Freud are from
the start part of a dialectic of energetics and hermeneutics, force *and*
meaning.[21] The universal instincts Freud posits (sexuality and aggression
or love and death) inaugurate a drama of human relationships in which
the biological is already interpersonal and incipiently cultural. Biological
forces undergo constant transformation as they are canceled, preserved,
and uplifted in human striving. Part of the pain of being human is the
consciousness that we can never successfully reify ourselves and attain a
self-reference where the hydraulic model of libido as pent-up soma demanding discharge would explain our experience. Instincts in dialectic
are their development. And that development must prove capable of pre-

serving and organizing the whole of things. The task of the dialectician is not to embrace *instinct* in the abstract, as in Brown or Marcuse, but to find those instincts that are totalizing.

The effort to articulate such a logic of instinctual "beginnings" informs Hegel's discussion of desire. Desire supplants both the apriorism of the Cartesian cogito and the empirical reduction of consciousness to a thing by establishing a prereflexive principle which is instinctually rooted in immediate experience yet oriented to experience's continual transformation. Caught up in the world, desire comes through frustration to that boredom which humanizes. That mood is the initial appearance of reflection as the dialectical force which will structure the *Phenomenology of Mind*. Reflection isn't superimposed on desire but arises out of it. In ontological terms, desire is reflexively related to itself and engaged, as a result, in a process of self-overcoming. As such, it is the first form of subject's noncoincidence with itself and the first concrete fusion of inwardness and existence. Desire catches up self and world in a process of reciprocal ontological determination.

Plato's and Hegel's "beginnings" point to a single conclusion. The relationship of opposites in a genuine dialectic is one of mutual self-overcoming. Insofar as dialectic begins with a primitive, instinctual opposition, it begins with an irreducible source of conflict that has its being in its becoming.

BEGINNING IN THE MIDDLE: DIALECTICAL NECESSITY AS
TRAGIC STRUCTURE

The same conclusion holds if one begins with a collection of oppositions. Since context is all, to understand any opposition one must establish its precise place and function within a total structure. The truth of any opposition is the contribution it makes to the development of the dialectic as a whole.

Throughout the *Phenomenology* Hegel emphasizes this characteristic of dialectic more than any other. Repeatedly he asserts the necessity of his transitions—each new position constituting the necessary outgrowth of the previous one—and the exhaustiveness of the total sequence. This claim has led to numerous misunderstandings which derive, for the most part, from an attempt to force the structure of Hegel's thought into a rationalistic straitjacket. Arranging the book's content into a sequence of mechanical triads, and charging that its "structure" depends on broad leaps and "transitions of sentiment," are opposite sides of the same coin.

Both derive from conceiving necessity of structure in narrowly syllogistic terms. The structure Hegel is after is a good deal more complex, and the connections he establishes are of a totally different order.[22]

The *Phenomenology* rearranges human thought in order to reveal the order implicit in the range of attitudes subject can take toward reality. The effort is to narrate a continuous movement from the least adequate stance subject can take toward its being to the most complex. Essential to the argument is the idea that the different attitudes subjects have taken on a variety of questions don't form an undifferentiated totality of opinions on diverse topics, but are responses to a single question and as such have a definite place in a single movement of thought. To attain the necessity he is after, Hegel must show that the place it has in the movement of subject toward "absolute knowledge" constitutes the "truth" of each attitude he considers, no matter how disconcerting that conclusion may be to that attitude's adherents.

Three important implications for the question of structure are immediately apparent. First, positions have already been reinterpreted when they enter the *Phenomenology*. Hegel reads other thinkers for what they reveal about subject's self-reference. Their failure to be aware of that dimension of their thought is irrelevant. Second, that dimension determines the structural place of each position included. The *Phenomenology* represents the order of self-mediations that constitute the subjectivity of subject. Given another problem—say, the rise of scientific method—a completely different structure would result. Third, liberating the understanding of subjectivity it contains constitutes the principle of interpretation for interrogating each position surveyed. Hegel's effort is not merely to trace the broad history of thought or the epigenetic course of lived experience. His "subject" is more philosophic.

There are important historical and epigenetic factors, but overemphasizing them obscures the work's structure. Hegel's main effort is to create a philosophic order that will describe the sequence of experiences any subject must go through in order to attain autonomy. His task is not to recount the vast number of attitudes toward reality subjects have held over time, but to reorder those views in a structure that will move from that which is logically and experientially first to that which is alone adequate. That structure will reveal the immanent order of human reflection on lived experience. Such an order does not correspond to the temporal order of experience. Its status is retrospective. It is the kind of order one can create only after one has taken up a variety of attitudes and now wants to record, in a sequential way, the contribution each has made to one's mature awareness.[23]

An understanding of the *Phenomenology*'s structure is considerably deepened and complicated when it is viewed along these lines. The *Phenomenology* constitutes, in effect, a philosophic *Bildungsroman*. Its task is to study thought in all its motivational and psychological complexity in order to force us, as readers, to undergo an engagement in which, after identifying with attitudes, we experience their breakdown from within. Reading the work correctly is a deeply disturbing and painful process for it demands that we constantly engage and then completely remake ourselves. Even the most speculative positions come alive for us—as they did for Hegel—in terms of the psychological forces and desires at work in them. Hegel offers what we may term a tragic drama of the philosophic passion. For the right reader, the *Phenomenology* becomes the drama of one's own personal and philosophic development, for its demand is that we live out the process of taking action within ourselves.[24]

To do so, it is not necessary that we adopt each position Hegel discusses with equal fervor; and we do his claim to be exhaustive no great injustice by noting that many of the positions he thought of great importance were but the passing fancies of his day. For the radical implication of Hegel's method is that the phenomenology of our time remains to be written. As history changes so does the labor of the negative. Because it articulates central problems subject must always face, the *Phenomenology* remains an invaluable guide to that task. But its value for an attempt to give dialectical order to the maze of contemporary attitudes and ideologies can be no more than methodological. Recapturing its repeatable possibilities requires applying its way of thinking to problems, attitudes, and movements of thought scarce dreamt of in Hegel's philosophy.[25]

Similar hermeneutic qualifications apply to the many connections between history and philosophy that are established in the book. Because the order Hegel is constructing is a philosophic one, many positions that occur fairly late in the history of thought are placed, with deliberate irony, at an early stage in the *Phenomenology*. Hegel reorders history at will. The epistemological problematic of section A, for example, is historically heterogeneous. Sense certainty is quasi-Cratylean and supposedly ancient; perception has more in common with Lockean empiricism and the ahistorical attitude of common sense than with any ancient text; while understanding is Hegel's first confrontation with Kant. Moreover, everything discussed in section A is historically posterior to the attitudes surveyed in section B.

That pivotal section, in turn, is historical only in a loose sense. It employs somewhat archaic historical examples to articulate universal structures of experience which transcend the moment of their historical emergence. Some historical experiences are essential to the emergence of subject because without them later developments would not have been possible. But it is a serious mistake to relegate history to the past or to overemphasize the historical at the cost of the universal principles it reveals. In a sense, section B jumps right out of history because it articulates principles of self-mediation that coincide with the very being of subject. Not to be outstripped, they underlie and undercut all attempts to avoid them.

Thought has its regressions, however, and in this regard Hegel, the progressive, is no friend of the ever-popular notion that the latest is the best. The most conspicuous example is the relegation of science and the epistemological fixation derived from its dominance to a decidedly secondary importance. Each time "science" trots forth its credentials, Hegel uses the occasion to reveal it as a prime instance of unhappy consciousness. Section C, "Observational Reason," about the triumphant advance which supposedly delivers us forever from unhappy consciousness, constitutes an extended and supremely comic demonstration of this point, culminating in the famous passage in which subject is reduced to a bone.[26] Such "advances" only return us to the unhappiness we hoped to transcend.

The necessity of such an advance is hardly syllogistic. It arises more out of an almost obsessional need to circle back to and reinterpret a set of recurrent problems. The subtext of sense certainty, for example, comes out only in the later discussion of hedonism.[27] Sense certainty then reveals itself not as the first position consciousness adopts toward experience but as the kind of intellectual rationale one develops fairly late in the game when one's motive is to construct an impregnable fortress by relativizing all positions. Sense certainty isn't the place where one begins, but the reductive posture one hardens into when more significant efforts have been renounced. Late in the order of personal experience, it is properly first in the dialectical reordering of experience because sense certainty is the most abstract and self-reifying effort one can make to escape unhappy consciousness.

Most of the problems commentators have with the work's structure derive from a mistaken attempt to impose a rationalist model of unequivocal logical progress onto a circular process which is necessarily full of abrupt reversals when solutions seem near at hand, striking advances hidden in positions that initially look unpromising, and ironic reinterpretations which reveal the regressiveness of "solid," well-established advances. Contra Hegel, "the cunning of reason" is not even a good metaphor for conceptualizing such processes. To a syllogistic gaze, the *Phenomenology* may look like a book in which we often wander aimlessly, threatened with a total collapse that will throw us back to the beginning. Breaking with the syllogistic model, we discover a structural logic that is just as rigorous but a good deal more complex. That logic is the logic of tragic drama.

If the *Phenomenology* has struck many readers, including Sartre and Hyppolite, as pantragicism rather than panlogicism, it is because the rationale behind its structure is the tragic rhythm of projection, reversal, and recognition. Through immanent critique, attitudes experience their internal contradictions and break down under their own weight. In pressing their case they bring destruction on themselves. In failing to know ourselves we engender the situations we most fear; in neglecting or repressing our conflicts we make it all the more likely that we will run into them—in monstrous form—somewhere down the line. Hegel demonstrates that similar processes define the life of thought. Attitudes, in the very act of trying to maintain themselves, give birth to their opposite. The necessity of the work's structure derives from such processes. Because that is so, many of Hegel's "transitions of sentiment" contain a complex psychological story that eludes rational interpretation. Two of the most striking examples are the abrupt change from the warm ethical aspirations of "The Law of the Heart" to "the Frenzy of Self-conceit" that erupts when that desire is frustrated, and the equally abrupt "transition" from that turbulence to the attitude of "Virtue" which endeavors to transcend interests and motives in order to achieve an ethic of pure duty. Syllogistic advance can't account for such a process because the subject generating it operates by a logic which transcends what reason can comprehend. The romantic longing for a world corresponding to the heart's desires contains, as its hidden contradiction, an opposition between narcissistic individuality and the "lawful" renunciations required for interpersonal living. When that contradiction surfaces, the unregenerate heart struggles to retain its precious individuality at all costs, resisting anything that would check its will. It is thereby driven to a solipsistic egoism and consumes itself in a fitful—and almost paranoid—effort to deny any limits. Terrified by that frenzy, it flees to the opposite extreme: the attempt to transcend all psychological factors. But "Virtue" is dense with unacknowledged motives. The attitude cannot sustain itself because a formalistic ethic of pure duty is unable to address concrete circumstances: a conflict of duties may be impossible a priori, but it is the primary fact of ethical choice in the real world.

It is well known that Rousseau and Kant are the thinkers Hegel has in mind in this section.[28] Less appreciated is the way the discussion complicates our understanding of both thinkers in a truly significant way by establishing motivational and psychological continuities between two positions that are usually regarded as antithetical. Those connections hold not by reason of a syllogistic connection but because Hegel discerns a tragic logic that binds both figures to the problematic of subjectivity he is constructing. Hegel's method brings this connection to the surface because the subject who moves through his narrative is engaged in the sufferance of a tragic process. Tragedy for Hegel, as for Nietzsche, is the true logic of subjective growth. It is tragedy, and not some abstract *Geist,* that is the "spirit" that moves through the *Phenomenology.* A narrative structure such as the one we've illustrated above brings that fact into view by relating Rousseau and Kant to a problem their thought contributes to whether they know it or not.

If the *Phenomenology* achieves necessity of structure, it does so not because it follows some abstract scheme of logical triads, but because it systematically enacts a logic of tragic interrogation and tragic growth. This understanding removes another common misinterpretation of the book. Tragedy is not the necessary outcome of attitudes but the best one, because tragedy alone turns the breakdown of a position into the movement toward a richer and truer possibility. As Hegel shows, tragic spirit does not refrain from death, but abides with it. The tragic outcome may be the exception rather than the rule, but Hegel's concern is not with the normal, self-protective fate of attitudes and the individuals who hold them, but with the exceptional case where the attitude suffers of itself and undertakes its self-overcoming. Hegel was well aware that most people maintain their "happy" resolutions and a stable "identity" in the face of an eternally deferred act of self-criticism. But he also knew that the tragic outcome is the one most worth studying because it alone brings unhappiness to the surface and makes it the basis for a new project. As in Nietzsche, every advance in the *Phenomenology* derives from that rarest of dispositions: "the courage" not "of one's convictions . . . but for an attack upon one's convictions."[29] Hegel's narrative is not that of every consciousness, but that of the exceptional self-consciousness. It depends on the desire to take issue with oneself, to tear one's beliefs to shreds, and to seek out the motives hidden within one's "reasons." Because he approaches positions from such a perspective, Hegel sees things in them that escape a purely rational gaze, and which the proponents of the positions have carefully concealed from themselves. In recapturing the existential density of philosophic positions, Hegel has not turned from objective analysis to motivism, but renewed philosophy as the "love of wisdom" by uncovering the profound passions that inform it.

The logic of tragic growth is one of reversal and recognition. In pushing its case, an attitude exposes its contradictions, bringing about its collapse. Then a self-analytic comprehension of the total experience of the previous attitude is made the basis for a new beginning. Often, of course, new attitudes simply try to smooth over contradictions and find the easiest solution. Such attitudes resist tragedy. But resistance always produces the same results: undoing, the flight into abstraction, and the inability to deal with the burden of previous experience. When there is genuine advance in the *Phenomenology* it is because the tragic is not denied but made the basis of an active reversal in which, by taking action within oneself, one produces a complete change in the nature of one's self-reference. The development of such an inwardness transforms one's existence.

The *Phenomenology* constitutes, in effect, the comprehensive tragedy of an agent who does not suffer death but lives on in the new attitude which his or her self-destruction makes possible. It dramatizes the movement of a subject who attains tragic dignity by systematically overcoming all attempts to arrest that progress. More often than not, both in life and in philosophy, attitudes consume themselves in resisting the tragic. Doing so, they end in impoverishment or, its philosophic equivalent, the spirit of abstraction. Ceaseless obsessional reiteration of stereotypes cancels any movement toward new possibilities. Tragedy remains the deferred self-knowledge underlying such practices. Ill will toward suffering is the essential barrier both to life and to authentic thinking. Knowing that, the tragic subject actively plunges into the dialectical process, eager to bring the negative home where it counts, where it hurts most.

Jacques Derrida begins his critique of structuralism with an incisive and gnomic statement. "The concept of centered structure—although it represents coherence itself, the condition of the episteme as philosophy or science—is contradictorily coherent. And as always, coherence in contradiction expresses the force of a desire."[30] It is a statement that could be made of every attitude examined in the *Phenomenology*. What Hegel's method brings to the surface is not a tissue of logical fallacies, but the founding desire that is their source. Desire is that force which, in trying to prosecute or to suppress itself, succeeds only in extending its contradictions. As long as it remains blind to itself, its practice remains unimpaired. By exposing conceptual contradictions, Hegel brings the life of desire back into the open. The most cunning thing about "the cunning of reason" is that rational explanations reveal and conceal (*alethia*) the deeper working of desire. In the effort to make necessary and give the stamp of fact and certainty to what it wants, desire becomes demand. This demand is reason—the insistence of desire on disguising itself in order to insulate itself from critique.

Like a good psychoanalyst, Hegel's method exposes the contradiction in such efforts in order to recapture their disclaimed core. Grasping positions in this way both reveals the persistence of desire and makes desire ripe for the movement of its critique and self-overcoming. Such a way of interrogating thought might be seen as the polar opposite of *resentment*. While the man of resentment, denying his desires, is unable to forget or work through anything, the Hegelian subject knows both the indestructibility of desire and the necessity of its self-transformation. Because this is its deepest knowledge, Hegel's book may be defined as the self-transformation of desire.

BEGINNING AT THE END: MIND AS INCARNATE PASSION

The same conclusion holds with regard to the third approach we can take to the problem of beginnings and ends. When the focus is on comprehensive oppositions—as is the case in critical and cultural theory today —the dialectical task is to find an opposition that is rooted in immediate experience in such a way that the movement from its initial to its final form will generate a necessary progression capable of comprehending the entire course of experience. If a comprehensive opposition is legitimate, it is not a hypostatized dichotomy under which a multiplicity of phenomena may be subsumed, but the single, immanent *end* from and toward which everything in experience proceeds, an indwelling rather than a transcendent cause, which requires the entire dialectical process for its actualization. In contrast to a subsumptive universal which is fixed a priori and remains outside the process of experience, a dialectical opposition is one with the order of phenomena that it generates. Abstract universals preserve their static identity, while a dialectical universal *mediates identity and difference* within itself. It is the universality of that which *becomes,* of that which *is* only in and through the act of continually transcending its previous forms.[31] This is the act that eventuates in what Hegel calls "the concrete universal."

The Concrete Universal

The concrete universal as a concept implies three distinct ways in which a comprehensive opposition coincides with its development. First, the initial form taken by the opposition both weds it to immediate experience and compels it beyond immediacy. Such an immediacy must be constituted by the demand for becoming through self-overcoming. Second, since the entire course of experience is required for its actualization, the universality of such a principle exists only at the end of the process. Universality is the product of a labor rather than the property of a substance. Finally, nothing outside it can ground its activity without compromising the dialectical process by introducing the search for that other starting point. The possibility of establishing absolute origins outside experience is a myth. The legitimacy of a comprehensive opposition thus depends on its ability *to generate its universality out of itself by progressively overcoming its own limitations.* Consequently, its achieved universality cannot be separable from the dialectical process, but must consist, rather, in the total order of experience established by that process. Dialectic can't transcend itself; its end must be its founding opposition brought to its ripest form. This distinction is crucial for clarifying the problems of closure and absolute knowledge. In its final form, a dialectical opposition must bear the full weight of all the experiential contexts it has organized. Transcendence violates concrete universality. There is no end to the dialectical process.

Hegel's dialectic of inwardness and existence ends in principle with the moment of Absolute Recognition between the philosopher, Hegel, and the world-historical agent, Napoleon. But that end is the concept of history and points to the future. To be aware of this limitation is to vow never to project beyond it. When inwardness recognizes world-historical existence as the true subject of reflection and the place where it must risk its life, and when existence thereby becomes infused with all the values thought has projected in its long cultural development, the dialectical process is "complete" in principle because subject has attained a self-conscious awareness that the dynamic which has shaped its previous development must now explicitly direct its future activity.[32]

The conclusion of a concrete dialectic necessarily incarnates that dialectic anew by bringing its founding opposition to its richest contemporary manifestation. The concrete universal is that end which is the determinate and open-ended logic of future development. Closure happens only through a failure—of imagination or of courage. Contra Plato and Hegel, the secret of the dialectic is the rejection of all transcendence, all contemplative ends to thought, and all utopian ends to history.

Once opened to the future, the entire dialectical process is explicitly raised to a new level of self-consciousness and of purposive activity. To cite one of the clearest examples: Marx's awareness of the history of thought as ideology is revolutionary not because it is just one more ideology, as Karl Mannheim would have it, but because it is an insight which initiates a new way of thinking about thought. Aware of the poverty of philosophy, thought transcends its previous forms and illusions and reconstitutes itself concretely as a search for social, economic, and historical motives. A further revolution grounds Marx's concepts in a richer appropriation of subjectivity: the only end possible for a dialectic of inwardness and existence is an explicit appropriation of the full subjectivity evolved through the dialectical process as the basis of a praxis which projects that awareness upon history. That act raises the dialectic to a new complexity, for through it the subject which reflects and the "object" upon which it reflects become one in the lived recognition that subject as being-in-the-world faces the task of totalizing historicity. Absolute knowledge lies neither in Hegel's "gray on gray" nor in Heidegger's vow of formalistic repetition, but in the demand for a historical concretization of the entire dialectic.

Contradiction and Determinate Negation

I have kept the terms *contradiction* and *determinate negation* in the background until now in order to avoid common misunderstandings. We are now in a position to define them in a truly dialectical manner by discussing first their methodological, then their ontological significance. If the whole is all there is, then our immediate knowledge of everything must be false. To restore our movement toward the whole, thought must, in Hegel's words, be "essentially the *negation* of that which immediately appears." And what immediately appears is relativism, common sense, and categorical understanding. To make the movement to dialectic natural and inevitable, one must begin with such positions and dramatize the internal contradictions whereby they destroy themselves. Fixed and hardened concepts thereby become fluid moments in a larger totality. By structuring his work as a series of such determinate negations, proceeding from the simplest to successively more complex positions, Hegel makes the movement of contradictions enact a gradual yet necessary ascent to the perspective of the whole. Beginning with sense certainty, the solipsism of the moment, the starkest and most immediate stance consciousness can adopt toward both the world and itself, Hegel shows how the common-sense attitude of perception which follows is both a natural outgrowth of the contradictions within sense certainty and the response most likely to provide a quick solution to those contradictions. When that position is then found to be fraught with contradictions of its own, understanding undertakes the effort to essentialize mind and fix its relationship to the world through the discovery of the a priori. But that effort reveals, on analysis, contradictions of an even more complex order. Thus, in each succeeding position the dialectician discovers new contradictions which force the movement to an even more complex position.

Such, in a nutshell, is the logic of dialectical advance. The negation of each position surveyed is *determinate* because it generates the position which follows. Every position from sense certainty on feels it has grasped the whole of things, and each time with a minimum of *mediation*. The contradictions in each position, however, generate the need for progressively more complex mediations. In this way, the dialectical process progressively expands both the scope of consciousness and the range of phenomena it comprehends. The necessity of further *mediation* at the end of each *determinate negation* is the fundamental circumstance that keeps the *Phenomenology* moving toward what Hegel calls the concrete. Sense certainty appears most concrete only because it is most immediate; the starkness of its contradictions demonstrates the abstractness of its apprehension. The concept of absolute knowledge, on the other hand, remains abstract only to those who have not enacted the self-movement of thought. For those who have, it is the most concrete position one can take toward reality because it has most fully incorporated the determinate structure of mediations required for a genuine reconciliation of inwardness and existence. It is the end to which all previous positions proceed.

Only in those thinkers who derive their dialectic secondhand and present it as an abstract dichotomy devoid of experiential genesis do we find the hypostatizations and dualistic bifurcations of experience that R. S. Crane correctly criticized. When concrete, the opposition between dialectic and other ways of knowing exists within dialectic and not outside it because dialectic articulates the logic of development that is present within thought from its inception. *Doxa* begets *pistis; pistis, dianoia;* and *dianoia, noesis.* All of the attitudes interrogated in the *Phenomenology* have their veracity, but their deepest truth lies in the contribution they make to the movement toward absolute knowledge. In this sense, dialectic may be seen as one realization of philosophic pluralism, but it is a pluralism in which contending voices don't persist in isolation—and friendly inability to relate to one another—but become contributing members of a larger vision. Dialectic feeds on the contradictions generated by other ways of thinking because immanence alone can wed it to the whole of things.

This demand for immanence is what gives contradiction and negation their ontological status. In Hegel, consciousness develops only through a process of *alienating itself from itself in the movement into otherness only to regain itself within that other, thereby enriching and transforming itself through the experiential process.* Contradiction and determinate negation are the basic principles of dialectical movement because they coincide with the inner dynamic consciousness requires for its actualization. Initially lost in external otherness—the this, here, and now of sensation—consciousness first finds itself trapped in sense certainty. It surmounts that otherness only by negating that which immediately appears. Consciousness thus actualizes itself through the determinate process of surmounting the very contradictions it introduces into reality. The voyage into otherness, the immersion in experiential difference, is not a holiday from some absolute status consciousness has prior to experience, but the very process required for consciousness to attain such a status. Alienation, unhappy consciousness, and the tragic anguish that characterize so much of the *Phenomenology* are not affairs to be bewailed or avoided, but essential experiences in the formation of subject. Contradiction and determinate negation are not impersonal logical operations grounded in some abstract, hypostatized *Geist,* but recurrent moments that constitute the innermost being of incarnate mind.

Referring the ontological understanding of contradiction and negation to the procedural gives us a deeper understanding of the former. At first glance, it may appear that dialectical thought confronts a number of independent nondialectical positions which it must somehow reinterpret and reorder. The truth of the matter, however, is that dialectic is omnipresent as subtext in all ways of thinking and gives birth to the inadequate positions it later surmounts. By successively positing and then overcoming its own limitations, thought becomes aware of its self-instituted criteria. Such a process constitutes the essence of Socratic questioning. Socrates saw that in advancing any opinion one posits far more than one imagines: in struggling to catch up with the implications of one's thought one is always led beyond one's initial assertions to new positions which only pose further problems. Negation and progression are reciprocal; once interrogated, any position becomes part of a dialectical process. This movement constitutes the hidden logic of all questioning.

While Socrates gives us an unforgettable picture of how that logic operates in everyday life, Hegel offers a rigorous methodological account of the process. For both thinkers, the first position adopted on any question is usually the simplest one, "common as common sense," because our initial tendency is to acquiesce in our limitations. Yet implicit in any position consciousness adopts—by reason of the very fact that a consciousness adopts it—is the possibility of a subsequent act of self-questioning which is simultaneously reflexive and progressive. That self-mediation structures the *Phenomenology*. Its operative principles, contradiction and determinate negation, are concrete rather than abstract universals, forms of becoming which have their being wholly in their movement. In contrast to abstract universals which stand above change and particularity, the concrete universal is the form of change itself.[33] Rather than arbitrarily lumping discrete experiences, it articulates a *hierarchy of integration*. Comprehending Hegelian self-consciousness thus requires that one see how all the attitudes surveyed in the *Phenomenology* constitute necessary stages in subject's self-realization. Unlike Kantian mind, Hegelian self-consciousness is not a fixed form existing prior to experience. Its universality depends, rather, on the ability to constitute itself in experience by constantly transcending its previous forms. Its universality is existential and historical rather than a priori and essentialistic. For Hegel, every property of "the human mind" is thoroughly historical.

There is thus a large irony in the claim that Hegel prefigures structuralism. The difference between two ways of thinking could not be more pronounced. Structuralism offers a static and spatialized system which schematizes binary oppositions that cannot be mediated; Hegel gives us an inherently dynamic and temporal system based on the mediation of conflicts. The first is a formalism resting on a reified concept of the human mind; the second a reflexive thought based on a principle which continually overcomes its own limitations. Lévi-Strauss's work derives much of its popularity from the satisfaction he offers to two persistent desires which Hegel directly challenges: (1) the quest to attain universals that are immune to change, and (2) the no less ardent belief that such essences are the proper objects of thought. Structuralism thus constitutes a wholehearted return to the very abstract universality Hegel had to overcome in order to initiate a study of the existing subject. It is also a single-minded return: fixed in the image of logical, scientific inquiry, the attempt by Lévi-Strauss and others to establish the mental sets and/or linguistic structures which determine the "unchanged and unchanging" nature of "the human mind" necessarily revives all of the antinomies of Kantian understanding. Because he rejects the possibility of mediation, Lévi-Strauss cannot move outside a formalistic circularity. His effort is to resolve the diachronous world of process, first liberated from abstract conceptualization by Hegel, into a synchronous order of static, spatial alignments among terms that necessarily remain frozen in their abstract opposition. Lévi-Strauss, not Sartre, is the ultimate Cartesian, and the movement he inspires is a regression of "the human sciences" to a pre-Hegelian understanding of the universal.

Dialectic vs. Deconstruction

The intellectual history of the past three decades often presents an ironic circularity. Structuralism may be seen as an attempt to save the traditional conception of humans as "rational animals" from the radically unsettling implications of the existential line of thought initiated by Hegel. A further line of defense derives from the opportunities for play provided by the binary oppositions structuralism generates. Many poststructuralists love such set-ups because frozen categories, incapable of mediation, are ripe for inversion. By showing how the lower or marginal term in the binary disrupts the "logic of the proper" or favored term, one employs a wholesale use of analogy to generate a new global understanding. The kind of mediation that takes place in a concrete dialectic is never addressed. It is the truly marginalized text.

We can conceptualize the three positions as three distinct logics. The logic of structuralism is one of binary oppositions which (1) split and (2) reify in order to (3) assimilate all of experience to a priori and subsumptive concepts. Concrete dialectic, in contrast, (1) cancels, (2) preserves, and (3) uplifts the conflicts of inseparable, mutually determining concepts. Deconstruction initially looks like an attempt to arrest such a possibility. Derrida sees the "logics" of *différance* and supplementarity as point-for-point replies to the logic of *Aufhebung*. The supplement (1) usurps, (2) separates, and (3) deprives. *Différance* (1) delays, (2) defers, and (3) differs. Both *différance* and the supplement identify forces that "no dialectic can comprehend."[34] But if by *dialectic* Derrida means "phallogocentric metaphysics"—and it is hard to find Derrida meaning anything else by it—then the primary object of his critique remains the binary world of structuralism. Finding the unguarded textual moment that convicts every thinker of falling into the dream of "self-presence" remains the Derridean operation. But traces and margins disrupt texts only where no process of mediation is in progress. Play disrupts order only when order is conceived of in severely logical terms. Fiction and metaphor unravel truth and the literal only when language and reality are conceived of along positivistic or Cartesian lines. Feminine consciousness is a source of terror only to the obsessionally phallic male. The marginalization of the feminine in his discourse is mirrored in those "deconstructive" systems in which a fixation on language, ontologized, produces through a stark inversion of "masculinist" discourse a pristine and utopian feminist consciousness. Concrete dialectic is untouched by such practices because it never posits the abstract oppositions one must attribute to it in order to deconstruct it.

The root error on which deconstruction depends is the structuralist assumption that thought can operate only by establishing binary oppositions among terms that must remain forever apart. Abstract inversion becomes *the* revolutionary intellectual act because it automatically assures one of a content. Binary logic thus remains the primary way of thinking. However, thanks to deconstruction, this characteristic degeneration that befalls dialectic when it loses contact with experience has perhaps seen its final days. Nevertheless, the lasting significance of deconstruction may lie in contributing to a renewal of concrete dialectics. The liberation of *différance,* of the marginal from abstract systematics, points to mediation as the concept we must reclaim.

Deconstruction might thus be seen as both a genuine and an arrested dialectic. In this regard, Derrida's ongoing critique of Hegel is invaluable because Derrida identifies every point where Hegel gives way to abstraction, every place where the endeavor to "collect meanings" is illegitimate or premature.[35] The solution, however, is not to construct the abstract counter to every one of Hegel's concepts—or to succumb to an equal fascination with the pure "logic" of one's discoveries—but to renew dialectic concretely by demonstrating that it makes progress not when meanings are collected toward some apocalyptic hosanna, but when the contexts of possibility wrestled from existence are used to maximize one's engagement in existence. The liberation of *différance* is an essential moment in that process, but it is in danger of remaining an abstract and merely antithetical one unless it becomes a moment in a larger dialectical effort.

I have no desire to minimize the difficulties of such a rapprochement. All the key words of deconstruction have *double contradictory meanings* which resist sublation. Reflection, for Derrida, identifies aporias that can't be resolved, while deferral supplants Heideggerian finitude in an arrested dialectic[36] which recovers repressed political and sexual energies but remains unable to constitute them. The hermeneutic circle of Derrida's thought refuses engagement in favor of charting intellectual binds that condemn us, in effect, to the solipsism of the linguistic moment.

Deconstruction shares the dialectical desire for concrete energetics but is unable to constitute it in any meaningful way. Like dialectic, it sees that the dichotomies of structuralism and Kantian rationalism never were binaries but are violent hierarchies full of suppressed conflict. But while the dialectician uses that discovery to construct a position in which conflict and its mediation become the focus for a concrete examination of experience, deconstruction exploits the situation abstractly by using binary oppositions to generate the pseudocontent that automatically accrues to the "outside" and either remains imprisoned in the logic of the dominant which it disrupts from within (Derrida), or proclaims its utopian potential by liberating the repressed (Irigaray). No operation is easier— or more practiced today. But it shares the defect of the abstract dialectics it would replace: a deduction of the particulars of experience rather than an experiential mediation of existing conflicts. That is why the formalistic practice of detecting aporias and the utopian, anti-oedipal versions of deconstruction have so much in common. Both generate their content by manipulating relations among terms that exist in a purely textual universe. To maintain one's belief in the ontological power of such operations one must believe, quite literally, Lacan's notion that "it is the world of words that creates the world of things"[37] because language is the only reality one inhabits. Deconstruction wages a concerted attack on nostalgia because nostalgia is the secret it must hide from itself. Utopianism is merely nostalgia projected into the future.

Here, then, are three "interpretations of interpretation"[38]—the attempt to identify aporias that can never be sublated; the attempt to generate a content by liberating the truth one finds in some privileged abstraction; and the effort to probe those tragic situations subject must mediate in order to maximize its existence. Even if all three interpretations bring us to a similar anguish, there remains a crucial difference regarding the situations and ways in which one is ready to suffer that "fact."

DIALECTIC AS SYSTEM: ITS CONTENT AND GROUND

The Nature and Content of Comprehensive Categories

In the *Phaedrus*, Plato describes dialectic as a method of generalization and division. Taken together, these moments define the ontological status and content of comprehensive categories. The moment of generalization binds together a plurality of separate phenomena under a single universal category or form. The moment of division makes explicit the precise way in which the plurality of phenomena contained in that form are preserved and ordered in it.

As they move through the conflicts and oppositions required for their development, dialectical categories undergo a constant expansion of meaning so that by the end of the dialectical process they have become comprehensive categories of being applicable to the whole of things. The previous section explained how such categories arise and develop in experience. Our task here is to articulate their internal structure and ground them in the unconditioned first principle that sustains them.

Comprehensive categories such as eros and knowledge in Plato and self-consciousness in Hegel are concrete universals which bind together diverse objects, experiences, and activities as moments in the hierarchy of ascent to a single goal. Their universality arises out of the movement of experience and remains one with it as a context of necessary connections and englobing relationships.

What is the nature of such connections and relationships? As Plato stresses repeatedly, perceiving the essence of a physical object, or any unity amidst multiplicity, initiates the dialectical process of relating dissimilar entities and activities. For once we perceive their essence, what are we to make of the similarities we subsequently discover in realities so apparently dissimilar as geometry, the state, and the soul? The discovery of such connections suggested to Plato that the true import of things resides in the larger complexes of meaning in which they participate. There is no way an ontology modeled on substance (Aristotle) or on the categorical relations of reciprocity among natural processes and things (Kant) can grasp such an evolving "language of forms." To articulate the perspective of the whole, Plato requires concepts of a fundamentally different order. As Sinaiko shows, he needs a language that in the physical discerns non-physical principles of self-motion that bring the soul into correspondence with the internal relations that animate "the whole of things." Eros is such a language: the order of experience it reveals requires a thinking that transcends *doxa, pistis,* and even *dianoia* because its attunement is to *nonperceptible internal relations.*[39] Unfortunately, internal relations are usually put in the wrong context thanks to Carnap's and Russell's positivistic attacks on Bradley's far from adequate attempt to rehabilitate this concept.[40] Internal relations are not causal relations among things, but relations of meaning. Rather than a preexistent state of affairs waiting to be apprehended, internal relations come into being as a result of an activity that moves through things, transforming the given and the fixed. As Hegel shows, internal relations first arise because consciousness, in its quest to achieve a coincidence of subject and object, negates that which immediately appears.

The connections thereby evolved have nothing to do with contiguous, causal, or reciprocal relationships between entities in space and time. They refer to a completely different order of being. The dialectician would be the first to admit that there is no external relationship among the successive loves that make up the hierarchy of Platonic eros and that from a disciplinary perspective the *Phenomenology* resolves itself into a number of separate inquiries. But these objections miss the point. Internal relations are relations of meaning. They unify experience by binding together a multiplicity of separate entities and activities into a hierarchy that is determined as a whole and in each of its parts by the evolution of a single, unconditioned principle.

An adequate theory of internal relations depends, accordingly, on an explanation of comprehensive categories as dynamic, experiential conflicts defined by the demand for development implicit in them. Lack and the need for self-differentiation commit them to a developmental process which defines phenomena by their place in a hierarchy that is created, not discovered. Such a conception of the "essential connections among things" is concerned not with things as isolated substances, but with the function phenomena have when caught up in a human quest in which value and being are finally indistinguishable. Dialectically, the reality of each thing is the "degree of being" it possesses, and that is determined by its place in such a hierarchy. The *content* of Platonic eros is such a graded hierarchy. The self-motion of *psyche* establishes a telos which is omnipresent in experience. Love for Plato is both sacred and profane, and requires all the speeches in the *Symposium*, including a great one by Aristophanes, to define it. The "form of beauty itself" is comprehended not when beauty is worshiped as an unchanging and transcendent end separable from the dialectical process, but when it is understood as the immanent and densely experiential order of internal relations that is brought into being by that process. As Sinaiko argues, a Platonic *form* is not a step beyond or outside the dialectical process, but an understanding of the process as a whole in the unity and necessity of its total development. Knowledge, as the *Republic* shows, is *doxa, pistis, dianoia, and noesis* because it comprehends the *unity* of the entire divided line.[41] The *content* of a comprehensive category is no more and no less than the total structure of internal relations its evolution establishes and sustains.

Reflecting on the logical implications of procedures such as Plato's led Hegel to conceive of subject as a totalizing process that requires the necessary sequence of positions traced in the *Phenomenology*. That process transforms both our understanding and the reality of objective being.

To understand how, we must take care once again to distinguish dialectic from substantialist thought. Dialectic makes no pretense to preserve things in their substantiality or activities in their isolation. It is quite content to leave the study of things in their particularity to disciplinary inquiry. For its concern is to apprehend "things" as participants in a process in which the given undergoes constant transformation. The implicit goal of dialectic, from its inception, is to rid reality of all substantiality. The true "nature" of each thing lies in the movement from its fixity and isolation to its development within a larger context of meaning.

Because internal relations are relations of meaning that are brought into being through human activity, their justification requires an explicit grounding in the single unconditioned principle which creates and sustains them. Lacking that ground, such relations appear little more than arbitrary and fanciful connections held together through visionary *analogies* that lack any ontological basis. Comprehensive categories hold only if they arise as the actualization of a single unconditioned principle which abides so deeply in experience that it requires the entire dialectical process to work out its inherent dynamic. Contra McKeon, unless this first principle is made the object of direct consideration, everything hangs in the air.

The Unconditioned First Principle: The Logic of Its Internal Structure

Once again, Plato provides a useful introduction to Hegel's achievement.[42] Once Plato transformed the diversity of everyday life into ultimate hierarchical forms such as Beauty, Knowledge, Virtue, and Truth, he faced an overwhelming question. If things are not what they seem but the inner principles that move through them, are there a plurality of independent dialectical wholes—a dialectic of love and a dialectic of knowledge, etc.—or can all of the forms be brought into a single alignment by a form of forms? The late dialogues take up this issue in pure and rather severely abstract logical terms. By trying to establish the dialectical relations among the ultimate terms of human thought and discourse—terms such as the one and the many, motion and rest, identity and difference, being and nonbeing—Plato tries to work out the basic logic needed to bring the forms discovered in experience together in a single system. That is why a work like the *Parmenides* speaks simultaneously of a single form, the forms as a single whole, and the one Form which comprehends and organizes the entire realm of forms.[43] Knowing "the whole of things" demands that the ultimate forms of thought and discourse, as well as the ultimate forms of concrete experience, be connected in a necessary unity through the efficacy of a single principle.

I think every reader of the late dialogues will admit that Plato handles these questions in a paradoxical and at times mystifying way. But where Plato leaves off, Hegel begins. The *Phenomenology* may, in fact, be seen as an attempt to integrate Plato's distinct dialectics (of love, knowledge, beauty, etc.) at one stroke and in a truly concrete manner. This is the rationale behind Hegel's decision to begin with desire and the natural consciousness. Beginning with the dialectical principle itself in its immediate and inchoate form, Hegel will show how the mediations of all the oppositions that constitute the course of experience derive from the inherent mediation of identity and difference that constitutes subject's internal unity. As a result of its internal constitution—and of the inner necessity that constitutes its self-reference and its innermost being —subject must, for Hegel, generate all of the differences which mark the development of experience, thought, and culture, thereby establishing the necessary place of all attitudes (and their objects) in the evolving whole which it alone produces and comprehends. And rather than just saying that subject does so, Hegel must make explicit the reasons why it must do so. The unconditioned first principle of Hegel's thought will be subjected to intense and intimate scrutiny.

The *Phenomenology* sets out to demonstrate that the progression of subject toward freedom necessarily entails not only a systematic knowledge of the whole of things, but the creation of that totality. The identity of the dialectical method with the self-motion of the human subject is the key to everything that happens in the book.

Hegel's "Preface" to the *Phenomenology* constitutes an extended reflection on the nature of that identity. Merely as an exercise in method it must be regarded as a classic. In it, Hegel works out the eight interdependent requirements for a *dialectical system* which will demonstrate that substance is subject. To state the entire formula: dialectic is a *comprehensive, self-contained,* and *circular* system that is *self-moved* in a *necessary* sequence by the single *unconditioned* principle which, in consonance with the *instability* that must characterize its "nature," demands the *open-endedness* of that system in its final form. For Hegel, previous dialecticians fail by not meeting one or more of these requirements.

It is essential to grasp the interdependence of the eight requirements. The dialectical quest for comprehensiveness creates the demand for self-containment. A system can explain the whole of things only by grounding itself in the single unconditioned principle which makes everything else intelligible. When a system depends on principles outside itself, it needs another system to ground it. It also leaves us with no way of either separating or relating things in a principled manner. One can separate entities only on the basis of a prior comprehension of them. Spinoza formulated this principle when he pointed out that "explanation implies monism." The only way a system can avoid infinite regress in the search for a principled *beginning* is by resting on nothing outside itself.

Determination from within implies the *circularity* of a dialectical system. A self-contained system finds its center everywhere because its central principle demands every other thing for its actualization. Organicism receives in dialectic its richest complication. Dialectic can't rest on fixed or unexamined first principles because everything is determined by the process of its coming into being. It allows for no untested or enabling assumptions because nothing can lie outside it. As Socrates illustrates, paralysis and aporia are only apparent consequences of the method. By refuting his auditors' untested assumptions, Socrates moves them toward the search for a principle that will be its own ground. Socrates will *begin* with any opinion. By tracing the circle of its implications and contradictions, however, dialogue moves toward an understanding that sublates the entire previous discussion. Such an understanding alone provides a *true beginning,* and through it everything previously discussed achieves definition. One can't begin with it, but one hasn't begun until one gets to it.[44]

In making self-questioning intelligence his founding principle, Hegel in effect ontologizes the Socratic method. Dialectical reflection is not the imposition of preestablished categories and functions upon reality, but an immanent dynamic which shapes the course of its development by the repeated transcendence of its own limitations. That self-reflexive process constitutes the circularity of dialectical thought—a circularity which is hermeneutic rather than tautological and radically different from anything that can be understood along substantialist lines.

Hegel rejects substantialism because he sees that a philosophy grounded in the principles of identity and noncontradiction necessarily reduces the intelligibility of things to what can be formulated in strict definitions. It is always embarrassed by those "realities" that have their being in their motion, i.e., by the very processes which constitute the "permanent" features of a world of conflict and human striving. Individuality may be unintelligible per se and discourse may depend on common terms which abstract from experience, but the underside of these long-standing philosophic pieties is the inadequacy of substantialist thought to the being of that being who is always a who, never a what, and whose very being is at issue as a matter of possibilities and projects. The liberation of such a problematic from substantialism entails major ontological readjustments.

A dialectic based on substance finally sacrifices everything to the criterion of self-containment. Spinoza exhausts its possibilities by making all appearances modes of a principle itself unchanged. And his remains the perfect philosophy of self-contained intelligibility. But to sustain the internal complexity of the world, dialectic requires a more dynamic first principle. Where a dialectic based on the philosophy of substance dissolves diversity into a one separated from the many (Parmenides), or a many resolved as modes in the one (Spinoza), a dialectic of the concrete must somehow preserve both.

By developing an unsuspected implication, Hegel shows that the demand for self-containment actually implies the destruction of substantialist thought. If nothing can be placed outside a dialectical system, its standard of truth and correct reasoning must arise out of its own movement.

The act of questioning must generate its own criteria. Hegel proclaims the interdependence of form and content, process and result, and grounds the possibility of philosophic truth in the very act of philosophizing out of philosophic necessity.[45] Dialectic must establish the meaning of all concepts (knowledge, truth, experience, subject, object, etc.) internally. This requirement implies the ontological primacy of the thinking subject and establishes the basis for the eventual identification of knowledge, truth, and being.

Hegel contends—and to understand him here is to see his "idealism" in a new light—that any a priori determination of either the mind, its objects, or the nature of truth leads to self-defeating contradictions which prevent our ever getting to experience. Kant is, for Hegel, the major sinner on all counts. Fitting the mind a priori with the concepts requisite for the "construction" of physical phenomena, Kant necessarily conceives of the object along Newtonian lines and models his concept of truth in the image of science. He preserves the independence of things (the noumenal order) only by rejecting the possibility of a holistic or dialectical perspective. Both science and the unconditioned are maintained, but their possible connection is sundered. It all works perfectly if we restrict ourselves to a scientistic concept of experience.

Yet, by these standards, phenomena and activities other than the "scientific" remain essentially unintelligible except by analogy. As Dewey notes, Kant is forced to divide into distinct *realms* concerns that are, in immediate experience, inextricably intertwined. The primacy of "science" in his thought results in the dualisms which mark its development, and he avoids Hegel's radical phenomenological grounding of all concepts in the *Lebenswelt* only by positing unintelligible limit concepts such as the *Ding-an-sich*. The "critical philosophy" thereby sacrifices on the altar of physical science both the concrete world of human engagement and subject's dialectical drive.

To counter Kant's powerful critique of dialectic and to satisfy the demand for self-containment, Hegel saw the need to begin in what he terms "absolute skepticism." All assumptions and a priori concepts are rejected. Truth, being, and knowledge must be generated reciprocally out of immediate experience. Is this too radical a move, even for Hegel? Beginning with the natural consciousness casts all traditional concepts of truth and correct reasoning into doubt. What status can one claim for a "truth" that is not preexistent, fixed, and independent of our activity, and how, bereft of the a priori logical canons needed to fix our thought,

can we ever overcome the distortions implied in the thinking of a consciousness that has become radically indeterminate? If philosophy must
generate its criteria experientially out of its own activity, consciousness
must prove adequate to a world in which, initially, all coherence is gone.
Such a reorientation of thought requires a fundamental reformulation of
philosophic logic. As Hegel sees it, the problem is to discover the principles of self-motion which force the natural consciousness to generate
"truth" by continually surmounting its own errors.[46] A truth so founded
must retain the conflicts required for its coming to be. Hegel foreshadows
Heidegger's redefinition of truth as *a-lethia*. Truth is a human act, dependent on struggle and suffering for its genesis, and implicated in error.
Only by putting a system's criteria of truth outside the system can one
avoid such unsettling reflections.

By centering his thought in the inherent instability of the natural consciousness, Hegel breaks with the controlling assumptions of substantialist
thought. While previous thinkers, following Aristotle and the Christian
tradition, regard motion as lack and even inherent imperfection, Hegel
sees it as the only possible source of self-containment *without exclusion.*
If a dialectical system simply resolves plurality into a single fixed principle, the autonomy of that principle, being merely subsumptive, inevitably
abstracts from experience. To become *concrete,* dialectic must overcome
the differences that characterize experience without compromising those
differences.

The only way Hegel can assure that possibility is by breaking down
the traditional opposition of *identity* and *difference* right within the first
principle of his thought.[47] Logically and methodologically that task is
enormous. Like Spinoza's Adequate Idea, Hegel's first principle must be
self-grounding—yet there is no way that its sufficient reason[48] can be
inferred from purely rational considerations. The natural consciousness
can't simply wander in a priori fixity through the world, but must be
embedded in it. Its dialectical *autonomy* is not the secure "property" of a
"substance," but the possibility of a labor. To assure the necessity of that
labor, a dynamic of self-transformation must be established *in principle*
within the immediate unity of the natural consciousness.

The revolutionary implication of that requirement is the transformation of dialectic from the search for knowledge of a preexistent "state
of affairs" that merely awaits apprehension to a process of comprehensive ontological transformation. The natural consciousness *in its immediate
unity* must both direct itself to a total involvement in the world and con-

tain the basis for that world's thoroughgoing ontological transformation. Unless the principles of self-motion informing the natural consciousness enable it to bring the world into ontological correspondence with itself, we must either abandon the dialectical "illusion" or search for some other first principle.

The initial situation of the natural consciousness is, admittedly, the opposite of such a correspondence. Consciousness is initially overwhelmed by a world pulsating with qualitative diversity. The whole, which "is all there is," initially is not. The possibility of its future existence depends on consciousness' ability to overcome all the forms of otherness into which it is thrown. For that to happen, consciousness must be internally constituted such that *it is forced to mediate the difference it encounters in the world in order to develop its own inherent mediation of identity and difference.*

For these reasons, the simple positing of *psyche* as *self-motion,* as in Plato's *Phaedrus,* is far from sufficient. In order to establish subject's dialectical force and experiential veracity, Hegel must formulate its internal logos. Methodologically, he faces four successive and inseparable problems. First, the principles of self-reference that "shape" subject cannot be substantialistic, as in Kant, but must arise existentially. Second, subject's self-reference must mediate the opposition of identity and difference. Third, subject must depend for its development on relation to the world, to external otherness or difference at large. Finally, the dialectic of that relationship, as the progressive overcoming of all otherness, must culminate in a specific knowledge of "the whole of things"—one in which that totality coincides with the complete actualization of subject.

Hegel begins by reversing the traditional idea that motion implies lack—a fall from the perfection that characterizes a world already substantially complete—by finding in lack and motion the true identity of subject. The difference whereby subject moves becomes the locus of its identity. Subject does not simply *contain* difference, nor is its development simply the fructification of a preestablished harmony. When identity is substantialistically conceived, motion and development are compromised. To make motion necessary, the self-moved must from the start be fundamentally *other to itself.* In fact, in an important sense difference must be given a controlling hand. But if difference were all, movement would be mere change, the gradual sundering of identity, and development a deconstructive process of self-unraveling. Rather than evolving dialectical unity, we would face continual dispersion and eventual entropy. The self-differentiation of motion must accordingly be *both* the continuous expression of subject's identity *and* the process necessary for its self-actualization. Overcoming its own initially abstract form by *intending* otherness, subject must continually evolve a new identity by surmounting the differences it generates. *Identity, so conceived, is a dynamic of progressive self-transformation.* Conceptualizing that possibility led Hegel to define subject as a process of thoroughgoing yet determinate *self-negation.*

Since the need for self-mediation constitutes the subject, an emphasis on difference and discontinuity does not, for Hegel, imply the death of subject as it does for many recent thinkers. The "scandal" of difference implies the end of "subject-ism" only if subject is conceived along Cartesian lines. If subject were not, as a consequence of its "identity," directed to something other than itself, it would remain locked in its immediate unity, incessantly revolving back upon itself. It would, perhaps, have wonderful tautological inner voyages, but experience would lack a dialectical core. As *the immediate unity of identity and difference,* however, subject *exists* as a demand for differentiation which can achieve determination only by relating to that which is outside itself: the world. Its immediate unity thus directs subject to an engrossment in the world so total that initially subject appears, with Sartre, as nought but a transcending projection of being. Consciousness is intentionality or *consciousness of,* and the otherness it *intends* must *be* even if this fact threatens to result in a Sartrean dualism of being and nothingness or a Kantian dualism of epistemology and ontology.

If the relationship between subject and the world involved nothing but pure, empty intentionality, however, subject would sunder itself wholly in intending its opposite. Shattered by the force and plenitude of differences it encounters, it would become the product of external relations.[49] As the immediate unity of identity and difference, however, *subject is both the principle that intends and the subsequent unity of relations intended.* So conceived, subject *is a process of ceaseless experiential self-mediation.* Subject progressively cancels, preserves, and uplifts the otherness it intends by continually sublating itself. Reflection always generates a new world and a new mode of intentional activity.

Logically, the Hegelian revolution in thought is complete once this conception of subject is attained. The shift from substance to subject frees dialectic from the need to purchase self-containment by insulating itself from experience. No longer need one dissolve reality in abstract constructs. Grounding philosophy in subject, Hegel roots thought in existence in a way that compromises neither, yet leaves neither ontologically stable. Subject, unlike substance, is dynamic self-reference containing *otherness in itself* and *existential becoming* in its very notion. A self-reflexive negativity maintains itself by generating then surmounting its own inherent contradictions as well as the contradictions which arise from its ongoing relationship to the world. As the dynamic unity of identity and difference, subject *exists* as a process of ceaseless yet determinate negation.

Once again, Plato helps us understand Hegel's admittedly difficult line of thought. For Plato, the architectonic principle which informs the self-motion of the *psyche,* eros, is the child of poverty and care, and is defined as nothingness.[50] The lack and unrest defining love mandate its total involvement in the world and its continual ascent beyond its objects. Love requires objects for its development. Yet with each attainment, it discovers the inadequacy of its object to its telos; the world thereby revealed becomes permeated with absence and nothingness. The negativity of love is thoroughly determinate and establishes an experiential hierarchy. To surmount the differences perceived by ordinary reason (*doxa* and *pistis*), Plato erects his dialectic on two reciprocal moments: the *discovery* of progressively more inclusive "forms" or internal relations, and their *connection* in an evolving hierarchy. Initially, of course, one sees no connection between Alcibiades' erotic love of Socrates, the art of politics, and Knowledge of the good and the beautiful. Yet both the *Symposium* and the *Phaedrus* demonstrate how love's self-motion binds such realities into a graded hierarchy which can, most properly, be termed the true or ultimate form of everything that participates in it, since the end of any thing or activity defines it. Love moves us from desire for a single, beautifully formed body and the nascent aesthetic appreciation of body in general, through involvement in the "higher" forms of order which inhere in noble laws and institutions, to a final, culminating insight into the idea which informs the entire movement of eros: the "form of beauty itself." That form, contra popular opinion, is no more and no less than everything making up the comprehensive *order of being* that is established through love's movement. The "form" of the body Alcibiades loves is, finally, the demand that he progress beyond it: it is, ultimately, what it is *not*. Contra Aristotle, Plato's philosophy is an ontology of movement. Rather than an unchanging, transcendent substance separable from experience, beauty is the immanent order which love, through its self-motion, reveals. The "language of forms" is the discovery of immanent principles of ascent in the phenomenal world which bind together apparently separate realities and activities.

Renewing that line of thought, Hegel found in the negativity of desire the possibility for a far more elaborate and concrete dialectic of experience. Desire reconstitutes "idealism" on phenomenological and appetitive grounds. Hegel never denies the existence of a world initially independent of our activity. With consciousness as the moving principle of that world, however, the problem of knowledge and reality becomes a question of how consciousness, through its development, transforms the given. Epistemology is no longer restricted to the question of how subject and object, fixed in their difference, ever gain relation. The independence of the physical world is finally only apparent; with the introduction of consciousness, nothing remains as it immediately appears. Initially independent, the world rests, ontologically, upon the transforming power of human activity. Epistemology, so conceived, has become ontology.

He may lapse later, but in beginning with desire Hegel transcends both subjective and objective idealism. Phenomenological interrogation is not the dissolution of resistant realities in abstract thoughts, but a study of the manner in which thought, through its presence in the world, produces the continuous transformation of both. "Idealism" is not a precondition of objective existence, but a direct consequence of the most hardheaded realism. Subject and object are, to use Heidegger's term, *equiprimordial*— and subject, rather than being "the basis of its being," a fixed center for rationalistic deduction, is the "being of its basis," a dynamic instability which destabilizes all else.[51]

The demand that all concepts be shaped from within the dialectical process gives us a final and specifically ontological understanding of why dialectical terms resist univocal definition. If language is the primary problem today, dialectic is the unacknowledged lesson in its suppleness. The architectonic vocabulary of philosophy must be initially indeterminate and flexible enough to accommodate the shifts and expansions of meaning required to evolve a single all-inclusive scheme. At each stage of the *Phenomenology*, accordingly, subject and object—and with them reality, truth, and knowledge—take on a new meaning. In the early chapters, subject gradually becomes the scientific knower, while object is the totality of physical things. With the shift to desire, the boundaries of epistemology are shattered. Subject, as unhappy consciousness, must realize itself through its own activity: knowledge becomes *Weltanschauung* with the cultural world of historical activity subsuming, as one of its moments, the physical world which has become the object of labor. By the conclusion of the work, subject and object have undergone the total series of transformations needed to establish their identity. The *object* of knowledge is the cultural *subjects* who are reflectively aware of their absolute status and fully *present* as a result in their historical situation. The only adequate definitions of subject and object must comprehend the unity of their entire dialectical transmutation. The same holds for all the other terms central to Hegel's dialectic: freedom, truth, knowledge, experience, and, of course, the whole of things. A dialectical term is a comprehensive category which has its being in the process of its becoming; its content is the hierarchy of relationships it establishes and sustains.

The shift from substance to subject, while it enables Hegel to orient philosophy to the concrete, has profound consequences for the *completion* of a system so grounded.[52] Assured of its dialectical autonomy only through a development that is necessary and total, subject must take on the project of bringing reality into correspondence with itself. Completion can reside, accordingly, only in a world which retains, at its core, a dynamic instability opened to the future. Closure is impossible—in principle. There is no way for a philosophy based on subject to take wing beyond its basis or to leap from the dialectical process to the arms of a transcendent absolute.

To reappropriate the concrete universality of subject, three negations are required. (1) There is no transcendent principle, either in a deity or in an essentialized human mind, that fits culture to predetermined forms and orders history to a predetermined goal. (2) There is no way to remove subject from its radical inherence in the dialectical process, and therefore, no way, through formalistic abstraction, to make humanity or the "human mind" objects of religious-humanistic reverence or detached structural investigation. (3) There is no temporal end to the dialectical process. God, or the world of metaphysical guarantees, is dead. All efforts to impose the eternal, or "the logic of the same," upon time must be purged from thought. In underscoring these negations we renew Hegel by identifying the internal contradictions he failed to overcome.

The end of the dialectical process must remain as dynamic as the principle that generates it. Grounding philosophy in subject requires that the "concrete infinite" lie in the infinite possibilities of future development contained in a finite absolute. In keeping with the principle of self-containment, the only absolute given to subject is "absolute knowledge"—a systematic understanding of our previous development which directs us to our present tasks. Because dialectic is necessarily circular, beginning and ending in immediate experience, and resting on nothing outside itself, its voyage of cultural *memory* must conclude with the historical *present* and the recognition that the true coincidence of subject and object resides in history. That recognition contains as its innermost meaning, for self-conscious subjects, the imperative that we become, through action, world-historical individuals. Though Hegel resisted it, the true "secret" of his thought is the recognition that a philosophy grounded in subject is a dialectic of finitude, a meditation on the tragic imperatives of being-in-the-world, and the call for a humanizing praxis.

The preface to the *Phenomenology* is the pivotal moment in the history of dialectic because it initiates the three crucial shifts that have shaped the development of dialectic since Hegel. (1) The principle of self-containment dictates an "absolute skepticism" which rejects the a priori constructs of traditional epistemology in favor of a radical immersion of subject in the world. (2) The need for a principle of self-motion within immediacy redefines consciousness as a self-reflexive negativity oriented from its inception to the ontological transformation of the given. (3) A phenomenological "description" of consciousness' experiential development constitutes a fundamental ontology ordered in such a way as to establish the coincidence of subject and object.

Such a project depends on reappropriating Hegel's demonstration that the natural consciousness is *autonomous, inherently dynamic, necessarily related to the world it transforms, total in its movement, and one, in its complete development, both with itself and with the whole of things*. For that concept to hold, the natural consciousness must be (a) unconditioned, non-hypothetical, and self-grounding since it can depend on nothing outside itself; (b) inherently dynamic or unstable since it is the source generating the oppositions and contradictions through which the dialectic proceeds; and (c) related, by its own internal necessity, to the many separate phenomena which it binds together into the whole.

The effort of Chapters 1–4 above was to root this concept of subject in experience. The present chapter articulates the ontological and methodological principles which ground that effort. Hegel's preface may look forward to the *Logic*, but its subject is the *Phenomenology*, and Hegel would be the first to admit that everything he says in the preface is abstract and remains no more than a speculative construct unless and until it is tested and rooted in experience. A logical and methodological reflection on the concept of subject merely suggests the possibility of an immanent dialectic of experience. It is in experience alone that the possibility can be assured and known for what it is. For that, one must turn to the *Phenomenology* proper to learn that the only way to understand the message of the book is by reconstituting it in the present. Chapters 1–4 and the present chapter are thus reciprocally determining. The circle of their relationship is now complete, but only insofar as it brings us back to experience as our unfinished task. Dialectic always ends by reentering itself in the desire for a deepened interrogation as prelude to a new self-mediation.

Notes

Index

Notes

THE NOTES are an important plank in my argument, a sort of intellectual itinerary of our time which attempts to place opposed thinkers and positions in a larger dialectical context that corrects their self-imposed limitations and renews their contact with experience. The notes also constitute an annotated bibliography of sorts. As critiques, the notes contribute to the concept of a hermeneutics of engagement by suggesting ways in which we must read our contemporaries against the grain. However, I comment only on those thinkers and controversies directly related to the problem of subjectivity and contrast my interpretations with others only when doing so significantly clarifies my position.

Chapter 1: Hegel: The Contemporary of the Future

1 My purpose in the first section of this chapter is to articulate the concept of consciousness that one can derive from the introduction to *The Phenomenology of Mind*, trans. J. Baillie, 2d ed. (New York, 1931), pp. 131–45 (hereafter referred to as *PhG*). Recapturing that concept is the first step toward constituting Hegel's contemporary significance. Unfortunately, however, Hegel conflates two concerns in the introduction: (1) the attempt to inaugurate a phenomenological method, and (2) the attempt to establish a necessary connection between it and the parousia of the absolute. As I will later argue, the latter is an abstract and a priori imposition which continually falsifies the experiential meaning and direction of Hegel's investigations. This contradiction, with which the *PhG* is repeatedly riven, constitutes the most salient fact about Hegel's text. In reading Hegel against the grain our purpose is to liberate the meaning he suppresses in his inexorable march toward a rationalistic absolute. Chapter 5 below takes up the ontological issues I have bracketed here in order to keep the discussion focused solely on the problem of consciousness. For a contrasting reading of Hegel's introduction where emphasis is given to the absolute at the expense of the experiential, see Martin Heidegger, *Hegel's Concept of Experience* (New York, 1970). I use the term *sublate* throughout as the equivalent for the key Hegelian term *Aufhebung* which carries the simultaneous meanings of to cancel, to preserve, and to lift to a higher level. The difference between Hegel's use

of this concept to collect meanings in a movement toward the absolute and my attempt to develop a specifically experiential meaning for it will become apparent as we proceed.

2 The descriptions offered below are, like Hegel's, summaries which omit the details of rationalist and empiricist epistemologies. My purpose is to articulate the shaping logos and identify the basic contradiction in both movements in order to reveal how inadequate they are to an understanding of the dynamics of reflection. Hegel follows a similar procedure throughout the *PhG*: allusions (the Law of the Heart, i.e., Rousseau, etc.) and brief sketches replace detailed commentaries because Hegel's purpose is to identify the central contradiction that will enable him to insert the movement of thought under investigation into the larger framework he is constructing. Following that model, I focus here on the central assumptions of rationalism and empiricism to indicate why both traditions—despite continued popularity—are no longer viable when our concern is to understand human subjectivity. Given a different concern one would naturally form a different judgment of their value.

3 John Dewey, *Experience and Nature* (Chicago, 1925), p. 131.

4 *PhG*, pp. 132–33. Heidegger discusses this aspect of the introduction at length in *Hegel's Concept of Experience*.

5 *PhG*, p. 140.

6 *PhG*, p. 143.

7 *PhG*, p. 143.

8 *PhG*, p. 138.

9 I should add that, while my effort is to join Hegel and existentialism, my interpretation of the introduction and later of the preface (see chapter 5, pp. 353–63) differs sharply from the readings developed by Heidegger and by his followers Hans-Georg Gadamer (*Hegel's Dialectic*, trans. P. Christopher Smith [New Haven, 1976]) and Werner Marx (*Hegel's Phenomenology of Spirit* [Boston, 1975]). While indebted to Kojève and Hyppolite, my attempt to recapture the existential dimension of Hegel's text also differs considerably from their readings. The academic contrast to my hermeneutic of engagement is best represented by the exhaustive historical reconstructions of Hegel's official intentions that have been developed most recently by Charles Taylor, Stanley Rosen, and H. L. Harris.

10 This discussion is in *PhG*, pp. 218–40.

11 This discussion is supplemented by the discussion of anxiety developed in Chapter 2, pp. 114–34, and in Chapter 4, pp. 266–73, below. The synthesis of these three discussions constitutes the dialectical understanding of that concept. I follow a similar procedure in defining a number of other concepts —love, the other, sexuality, self-identity, etc. This procedure is one of the ways in which I try to indicate that the four chapters are suspensive and

progressive and need to be superimposed upon one another in order to be understood.

12 Hegel's discussion contains, before the fact, a systematic working out of the logic of the "always already" which Derrida derives primarily from Freud and Heidegger.

13 Gustave Flaubert, *Madame Bovary*, trans. Francis Steegmuller (New York, 1957). See pp. 215–16.

14 Hegel, as phenomenologist, thus subverts what Derrida, as deconstructionist, terms his logocentric paralysis before the scandal of "origins."

15 This is one of the more important contrasts between Hegel and Derrida. For Derrida on the trace, see *Speech and Phenomena* (Evanston, 1973), pp. 23, 47–49, and *Of Grammatology* (Baltimore, 1974), pp. 65–73.

16 The two best recent examples of the traditional reading are Charles Taylor, *Hegel* (London, 1975), and Stanley Rosen, *G. W. F. Hegel* (New Haven, 1974). My attempt is to chart an understanding which cuts between this rationalist reading of Hegel and the Bataille-Derrida deconstruction. The *für uns* and Absolute Knowledge are dissolved not through the elimination of subject but through the liberation of an existential *für uns* which emerges once the contradictions of rationalist subjectivity become apparent. The articulation of that existential subjectivity is the thread unifying the series of propositions the present chapter advances as the experiential self-references that constitute the self-mediation of subject.

17 *PhG*, p. 226.

18 I shall draw on a number of competing psychoanalytic sources including Melanie Klein, Mahler, Lichtenstein, Kohut, and Lacan. The dialectical rationale for extending the discussion in this way is worked out in Chapter 4, below.

19 Heinz Lichtenstein, *The Dilemma of Human Identity* (New York, 1980), especially the chapter "Identity and Sexuality: A Study of Their Interrelationship in Man."

20 Jacques Lacan, *Ecrits: A Selection*, trans. Alan Sheridan (New York, 1977), and *The Four Fundamental Concepts of Psychoanalysis*, trans. A. Sheridan (New York, 1978).

21 Lacan (repetition) and Derrida (supplementarity) represent the two alternatives to the position we are developing.

22 This phrase is taken from the central chapter in Jean-Paul Sartre, *Being and Nothingness*, trans. Hazel Barnes (New York, 1956), pp. 361–413. For its Hegelian reinterpretation, see below, pp. 119–26.

23 See below, pp. 71–94.

24 Bataille is one of the few commentators who see the deeper layer of the discussion—and its similarity to Nietzsche's *Genealogy of Morals*. Even Hyppolite and Kojève remain curiously literal in reading this section of Hegel.

25 The Heideggerian concept which the next chapter will develop is introduced
    here in order to establish the necessary connection between the two chapters
    at the precise moment in Hegel where the experiential ground for that
    connection emerges.

26 The need to break with a quasi-historical reading of Hegel is crucial. History
    in this part of the *PhG* is purely philosophic in the best sense of the term. As
    in Heidegger's existential analytic, Hegel here meditates on the nature and
    significance of an experience that founds history even if it itself was never
    experienced by the transparently clear self-consciousness used to articulate
    its significance. The power of such a conceptualization is its ability to explain
    the ontologically derivative nature of a multitude of behaviors which are
    defined by their desire to escape the experience it articulates. A similar
    logic is developed in Heidegger's discussion of anxiety, authenticity, and the
    derivative nature of ordinary, inauthentic living. See Chapter 2, pp. 114–34,
    below.

27 This reading demystifies the romantic and humanistic readings of slavery
    (often based on Marx's 1844 Manuscripts) as the experience which issues
    in a transparent consciousness of one's essential human dignity, etc. It also
    undercuts Hegel's later theory of how the three modes of "absolute spirit"
    (art, religion, philosophy) transcend history. These activities harbor a deeper,
    more conflicted text than either romantic or rationalist readings of their
    development can fathom. Marx, Lukács, and Hannah Arendt do much to
    establish the ontological significance of labor. But labor, being human, har-
    bors the full weight of unhappy consciousness and engenders a much more
    complex dialectic than a purely historical account of the genesis of concepts
    can comprehend. The dialectic of master and slave began with the insight
    that desire is intersubjective; it ends with the recognition that it is political,
    with politics seen, as in the ancients, not as something external to human
    beings but as an immediate and necessary determination of their being. The
    struggles characterizing human relations are objectified in institutions and
    social structures. The positions we occupy, or seek to occupy, in the social
    world are a primary context in which each person suffers and discovers
    his subjectivity. Class consciousness is a condition to which we are all con-
    demned not because we are, by natural endowment, master and slave, male
    and female, but because we find ourselves so situated and come to our sub-
    jectivity bearing the contradictions those positions entail. For a development
    of these ideas and an argument that politics is an existential a priori, see
    Chapter 3, below.

28 This paragraph indicates why, although Hegel's and Heidegger's texts
    deepen and reinterpret each other, Hegel's existential analytic remains the
    more basic text which prevents Heidegger's thought from lapsing into for-
    malism. See Chapter 2, pp. 142–46, below.

29 Jean Hyppolite, *Genesis and Structure of Hegel's Phenomenology of Spirit*, trans. Samuel Cherniak and John Heckman (Evanston, 1974), pp. 190–91. Hyppolite's superb discussion of noncoincidence is one of the sources of Sartre's thought. The other is its denser source: Alexandre Kojève's *Introduction to the Reading of Hegel*, trans. James H. Nichols, Jr. (New York, 1969).

30 Thus, for *stoicism* read *structuralism;* for *skepticism* read *deconstruction;* and for *unhappy consciousness* read *existentialism*.

31 Jacques Derrida, "Structure, Sign, and Play in the Discourse of the Human Sciences," *Writing and Difference*, trans. Alan Bass (Chicago, 1978), p. 279.

32 See especially Rosen, *G. W. F. Hegel*, pp. 132–34, where the sigh of relief at this definitive transition is almost audible. Existence will no longer intrude on the march of reason. See also Taylor, *Hegel*, pp. 161–62.

33 The notion that this is the primary meaning of the slave's experience is the excessively rationalist construct of Charles Taylor. One would be hard pressed to find a better—and given its occasion, more ironic—example of the "philosophic" effort to ascend to reason and leave desire far behind. Existence, in Taylor's reading, is that thing one must get beyond as quickly and definitively as possible.

34 Derrida made this statement in reply to a question after the initial presentation of "Structure, Sign, and Play." In a sense this idea has been mainline truth since Kant.

35 Paul de Man, *Allegories of Reading* (New Haven, 1979), p. 10. The following discussion can be taken as a "deconstruction" of de Man. The deconstruction of Derrida is a more complicated matter: see Chapter 5, pp. 346–49 and passim, below.

36 Pun intended, thereby inverting Derrida's discussion of keeping in reserve vs. expenditure without reserve in *Writing and Difference*, pp. 251–77.

37 Unhappy consciousness originates in the recognition of this necessity. That is why throughout *Blindness and Insight* (New York, 1971) de Man labors to deconstruct the unhappy consciousness. His work may be seen as an attempt to reverse the movement from skepticism to unhappy consciousness in order to circumvent the possibility of a dialectic of experience. Only when so protected can he go on to elaborate the linguistic aporias of his later thought. Existence will not intrude.

38 On this concept see Soren Kierkegaard, *Concluding Unscientific Postscript*, trans. David F. Swenson and Walter Lowrie (Princeton, 1941). The present section might be taken as an attempt to write what Kierkegaard would have said about section B in the *PhG* had he taken it seriously and read it with infinite concern. Had he done so he'd have seen that the arch-rationalist he attacks is open to experiences that bar the religious hierarchy Kierkegaard wants to confer upon existence. Kierkegaard's understanding of

the methodological implications of "subjective thinking" is unparalleled, but insufficient engagement in the critique of his own subjectivity prevented his letting Hegel's understanding of unhappy consciousness impinge too deeply on his awareness. The choice is not Hegel or Kierkegaard; adequacy to subject requires a more difficult kind of conceptualization.

39 For a contrasting discourse see Emil Fackenheim, *The Religious Dimension in Hegel's Thought* (Boston, 1970). Fackenheim's superb book traces the series of religious sublations which I—by recapturing the experience from which religion derives its origin—negate. That origin convicts religion of irretrievable bad faith. A psychological reading of religion restores the dissembled subtext that shapes even its most exalted affirmations.

40 Lukács, Meszaros, Ollmann, Schacht, and others enter the movie too late —i.e., the discussion of alienation (and Rameau's nephew) in the section on culture—and thus fail to establish a concept of alienation that is not subject to sociological and structuralist reduction once social situations change, as they did from the turbulent 1960s to the present slumber. The academic discourse about alienation collapsed into an abstract debate over the difference between *Entäusserung* and *Entfremdung* because the existential ground for both concepts, which we try here to articulate, was neglected.

41 The subliminal connection between Hegel and Derrida on this point is the key to moving beyond their respective solutions—the *für uns* and *différance*. It's also a perfect example of their unacknowledged similarity: Derrida opts for an infinite regress—the trace of the trace of its obliteration—which is an inverted parallel, an anti-*Aufhebung,* of Hegel's infinitely progressive collecting of meanings. Both thereby escape the "scandal" of existence—and of engaged thinking. See Chapter 5.

42 For Derrida's attempt to circumvent reflection by indefinitely delaying the moment when it might achieve self-mediation, see especially *Writing and Difference*, pp. 251–76, *Of Grammatology*, pp. 260–75, and *Margins of Philosophy* (Chicago, 1982), pp. 88–108, 113–36, 258–71. Rodolphe Gasche discusses this problem at length in *The Tain of the Mirror* (Harvard, 1987). The opposition between reflection and *différance* may represent the true contradiction defining the situation currently termed "postmodern."

43 *PhG*, p. 252.

44 Ibid., pp. 254–55.

45 Ibid., p. 255.

46 Difference is here established as the experience necessary for dialectic and not the force that disrupts and deconstructs it.

47 Hegel will return the favor in Chapter 4 when we offer a dialectical reinterpretation of the core of psychoanalytic theory.

48 *PhG*, p. 257.

49 Two of the best psychoanalysts on this are Melanie Klein and Hans Loewald.

See Melanie Klein, *The Psychoanalysis of Children* (New York, 1975), and *Love, Guilt and Reparation and Other Works, 1921–1945* (New York, 1975); Hans Loewald, *Papers on Psychoanalysis* (New Haven, 1982).

50 Melanie Klein, "Mourning and Its Relation to Manic-Depressive States," *Love, Guilt and Reparation*, pp. 344–69.

51 This is the kind of perception that Hans Kohut and Otto Kernberg have brought to the center of current psychoanalytic theory.

52 *PhG*, p. 259.

53 Ibid., pp. 259–60.

54 Ibid., p. 260.

55 Ibid., pp. 261–62.

56 Ibid., p. 261.

57 Ibid., pp. 261–62.

58 Ibid.

59 Ibid.

60 Ibid., pp. 262–64.

61 Ibid.

62 The dialectic of sex conceptualized in the course of this book coordinates this section with Chapter 2, pp. 119–26, Chapter 3, pp. 218–21, and Chapter 4, passim, especially pp. 296–307.

63 *PhG*, p. 264.

64 Hegel foreshadows Foucault's study of the connection between the history of sexuality and the history of discourse about it. Here he articulates the initial experiential motive for this particular "incitement to discourse." See Michel Foucault, *The History of Sexuality*, Vol. 1: *An Introduction*, trans. R. Hurley (New York, 1980).

65 *PhG*, p. 264.

66 Harry Stack Sullivan, *Clinical Studies in Psychiatry* (New York, 1956), pp. 229–83, sees this as the essential operation that constitutes the unending defeat of the obsessional process.

67 Unlike Derrida, we deconstruct "self-presence" experientially rather than linguistically thereby preserving the possibility of an existential self against the unraveling of that concept.

68 For the concrete development of this idea, see Chapter 4, pp. 296–307, below. Within psychoanalysis Lichtenstein comes closest to seeing the connection, but unfortunately arrests its dialectic in a substantialistic theory of identity formation.

69 Sartre is especially good on this phenomenon. In fact, one might argue that the limitations in Sartre's study of human relations derive not only from his Cartesian dualism but from his inability to sublate shame. On the psychological value of shame and its connection to identity, see also Helen Lynd, *Shame and the Search for Identity* (New Haven, 1969).

70 *PhG*, pp. 265–66.
71 Lacan, *Ecrits*, p. 153.
72 *PhG*, pp. 265–66.
73 Ibid., p. 266.
74 Ibid., p. 266.
75 See Jean-Paul Sartre, *Critique of Dialectical Reason*, trans. Alan Sheridan-Smith (London, 1976), vol. 1, for a brilliant study of the ontopsychology of groups.
76 *PhG*, pp. 266–67.
77 Ibid.
78 Ibid.
79 *PhG*, section C, "Reason." This chapter is finally a great comic episode: the comedy of convalescence from unhappy consciousness, an extended parody of the obsessional attempt of reason to assure itself that substance exists secure in a fixed external order. Its ironic culmination results in one of Hegel's more delightful puns. See *PhG*, p. 362.

Chapter 2: Existentialism: The Once and Future Philosophy

1 This is the central issue in our interrogation of *Being and Time*, trans. John Macquarrie and William Richardson (New York, 1962) (hereafter designated *SZ*). The critical rethinking of *SZ* we carry out in this chapter is methodologically equivalent to the critique of Hegel we developed in Chapter 1. In terms of the hermeneutic of engagement we are constructing, the task of this chapter is to recapture the existential dimension of Heidegger's thought by freeing it from the limitations of his formalism. Such a recovery will have important implications for the way phenomenological studies are generally conducted. In its current self-understanding, phenomenology is an arrested dialectic which attempts to identify as topics for separate description experiences that can be understood only when grasped in their necessary dialectical and existential connections.

2 In developing this idea our effort will be to recapture the existential dimension of the hermeneutic circle in order to show how engagement revolutionizes all other conceptions of the circle, especially Heideggerian formalism. For Heidegger's discussion of the hermeneutic circle, see *SZ*, pp. 24–31. Heidegger's formalism depends on the important distinction he makes between an *existentiale* analytic of the existence structure and the *existentiell* study of particular acts, choices, etc. (*SZ*, pp. 32–34). We will argue below, pp. 144–56, that this distinction cannot be maintained.

3 Heidegger's refusal to let his ontological inquiries be reduced to separate, isolated disciplines such as sociology, psychology, or ethics is laudable. But

the possibility of a philosophic anthropology and a genuinely dialectical ethic gets lost in the process. Our effort is to recover such possibilities by showing, for example, that ontological questioning is ethical questioning, a point which Heidegger acknowledges in *An Introduction to Metaphysics*.

4 The problem of "beginnings" is here conceptualized in a hermeneutics of engagement in a way that provides a meaningful contrast to Derrida's concept of the trace. Each section of this chapter shows how in grasping existential time we cancel the myth of origins while avoiding the infinite regress of deconstructive formalism.

5 The following discussion is an existential corollary to the discussion of the other in Chapter 1. I discuss the other from a marxist perspective in Chapter 3, pp. 211–18, and in a psychoanalytic context in Chapter 4, pp. 242–50. Together these four discussions constitute a dialectical definition of the other.

6 This is where Husserl gets trapped and where any epistemologically oriented phenomenology begins to unravel. See especially *Cartesian Meditations*, trans. Dorion Cairns (The Hague, 1962), chap. 5.

7 See *SZ*, pp. 210–24. Part of the irony of Heidegger is that on one level he contributes to the "death of subject" while on another he points toward a new understanding of subjectivity.

8 T. S. Eliot, "Four Quartets."

9 Jacques Derrida, "Differance" *Speech and Phenomena* (Evanston, 1973), pp. 129–60, and *Of Grammatology*, (Baltimore, 1974), pp. 166–85. As we'll see, the existential reference of anxiety both arrests and grounds Derridean play, referring it to a concept of authenticity, which is of necessity a matter not of presence but of choice and will. See below, pp. 346–49.

10 For a marxist understanding of how fear is the engine producing the internalizations needed to sustain the capitalist machine, see below, pp. 215–18.

11 Heidegger's key statements on the ontological primacy of existence are in *SZ*, pp. 168, 179–82, 230, 234, 303.

12 The deconstruction of existentialism along the lines of a myth of self-presence—here self-presence through *Angst*—is thereby cut off. Existentialism rests on a logic that transcends the social-individual dichotomy, demonstrating both the dominance and the derivate nature of the sociological.

13 This discussion bears the full weight of Hegel's concept of desire as the context it tries to sublate. The present discussion is, in turn, concretized and challenged by the discussions of love in Chapters 3 and 4.

14 Heidegger argues the ontologically revelatory power of mood (*Befindlichkeit*) in *SZ*, pp. 172–78. In the even finer discussion of mood in "What Is Metaphysics?" (*Existence and Being* [Chicago, 1949], pp. 353–92), Heidegger lists love as one of the "moods" of ontologically revelatory significance. In placing the discussion of love between two discussions of anxiety, my purpose is to cancel Heideggerian formalism by showing that anxiety and love are equi-

primordial in a relationship where they question and attune themselves to one another in a way that establishes the interpersonal nature of existence, which is a dimension Heidegger always marginalizes.

15 Merleau-Ponty's great text on the body in *The Phenomenology of Perception*, trans. Colin Smith (New York, 1962), pp. 67–202, proceeds along similar lines, though without using love as an example.

16 See *SZ*, pp. 229–35.

17 Love thus gives one of the best examples of a theory of self and of identity that cuts between substantialism and deconstruction. I develop the psychoanalytic implications of this concept of love in Chapter 4. Both discussions point to one conclusion: one cannot avoid having one's being defined by love.

18 Heidegger's great discussion of time and the *ex-states* of temporality is in *SZ*, division 2, pts. 3–4. See especially pp. 377, 281–82, 390, 401, 437.

19 Methodologically, engagement always goes in a circle in which each discussion ends or concludes with a return to the beginning and the recognition of the need to undertake a deeper reflection on the problems and phenomena it has discussed. The interdependence of my first four chapters is an attempt to enact this process.

20 Heidegger's key discussions of anxiety are in *SZ*, pp. 229–34, and in "What Is Metaphysics?"

21 *SZ*, p. 193.

22 Existential engagement blocks the *Kehre* which initiates the later thought of Heidegger. For a contrasting view which praises Heidegger's development, see William J. Richardson, *Heidegger through Phenomenology to Thought* (The Hague, 1967). Heidegger's debt to Kant is considerable. Heidegger makes one of the clearest statements of what he will attempt in *SZ* in *Kant and the Problem of Metaphysics*, trans. James S. Churchill (Bloomington, 1962). See especially section 4. For an extended quarrel with the Kantian analogy and an attempt to formulate a different concept of the existential a priori, see below, pp. 140–46.

23 On this charge see Lukács, *History and Class Consciousness* (Cambridge, Mass., 1971), passim, and Theodor Adorno, *The Jargon of Authenticity*, trans. E. B. Ashton (Evanston, 1983).

24 The best critique of Kant and ethical formalism remains Max Scheler, *Formalism in Ethics and Non-Formal Ethics of Value*, trans. Manfred S. Frings and Roger L. Funk (Evanston, 1973). This major and unjustly neglected work is one of the finest discussions of the appeal of formalism. Heidegger's strenuous objection to ethics is a function of his formalism. The greatest value of existentialism may lie, however, in moving ethics beyond its Kantian limits. For a contrasting argument that sees existentialism as voluntarism, see Frederick A. Olafson, *Principles and Persons* (Baltimore, 1967).

25 An existential understanding of death thus gives a new slant to the Hegelian argument developed on pp. 39–42. Death humanizes desire and situates inwardness in the world.

26 See *Metaphysics*, 9; *Physics*, 2; *Nicomachean Ethics*, 2; and *De Anima*, 3. 431–33.

27 For the marxist development of this idea see below, pp. 223–31.

28 Thereby pop existentialism on the right is also canceled. But for a curious example see K. Wojtyla's *The Acting Person*, trans. Andrzej Potocki (Boston, 1979), that strange amalgam of Husserl, Kant, and traditional Christian ethics.

29 *SZ*, pp. 393–96.

30 *SZ*, p. 355.

31 The *Seinsmystik* of his later thought necessarily follows, its primary lesson being that when one has nothing to do one reverts to cosmology and theology.

32 Rilke, "Torso of an Archaic Apollo."

33 Though it goes under many names, often without any explicit reference to Kant, neo-Kantian formalism is one of the major movements of modern thought. It includes Cassirer, the New Critics, Lévi-Strauss, structuralism, and Chomsky.

34 The rescuing of existentialism from what Robert Denoon Cumming terms its American "vagabondage" is a redoubtable task. Cumming clears much of the ground in his *Starting Point* (Chicago, 1979). Other noteworthy efforts include Calvin O. Schrag, *Existence and Freedom* (Evanston, 1969), and Richard J. Bernstein, *Praxis and Action* (Philadelphia, 1971).

35 Michel Foucault, *The Order of Things* (New York, 1970), pp. 303–43. See also the fine book on Foucault by Hubert L. Dreyfus and Paul Rabinow, *Michel Foucault: Beyond Structuralism and Hermeneutics* (Chicago, 1982). Because he does not take a sufficiently dialectical view of this problem, Foucault dissolves subject and lapses into his own form of structuralist formalism, a historical Kantianism of "epistemes."

36 See Paul Ricoeur's discussion of the concept of a hierarchy of integrations in *Freud and Philosophy*, trans. Denis Savage (New Haven, 1970), pp. 37–56.

37 As in Erik Erikson, whose thought is not the coming of existentialism to psychoanalysis but the antithesis of that possibility. See Chapter 4, pp. 257–58, below.

38 Immanuel Kant, *Works*. (Cass.), 8: 343–44.

39 *SZ*, pp. 184–88. Heidegger's important concept of the equiprimordial is one of his most conspicuous efforts to work out a logic that is free of the concept of presence. Derrida's more systematic effort to spell out this logic derives from Heidegger's lead.

40 See Jean-Paul Sartre, *Search for a Method*, trans. Hazel Barnes (New York, 1963).

41 This is one of the reasons why literature is a primary mode of existential knowledge and a way of thinking about experience that reverses the ancients' resolution of the quarrel between literature and philosophy in favor of philosophy. Rather than oppose literature and philosophy, we need to establish the nature of their dialectical relationship. For that to take place, neither can be set up as primary and the other marginalized. A concrete understanding of their connection requires a dialectic in which philosophy will transform itself by thinking through the implications of literature's primary access to experience. The present work is but a prelude to that effort.

42 In so doing, crisis concretizes Heidegger's formalistic understanding of the *ex-states* of temporality.

43 Deconstruction encourages the idea that we can always start again because we've never started. This is its most conspicuous point of contact with its "origin" in the spontaneity of the Sartrean *pour-soi*. Crisis, in contrast, is the situatedness that restores our contact with the world.

44 This discussion attempts to correct the dilemmas in which Sartre's concept of the *pour-soi* lands him.

45 See Norman K. Denzin, *On Understanding Emotion* (San Francisco, 1984), for a fine overview of theories of emotion organized in terms of the progression toward a phenomenological and Sartrean understanding. See also Jean-Paul Sartre, *Sketch for a Theory of the Emotions*, trans. P. Mariet (London, 1962), and, for the notion of incipient action, Kenneth Burke, *A Grammar of Motives*.

46 *SZ*, pp. 182–88.

47 *SZ*, pp. 416–17. In many ways this statement completes the existential ontology of *SZ*. Heidegger's subsequent thought will try to transcend this connection, but the truth of the matter may be that it is unsurpassable. Rather than take wing beyond existence, we must deepen it by probing all of its ontological implications. In that sense, this chapter constitutes an attempt to reverse the *Kehre*. As a conceptual transition to the next two chapters, what follows moves the idea of world in the two directions that Heidegger's formalism prevented him from taking.

48 *SZ*, pp. 437–38. Heideggerian repetition attempts to formalize this insight. Our effort, in contrast, is to make it the critical edge that enables us to dive into the past alive to the past's contradictions as well as its possibilities. Often the repeatable possibility is the one a thinker spent all his time covering up. So it is, in many ways, with both Hegel and Heidegger. The task of a hermeneutics of engagement is to foreground that possibility as the ground of the deepest relationship we can have to previous thought. But we can sustain it in the present only by remaining harshly critical of ourselves. Engagement

always cuts both ways. For a different, more traditional, and humanistic concept of hermeneutics, which is also much closer to the contemplative, lyric, and romantic directions of Heidegger's later thought, see Hans-Georg Gadamer, *Truth and Method* (London, 1970), and *Philosophical Hermeneutics*, trans. David E. Lingis (California, 1976).

49 See *PhG*, pp. 644–79; Georg Lukács, *History and Class Consciousness*; and Thomas Mann, *The Magic Mountain*.

Chapter 3: Subject in a Marxism without Guarantees

1 While I focused on the interrogation of a single thinker in the first two chapters, the methodology of a hermeneutics of engagement will be developed in the next two chapters by taking a diverse body of thinkers and texts and subjecting them to critical reflection. In Chapter 3, I show how the broad line of development of marxist theory enables us to purge marxism of the contradictions and dogmas that have frustrated its development. In Chapter 4, I take psychoanalysis from Freud to the present as a single text from which we can derive a core theory that liberates a new self-understanding for psychoanalysis. The theories thereby constructed in these chapters are not equivalent to anything one could find in any of the thinkers under investigation. They are products, rather, of an engagement looking to constitute repeatable possibilities in the present.

2 Stuart Hall, Public Lecture, University of Illinois, June 1983.

3 Louis Althusser, *Lenin and Philosophy*, trans. Ben Brewster (New York, 1971), pp. 170–83.

4 Gayatri Spivak, "Marx after Derrida," in *Philosophy and Literature*, ed. William Cain (Lewisburg, Pa., 1983). Spivak distinguishes antiscientific antihumanism (Derrida) and scientific antihumanism (Althusser) as the two alternatives open for contemporary marxism. We offer a third, which transcends both Spivak's framework and the humanistic marxism to which it is opposed. By so doing, this chapter constitutes a further step in our effort to transcend the alternatives of humanism and deconstruction.

5 The focus on ideology connects this chapter with the effort defining the previous ones. Ideology is here the main thing we must experience and think through because it is the concept within marxism—and within sociology in general—which bears most directly on the question of subject and on the task of rethinking reflection outside rationalist limits. Rather than oppose reflection and ideology, as most contemporary marxists do, our effort is to establish their dialectical connection as the basis for a marxism of experience. It also constitutes a further development of our reflection on the nature of reflection.

6 Chapter 2 is here *thrown* into a *situation* or situatedness—ideology—to test

whether the possibility it establishes can be concretely earned in the belly of the beast. An analogous test is performed on the Hegelian subject in Chapter 4.

7   This is Paul Ricoeur's term. See *Freud and Philosophy*, trans. Denis Savage (New Haven, 1970), pp. 32–36.

8   By sublating this view, the present chapter incorporates and reverses the impact of deconstruction on marxism by opposing reflective engagement to the generation of content through abstract logical games and through the manipulation of terms in a purely textual universe. For a different assessment of the relationship between marxism and deconstruction, see Michael Ryan, *Marxism and Deconstruction* (Baltimore, 1982).

9   The concept of reflection we constructed in Chapter 1 is here used both to criticize current marxism and to transform itself through that act. Reflection proves itself concrete and self-transforming by here performing the labor of the negative on a dominant conception of itself. The chapter thus constitutes a further critique and reconstruction of Hegel that circumvents the recent arguments of Althusser, Coletti, Della Volpe, and others that we must purge the Hegel in Marx. Neither Hegel nor Marx is here set up as the stable meaning that enables us to read the other. They read one another.

10 As a "scientific" discipline sociology is generally loath to take this step, preferring to acquiesce in an inherently positivistic posture. Alvin Gouldner sees this as sociology's coming crisis. As with the other great sociologists (Weber, Mead, Dewey, Burke, Schutz), Marx's essential contribution is to move the discipline toward that crisis.

11 With reference to marxism, see Jacques Derrida, *Positions*, trans. Alan Bass (Chicago, 1981), pp. 39–96.

12 See Adorno's great chapter "The Culture Industry" in Theodor Adorno and Max Horkheimer, *Dialectic of Enlightenment*, trans. John Cumming (New York, 1972), pp. 120–67. What Adorno's study lacks is the Althusserian insight that the glue holding the whole industry together is the interpellation of subjects.

13 Marx's best discussions of this are in *The German Ideology* and *The Holy Family*. Lukács is the one who most fully develops the idea in his great critique of Kantianism, "The Antinomies of Bourgeois Thought," in *History and Class Consciousness* (Cambridge, Mass., 1971), pp. 110–48.

14 The history of marxism is littered with attempts to circumvent Mannheim both before and after the fact by claiming that marxism is beyond ideology. Marx was the first to think so, Althusser the latest. The claim of scientific status is also a recurrent theme in marxist thought.

15 Lukács, *History and Class Consciousness*, pp. 110–49. See also Herbert Marcuse, *One-Dimensional Man* (Boston, 1964), especially chap. 6, and the major critiques of reason developed in the Frankfurt school. The best source on the latter remains Martin Jay, *The Dialectical Imagination* (Boston, 1973).

16 For the critique of class reductionism see Antonio Gramsci, *The Prison Notebooks*, trans. Quintin Hoare and Geoffrey Nowell-Smith (New York, 1971), and Ernesto Laclau, *Politics and Ideology in Marxist Theory* (London, 1977). See below, pp. 196–98.

17 Derrida does not take these steps, but he makes them ideologically fashionable and perhaps irresistible. On *écriture féminine* see Hélène Cixous, "The Laugh of the Medusa," *Signs* (Summer 1976). For a more complicated and thoroughly Derridean feminism, see Luce Irigaray, *Speculum of the Other Woman*, trans. Gillian C. Gill (Ithaca, 1985). On schizoanalysis, see Gilles Deleuze and Felix Guattari, *Anti-Oedipus: Capitalism and Schizophrenia*, trans. R. Hurley, M. Seem, and H. Lane (New York, 1977).

18 See especially Jürgen Habermas, *Communication and the Evolution of Society*, trans. Thomas McCarthy (Boston, 1979), and Habermas' critique of Adorno, "The Entwinement of Myth and Enlightenment," *The German Critique*, 26 (1982), 13–30. Kant vivant. For a superb overview of Habermas' work, see Thomas McCarthy, *The Critical Theory of Jürgen Habermas* (Boston, 1982). The loss of the energies of the Frankfurt school in the movement from Adorno to Habermas is considerable. That decline may be the best example of how difficult it is to maintain a dialectical understanding of experience and of how ready reason, Kantian or otherwise, is to step in to fill the breach when more tragic and psychoanalytically attuned energies burn out. Habermas' neat symmetry of reason with universal pragmatics, moral development, and ego identity, and the inevitable alignment of all the above goods with the dominant social order, are the parody repetition of all that Adorno subjected to unremitting critique. Habermas' handling of Freud and Nietzsche is the clearest index of what happens in Frankfurt's erasure of its origins.

19 See especially *The Savage Mind* (London, 1962). As we'll see, structuralism is late capitalism incarnate. Lévi-Strauss correctly sees his work as a contribution to the analysis and critique of the "superstructure," and as such it is of great value; however the superstructure is not an eternal idea but a historical reality.

20 Jacques Lacan, *Ecrits: A Selection*, trans. Alan Sheridan (New York, 1977), especially pp. 30–113, 114–45; and Althusser, *Lenin and Philosophy*, pp. 189–221. For a more doctrinaire marxist critique of psychoanalysis, see Russell Jacoby, *Social Amnesia* (Boston, 1975).

21 In this sense, herstory repeats the oldest and most disposable story/concept in marxism. Marx saw the fallacy of all utopian socialisms, but indulged in his own bow to their appeal when he distinguished prehistory and human history.

22 Nietzsche makes this statement about language. The same question, of course, applies to the subject, which as we've now been instructed is merely a language effect.

23 Foucault traces this process in detail, while Althusser provides its basic concept—the interpellation of subjects.

24 Perry Anderson, *In the Tracks of Historical Materialism* (Chicago, 1984). The real tracks here are the rationalist-deconstructive dichotomy and the conceptual framework that makes rationalism and deconstruction exclusive and exhaustive alternatives, leaving no room for the concrete perspective that transcends their binds.

25 James McMurtry, *The Structure of Marx's World-View* (Princeton, 1978), chaps. 5 and 6. The following paragraph summarizes the argument of those chapters.

26 McMurtry, *Structure of Marx's World-View*, pp. 148–50.

27 This is one of the key reasons why ideology is the other side of the psychoanalytic idea of the unconscious. Together they put an end to the notion of conscious intentionality as a likely or sufficient account of our activities.

28 Thus Althusser and Lenin.

29 Thus Lukács, Adorno, Marcuse, and Fromm.

30 The assumption Althusser and Habermas share.

31 The assumption that Lukács and modern French feminists share. See also Jean Baker Miller, *Toward a New Psychology of Women* (Boston, 1976), where Lukács's adaptation of Hegel's master-slave dialectic—the claim that the proletariat is the identical subject-object of history—is taken over unchanged to argue that women necessarily understand both their own consciousness and that of their oppressors.

32 Thus Marcuse, Reich, Deleuze/Guattari, Irigaray.

33 We here make our initial bow to Althusser's concept of ideology and begin the long process of reversing the conclusions Althusser draws from it. See below, pp. 207–10.

34 Gramsci's best discussion of this is in *Prison Notebooks*, pp. 381–419. See also Raymond Williams, *Marxism and Literature* (Oxford, 1977), and Chantal Mouffe, ed., *Gramsci and Marxist Theory* (London, 1979). Habermas' concept of legitimation attempts to conceptualize some of the same phenomena from a much more rationalistic point of view. See *Legitimation Crisis*, trans. Thomas McCarthy (Boston, 1975).

35 For Gramsci on this, see *Prison Notebooks*, pp. 171–75.

36 Althusser will later rethink this important idea of Gramsci's in structuralist terms. See below, pp. 202–6.

37 For Althusser's critique of expressive causality and his development of a Spinozistic concept of structural causality, see Louis Althusser and Etienne Balibar, *Reading Capital* (London, 1970), pp. 112–17.

38 For Henri Lefevbre's major contribution to marxism, see *Everyday Life in the Modern World*, trans. Sacha Rabinovitch (London, 1971). On docility, see Michel Foucault, *Discipline and Punish*.

39 Kenneth Burke's focus on drama and literature gives his understanding of

experience a concreteness that eludes Gramsci. Robert Wess is currently developing a "marxist rhetoric" based on Burke. For a consideration of Burke and the politics of critical theory, see Frank Lentricchia, *Criticism and Social Change* (Chicago, 1983).

40 Hegel in *PhG*, pp. 514–20, sees the connection between the fractured negative consciousness of Rameau's nephew and "society as a community of animals" as defining the historical situation which we, coming at a later stage of its development, term modern. We here introduce the concept of alienation in a context quite different from the one that prevailed during its recent heyday when Fromm, Schacht, Ollmann, and others used it to claim an essentialistic humanism for Marx.

41 The same can be said of Sartre, Burke, Bakhtin, and Adorno. The dismissive code word for all such ways of thinking is left Hegelianism.

42 See especially Althusser, *Lenin and Philosophy*, pp. 170–83, and *Essays in Self-Criticism*.

43 Althusser, *Lenin and Philosophy*, pp. 170–83.

44 Althusser, *Lenin and Philosophy*, pp. 143–62. How marxists, as dialectical materialists, managed to ignore this for so long in the study of ideology is a curious thing. The base-superstructure distinction is one of the surest ways of making oneself blind.

45 Burke calls such rituals "rhetorics." Burke's work deconstructs the thought-persuasion distinction on which classical and rationalist rhetoric is based. With that deconstruction, preexistent ideas and the form-content distinction are abolished; everything in consciousness and language becomes a matter of rhetoric. For Burke's attempt to rethink social theory from the point of view of rhetoric and literature, see especially *Permanence and Change* (New York, 1935) and *Attitudes toward History* (New York, 1937). Burke schematizes his concepts in *A Grammar of Motives* (New York, 1945). He then develops in *A Rhetoric of Motives* (New York, 1945) the main categories needed to understand literature and the social process in their necessary dialectical connection.

46 In Althusser we have, in effect, the marriage of Gramsci and Lacan, performed by Lévi-Strauss.

47 On the logic of the supplement, see Jacques Derrida, *Of Grammatology* (Baltimore, 1974), pp. 141–64. On its political implications, see *Positions*, pp. 56–91, and Ryan, *Marxism and Deconstruction*, pp. 43–81.

48 Althusser, *Lenin and Philosophy*, pp. 159–62. Lacan's statement is "The unconscious has no history."

49 Althusser and Balibar, *Reading Capital*, pp. 112–17. See also Fredric Jameson, *The Political Unconscious* (New Haven, 1983), pp. 51–75, and its parent text, Pierre Macherey, *A Theory of Literary Production*, trans. Geoffrey Wall (London, 1978).

50 The clearest initial formulation of Barthes's project is contained in *Mytholo-*

gies, trans. Annette Lavers (New York, 1972); its most sophisticated development is in *S/Z*, trans. Dick Howard (London, 1976). Many structuralists and semioticians find Barthes's psychoanalytic and political extensions of their rarefied methodologies "unscientific," when actually they constitute the immanent critique and redirection of those disciplines. Barthes, in effect, sublates both phenomenology and semiotics in a marxist concept of ideology.

51 In this way, Barthes historicizes Lévi-Strauss and thereby brings the whole structuralist enterprise to the point of critique. Barthes doesn't solidify structuralism, but performs an immanent or autocritique that is more solid than Derrida's critique because it has a content and brings out the historical and existential realities that slumber in structuralist descriptions.

52 On this concept, see Jean-Paul Sartre, *Critique of Dialectical Reason*, trans. Alan Sheridan-Smith (London, 1976), passim; Herbert Marcuse, *Reason and Revolution* (Boston, 1960), pp. vi–xiv; and Lukács, *History and Class Consciousness*, pp. 1–24.

53 For Althusser's critique of the humanistic Marx, see *For Marx* (New York, 1969), pp. 219–48.

54 See, in Karl Marx, *Economic and Philosophic Manuscripts* (New York, 1964), "Estranged Labor" and pp. 165–69.

55 The term is introduced by Raymond Williams in *Marxism and Literature*.

56 This methodological point is crucial to Marx's conceptualization of the bourgeois need to incorporate previous historical meanings. *Capital* is a structural study of that need in terms of the economic relations of production. Its mirror is bourgeois inwardness. Following the method of *Capital*, I here try to construct a model that brings out the laws or tendencies of a process—in this case the development of capitalist inwardness. It is not intended as an empirical sociological description. Nor does it enter into all the details of capitalist everydayness. The effort, instead, is to describe what the perfected product of that system would be like. On *Capital* as a conceptual model rather than a historical description, see Althusser, *Reading Capital*, pp. 158–64, 182–93. It is worthwhile to think of *Capital* as in part a mimetic or phenomenological work, analogous in method to Hegel's *PhG*. Marx represents the mind and way of thinking of the capitalist, excluding all that is not integral to that attitude and its immanent critique. From this perspective, *Capital* is merely one chapter in the philosophic anthropology of Nietzsche's last man. For an update on the economic side of that story, see Paul A. Baran and Paul M. Sweezy, *Monopoly Capital* (New York, 1966), and Ernest Mandel, *Marxist Economic Theory*, 2 vols. (New York, 1962).

57 In this section we try to give a phenomenological description of how ideology operates within the "stream" of everyday life. As a "return" to phenomenology, the discussion attempts to concretize what is left formalistic and ahistorical in discussions of the "they" such as Heidegger's. We here describe

the logic of the process whereby ideology becomes an immediacy; and the way in which those lulled by it experience their existence. The pessimism of the section, like Adorno's in *Dialectic of Enlightenment*, derives from an attempt to situate "residual meanings" in the Waste Land. The only consolation is that the totalization described here is still in process; until capitalism perfects its "Idea" it won't have attained the absolute security required for reproducing within subjects the conditions of its reproduction.

58 Max Weber, *The Protestant Ethic and the Spirit of Capitalism*, trans. Talcott Parsons (New York, 1958), still gives one of the best examples. Weber is also the source of the critique of rationality developed by Lukács, the Frankfurt school, and Marcuse.

59 This is where Lukács, Marcuse, and the Frankfurt demonstration that "reason" necessarily becomes positivism in the capitalist order proves invaluable.

60 See D. H. Lawrence, "The Rocking-Horse Winner."

61 Karl Marx, *Early Writings*, trans. Tom Bottomore (London, 1956).

62 This is the utopian line of thought pursued by Reich, Marcuse, Laing, and Norman O. Brown.

63 The last two forms of alienation discussed in the 1844 Manuscripts—alienation from one's fellow workers and from one's own humanity—establish species-being as the basis, not for a humanistic essentialism, but for a marxist phenomenology. See Hannah Arendt, *The Human Condition*, and for one of the better updatings of Marx's phenomenology of labor, Harry Braverman, *Labor and Monopoly Capital* (New York, 1974).

64 The following discussion of the family is grounded and sublated psychoanalytically in Chapter 4, pp. 242–48, 307–13. The purpose in taking up the family in both chapters is to refer Althusser's notion of "ideological state apparatuses" to the most formative site of interpellation. The family is the primary institution in which everything comes together in the concrete universality of that which is not a human essence but a historical reality.

65 This project will be sketched in Chapter 4, pp. 242–48. The historicity of the family is the insight Hegel will not quite let himself have; as a result, his discussion lapses into a nostalgic discussion of Greece—and the brother/sister relationship—in an effort to conjure up, if only for the moment, an ideal of the family he can somehow place outside history.

66 I am not claiming Hegel knew this; it is, rather, the knowledge his text yields in spite of his effort to conceal it.

67 Walter Benjamin, *Illuminations*, trans. Harry Zohn (New York, 1969).

68 This is the position Hegel finds himself in once he tries, unsuccessfully, to cancel the alienation of Rameau's nephew. For a more sympathetic reading of Hegel's argument, see Charles Taylor, *Hegel* (London, 1975), pp. 171–96.

69 Marcuse and recent deconstructive notions of art as the liberation of suppressed energies are the most conspicuous examples of this romanticism

within marxist aesthetics. Notes 68–76 constitute an outline for a dialectic of marxist approaches to literature and art.

70 See Macherey, *Theory of Literary Production*.

71 Lévi-Strauss is the current formalistic champion of this position. Kenneth Burke offers a more historically open construction of its implications for aesthetic form as social act.

72 Barthes argues this eloquently throughout his work, especially in *SZ*. As he knew, those who don't learn to read in this way are condemned always to read the same book without knowing it. Bakhtin's method of dialogal reading opens up similar lines of complication. See *The Dialogic Imagination*, trans. Caryl Emerson and Michael Holquist (Austin, 1981).

73 Williams, *Marxism and Literature*. pp. 128–35.

74 To get the main implications of this connection for the interpellation of subjects, substitute gender for genre.

75 Representation, or mimesis, and textuality aren't opposed but dialectically related. Mikhail Bakhtin, *Problems in Dostoyevsky's Poetics* (Minnesota, 1983), explores Dostoyevsky from this perspective. Jacques Derrida, "The Law of Genre," *Glyph*, 7 (1980), 176–201, presents a more abstract argument for similar considerations. Contrary to popular opinion, all the great marxist aestheticians have been preoccupied with form. See Eugene Lunn, *Marxism and Modernism* (California, 1984), for a fine overview.

76 This proposition endorses the deconstructive moment in order to sublate it.

77 For a critique of the current state of academic literary criticism from this perspective, see my essay on Stanley Fish, "The Fisher King: *Wille zur Macht* in Baltimore," *Critical Inquiry*, 10 (June 1984), 668–94.

Chapter 4: The Drama of the Psychoanalytic Subject

1 *Freud* and *psychoanalysis* are shorthand terms for a body of texts stretching from the Complete Standard Edition to recent work by analysts as diverse as Schafer, Kohut, Fairbairn, and Lacan. In rejecting the notion of a privileged text or the limitation of psychoanalytic theory to the interpretation of Freud, this chapter breaks both with the Lacan/Derrida line, which focuses its considerable energies almost exclusively on the slipperiness of Freud's texts, and with the more traditional and decidedly nonpsychoanalytic effort of Adolf Grunbaum in *The Foundations of Psychoanalysis* (California, 1984) to establish once and for all the univocal meaning of Freud's texts and their scientific status. While my effort is similar to the hermeneutic interpretation of psychoanalysis that Grunbaum scorns, I take issue with the shared assumption of Ricoeur, Habermas, and Derrida that one can understand psychoanalysis without having been analyzed. To understand and interrogate psychoanalysis, a personal analysis is the sine qua non for entering the hermeneutic of engagement. If we want to talk, in the current jargon, about

how "the psychoanalytic text reads us" we should not abridge its power to do so. My interpretation also endorses the critique of metapsychology that has been developed within psychoanalysis—see *Psychology versus Meta-psychology: Psychoanalytic Essays in Memory of George S. Klein* (New York, 1976)—and is indebted to the major reformulations of psychoanalytic theory developed by W. Ronald D. Fairbairn, Roy Schafer, and George S. Klein. My effort, however, is to show that these theories are insufficiently drama-tistic and nondialectical. I note my debts and disagreements with different psychoanalytic theories in the proper place as we proceed.

2   Following Derrida, deconstructive responses to Freud have remained single-mindedly fascinated with this game. See, for example, Shoshanna Felman, "Turning the Screw of Interpretation," *Yale French Studies* 55–56: 94–207, where the practice convicts itself of the very desire for mastery it criti-cizes, and where sexuality is conveniently transformed into textuality. Samuel Weber, *The Legend of Freud* (Minnesota, 1982), shows how a restrained and rigorous Derridean approach renders truly provocative readings. The vital line in such efforts is methodological: how does a text reveal/conceal and resist its discoveries? In the hands of Hegel, Marx, Nietzsche, Freud, and Heidegger this methodological axiom has far more disruptive and experi-ential implications than it has in the current practice of showing how every text unravels itself.

3   This was the line of early feminist attacks on psychoanalysis as well as the source of the traditional and foolproof academic refutation of Freud, i.e., "Freud claims that if I disagree with him that means I'm resisting. This is a vicious circle and robs psychoanalysis of scientific status." Juliet Mitchell in *Psychoanalysis and Feminism* does a good job of sorting out Freud's thoughts on women, and Roy Schafer contributes a fine brief statement in "Problems in Freud's Psychology of Women," *Journal of the American Psychoanalytic Association* 22: 459–85. I have no desire to minimize the dogmatism of the average analyst, the sorry state of psychoanalysis as a profession, or its vast and unacknowledged complicity with capitalist society. But a reductive and self-protective dismissal of psychoanalysis misses the true opportunity: a psychoanalytic critique of what is false and a reformulation of what is sound and true in psychoanalytic theory.

4   Trauma does not consign one to error or neurotic blindness. It is, rather, the experience that puts us in a position to understand psychoanalysis from within. As Freud knew, having written *The Interpretation of Dreams*, self-analysis is the condition for laying the foundations of psychoanalysis. It is also the primary source for further conceptual progress in it. Subjectivity is the subject here, and those who want to eliminate it are guilty of the very charge they make. The constraints of their hermeneutic circle derive from the self-protective motives that sustain it.

5   *Dramatistic* and *dramatism* are terms adapted from Kenneth Burke. The

reconstruction of psychoanalytic theory I offer has little in common with Burke's sociorhetorical theory of motives, however, and even less with his reading of psychoanalysis.

6 Derrida's reading of Freud begins with an intricate discussion of the mental apparatus as slate in "Freud and the Scene of Writing," *Writing and Differ-ence*, trans. Alan Bass (Chicago, 1978), pp. 196–231. The centrality of the same Freudian texts to the Lacanian school is revealed in Jean Laplanche and Serge Leclaire, "The Unconscious," trans. P. Coleman, *Yale French Studies* 48: 118–78.

7 The theory of subject worked out in Chapter 1 is the one psychoanalysis needs in order to ground its perceptions, and vice versa: psychoanalysis is what the Hegelian subject needs for its concretization. Engagement in this circle constitutes the dialectical connection of chapters 1 and 4.

8 Sigmund Freud, *The Complete Introductory Lectures on Psychoanalysis*, trans. James Strachey (New York, 1966), pp. 378–91.

9 Trauma is the concretization in psychoanalysis of Heidegger's concept of anxiety; that is why it has the power to expose the contradictions in in-authentic comprehensions of psychoanalysis and give us a standpoint which cuts through the opposition between the adaptational ego of American psy-chology and the Lacan deconstruction of subject. These alternatives are the equivalent within psychoanalysis of the rationalism-deconstruction opposi-tion which it is our purpose to transcend.

10 No one has done more to develop such a language for psychoanalysis than Roy Schafer in *A New Language for Psychoanalysis* (New Haven, 1976). But Schafer's desire to preserve the purity of his "action language" and to rid psychoanalysis of all traces of substantialism leads to a descriptive hyper-empiricism that renders the possibility of dramatic, experiential connections moot. It also creates a curious rapprochement with the leveling tendencies of common language philosophy. My debt to Schafer is considerable, but my effort will be to move his insights in a dialectical and existential direction.

11 Three examples: Erik Erikson, *Identity and the Life Cycle* (New York, 1959); Heinz Kohut, *The Analysis of the Self* (New York, 1971); Norman Holland, *Five Readers Reading*. Erikson imports every humanistic ideal available to give psychoanalysis ethical and personal values; its need for same is attested by the enthusiasm of a great traditional metapsychologist, David Rapaport, for Erikson's work. As Rapaport sees it, combine Heinz Hartman with Erikson and psychoanalytic theory will enter its golden age. See *The Col-lected Papers of David Rapaport*, ed. M. Gill (New York, 1967). Much later in the history of psychoanalysis, Kohut uses his superb clinical studies on the neglected topic of narcissism to graft a concept of "self" onto meta-psychology. Holland is perhaps the definitive representative of the recent tendency to make the "self" (and its "humanistic" defense) serve as the blank

check for a psychological self-indulgence that preserves everything defensive, adaptational, and conservative in ego psychology.

12 Sigmund Freud, "Some Character Types Met with in Psychoanalytic Work," *Character and Culture*, ed. Philip Rieff (New York, 1963), pp. 157–81.

13 For two contrasting views, see Otto Fenichel's classic *The Psychoanalytic Theory of the Neuroses* (New York, 1945) and the recent Kohutian scheme proposed by John E. Gedo and Arnold Goldberg in *Models of the Mind* (Chicago, 1973).

14 The best discussion of this line of thought is in George S. Klein, *Psychoanalytic Theory: An Exploration of Essentials* (New York, 1976).

15 I realize that in some quarters everything said above marks me as one out to domesticate Freud's truly radical discoveries: alterity; utter difference; energetics freed from hermeneutics and its logocentric correlates; the impossibility of tracking down, let alone sublating, the self-dispersing *traces* of the unconscious, that other site radically separate from consciousness and operating with a will and a word of its own. But the methodological weakness of this radical view—usually termed "French Freud"—derives from two factors: (1) its need to identify psychoanalysis with the ornate reading of certain canonical texts by Freud; and (2) its curious argument that it is impossible to test its concepts clinically or experientially since the very possibility of experience is what the approach calls into question. Though Lacan is the main representative of some of these concepts, Derrida is the one who picks up and celebrates their most disruptive implications. As *La carte postale* (Paris, 1980) shows, Freud has always been central to Derrida's project. The logic of the trace may be seen, in fact, as an attempt to formulate the philosophic implications of Freud's discoveries.

16 On the distinction between primary and secondary repression, see Sigmund Freud, "Repression" and "The Unconscious," *Standard Edition*, vol. 14 (London, 1957), pp. 146–58, 162–73.

17 Schafer, *New Language for Psychoanalysis*, pp. 127–78. For a good discussion of this issue which directly confronts the contradictions in Freud's texts see Hans Loewald, "On Motivation and Instinct Theory," *Papers on Psychoanalysis* (New Haven, 1982), pp. 102–38.

18 For the critique of metapsychology within psychoanalysis, see M. Gill, *Topography and Systems in Psychoanalytic Theory* (New York, 1963), as well as the works of Schafer, Klein, and Loewald.

19 Fairbairn uses this concept to undertake a complete reformulation of psychoanalytic theory in *An Object-Relations Theory of the Personality* (New York, 1952).

20 "Adultomorphism" is the critique usually made (incorrectly, I think) of Melanie Klein's major contributions to psychoanalysis. To understand the inception of psychological processes, we need to cut through the dichotomy

between instincts and conscious ideas. Klein's concept of unconscious fantasies is an attempt to conceptualize early psychological development within
the limits that "adult" language imposes on us. My use of the concept of
delayed effect (*Nachträqlichkeit*) offers a more dramatistic logic for such processes.

21 To comprehend the temporality of psychoanalytic experience we need to
supplant the dichotomy of rational causality–deconstructive alterity with an
existential understanding of time. Freud wrestled with this problem as clini-
cian in his three revisions of the "seduction theory" without ever coming up
with the concept of time needed to conceptualize the connection between
fantasy, delayed effect, and the action of all parties in the family complex.

22 The virtue of this formulation is that it gets us out of the blame game which
provides such a neat defense against psychoanalysis. Even if psychoanalysis
never "blamed mothers," its dyadic language left this interpretation open.
Current efforts to liberate the mother from her patriarchal and Lacanian
task of preparing the way for the Law of the Father merely present the flip
side of an abstract conceptualization. For a balanced and interpersonal feminist view, see Nancy Chodorow, *The Reproduction of Mothering* (California,
1978).

23 This is a more concrete formula than the one Lichtenstein proposes when he
claims identity is formed by the infant's response to the mother's unconscious.
See Heinz Lichtenstein, *The Dilemma of Human Identity* (New York, 1974).
Lichtenstein's powerful theory that the mother imprints an identity theme
on the child who is then incapable of doing more than working out its
variations is marred by the fact that he uses a passive schizoid patient as
his clinical example. Long before Lichtenstein, Harry Stack Sullivan based
his interpersonal theory of the self-system on the notion that response to
the mother's anxiety is the original experience. The most extensive clinical
investigations of mothering are by Margaret Mahler in *On Human Symbiosis
and the Vicissitudes of Individuation* (New York, 1968) and, with F. Pine
and A. Bergman, *The Psychological Birth of the Human Infant* (New York,
1975). Lacan's concept of the mirror stage, however, develops the disruptive
implications of infantile experience for substantialist ways of conceptualizing
identity such as Mahler's.

24 This is the main difference between my use of oedipal terminology and its
abstract use by Lacan and by those feminists such as Irigaray who simply
invert the Lacanian abstraction. Lacan's Symbolic merely maps one dissolution of drama; as such, it covers over the vast conflicts that fester within
its dominance. For a nonreductive view of gender and sexual difference, see
section entitled "Subject and 'The Large Glass,'" pp. 296–313.

25 One of R. D. Laing's finest contributions to psychoanalysis is his recognition
that attribution not prohibition is the language that binds the psyche. Telling

us who we are is the subtlest communication/torture the family inflicts on us. See especially R. D. Laing, *The Self and Others* (London, 1961).

26 This is how psychoanalysis renews and concretizes Hegel's concept of the primacy of the struggle for recognition. Lacan is onto this connection, but in his desire to be the "antithesis" of Hegel—and of the possibility of any dialectical movement of the psyche—he schematizes logical permutations under the dominance of a single "symbolic" model or law rather than opening up phenomenological complexities. Lacan's seminar 11, now published under the title *The Four Fundamental Concepts of Psychoanalysis*, trans. Alan Sheridan (New York, 1978), contains some of the sharpest contrasts between Lacan's position and the direction of Hegelian and existential explanations of experience. "The Subversion of the Subject and the Dialectic of Desire in the Freudian Unconscious," *Ecrits: A Selection*, trans. Alan Sheridan (New York, 1977), pp. 292–325, is a more direct reflection of Lacan's debt to Hegel and Sartre. Lacan's purpose, however, is to welcome the dialectical subject into his thought so that he can confine it to the imaginary.

27 The ability to move to the "oedipal" is the dividing line between borderline disorders and neurosis. That movement is impossible unless a sufficient degree of self and object constancy or stable internalizations exists. But the Oedipus never simply casts off the prior: it sublates it by adding further complications. These complications get leveled off in Lacan's imaginary/symbolic distinction as well as in Gedo and Goldberg's Kohutian scheme for classifying psychic development. Dramatistic understanding restores the connections that are severed in a logic of discrete experiential stages.

28 Lacan's mistake is to give us only one version of this drama; Irigaray's to think its simple inversion a source of liberation. In both cases the complexity of those disruptive interpersonal phenomena from which one must begin gets lost. I use the term "Oedipus" as shorthand metaphor to designate this stage; the term is not tied to gender. As Chodorow shows, the crisis marking this development of experience takes on characteristically different ramifications for men and women; however dominant, the Lacanian patriarchal model is but one term in a complex drama. For Lacan's complex thoughts on this issue, see *Feminine Sexuality*, trans. Juliet Mitchell and Jacqueline Rose (New York, 1983). Lacan is perhaps the unhappy consciousness of structuralism.

29 This is one of the places where the psychoanalyst's desire to assert control over the phenomena is conspicuous. Freud's version of the Oedipus is the paradigm of patriarchal vision. Lacan's Symbolic hypostatizes that paradigm. In experience, however, the paradigm never functions without hindrance. The beauty of mothering is that it engenders conflicts that challenge all abstract positionings of subjects. Patriarchy rarely superimposes itself on experience without engendering discontents. The patriarchial father may

wish for the symbolic law, but everything in his household gives the lie to his desire. In view of the mutual cruelty that operates independent of gender, we must view Lacan's symbolic order as a mystification, a dream of order, and a protest against the disruptiveness of actual interpersonal experience.

30 This concept of the family is an attempt to concretize Fairbairn's great insight that the therapeutic task is to break into a closed system and introduce new possibilities.

31 The contrast here is to the founding gesture of ego psychology: Heinz Hartmann's notion of adaptation and development of "the conflict-free ego sphere" as the goal of analysis. See Heinz Hartmann, *Ego Psychology and the Problems of Adaptation* (New York, 1958); *Essays on Ego Psychology* (New York, 1964); and, with Ernst Kris and R. M. Loewenstein, *Papers on Psychoanalytic Psychology* (New York, 1964).

32 The life process approach of Erikson blurs this focus. In contrast to Erikson's focus on the attainment of certain general humanistic values and stable "ego functions," our emphasis on interpersonal conflict disrupts all stabilities. Erikson was among the first to see the need for a psychological reinterpretation of Freud's discussion of infantile sexuality, and Erikson's reformulation in *Childhood and Society* (New York, 1950) remains a major contribution. Unfortunately, both psychosexuality and the complexity of conflict are progressively leveled off as Erikson's work proceeds. Sex becomes something one more or less gets beyond in order to achieve that social generativity which transforms conflict into a matter of affirming certain essentialistic human values.

33 Fairbairn makes this operation central in his reformulation of the dynamics of intrapsychic structure. Melanie Klein lays the basis for this effort; Klein sees splitting as the primary operation that generates the first position the infant takes toward its conflicts.

34 See "Splitting in the Mechanisms of Defense," *Standard Edition*, 23:275–78. Splitting has since been given a much larger role in developmental schemes which try to coordinate specific defenses with specific stages of ego development. For a fine overview of this connection see Gertrude Blanck and Ruben Blanck, *Ego Psychology*, vol. 1 (New York, 1974).

35 George S. Klein is especially good at explaining repression in terms of the cognitive and motivational schemata it establishes. See *Psychoanalytic Theory*, pp. 223–58.

36 The concept of the unconscious outlined here stands in opposition to the traditional one—which Sartre correctly terms a blank check for reductive explanations—and to the notion of the unconscious as wholly other site that is developed, following Lacan's lead, by Laplanche and Leclaire, "The Unconscious."

37 Fairbairn, *Object-Relations Theory of the Personality*, pp. 36–45. See also the

work by Fairbairn's best expositor, Harry Guntrip, *Schizoid Phenomena, Object Relations, and the Self* (New York, 1969).

38 Klein, *Psychoanalytic Theory*, pp. 259–311. The characterization of these principles which I offer below reconstructs Klein's discourse within a dialectical context.

39 Lawrence Kubie, "The Fundamental Nature of the Distinction between Normality and Neurosis," *Symbol and Neurosis* (New York, 1978), pp. 127–61. A superb article, perhaps the finest discussion of its topic.

40 Klein, *Psychoanalytic Theory*, pp. 239–58.

41 Clara Thompson, *Interpersonal Psychoanalysis*, ed. M. Green (New York, 1964).

42 Sigmund Freud, *Therapy and Technique*, ed. Philip Rieff (New York, 1963). The papers collected in this volume are an inexhaustible supply of clinical insights that show how alive Freud was to dramatic complexities that exceeded his theoretical frameworks.

43 Roy Schafer, "The Psychoanalytic Interpretation of Reality," *New Language for Psychoanalysis*, pp. 22–56.

44 The maxim of the early Freudian Hans Sachs: "The analysis is over only when the patient realizes that it could go on forever."

45 Freud, *Therapy and Technique*, pp. 157–66, the great discussion of "recollection, repetition, and working through."

46 In this sense, our theory of the psychoanalytic subject may be aligned with the work of Reich, Norman O. Brown, Marcuse, and Laing. But our attempt is to recover an erotics of the self-in-conflict, not a utopian self-presence via the orgasmic or the recovery of the polymorphous perverse.

47 In *Freud and Philosophy*, Ricoeur identifies this Spinozistic heritage as the context which informs Freud's understanding of the tragic. Our effort is to set Freud's great vision of necessity within a more active and dialectical concept of the tragic.

48 Only mature loving can replace this attachment. See below, pp. 307–13.

49 Aristotle, *Poetics*, chap. 6, sect. 2. The concepts of reversal and recognition, which we derive from Aristotle, are used throughout this discussion in a context that breaks sharply from the essentialistic view of human nature and conduct Aristotle develops in the *Nicomachean Ethics*. By making poetics a separate discipline, Aristotle was able to isolate the tragic and keep its principles from impinging on his ethic of the good life.

50 Roy Schafer, "The Mechanisms of Defense," *International Journal of Psychoanalysis*, 49: 49–62, opens up this issue brilliantly.

51 Grete L. Bibring et al., "A Study of Pregnancy," in *Affective Disorders*, ed. P. Greenacre (New York, 1953), remains the best overview. Incisive definitions of over forty defenses are offered.

52 We here renew the discussion of anxiety developed in Chapter 2, pp. 114–34.

Heidegger and Freud clarify and concretize one another: Freud's clinical focus saves Heidegger from formalism; Heidegger's existential focus cancels Freud's scientistic reductions.

53 For a good discussion of this position and the alterations it required in Freud's theorizing, see Roy Schafer, "Danger Situations," *Journal of the American Psychoanalytic Association* 24: 1–32.

54 Harry Stack Sullivan, *The Interpersonal Theory of Psychiatry*, pp. 113–15.

55 Sullivan, *Interpersonal Theory of Psychiatry*, pp. 113–22.

56 For a good statement of this shift, which, unlike others, does not admit problems only to slip back into the old ways of conceptualizing the ego, see Loewald, *Papers on Psychoanalysis*, especially "On Motivation and Instinct Theory." Loewald's critique of ego psychology begins with an attempt to root out substantialistic conceptualizations. Ego psychology prides itself on having studied the defenses. But an understanding of their dynamic functions is incompatible with the substantialism that controls its theory of subject.

57 Schafer, "Mechanisms of Defense," p. 51.

58 Hartmann deserves the major credit for having expanded the understanding of intersystemic and intrasystemic conflict. More's the pity that his adaptational view of expanding the "conflict-free ego sphere" and his desire to gain psychoanalysis academic respect as a general psychology forced him to close down everything he opened up. Anna Freud's classic *The Ego and the Mechanisms of Defense* (New York, 1936) performs a similar operation. As Lacan shows, ego psychology suppresses its own dialectic by refusing to see that the "I" is the other, that the origins of the ego lie in its perpetual discontent with its capture by the other.

59 Schafer, "Mechanisms of Defense," p. 55.

60 Robert Waelder, "The Principle of Multiple Function," *Psychoanalytic Quarterly* 15: 45–62.

61 Schafer, "Mechanisms of Defense," pp. 59–61.

62 Derrida does even more than Lacan to liberate the disruptive energies and implications of Freud, but he does so in a characteristically abstract and formalistic way. Refusing to see energy as more than dispersal and difference, he sacrifices the possibility of discovering dramatistic or experiential connections in favor of what is finally a reified praise of the unconscious for its incessant ability to resist any limitations we try to place upon it. Ironically, the unconscious Derrida valorizes is the unconscious as it appears at the beginning of analysis; his reading of Freud is thus the last in a long line of romanticisms, this time recycled as a theory of the force of language.

63 Schafer, "Mechanisms of Defense," p. 57.

64 Its domination by the economic point of view makes the metapsychological explanation of affects in traditional psychoanalysis a model of reductionism: pent-up drives and other impersonal and quasi-somatic processes crave discharge and have little significance beyond that fact.

65 Franz Alexander, "The Logic of Emotions and Its Dynamic Background," *The Scope of Psychoanalysis, 1921–1961* (New York 1961), pp. 116–28, a great and neglected article, full of dramatistic implications poorly served by the quasi-biological framework Alexander relies on.

66 Spinoza, *Ethics*, bk. 4, prop. 7.

67 In the notion of unconscious affects, psychoanalysis is onto a dramatistic reality that gets lost in the substantialism of metapsychology. We here offer a dramatistic and existential explanation of the scandalous notion that we are seldom aware of how we really feel. No substance is needed to sustain the gaps in our self-awareness. We act and project them constantly. They are our way of being in the world.

68 Nunberg was the first of Freud's immediate followers to insist on such a distinction, Erikson the first to give it systematic development. For a good overview, see Schafer, "The Loving and Beloved Superego in Freud's Structural Theory," *Psychoanalytic Study of the Child* 15: 163–88.

69 J. Arlow and C. Brenner, *Psychoanalytic Concepts and the Structural Theory* (New York, 1964).

70 Erikson first develops this in 1941 in *Identity and the Life-Cycle*.

71 Twenty years after Erikson, Kohut took this step in *The Analysis of the Self*. The book is a systematic attempt to introduce a concept of subject within the confines of traditional metapsychology.

72 Klein, *Psychoanalytic Theory*, p. 158. (Klein's survey treats ego psychology up to 1976.)

73 Hartmann's original program for ego psychology is developed in Hartmann, Kris, and Loewenstein's *Papers on Psychoanalytic Psychology* (New York 1964) and Hartmann's *Essays on Ego Psychology*. Klein's survey in *Psychoanalytic Theory* shows that the conceptual framework that traps ego psychology in Hartmann's contradictions has remained in control throughout its development.

74 Even Kohut's formula levels the complexity of the phenomena because it assumes that the analyst has mastered his unconscious. The analytic interaction is a two-way street, and what is called countertransference is a vital part of the action. Neither participant possesses a transparent self-knowledge. The analytic interaction deserves its status as the main source of new knowledge in psychoanalysis only if it remains open on both sides to the shock of recognition.

75 See "The Freudian Thing," *Ecrits*, pp. 114–45, for Lacan's discussion of this statement. See also Ellie Ragland-Sullivan, *Jacques Lacan and the Philosophy of Psychoanalysis* (Urbana, Ill., 1986), for a superb and lucid overview of Lacan's thought.

76 Freud's *Group Psychology and the Analysis of the Ego* is only a beginning. For a good overview of subsequent developments, see *Psychoanalytic Group Dynamics: Basic Readings*, ed. Saul Scheidlinger (New York, 1980).

77 E.g. (Joyced), the cathexis of the internal parental prohibition reacted against the libidinal decathexis of the projected transgression to produce hysterical arrest prior to the analytic intervention . . . Such formulas are the inadvertent parody of dialectical descriptions.

78 Ernst Kris, "Regression in the Service of the Ego," *Psychoanalytic Explorations in Art* (New York, 1952). For a more dynamic account of such processes, see Anton Ehrenzweig, *The Hidden Order of Art* (California, 1967).

79 Hans Loewald, "On the Therapeutic Action of Psychoanalysis," *International Journal of Psychoanalysis* 41: 16–33.

80 This paragraph recapitulates, in a quite different context, the main ideas developed in Freud's *Three Essays on the Theory of Sexuality*.

81 This is the thread—via Lacan—that Derrida, Irigaray, and Cixous use as the privileged point from which to construct their theories. Sex is, indeed, a challenge to logic and to rationalist conceptualization. But it is so as an experience. And as such it raises many questions that get short shrift when its only significance is as a contribution to deconstructive logic or *écriture féminine*. Sex puts us on trial, not in play or on display. For a significant attempt to sustain its dynamic within a deconstructive and feminist viewpoint, see Julia Kristeva, *Revolution in Poetic Language*, trans. Margaret Waller (New York, 1984).

82 George S. Klein, "Freud's Two Theories of Sexuality," *Psychoanalytic Theory*, pp. 72–120.

83 Roy Schafer, *Language and Insight* (New Haven, 1978), pp. 139–72.

84 This concept suggests a way out of the current impasse of some feminist theories, since it refers not only to how men conceive of women, but vice versa. In so doing it points to the mutual cruelty and aggression that inform most of the ways we represent and relate to one another.

85 Sullivan, *Interpersonal Theory of Psychiatry*, p. 303.

86 This statement both employs and negates Sartre's discussion of human relations in *Being and Nothingness* by taking the problem that for Sartre convicts all relations of perpetual failure and using it to suggest the bare possibility of another outcome that depends on going through, rather than around, the conflicts Sartre describes.

87 Freud's best discussion of this is in the essay "On Narcissism: An Introduction." *Standard Edition* 14: 67–102.

88 Clinicians now generally see the Don Giovanni type as the male version of hysteria. As usual, masked behavior acts out the male predicament: fear of feeling, flight from inwardness, and the need to keep everything safely externalized in roles.

89 For different and more optimistic views of love, see Erich Fromm, *The Art of Loving* (New York, 1956), and Martin Buber, *I and Thou*, trans. Walter Kaufmann (New York, 1970). Irving Singer, *The Nature of Love*, 2 vols.

(Chicago, 1983), traces the philosophic and literary representation of love in Western culture through the nineteenth century.

Chapter 5: Methodology Is Ontology

1   Each section of this chapter is dialectically suspensive; it takes its concepts to a point that requires the entire next section for their development. In this way the account of dialectic constitutes a dialectic of understandings of dialectic. The placement of other accounts thereby becomes a critique and sublation of them.

2   See R. S. Crane, *The Idea of the Humanities*, 2 vols. (Chicago, 1967), and *The Languages of Criticism and the Structure of Poetry* (Toronto, 1953). The most important works for Richard McKeon's concept of dialectic are: "Philosophy and Method," *Journal of Philosophy* 48 (October 1951), 653–82; *Thought, Action, and Passion* (Chicago, 1954); "Philosophic Semantics and Philosophic Inquiry," manuscript (Chicago, 1967). The account of the four modes of human thought that I present in chapter 3 of *The Act of Interpretation* (Chicago, 1977) is derived from the last McKeon essay listed above.

3   McKeon, "Philosophic Semantics and Philosophic Inquiry," p. 1; "Philosophy and Method," pp. 662, 665–66.

4   In describing such procedures McKeon's attempt is to account for the distinct nature of dialectical thought and to place it within a pluralistic system that is grounded in principles that dialectic necessarily violates. The metaphysical implications of McKeon's philosophic pluralism are developed in his essay "Being, Existence, and That Which Is," *Review of Metaphysics* 13, no. 4 (June 1960), 539–54.

5   Martin Heidegger, *Being and Time*, trans. John Macquarrie and William Richardson (New York, 1962), p. 175. Also "What Is Metaphysics?" *Existence and Being* (Chicago, 1949); and *Poetry, Language, Thought*, trans. Albert Hofstadter (New York, 1971).

6   This is the definition of dialectic Plato develops in his most systematic discussion of the method in *Republic*, bk. 7.

7   McKeon, "Philosophy and Method," pp. 662, 665, 678.

8   This is a paraphrase of the account offered by McKeon in "Philosophic Semantics and Philosophic Inquiry."

9   Herman Sinaiko, *Love, Knowledge, and Discourse in Plato* (Chicago, 1965). Beginning with the recognition that dialogue is not simply a literary, rhetorical device but an integral part of the content of Plato's philosophy, Sinaiko develops an interpretation of Plato that preserves the experiential content of Plato's thought while liberating it from many of the hypostatizations that have become synonymous with Platonism.

10 Aristotle originates the way of thinking that is here contrasted with dialectic.

For McKeon's unrivaled description of Aristotle's philosophic method, see "Philosophy and Method"; "Rhetoric and Poetic in the Philosophy of Aristotle," in *Aristotle's Poetics and English Literature*, ed. Elder Olson (Chicago, 1965), pp. 201–36; and "The Philosophy of Aristotle," manuscript (Chicago, 1940).

11 See McKeon, "Imitation and Poetry," *Thought, Action, and Passion*, pp. 108–11. While indebted to McKeon for the concept of logistic thought, I am solely responsible for its application to Anglo-American analytic philosophy.

12 This is pluralism's main methodological and ontological canon. For more on the implicit critique of pluralism I am developing throughout this chapter, see below, pp. 349–56.

13 McKeon distinguishes universal methods from distinct particular methods for the treatment of different questions and problems. R. S. Crane sharpens this distinction polemically throughout his work. The insistence on keeping questions and disciplines separate is the hallmark of his pluralism.

14 See McKeon, "Philosophy of Aristotle"; Aristotle, *Metaphysics*, bks. 1–5; *On Interpretation*; *Posterior Analytics*.

15 McKeon, "Philosophy and Method," pp. 662, 665–66, 673.

16 See especially Epistle 7 and *Phaedrus* 258d–279c. Most interpretations of Plato are vitiated by the failure to appreciate dialogue as more than a rhetorical device. For Plato dialogue was a philosophic necessity and implied the inseparability of the content of philosophy from the act of philosophizing. Dialogue is not something from which one abstracts doctrines. The dialogue is the doctrine. Plato's use of myth is usually given short shrift by commentators in search of abstractable propositions. Myth, like dialogue, is integral to Plato's thought. The myth of eros in the *Symposium* and the allegory of the cave are precisely the kind of linguistic acts Plato required in order to affirm paradoxes and figure forth ideas that transcend ordinary philosophic conceptualization. Without dialogue, symbol, myth, allegory, paradox, and poem Plato could not have *said* what he was trying to say about language, its modes, and its limitations. If Plato has a "doctrine" it lies within the immense complexities and multiple ironies of his dramatic method. "The ancient quarrel" between philosophy and poetry may, in fact, be one of Plato's greatest ironies since everything in his dialogic method suggests the philosophic superiority of literary language.

17 Spinoza, *Ethics*, pt. 1.

18 Dualistic oppositions are thus ripe for the inversion practiced by Derrida and Irigaray. Unfortunately, that act sustains for many of their followers the illusion that the inversion of phallogocentric discourse liberates the truth of experience. The proper name for this new illusion is linguistic formalism.

19 See Gustav E. Muller, "The Hegel Legend of 'Thesis-Antithesis-Synthesis,'" *Journal of the History of Ideas* 19, no. 3 (June 1958), 411–14.

20 For Crane's unjustly neglected critique of dialectic, see "Critical and Historical Principles of Literary History," *Idea of the Humanities* 2: 45–156, and *Languages of Criticism and the Structure of Poetry*, passim.

21 See Paul Ricoeur, *Freud and Philosophy*, trans. Denis Savage (New Haven, 1970), pp. 117–34, 149–51.

22 I use Hegel as my sole example in this section because he (1) thought through the problem of structuring opposites more thoroughly than any other dialectician and (2) made that problem more difficult than any other thinker by bringing so much of experience into his structure. Kierkegaard's three stages and Plato's four kinds of knowledge are abbreviated phenomenologies by comparison. They are less adequate to experience in proportion to the amount of drama they eliminate.

23 In this sense the interdisciplinary position I have constructed may be termed dialectical pluralism to mark it off from those pluralisms that depend on separating questions and disciplines. My argument is that the latter cannot maintain themselves and that they become, on interrogation, moments in a dialectical understanding. See below, pp. 343–46.

24 One invokes the tragic in a discussion of philosophic "truth" at the risk of losing several audiences. But tragedy has been with us all along. Chapters 1–4 can be taken as an argument for its ontological and experiential primacy. The present section is a retrospective attempt to make explicit the logic that structured Chapters 1–4. Tragedy is *the* philosophic category but only for those who are "profoundly wounded and profoundly consoled" by the hermeneutic of their engagement in its conceptualization. To them it reveals itself as the concrete universal that supplants both rationalism and deconstruction.

25 In this sense Chapters 1–4 constitute a rewriting of the *Phenomenology of Mind* in the context of contemporary thought.

26 G. W. F. Hegel, *The Phenomenology of Mind*, trans. J. Baillie, 2d ed. (New York, 1931), pp. 371–72 (hereafter cited as *PhG*).

27 *PhG*, pp. 384–89. Santayana's discussion of the "solipsism of the moment" in *Skepticism and Animal Faith* (New York, 1923) makes a similar point.

28 Whether Kant held such motives is finally irrelevant, for Hegel's concern is with the appeal of the Kantian ethic to the unhappy consciousness. The issue is developed further in what is a key text for Lacan, the discussion of "the beautiful soul," *PhG*, pp. 645–67.

29 Friedrich Nietzsche, *Beyond Good and Evil*, trans. W. Kaufmann (New York, 1966), passim. See especially pt. 6, "We Scholars."

30 Jacques Derrida, "Structure, Sign, and Play in the Discourse of the Human Sciences," *Writing and Difference*, trans. Alan Bass (Chicago, 1978), p. 263.

31 Hegel terms such a logic that of the notion (*Begriff*). To avoid the unfortunate connotations of that term I've avoided it. This section is an attempt to provide

a conceptual equivalent of that concept. In addition to *PhG*, pp. 100–105, 119–24, 613–16, 623–29, 645–52, 664–79, one should consult the following for Hegel's key discussion of the logic of notional thinking and the concrete universal: *Hegel's Science of Logic* [The Greater Logic], trans. A. V. Miller (New York, 1969), pp. 43–56, 600–622, 755–61, 825–44; and *The Logic of Hegel* [The Lesser Logic], pp. 30–50, 141–49.

32 This contradiction is at the center of the last chapter of the *PhG*. "Absolute Knowledge" is a model example of a self-deconstructive text.

33 For Hegel's idea of the concrete infinite and its contrast with the mathematical infinite, see *PhG*, pp. 100–105; "The Greater Logic," pp. 137–56, 225–34; and "The Lesser Logic," pp. 174–76, 194–98.

34 Jacques Derrida, *Of Grammatology* (Baltimore, 1974) pp. 198–260; *Writing and Difference*, pp. 217–32.

35 Derrida's clearest argument that this is the error that inscribes Hegel's discourse within logocentric metaphysics is in *Writing and Difference*, pp. 251–77. See also "The Pit and the Pyramid: Introduction to Hegel's Semiology," *Margins of Philosophy*, trans. Alan Bass (Chicago, 1982), pp. 69–108, for a more formalistic critique of Hegel's concept of *Aufhebung* (*relever*). *Glas* stages the confrontation with Hegel at great and comic length.

36 Derrida has described his thought as an endless commentary on Hegel. He also sees the edging of Heidegger as of equal importance. My dialectical effort, in contrast, is to refer both deferral (Derrida) and finitude (Heidegger) to situatedness. On the Derrida-Heidegger connection, see Robert Denoon Cumming, "The Odd Couple: Heidegger and Derrida," *Review of Metaphysics* 34 (March 1981), 487–521.

37 Jacques Lacan, "Of Structure as an Inmixing Prerequisite to Any Subject Whatever," in *The Structuralist Controversy* (Baltimore, 1975), pp. 180–92.

38 The allusion is to Derrida's statement at the end of "Structure, Sign, and Play" where he says that there are two interpretations of interpretation, the sad, guilty Rousseauistic one and the Nietzschean liberation of "free play." A hermeneutics of engagement suggests a third.

39 Sinaiko, *Love, Knowledge, and Discourse in Plato*.

40 Bradley develops the concept in *The Principles of Logic*, 2 vols. (Oxford, 1950) and *Appearance and Reality* (Oxford, 1969), chap. 3. The concept is restated brilliantly by Brand Blanshard in *The Nature of Thought* (London, 1939), vol. 2, pp. 475–519, and throughout *Reason and Analysis* (La Salle, Ill., 1962). R. G. Collingwood's discussion of "the scale of Forms" in *An Essay on Philosophic Method* (Oxford, 1953) is another valuable contribution to the problem. For a critique of internal relations, see Bertrand Russell, *Philosophical Essays* (London, 1910), chap. 6, and "Symposium: Internal Relations," *Aristotelian Society Proceedings* 14, supp. (1936).

41 Sinaiko, *Love, Knowledge, and Discourse in Plato*, pp. 119–66, 300–308.

42 This section conceptualizes the ontological and methodological bases for the experiential theory of subject constructed in Chapters 1–4. The focus on Hegel here merely provides the ground for initiating the circle of engagement which those chapters carry out.

43 Sinaiko outlines Plato's response to the problem on pp. 199–207, 234–40 of *Love, Knowledge, and Discourse in Plato*. That provocative discussion would strike Hegel as far too abstract and paradoxical precisely because the ground or first principle of the entire argument remains unexamined and opaque.

44 The processual beginnings articulated here are quite different from those beginnings Derrida criticizes for their implication in the myth of originary self-presence.

45 *PhG*, p. 1. The discursive, conceptual, and real orders are necessarily one in dialectic, but as this paragraph shows, this is true as a result of the dialectical process, not as a preexistent condition.

46 The circle of Hegel's existential thought is such that what is in the "Preface" a hypothetical discussion of the possibility of a self-grounding system is established in the *Phenomenology* itself as a description of the experience of the natural consciousness. Try as he may, Hegel can't transcend this circle of engagement without contradiction.

47 For an analogous attempt by Plato to mediate these concepts, see the *Parmenides* and the *Sophist*. In "What Is Metaphysics?" and *The Essence of Reasons* Heidegger develops dialectical companion meditations on nothingness and the ontological difference.

48 For a superb rethinking of the principle of sufficient reason from the perspective of being-in-the-world, see Heidegger's *The Essence of Reasons*.

49 Something like this is developed in Derrida's "absolute expenditure without reserve" interpretation of the significance of *différance*. For Derrida's most rigorous attempt to think through this "logic" in purely conceptual terms, see "Differance," in *Voice and Phenomena*, pp. 129–60.

50 *Symposium*, 202c–204d. Heidegger's notion of Care (*Sorge*) as the being of *Dasein* is a somewhat formalistic repetition of Plato's deeply erotic concept.

51 An existentialized Hegel thus points the culminating insight of *Being and Time* toward an experiential concretization that puts an end to formalism.

52 This is, of course, the problem of absolute knowledge. For Hegel's discussion of this concept in the *PhG* the key pages are 792–93, 795, 798, 804–5, 807–8. The existentialized concept of absolute knowledge I have developed should be contrasted not only with the traditional view of Hegel's position (see, for example, Charles Taylor, *Hegel* [London, 1975], pp. 214–21) but with the discussions of absolute knowledge developed by Kojève (*Introduction to the Reading of Hegel*, trans. James H. Nichols, Jr. [New York, 1969], pp. 100–

149) and Hyppolite (*Genesis and Structure of Hegel's Phenomenology of Spirit*, trans. Samuel Cherniak and John Heckman [Evanston, 1974], pp. 553–83). As in Chapter 1, my effort is to rethink Hegel's thought by liberating the contradiction in his text in order to sublate the unhappy consciousness that engendered it. This operation constitutes the *für uns* of a hermeneutics of engagement.

Index

Alienation (*continued*)
culture and, 227; labor and, 78, 222;
in Marx's 1844 Manuscripts, 385;
subject formation in *PhG* and, 344.
See also Marx, Karl
Althusser, Louis: "ideological state
apparatuses," 385*n*64; ideology for,
175, 184, 203–4; "science" of and
ideology, 182, 208; structural causality
and, 207; subject for, 203, 205
"Always already," Derrida's logic of the,
and Hegel, 369*n*12
Analysis: authentic, as necessarily lived,
291; autonomous ego and, 290; critique of American mental health
professions' use of, 260; of defenses,
266–7; demystification of immediacy
in, 280; displacement and hyper-
empiricism of, 260; exacerbating
conflicts in, 279; love and, 307; movement of and ego, 289; as quest, 232;
sadomasochism and, 308; sexuality
and, 296; of superego, 286
Analytic: movement, ontology of,
320–21; reduction of subject versus
dialectic, 321
Analytic formalism: versus existential
engagement, 4
Analytic process: methodological
clarifications of, 232–33; recovery of
repressed, 240
Analytic thought versus dialectic, 320
Analytic tradition as an epistemology,
320
Anglo-American thought versus continental, 320
Anti-*Bildung*: and Hegel, 223; reversal
as, 212
Antidialectic: death drive as, 103;
within dialectic, 72; as dialectic in
skepticism, 57
Anxiety: absence of, 269; as basis for
action, 170; the body and, 127; choice
in the face of, 132; contingency
and, 130; consciousness, effect on,
137; death and, 135, 136; defenses

connected to, 267; Derridean play
and, 375*n*9; dialectical understanding
of, 368–69*n*11; ego psychology and,
128; existentialism and, 119, 127, 129,
142, 158, 270; experience of, 114;
flight from, 118; Freud and, 268,
393–94*n*52; in Heidegger, 128, 131,
144, 388*n*9, 393–94*n*52; interrogating,
270; inwardness and, 131; love
and, 121–22, 126; as a mania of
the self, 129; phenomenological
character of, 126, 129; repressed
motives and, 294; as response to
the world, 134; situated subjectivity
and, 130, 133; subject and, 112, 127,
133; subjectivity and, 130–31, 159;
sublation of, 259; Sullivan on, 268
Aporia, 348–49; paralysis in dialectic
method and, 353
A priori: determination for Hegel, 355;
existential, 132, 140–41; knowledge,
and Kant, 10; neo-Kantian, 141;
rationality, and reason in Hegel, 97.
See also Existential a priori; Hegel,
G. W. F.; Kant, Immanuel; Reason
Aristotelian discourse versus dialectic,
321
Aristotle: logic of, versus dialectic, 317,
323; ontology of, 349–50; versus
Plato, 359
Arlow, J., and C. Brenner, ego functions
in, 287
Asceticism, erotics of, and subjectivity,
86
Atomistic individualism, versus social
determinism, 199, 200
Aufhebung: capitalism as, 215; dialectic
process and, 328; as inversion of defense development, 272; versus logic
of *différance* and supplementarity,
347; sublation and, 367–68*n*1; of the
unhappy consciousness, 225
Authorial intention, sovereignty of, 3
Autonomy: desire for, 31, 35; quest for,
versus ontological insecurity, 36

Freud and, 387*n*2; conflict with humanism, 3; and interpretation of interpretation, 349; on Kantian rationalism, 348; marxism and, 380 *n*8; pseudocontent generated by, 348; root error of, 347; on structuralism, 348; of subject, 55; versions of, 348

Defenses: affects and, 267; analysis of, 266–67; anxieties and, 267; desire and, 271–72; drama and, 252, 273; dramatistic doubling and, 255, 270, 272; as dynamic tendencies, 270; enactments of unconscious ego, 272; intellectualization of, 255; keys to, 273; like emotions, 279; logic of development of, 272–73; maintenance of, 271; projection of, 260; reason *why* of, 261; retracing, 252; Schafer's double agent's, 271; and sex, hermeneutically, 297; splitting as one of our, 252; as substitutes, 272; uncovering of, 260–61

Deferral and reflection for Derrida, 348

de Man, Paul, deconstructed as unhappy consciousness, 54, 371*n*35

Demand: impossibility of and dialectic, 36; and need in Lacan, 36; supplementarity and, 36

Depression: as psychological subtext of skepticism, 56; negativity and, 103. *See also* Skepticism

Derrida, Jacques: the "always already" in, and Hegel, 369; on dialectic versus Hegel, 147, 347–48; *Différance* and supplementarity in, 347; *Différance* in and the unhappy consciousness, 66; play and anxiety, 375 *n*9; reflection and, 348, 372*n*42; the self for, 180; critique of structuralism in, 339–40

Descartes, René, subjectivity and the scientific cogito, 120

Desire: for autonomy, 31, 35; awareness of oneself as, 34; in capitalism, 216; for death, 118; defense and, 271–72; of desire, 27, 34; as devotion to extinguish desire, 86; dialectic of,

26, 30, 32, 45; dissatisfaction and, 29, 31, 67; experience and, 28; for father, 248; formulation of, 246; Freud on, 312; gender confusion and, 245; genesis of, in intersubjective experience, 38; of the hedonist, 30; Hegel on, 26, 29, 304, 317, 329, 340, 360, 375*n*13; homosexual, 271–72; impossibility of, 246; and instinct in *PhG*, 333; for Lacan, 35–36; for the masochist, 72; and neurotic process, 251; for object, 27; the other and, 38; psychoanalysis and, 35, 391*n*26, 391–92*n*29; pulsion of, 252–53; reclaiming of, 262–63; for recognition, 32, 39, 42; as rejection, 312; and relationship to the mother, 35, 248; religious, 69; renunciation and, 85, 263; repression of, 242, 251; self-consciousness and, 25, 27, 33; self-mastery and, 66, 77; in skepticism, 52; in the slave, 41; subjectivity and, 22, 26–29 passim, 59; sublation of, 62, 65–66, 82, 96, 98, 101; for the transcendent, 68; transference of, 265; triangular, 247; for the unchanging, 64. *See also* Hegel, G. W. F.; Sexuality; Unhappy consciousness

Determinate negation: consciousness and, 22; dialectic and, 20, 342–44; process of in subject, 106

Devaluation, as love conflict, 309–10

Devotion, for Hegel, 72, 73

Devotional project, psychosexual denial of the body, 86

Devout consciousness, and the master-slave dialectic, 75–76

Dewey, John, phenomenal world of, 11

Dialectic: abstraction of, 55, 187, 316, 330–31, 343–44; action and, 96; analytic subject and, 321; antidialectic within, 72; anxiety understood through, 368–69*n*11; versus Aristotelian and Cartesian discourse, 321, 323; arrested, deconstruction as, 347; arrested, phenomenology as, 374*n*1; *Aufhebung* and, 328; in

Existential a priori (*continued*),
versus Heidegger, 145; Lukács and,
132; subject and, 141–42
Existential engagement, versus analytic
formalism, 4
Existentialism: as the absurd, 4; anxiety
and, 119, 127, 188, 270; Cumming
on, 377*n34*; death and, 377*n25*;
deconstruction and, 57, 153, 375*n12*;
dialectic and, 3, 137; existentially
read, 5, 132; experience and, 146–47;
fractionation and, 257; Hegel and,
368*n9*; inwardness and, 142, 159, 160,
172; Kant and, 4, 144; love and, 122;
on literature, 378; as passion, 113;
possibility, 138, 151; and question,
138; relativism and, 4, 162; sociology
and, 119; as subjectivism, 4; world
and, 167
Existential reflection: anxiety and, 129;
questions and, 108; subjectivity and,
108
Existential subject, 150; action and, 172;
anxiety and, 158; choice and, 108; in
crisis, 153; death and, 152; dialectic
agency and, 151; and engagement,
162; inwardness of, 145; logic and,
111; self-reference and, 107
Existential subjectivity, 107, 119, 148–
49, 160
Existential thought, Hegel's circle of,
401*n46*
Existential time, unity of, 153
Experience: absolute knowledge and,
32; comprehensive opposition and,
331; conflicts and, 257; consciousness
and, 15, 32; death and, 61; dialectic
and, 9, 86, 105, 140, 146, 325, 326,
358; desires and, 28; as drama,
5, 254; epistemology and, 25; for
existentialism, 146; Hegel and, 13,
355; "labor of the negative" and,
18; love and, 120; phenomenology
of reflection and, 20; as process of
relation, 10; as questioning, 138;
psychoanalytically defined, 266,

390*n21*; reflection and, 19, 22;
repression and, 255; self-interrogation
as, 17; self-mediation as, 147; self-
questioning as, 146; skepticism and,
56; the stoic and, 51; subject and, 141,
154, 158, 175; subjectivity and, 107;
unhappy consciousness and, 57

Fackenheim, Emil, on religious sublation in Hegel, 372*n39*
Fairbairn, R. W. D.: on paranoid
displacement, 257; on splitting, 392
n33
Family: as conflict, 243; in Hegel, 385
n65; as historical institution, 225;
psyche and, 245; psychoanalysis and,
224–26; subject and, 224–26; theory
of, 242; unhappy consciousness and,
225
Fear: anxiety and, 117; Freud on, 312;
Heidegger on, 117–18; identity and,
117
Feminism: abstract inversion and,
299; Lacan and, 299; Lukács and,
382*n31*; modern French, 382*n31*;
oedipal terminology and, 390*n24*;
psychoanalysis and, 387*n3*
Form: ideology and, 229–30; limits of,
230
Formalism: Chicago pluralism and,
322; versus existential a priori,
145; Heideggerian, 144–45, 374*n2*;
neo-Kantian, 377*n33*
Foucault, Michel: on history and
sexuality, 373*n64*; on power and
sexuality, 220; on subject, 188
Fractionation: versus active reversal,
264; existentialism and, 257; Klein
on, 257; psyche and, 258–59
Frankfurt school: from Adorno to
Habermas, 381*n18*; on contradictions,
329
Freedom: and death, 136; and determination, 56; and possibility, 99, 155;
Sartre and, 154; and stoicism, 48–49
Freud, Sigmund: anxiety and, 393–

94*n*52; clinical insights of, 5; on danger situations, 268; deconstruction and, 287; distinctions in, 244; on emotions, 274; on fear and desire, 312; infantile seduction, 249; instincts for, 332; interpretation of, and Hegel, 78; interpretation of Dora by, 281; *Interpretation of Dreams*, 387*n4*; language of activity and passivity in, 299; as liberated by Derrida, 394*n62*; love relations and, 249; overdetermination and, 292; psychoanalysis and, 386–87 *n1*; psychobibliographical issues and, 233; on renouncing desire, 263; revisions of, 238; on sex and situatedness, 297; sexuality and, 298; scientism of, 5; shift in methods by, 238; structural theory of id, ego, superego in, 283–88; on therapy and technique, 263–64; on trauma, 235; on the unconscious, 240; vacillations on anxiety, 268

Frigidity and subjectivity, 305

Frye, Northrop, on literary modes, 261

Fundamental ontology, philosophic anthropology as, 321

Für uns: Absolute Knowledge and, 369 *n16*; *différance* and, 372*n41*; problem of, 32

Gender: confusion of, 245; false issues of, 243; as mutual cruelty, 299

Genetic fallacy, 246

God: as absolute source of value, 78; death of, 62, 93; as desire for self-mastery, 66; disappearance of, 77; as principal of internal torture, 77; recognition from, 68; as Supreme Other, 68; and unhappy consciousness, 62, 66, 70

Gramsci, Antonio: collective consciousness and, 198; hegemony and, 195; ideology and, 197; marxism and, 183; subject and, 200–201

Grounding, phenomenological, in *Lebenswelt*, 355

Guilt: inwardness and, 102; the priest and, 88, 98; psychic autonomy and, 102; self-mastery and, 88; subject and, 103–4; as synthesis of shame and sin, 88

Habermas, Jurgen: on concept of legitimation, 382*n34*; and Frankfurt school, 381*n18*; marxist ideology and, 184

Hall, Stuart, on "marxism without guarantees," 173

Hartmann, Heinz: intersystemic and intrasystemic conflict, 394*n58*; on psychoanalysis, 254

Hedonism: desire and, 30; in the *PhG*, 336

Hegel, G. W. F.: absence and presence in, 28; Absolute Knowledge in, 32; "absolute skepticism" in, 14, 317–18, 355; a priori determination in, 355; consciousness and, 9, 14, 21–23, 28, 77; Derrida and, 67, 147, 347–48, 369 *nn12, 16*; on desire, 28–29, 85, 317, 329, 333, 340, 360, 375*n13*; determinate negation and, 20; devotion in, 72; on dialectic, 9, 15, 20–21, 38, 147, 314–15, 325, 333, 341–42, 352, 355; dialectical method and absolute skepticism in, 317–18; dissatisfaction and desire in, 29; epistemology, response to classical, by, 21, 25–26; existentialism and, 368*n9*, 401*n46*, 401–2*n52*; the *für uns* and, 32; Heidegger's *a-lethia* and, 356; historicity of family, 385*n65*; on identity and difference, 356; on internalizations, 78; on internal relations, 350; inwardness and existence and, 8, 330; on Kant, 11, 18, 355; on labor, 221; master-slave dialectic in, 41; nature of mind for, 13; on mood(s), 67; on natural consciousness, 16, 356, 362; on the Objective Spirit, 223; phenomenological method of, 3, 13, 355, 399*n22*; *PhG* of, as narrative of self-

99; inwardness and, 35, 121; love
and, 120; master-slave struggle and,
41; narcissism and, 74; self and, 115;
self-knowledge and, 124; self-mastery
and, 39; subject and, 115; as threat,
35
Otherness: capitalism and, 215–
16; idealization and, 301; self-
consciousness and, 25; unconscious of
subject and, 240
Overdetermination, principle of, 292–94

Panlogicism: dialectic and, 51; *PhG* as,
337
Pantragism: dialectic and, 51; *PhG* as,
337
Paralysis, aporia and, in dialectic
method, 353
Paranoid displacement, Fairbairn on,
257
Passion: as existential act, 24, 113;
primacy of over epistemology, 113;
thinking as discipline of, 163
Passive aggressive personality, 72;
schizoid withdrawal and, 267; sex
and the, 303; in the slave, 41
Passivity: Freud's language of, 299; in
the unhappy consciousness, 78
Patriarchy, oedipal model of, 244–45
Phaedrus (Plato): dialectic in, 324,
349; psyche as self-motion in, 357;
self-motion of love in, 359
Phallogocentrism, identity and, 184
Phenomenal world for Plato, 318–19
Phenomenological method: of Hegel,
13–14; of interrogation, 360; and
parousia of the absolute, 367*n1*; as
unhappy consciousness, 14
Phenomenology: as arrested dialectic,
374; of experience in reflection, 20;
of Hegel, Kierkegaard, and Plato,
399; of labor in Marx, 221; oedipal
separation and, 244; as route to
dialectic, 331; of the superego, 285;
of the unhappy consciousness, 60
Phenomenology of Mind, The (PhG)

(Hegel): comprehensive tragedy of
an agent in, 339; consciousness and,
32, 345, 367–68*n1*; epistemological
problematic of section A of, 335–
36; formation of subject in, 344;
as guide to "our" phenomenology,
335; hedonism discussed in, 336;
Hegel and, 4; Hegel's dialectic
emphasis and, 333; Hegel's tracing
of inwardness and existence in, 330;
hierarchy of integrations in, 345;
historical problematic of section B
of, 336; historical reading of, 41, 44;
history in, 370*n26*; as integration of
Plato's dialectic, 352; Kierkegaard
on, 371–72*n38*; logic of instinctual
beginnings and desire in, 333; logic
of tragic interrogation and growth in,
338–39; natural consciousness in, 15;
as panlogicism, 337; as pantragism,
337; preface to, 353, 362; principle of
interpretation in, 334; psychological
and motivational forces in, 335;
psychological implications of, 6;
rationalist problem of structure
in, 336–37; reflection and, 20, 23;
relation of questions in, 323; and
requirements for dialectical system,
353; Rousseau and Kant in section
C of, 338; scientific problematic of
section C of, 336; section C of as
comedy, 374*n79*; self-consciousness
in, 339; self-mediation as structure
in, 345; structure of, 334; subject
in, 315, 319, 334–35, 339, 351, 353;
"transitions of sentiment" in, 337; the
unhappy consciousness in, 43. *See also*
Unhappy consciousness
Philosophic anthropology: the development of subject in, 44; as fundamental ontology under dialectic, 321;
history and, 45; task of, 44
Philosophy: access of, to reality, 320;
Aristotelian distinctions of, 12; for
Hegel, 8, 46–47; history and, 183;
ideology and, 183, 192; literature and,